Megha Kumar is Deputy Director of Analysis at Oxford Analytica, the global analysis and advisory firm, where she has also been Senior Analyst for South and South-east Asia. She holds a DPhil in Modern South Asian History from the University of Oxford and an MSt in South Asian Colonial History from the University of Oxford. In addition, Megha Kumar has acquired a wealth of knowledge through her writing and journalism in India. Her research has appeared in the journal *Social Scientist* and in a human rights report on violence against women for Sahmat Publications.

'The book combines fine-grained empirical research with considerable conceptual acumen and penetrating analysis. Megha Kumar has taken on a particularly difficult theme to write about and she writes with great honesty and meticulous scholarship.'

Tanika Sarkar, Retired Professor of History,
Jawaharlal Nehru University, Delhi

'Megha Kumar's book is important because of its subject and because of the way she approaches it. Sexual violence during communal riots has been a recurring feature of the Hindu–Muslim conflict, at least since Partition. Kumar shows that when it is exerted by Hindu nationalist activists, it is directly connected to their ideology, including the muscular, machist dimension of this repertoire. She makes this point by presenting a detailed ethnographic account of three violent episodes of the history of Ahmedabad, the Gujarati city where the number of casualties of Hindu–Muslim riots has been the largest in India since 1947. This book makes it clear that social scientists can approach analytically the question of sexual violence at the time of communal conflicts.'

Christophe Jaffrelot, Senior Research Fellow at CERI-Sciences
Po/CNRS and Professor of Indian Politics and Sociology,
King's College London

'This is a gripping and, unfortunately, apparently accurate account of the largely hidden and silently tolerated victimisation of mostly Muslim women and men by a vast segment of Indian society that, for the most part, turns a blind eye to it.'

Paul R. Brass, Professor Emeritus of Political Science and
South Asian Studies, University of Washington

COMMUNALISM AND SEXUAL VIOLENCE IN INDIA

The Politics of Gender, Ethnicity and Conflict

MEGHA KUMAR

I.B.TAURIS

LONDON · NEW YORK

Published in 2016 by
I.B.Tauris & Co. Ltd
London • New York
www.ibtauris.com

Library of Development Studies 7

ISBN: 978 1 78453 530 8
eISBN: 978 1 78672 068 9
ePDF: 978 1 78673 068 8

A full CIP record for this book is available from the British Library
A full CIP record is available from the Library of Congress

Library of Congress Catalog Card Number: available

Typeset in Garamond Three by OKS Prepress Services, Chennai, India
Printed and bound by CPI Group (UK) Ltd, Croydon, CR0 4YY

For Jonah

CONTENTS

List of Abbreviations   ix
List of Maps and Figures   xi
Acknowledgements   xiv

Introduction   1

1. 1969   52
2. 1985   105
3. 2002   148
4. Aftermath   217

Appendix   Hindu Nationalist Propaganda Materials   255
Glossary   262
Notes   266
Bibliography   285
Index   299

LIST OF ABBREVIATIONS

ABVP	Akhil Bharatiya Vidyarthi Parishad (All India Students Union)
AGRS	Akhil Gujarat Navrachna Samiti (All Gujarat Committee for Reconstruction)
AMC	Ahmedabad Municipal Corporation
AWAG	Ahmedabad Women's Action Group
BJP	Bharatiya Janata Party
CCT	Concerned Citizens' Tribunal
CJP	Citizens for Justice and Peace
CPI	Communist Party of India
CPI-M	Communist Party of India (Marxist)
FIR	first information report
HDRS	Hindu Dharma Raksha Samiti (Committee for the Protection of Hindu Religion)
HJM	Hindu Jagran Manch (Forum for Hindu Awakening)
HPSS	Hullad Pidit Sahayta Samiti (Relief Committee for Riot Victims)
IMF	International Monetary Fund
KHAM	Kshatriyas, Harijans, Adivasis, Muslims
MGJP	Maha Gujarat Janata Parishad (Grand Gujarat People's Council)
MLA	member of the legislative assembly
MP	member of Parliament
NGO	non-governmental organisation

NPYC	Naranpura Patel Yuvak Mandal (Naranpura Patel Youth Committee)
OBC	Other Backward Class
RSS	Rashtriya Swayamsevak Sangh
SIT	Special Investigation Team
SRPF	State Reserve Police Force
TLA	Textile Labour Association
UP	Uttar Pradesh
VHP	Vishwa Hindu Parishad

LIST OF MAPS AND FIGURES

Maps

Map 1. Districts of Gujarat   xii

Map 2. Ahmedabad City   xiii

Figures

Figure 3.1. VHP's 'Savadhan Campaign'   185

Figure A.1. Reverse of Pamphlet in Figure 3.1   256

Figure A.2. Bharat ke Isaikaranka Shadyantra   257

Figure A.3. Reverse of Pamphlet in Figure A.2   258

Figure A.4. Bajrang Dal-Vishwa Hindu Parishad   259

Figure A.5. Jai Bharat Mata   260

Figure A.6. Navchetan Group   261

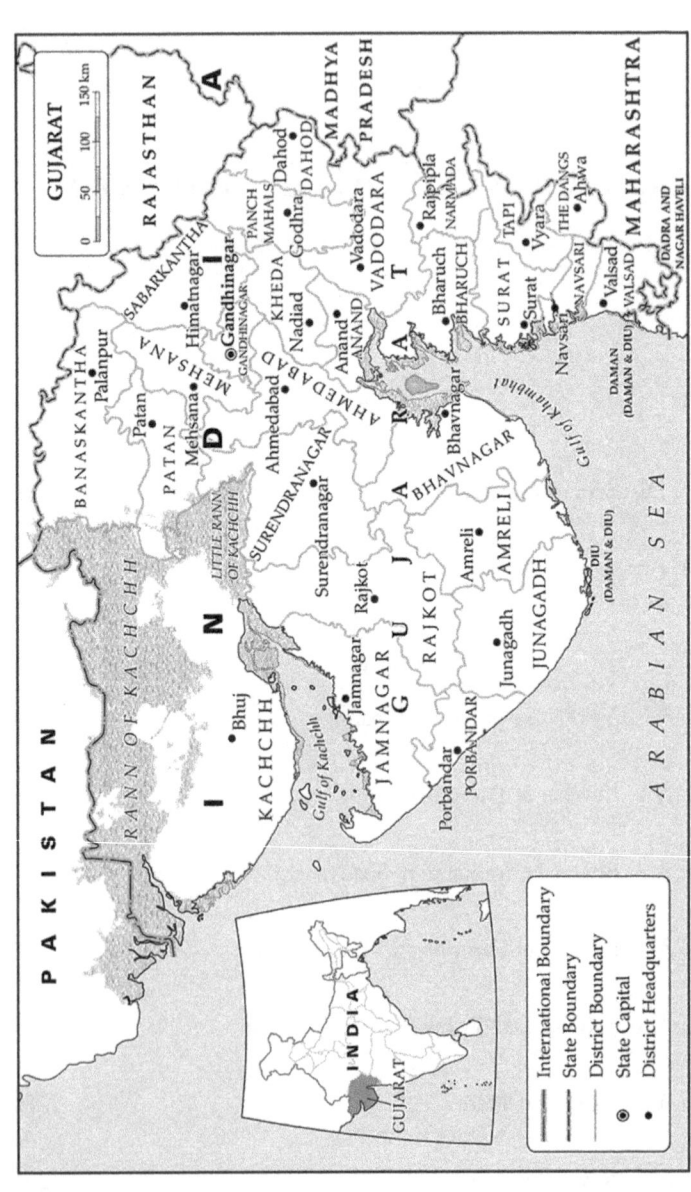

Map 1   Districts of Gujarat

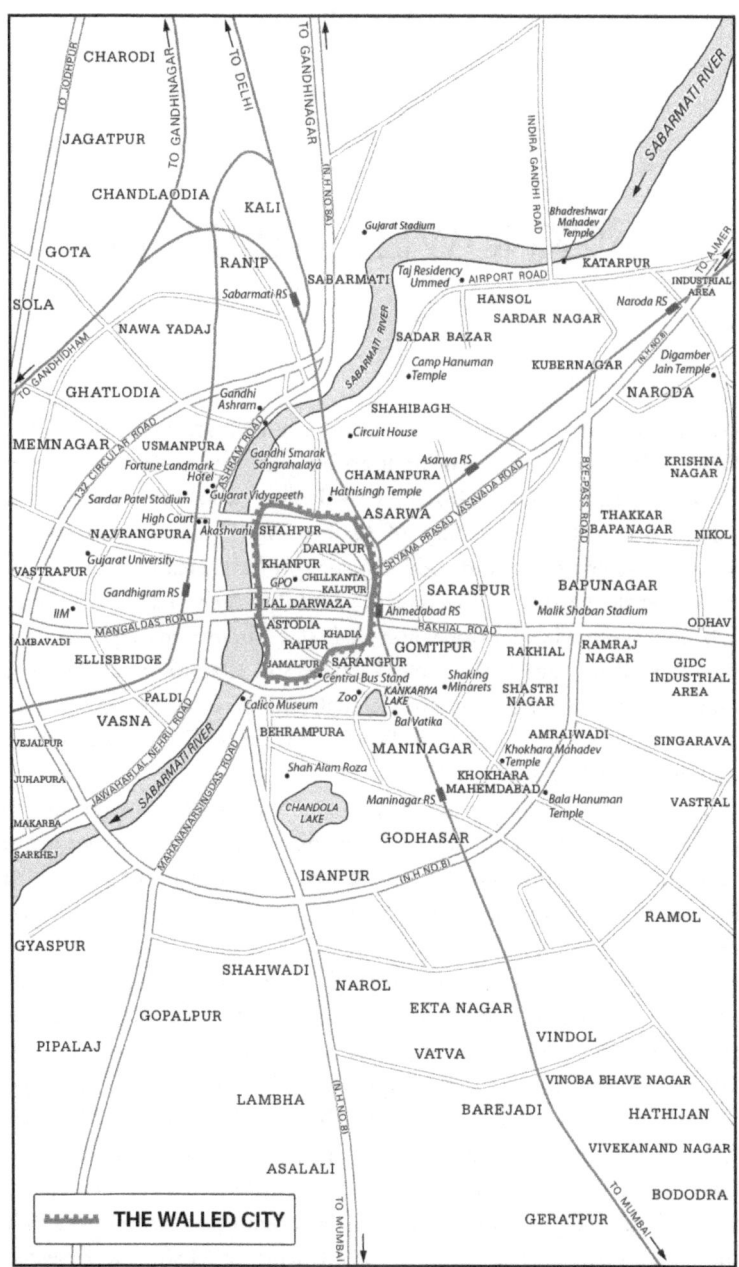

Map 2   Ahmedabad City

ACKNOWLEDGEMENTS

Over the course of writing this book, I have incurred numerous debts. First of all, I want to express my heartfelt gratitude to Professor Judith M. Brown and Professor Rosalind O'Hanlon, who were my doctoral supervisors at the University of Oxford. Their incisive comments, constructive criticisms and enduring support have greatly enriched my work over the years; I will be forever grateful to them. I also owe a huge debt to Professor Lyndal Roper and Dr Lesley Abrams, my supervisors at Balliol College. From the time I arrived in Oxford in 2003, they supported me through my intellectual and personal struggles with ingenuity, love and compassion. Dr (Rev.) Douglas Dupree was a most supportive mentor.

Dr David Washbrook generously took time from his busy schedule to give me constructive feedback on the manuscript and encouraged me to persevere. As examiners of my doctoral dissertation, Professor Jan Breman and Dr Nandini Gooptu offered invaluable insights on the first version of this project.

During the course of my doctoral work (2005–09), I had the privilege of discussing ideas in the first iteration of this book with the participants of various conferences and seminars: I am grateful to them for their recommendations and suggestions. I am particularly indebted to Professor Roger Jeffery, Professor Thomas Blom Hansen, Professor Kumkum Sangari, Professor Sudhir Chandra, Dr Pratiksha Baxi and Dr Rohit Barot. Dr Nikita Sud and Dr Rubina Jassani generously shared their work, insights and knowledge of sources with me. As a Past and Present Research Fellow at the Institute of Historical Research (2009–10), I had several invaluable opportunities to discuss my work

with my peers and with Professor Miles Taylor. I am grateful to all of
them.

I also take this opportunity to thank the people who made my
fieldwork in Ahmedabad, Surat, Vadodara, Mumbai and Delhi feasible
and enjoyable.

In Ahmedabad, Achyut Yagnik (SETU: Centre for Social Knowledge
and Action), Cedric Prakash (Prashant), Girish Patel and Sophia Khan
(Safar) were most generous in taking time out for repeated discussions
and in sharing their documentation with me. I especially thank Bina at
Prashant, whose resourcefulness enabled me to access some of the most
important sources for this study. Bina Jadhav and Afroze Jahan
(ActionAid) helped me secure initial introductions to survivors in Vatva
and Ekta Nagar; Stalin K. and Nimmi Chauhan introduced me to
survivors in Juhapura; Rehana Pathan (Video Volunteers) was most
generous in coordinating interviews with Dalit and Muslim families in
Behrampura; and Bharat Rathod accompanied me on some trips to
Naroda Patiya. Hiren Gandhi (Darshan) put me in touch with some
members of Hindu nationalist organisations. Without their help this
book would not have been possible.

The debt I owe to people at Drishti can never be repaid. Neerav,
Pushpa, Gaurang, Dhiren, Rajat and Arun made visits to Ahmedabad
possible, bearable and enjoyable in their own wonderful ways. Neerav's
wife Bhamini and daughter Khushi welcomed me into their family and
were a source of warmth and compassion. Nimmi Chauhan and Kavita
Das Gupta were the sort of friends one needs when working on
emotionally gruelling issues; their constant support helped me cope
with the pain inherent in the subject of this study. I thank Stalin K. and
Jessica Mayberry for hosting me during my first field trip, and the Bhatt
family for making my stay in their house during the second trip
anything but boring.

Dr Lancy Lobo at the Centre of Culture and Development in
Vadodara, and Dr Biswaroop Das at the Centre of Social Studies in Surat
were kind hosts. The sources they let me access at their respective
institutions, through their supportive library staff, were most useful.

In Mumbai, Teesta Setalvad, Javed Anand, Tamara Anand and Jibran
Anand welcomed me into their home and lives in a way I thought only
family could. Teesta also generously shared with me her boundless
knowledge on Gujarat, and gave me access to critical sources, for which I

am deeply indebted to her. I am also grateful to the staff of Sabrang for making sources available to me at short notice. The support and encouragement of Dr Rajendra Prasad (SAHMAT) in Delhi played a major role in enabling this book to see the light of day. I am also grateful to Deepak Dholakia and Jhanvi Bhatt, who have taught me all the Gujarati I know. Special thanks are due to Rupa Mehta, who very kindly agreed to help me with some translations at very short notice. Will Arthur and Dhvani Mehta went out of their way to help me with some last-minute research, for which I am very thankful. Jayna Kothari, Rajeev Dhavan, Dev Gangjee and Sudhir Krishnaswamy magnanimously offered advice on legal issues involved in publishing this book; I cannot thank them enough.

Most of all, my gratitude is due to all my interviewees. Their generosity with their time and knowledge has made this book possible. I am particularly grateful to the men and women who have shared with me some of the most traumatic experiences of their lives. I have learnt a lot from them. I hope they find my reflections on their experiences responsible and compassionate.

For their generous financial support over the years, I am grateful to the following trusts and institutions: Rhodes Trust, C. R. Parekh Foundation, United Nations Educational, Scientific and Cultural Organization (UNESCO), Wingate Foundation, Balliol College, Andrew Smith Memorial Foundation and the Past and Present Society. The funding provided by the Beit Fund, Radhakrishnan Grant, Frere Exhibition and Vice-Chancellors Fund also made this research possible.

I am also grateful to the anonymous reviewer of my manuscript, and to Tulika Books and I.B.Tauris for publishing this book (under slightly different titles) for South Asia and the rest of the world, respectively. In particular, I am indebted to Indu Chandrasekhar of Tulika and Sophie Rudland and Dan Shutt of I.B.Tauris for the care and diligence they have shown in producing this book.

Friends and family have been supportive in numerous ways over the years. It is a pleasure to thank my friends Abhishek Singh, Akanksha Dureja, Ashish Kumar, Azar Zaidi, Kanishka Prasad, Manak Matiyani, Namita Gupta, Namrata Nyasi, Shantanu Grover, Shubra Hajela and Tarun Khanna, who make my visits to Delhi truly memorable and thoroughly relaxing. Paul Petzschmann always looked out for me in Oxford. Arindam Dutta and Annie Reinhardt have seen me through my intellectual struggles and personal turmoil several times over the past few years. Ruma Gupta and Amna Khalid are especially dear to me; I have come to rely on them for warmth, love and healing. I am also grateful to my colleagues at Oxford Analytica, who have been a constant source of encouragement. Special thanks are due to my wonderful friends/colleagues Alison Baily, Benjamin Charlton, Jill Hedges, Katerina Fytatzi, Sarah Michaels, Stephanie Hare and Yulia Rusanova for enabling me to look past my doubts on particularly difficult days. Benjamin also gave useful feedback on some of my chapters. My brother Siddharth Goel, sister-in-law Tina Tandon and nephew Viraj bring much joy to my life. Gerlinde Wilberg has been an enduring source of love.

I thank my mother Ashok Kumari who, with her intellectual curiosity, commitment to secular politics and women's rights, and her unconditional love, inspires and sustains my life. Finally, I would like to express my deepest gratitude to Jonah Wilberg, my intellectual companion and life-partner for over 12 years. His rigorous and incisive feedback on every chapter helped me develop my ideas and refine my writing. Without his patience and support I could not have worked on such an emotionally taxing subject for the most part of a decade. Since this book would simply not exist without Jonah, it is to him, my *jaano-dil*, that this work is dedicated.

INTRODUCTION

I arrived in Ahmedabad for the first time in May 2002. A 20-year-old history undergraduate at Delhi University at the time, I was in the city to assist a prominent Indian human rights activist in her work with Muslim women who had been raped, gang-raped or genitally mutilated by Hindu activists during the anti-Muslim massacre in Gujarat in the summer of 2002. The massacre had begun on 28 February and lasted two months. Although the violence was confined to Gujarat, with Ahmedabad as its epicentre, at least 18 other districts of a total of 26 in the state were affected as well. The massacre left some 113,697 refugees languishing in 103 temporary relief camps established across the state; at least 44 camps were located in Ahmedabad, together housing more than half of all the refugees (66,292).[1] At least 150–200 women, the overwhelming majority of whom are believed to have been Muslims, were raped or gang-raped, and in many cases mutilated with swords, wooden sticks and iron rods (CCT 2002, 1:226). Most of the victims were between 20 and 45 years of age, but some were as young as three. Many were burnt afterwards to obliterate evidence.

During my stay in Gujarat, which lasted nearly a month, I visited at least a dozen relief camps in Ahmedabad, and the main camps in the districts of Panch Mahals and Dahod, all of which housed victims of and witnesses to gory sexual violence. Some rape survivors could barely describe their experiences, tears and trauma choking their voices. Others were calm and matter-of-fact, their composure striking me as almost otherworldly. Sultani Feroze Rasul Sheikh, who was gang-raped on 28 February in Eral village in Panch Mahals, was one such individual.

When speaking of the number of men who had attacked her, she gave a terse and calm response: 'The men caught me from behind and threw me on the ground. Faizan [her son] fell from my arms and started crying. My clothes were stripped off by the men and I was left stark naked. One by one the men raped me. All the while I could hear my son crying. I lost count after three' (Citizens' Initiative 2002: 76).

Some were angry and demanded answers to difficult questions. An unmarried Muslim woman in her 20s who had been gang-raped and beaten in the Naroda Patiya neighbourhood of Ahmedabad on 28 February asked: 'Why did this happen to us? Did I not remind them of their sister?'[2] Medina Sheikh witnessed her daughter and niece being beaten, gang-raped and killed after their breasts were cut off, on 1 March in Eral village in Panch Mahals. She asked repeatedly, 'My daughter was like a flower, still to see life. Why did they have to do this to her? What kind of men are these? The monsters tore my beloved daughter to pieces'.[3] With these questions in my mind and the voices of these women in my heart, I began this research in 2005 as a doctoral student at the University of Oxford. Examining the motivations behind and modalities of the perpetration of sexual violence against Muslim women during Hindu–Muslim conflicts in Ahmedabad became a priority for me.

Nirbhaya and 'everyday' sexual violence

The publication of my findings comes at a time when the 'everyday' sexual victimisation of women has become an urgent issue in India. On a daily basis, viewers of Indian and international television news programmes and readers of Indian newspapers learn about outrageous attacks against adult women and female minors by their family members, neighbours, employees, employers, or by strangers on public transport. An incident that gave rise to unprecedented media coverage and sparked widespread public anger over sexual violence occurred in December 2012. At around 9 p.m. on 16 December 2012, a 23-year-old female physiotherapy student boarded a bus with a male friend after watching a movie in one of the cinemas in south Delhi. Six men who were on the bus first taunted her for being out late at night with a man she was not married to. When she fiercely resisted their misbehaviour, the men beat her, gang-raped her and mutilated her abdomen with what is believed to have been an iron rod. One of the assailants reportedly tore out parts of her intestines with his bare hands. The male companion of the student was also beaten when he tried to intervene. After the attack, both the student and her friend were thrown out of the bus. The bus driver, who was one of the assailants, tried to run the student over, but her friend pulled her aside just in time. Six days later, the student succumbed to her grievous injuries.

The incident provoked unprecedented public outrage in Delhi and other major Indian cities such as Mumbai and Kolkata, with protesters demanding justice for the student whom they named Nirbhaya, the fearless one; harsh punishment, even the death penalty, for the accused; and greater state responsiveness to violence against women. The utter savagery with which Nirbhaya was attacked horrified sizeable sections of the urban public, not just in India but also overseas.

The protests by citizens and civil society organisations, together with media campaigns and international condemnation, forced a reconsideration of the legal apparatus and its responsiveness to sexual violence. Notably, on 22 December 2012, the Congress Party-led national coalition government appointed a committee under former chief justice of India J. S. Verma to propose, within 30 days, amendments to the sexual violence laws. A fast-track court was established in Delhi to expedite proceedings in cases of sexual violence, since the delay in trials often deters the pursuit of justice. A 13-member task force headed by the union home secretary was set up on 1 January 2013 to review police handling of such cases on a fortnightly basis, not least because the lack of police sensitivity in handling such crimes has long been criticised. The government also secured the passage of the Criminal Law (Amendment) Act through Parliament in March 2013.

The act, ordinarily referred to as the new 'anti-rape law', falls short in key areas, particularly in failing to recognise marital rape and sexual violence against men as crimes punishable under the Indian Penal Code. Nonetheless, the act constitutes an important intervention, since the law exercises significant social and political power, and is a reflection and extension of dominant discourses (Cahill 2000). For the first time, sexual harassment (unwelcome physical, verbal or non-verbal sexual overtures), the stripping of women, stalking, and the abuse of power to demand or request sexual favours have been explicitly recognised and categorised separately as crimes (Government of India 2013: 2–6). This is a welcome change, since the law now recognises subtler and more pervasive forms of abuse of women, and is more sensitive to women's perceptions of such actions.

Moreover, the act marks a sharp departure from long-criticised previous laws that deemed sexual intercourse necessary to the offence of rape.[4] Now, penetration of any part of the body of the victim by any part of the assailant's body or an object constitutes 'rape', and is punishable by at least seven years' imprisonment (Government of India 2013: 5–8). This constitutes an important intervention because, by focusing previously on only penile penetration, the law placed a premium on notions of chastity, virginity and marriage (Agnes 1992: 21). Gang-rape, 'where a woman is raped by one or more persons constituting a group or acting in furtherance of a common intention', is also now recognised as an offence separate from 'rape' and is punishable by at least 20 years' imprisonment (Government of India 2013: 8). By including this provision, the law brings within the judicial purview the range as well as the gravity of gendered crimes committed against women and girls.[5] Throughout this book, the terms 'rape' and 'gang-rape' refer to the revised definitions of these crimes in the Indian Penal Code. 'Sexual violence' is used more broadly to refer to any sexually oriented act experienced by the victim as abusive, ranging from rape and gang-rape, on the one hand, to the use of sexual profanities and the exposure of male genitals to women, on the other.

Last but not least, the act introduces a special provision for sexual violence committed against women during communal violence, making such crimes punishable by a minimum sentence of seven years that can be extended to lifelong imprisonment (Government of India 2013: 6). By including this provision, the law now acknowledges the particular gravity of sexual violence committed during large-scale, ethnic-identity-based conflict. This is especially welcome since the Prevention of Communal and Targeted Violence (Access to Justice and Reparations) Bill, which could include provisions for redressing sexual violence committed during communal conflict, has not secured parliamentary approval.[6]

Amid these structural and legal reforms, mainstream Indian newspapers have reported numerous further cases of severe sexual violence since December 2012. One of the most horrifying cases was reported in mid-April 2013. On 15 April, a five-year-old girl, apparently called Gudiya, from an east Delhi neighbourhood, was abducted by her 22-year-old neighbour (possibly with an accomplice), and raped repeatedly. She had pieces of candle and a bottle thrust into her vagina, and was left to die without food or water for over 40 hours in a locked room. The incident once again brought hundreds of protesters onto the streets of Delhi, especially following revelations that local police officials had initially ignored complaints from the family about the girl's abduction. They also allegedly offered to purchase the family's silence with Rs 2,000 (around $37). An additional commissioner of police in Delhi had slapped a young woman for protesting against the incident and the police's mishandling of the case.[7] These events, and the widespread national and international coverage given to them, embarrassed the national government, forcing then Prime Minister Manmohan Singh to publicly express regret, and the Delhi police to suspend malfeasant officials.

The cases of Nirbhaya and Gudiya sparked unprecedented outrage partly because the brutality inflicted seemed exceptional. However, this sense of exceptionality was lacking in historical perspective: the Indian subcontinent had witnessed savage sexual violence against Hindu, Muslim and Sikh women during Partition, and against Muslim women in 1969 and more recently in 2002. Indeed, the violence inflicted against the two victims from Delhi horrifyingly resembles the brutalities inflicted upon Muslim women in 2002. In its detailed inquiry into the violence inflicted during the 2002 massacre, the Concerned Citizens' Tribunal (CCT) noted the following:

> Before they were finally killed, some were beaten up with rods and pipes for almost an hour. Before or after the killing, their vagina would be sliced, or would have iron rods pushed inside. Similarly, their bellies would be cut open or would have hard objects inserted into them. A 13-year old girl, had a rod pushed into her stomach, and was then burnt. A mother reported that her three-year old baby girl was raped and killed in front of her, while elsewhere daughters reported on the rapes of their mothers, now dead. Kausar Bano, a young girl from Naroda Patiya, was several months pregnant. Several eyewitnesses testified that she was raped, tortured, her womb was slit open with a sword to disgorge the foetus which was then hacked to pieces and roasted alive with the mother. (CCT 2002, 2:40–1)

Mumtaz Bano, who lived in Naroda Patiya in Ahmedabad before 2002, confided to a fact-finding group about the condition in which victim-survivors of rape had been brought to a relief camp soon after the massacre began on 28 February. She said:

> There were 13 girls among the women the first night [...] they were all bleeding so profusely [...] we scavenged for paper, that was all we could find, and stuffed them with it to hold blood [...] Some of them were in terrible agony, that had pieces of wood inside them, you know like those stumps in cricket [...] remove mine first, please remove mine [...] they kept screaming in pain. (Lahkar and Dhanushkodi 2002: 31)

When juxtaposed with the recent Delhi cases, the depravity suffered by Muslim women in 2002 seems to be a more targeted manifestation of the brutality suffered by Nirbhaya and Gudiya. In both contexts, brutal sexual violence against women drew partly on patriarchal ideas that normalise such acts as 'sex', converting the act of inflicting violence into an erotic, natural and pleasurable experience. For example, the prime accused in the Nirbhaya rape case, Ram Singh, who committed suicide in jail in March 2013, reportedly told his police interrogators that he did not regret raping the 23-year-old female physiotherapy student, partly because he and his friends were out 'to have fun', since they had met after a long time.[8] Some of the perpetrators of sexual violence during the 2002 massacre saw their actions in a similar light. Notably, Suresh Chara, who has been sentenced to 12 years' imprisonment for raping Naseemo, a 16-year-old Muslim girl, in Ahmedabad's Naroda Patiya area during the carnage, justified his actions to an undercover journalist in the following words: 'When thousands of hungry men go in, they will eat some fruit or the other [...] who wouldn't, when there's fruit?'[9] For both Ram Singh and Suresh Chara, their victims were sexual objects who could be used to satiate their 'hunger' and desire 'to have fun'. (The significance of patriarchal ideas in motivating sexual violence during communal conflict is discussed in detail at a later stage.)

Yet there are crucial differences between these 'peace-time' and 'conflict-time' sexual brutalities, the two most important being the role of ethnic identity in motivating the violence, and the role of the state in preventing or facilitating it. First, according to the available evidence,

Muslim women were attacked during the 2002 massacre by activists associated with the chauvinistic and xenophobic Hindu nationalist movement; these attacks were motivated by the ethnic as well as the gender identity of the victims.[10] Indeed, the violence in 2002 was so targeted that many have described it as a pogrom, even as genocide, since the events conform to the United Nations' (UN's) definition of genocide as acts committed with the intent to destroy, in whole or part, a national, ethnic, racial or religious group.[11] In the Delhi cases cited earlier, the violence was not motivated by the victims' ethnic identity (both the victims and all the assailants were Hindus).

Second, many media commentaries, academic accounts and the reports of citizens' groups have alleged that in 2002, large segments of the state apparatus, including senior government officials, politicians and police officers, either turned a blind eye to the violence, or may have even actively connived with the rioters, providing them with ideological and logistical support.[12] Some police officials also beat Muslim women in their private parts, hurled sexual obscenities at them and stripped before them.[13] In the Delhi cases, the state apparatus is guilty of acts of omission, but not necessarily of commission. The police, for example, failed to ensure the safety of women in the capital, neglected its duty to act on the report filed by Gudiya's family, and sought to pervert the course of justice by attempting to bribe her family. However, in these specific cases no questions have been raised regarding the state's involvement in the violence.

These two central differences in the political contexts of the events in Delhi and Gujarat have profoundly shaped the responses of Hindu nationalist leaders and organisations. In the case of the Delhi incidents, Hindu nationalists condemned the violence, called for tough sentences for the accused, and criticised the local authorities for inadequately maintaining law and order in the national capital. However, on sexual violence committed against Muslim women in 2002, these leaders were far more reticent, their responses betraying their apparently hypocritical views on gendered crimes. They have been criticised for implicitly condoning sexual violence against Muslim women, while viewing sexual attacks against Hindu women as morally unacceptable and as evidence of the (Congress-led) Delhi government's failure to preserve the safety and bodily integrity of (Hindu) women. (Moral relativity with regard to sexual violence against Muslim and Hindu women is an essential element of Hindu nationalist ideology. This aspect is discussed in detail later in this Introduction.)

A few examples of such dual standards would be illustrative. Two weeks after the Nirbhaya case, on 2 January 2013, Mohan Bhagwat, the *sarsanghchalak* (supreme philosopher-guide) of the Rashtriya Swayamsevak Sangh (National Volunteer Corps, hereafter RSS), an organisation that spearheads the Hindu nationalist movement, called for stronger anti-rape laws. He added that such crimes 'hardly take place' in rural India but occur frequently in 'some urban belts', and that he would favour capital punishment for those convicted of rape.[14] However, Bhagwat ignored the fact that in 2002, activists associated with the Hindu nationalist network sexually brutalised Muslim women in urban areas such as Ahmedabad as well as in Gujarat's rural districts of Panch Mahals and Dahod.[15] He also did not call for a tightening of laws on sexual violence, or for tough sentences for those implicated in these crimes.

Meanwhile, leaders of the Bharatiya Janata Party (BJP), the electoral wing of the RSS, attempted to mobilise political capital from the recent cases in Delhi, where the Congress was in power until 2013. As the main opposition party, the BJP had the democratic right and the responsibility to demand better governance from the Congress-led Delhi administration. However, the party failed to direct this critique inwards. Narendra Modi, now Prime Minister, led the BJP government in Gujarat as Chief Minister when the massacre occurred in 2002, and his party has since then won three more terms in power (in 2002, 2007 and 2012). His administration has been widely accused of aiding and abetting the massacre of Muslims. Despite repeated calls for public apology, Modi has thus far refused to apologise for his government's failure to prevent the killings and rapes of Muslim women, men and children.[16] However, Modi openly expressed condolences and regret with regard to the Nirbhaya case via social media, publicly stating that 'providing safety to women is a matter of concern'.[17]

Similarly, Sushma Swaraj, a veteran woman BJP politician and then leader of the opposition in the lower house of Parliament, visited Gudiya in hospital and called on then Prime Minister Manmohan Singh to organise a cross-party meeting on the issue. 'Nothing short of death sentence in cases of rape of children and cases involving brutality and barbarity will help', she said.[18] However, Swaraj neither visited the relief camps in the aftermath of the 2002 massacre in Gujarat, where so many Muslim rape victims sought refuge, nor called for tough sentences for those accused of raping Muslim children in the massacre.[19] This omission is particularly striking given that, by mid-April 2002, incidents of gory sexual violence against women and girls in Gujarat had been brought to public attention by a women's panel in India (Citizens' Initiative 2002),[20] as well as by the international press.[21]

The BJP's women's wing, the Mahila Morcha (Women's Forum), on 21 April 2013 organised a protest over the Gudiya case outside the residence of Congress president Sonia Gandhi, strongly condemning the incident and the Congress Party's governance record in Delhi.[22] However, the Mahila Morcha organised no such protest against the BJP in Gujarat or elsewhere after the violence of 2002. In fact, the organisation's handling of Maya Kodnani speaks volumes about the duplicity of its stand on sexual violence against women and girls. Kodnani is a former general secretary and president of the Mahila Morcha in Gujarat. In 2002, she was the BJP member of the legislative assembly (MLA) from Ahmedabad's Naroda constituency, where the worst forms of sexual violence were committed against Muslim women and girls. Despite being accused of orchestrating violence in Naroda, she was elevated to the Gujarat cabinet in 2007 and appointed minister for women and child development. In August 2012, she was sentenced to 28 years' imprisonment for her complicity in the violence. However, the Mahila Morcha and the BJP have yet to issue any public apology or statement condemning the complicity of one of their former senior officials in the brutal sexual victimisation of Muslim women.

Sexual violence during communal conflict: Burdens of patriarchy and history

Sexual violence has been a regular feature of communal conflict in India since independence in 1947. Indeed, the country took its first steps as a sovereign nation-state under the dark shadow of Partition, which saw the rape, gang-rape and mutilation of thousands of Muslim, Hindu and Sikh women in Punjab and to a lesser extent in Bengal (Bagchi and Dasgupta 2006: 4). Although authoritative statistics are unavailable, according to G. D. Khosla, the Punjab High Court judge appointed by the Indian government to collate the findings of its fact-finding committee, some

100,000 women were raped and abducted on both sides of the border during Partition (Das 2006: 20). Since Partition, mercifully, no episode of communal conflict has witnessed sexual violence on a similar scale.

However, between 1947 and 2013, several episodes of religiously motivated conflict have been accompanied by sexual violence that resembles the Partition experience in terms of brutality. In each of these episodes, the perpetrators of gendered violence were Hindu men and the victims mostly women belonging to Muslim and Christian minority groups. Such violence has occurred in several states of India, particularly Gujarat, Maharashtra, Madhya Pradesh and Odisha (called Orissa until 2011). In 1969, several Muslim women were raped, gang-raped and mutilated during communal rioting in Ahmedabad.[23] The next worst episode occurred in the aftermath of the demolition of the Babri Mosque by Hindu nationalist activists in the northern Indian town of Ayodhya on 6 December 1992. The demolition triggered a wave of communal riots across the country. The worst-affected cities were Mumbai (called Bombay until 1995) and the Gujarati city Surat.[24] Besides killing, looting and arson, violence inflicted by Hindus against Muslims in these cities included sexual atrocities against Muslim women, who were paraded naked on the streets, raped, gang-raped and mutilated (Chandra 1993; Lobo and D'Souza 1993; Patwardhan 1994; Srikrishna 1998).

Since 1992, sexual violence has been a feature of several episodes of communal violence across India. As mentioned earlier, in 2002, at least 150–200 women (the overwhelming majority of whom were Muslims) were sexually brutalised in three districts of Gujarat: Ahmedabad, Panch Mahals and Dahod. In August 2013, at least five Muslim women were gang-raped during communal rioting in Uttar Pradesh's (UP) Muzaffarnagar district. Christian women, especially nuns and tribals, have been targets of similar violence, albeit less frequently than their Muslim counterparts. In 1998, three Catholic nuns were gang-raped in Jhabua district of Madhya Pradesh (Venkatesan 1998). Two Christian tribal women were gang-raped in another Madhya Pradesh district, Khargone, in 2006 (Carvalho 2006). In 2008, a Catholic nun was raped in Kandhamal district of Odisha.[25]

This book investigates the incidence of sexual violence against Muslim women during communal conflicts in Ahmedabad between 1969 and 2002. It examines the three deadliest episodes of organised communal violence that occurred in 1969, 1985 and 2002 in Gujarat, with a view to exploring the processes involved in the infliction of sexual atrocities, in both aggravated and less extreme forms, against Muslim women. Ahmedabad was the epicentre of each of these episodes of violence, and the discussion in this book is confined to events that occurred in the city. Except for parts of the discussion on the 1985 riot in Chapter 2, the present volume does not examine the victimisation of women from other religious backgrounds. This is mainly because Muslim women have been the prime, even exclusive, targets of sexual violence in the episodes of conflict covered in this book.

The motivations for sexual atrocities committed against women of minority communities during communal conflict have drawn considerable scholarly attention in India. The predominant academic consensus has unequivocally assigned responsibility to Hindu nationalist ideology for encouraging its supporters to inflict such violence against Muslim and, to a lesser extent, against Christian women. It has been argued that ideologically motivated men inflict such violence in order to destroy the symbols of honour, the biological reproducers and the property of the 'enemy' Muslim community. These explanations have drawn on and contributed to analyses of the occurrence of sexual violence in large-scale ethnic conflicts elsewhere in the world. Here, I will describe the prevailing approaches to the interpretation of sexual violence during communal or ethnic conflicts. Later sections will lay out in detail the overall perspective and methodology adopted in this book.

According to the scholarship, communal Hindu activists sexually victimise Muslim women with a view to 'dishonouring' them and their community (Agarwal 1996; Bagchi and Dasgupta 2006; Butalia 1998; Chandra 1993; Pandey 2001; T. Sarkar 2002). In most patriarchal worldviews, the sexual purity of women is conflated with the honour of the family, the ethnic community and the nation. The forceful appropriation of female sexuality outside the realms of legitimate structures such as the family or the community is then construed as a symbolic humiliation of the male enemy and a demonstration of the virility of the victorious male. As linguist and political analyst Purushottam Agarwal (1996: 39) argues, 'Women are metamorphosed into a metaphor of both sacredness and humiliation. And virility comes to hinge upon defending one's honour and humiliating the "Other" through the agency of the sexuality of women'. During communal conflicts in post-independence India, Hindu nationalists have often drawn on this patriarchal notion to 'dishonour' the Muslim enemy. By inflicting sexual violence against the woman, men humiliate her and, through her bodily violation, the male members of her family and community. This explanation has featured frequently in the writings of scholars working on conflicts in other parts of the world as well, including Mozambique, Rwanda and Bangladesh.[26]

Such violence, according to the extant historiography, is also motivated by a desire to 'violate' the sanctified property of the male members of Muslim families and the Muslim community (Bacchetta 1994; Kannabiran and Kannabiran 1996). Since women are perceived as the sexual and productive property of the family and the community, violation of the Muslim female robs the Muslim male of the right to his property (Bacchetta 1994). Political scientist Meredith Turshen (2005) endorses this explanation in her analysis of gendered violence during the genocide in 1994 in Rwanda, where, according to the UN, from 100,000 to 250,000 women were raped. According to Turshen, women's productive and reproductive labour comes within the ambit of transferable property during conflict, when they are abducted to do menial jobs, farming, sex work, etc., or are sexually abused to bear children.

The desire to usurp or destroy the biological reproducers of the Muslim community is cited as another key motivation behind such sexual violence (Butalia 1996; Kishwar 1993). On the one hand, perpetrators seek to impregnate Muslim women with the seed of the 'superior' Hindu race, thereby to assuage their anxiety about the imagined diminution of the Hindu population. On the other hand, the evisceration of Muslim women's reproductive organs destroys the reproductive autonomy of Muslims, in order to diminish the Muslim population. In her work on Bangladesh's struggle for independence from Pakistan in 1971, feminist activist-writer Susan Brownmiller (1975) supports this view. She argues that sexual violence against Bangladeshi women by the Pakistani military was used as a 'weapon of war' whereby the enemy could be impregnated by the Pakistani victor. This explanation also finds favour with legal theorist Siobhan Fisher (1996) in her work on the genocide in the former Yugoslavia between 1992 and 1995, where, according to UN statistics, some 50,000 women and girls were raped. Fisher argues that during the protracted military conflict, rape may have been used 'not only as a tool of war, but also to implement a policy of impregnation in order to further the destruction of one people and the proliferation of another' (ibid.: 92). Bluntly speaking, forced impregnations became a tool for cleansing the nation of its enemy population and creating a 'purer' race.

Other scholars attribute the infliction of sexual violence upon Muslim women in independent India not only to patriarchal ideologies, but also to the unique history of India (Bagchi and Dasgupta 2006; Das 2006; D. Mehta and Chatterji 2001; Robinson 2005; T. Sarkar 2002). For them, the sexualised targeting of Muslim women during communal riots is a legacy of one 'critical' historical event: Partition. They argue that gendered violence against Hindu (and Sikh) women by Muslim men during Partition confirmed and intensified fears of alleged Muslim male sexual depredation and purported Hindu impotence. Whereas rapes of Hindu women during Partition re-entrenched stereotypes about the hyper-virility and degeneracy of the Muslim male, abductions and forced impregnations deepened Hindu anxiety about the diminution of the Hindu population. The failure of the Hindu male to prevent miscegenation lent force to the anxiety about Hindu weakness, making the appropriation of Hindu wombs by the Muslim 'enemy' a humiliating symbol of Hindu emasculation. Such stereotypes about Muslim and Hindu sexuality animated the public domain in the late nineteenth and early twentieth centuries in the form of cartoons, posters, pamphlets, comic strips and vernacular books, and newspapers (C. Gupta 2001). These stereotypes continue to impinge on the violence inflicted during contemporary riots. Moreover, these stereotypes acquire greater significance since they draw on patriarchal conceptions of women as symbols of honour, as sanctified property, and as the biological reproducers of family, community and nation.

Together with gendered communal stereotypes, these conceptions of sexuality make possible the memorialisation of Partition through the vocabulary of masculine victory/humiliation. According to historian Tanika Sarkar (2002: 2874), the memory of this Hindu male humiliation, and a 'dark sexual obsession about allegedly ultra-virile Muslim male bodies and overfertile Muslim female ones', motivated and sustained Hindu men during the 2002 massacre. Subscribing to Sarkar's exposé of the connections between the sexual brutalities inflicted during Partition and those that occurred during the 2002 massacre, sociologist

Rowena Robinson (2005: 19–20) argues that such analysis is vital, because it reveals 'not only a frightening repetition of particular kinds of violent acts, but also, sometimes, peculiarly precise gradations in the texture of torture'.

The extant scholarship has done much to enhance our understanding of the ideological motivations behind the sexual victimisation of minority women in India. However, this book departs from the preceding approaches by uncovering the actual dynamics involved in the unfolding of such violence on the ground. Further, it pays attention not only to the occurrence of sexual violence, but also to episodes of communal rioting in which such violence has been rare or absent. This enables us to identify and examine the conditions that facilitate the infliction, as well as those that result in the avoidance, of sexual violence against Muslim women during communal conflicts. I argue that the perpetration or avoidance of such atrocities during large-scale communal violence in 1969, 1985 and 2002 in Ahmedabad was governed by the interaction between Hindu nationalist ideology and the economic, political and social dynamics in operation at the local level. I hope that, as the first book to undertake an in-depth and grassroots-level analysis of the sexual victimisation of minority women in any communal conflict anywhere in India since 1947, the findings of this study will complement the existing literature on the motivations for sexual violence during conflict. I also hope that these findings will be of some relevance to studies of ethnic conflict in other parts of India, and elsewhere in the world.

Ahmedabad: The emergence of a riot city and the experience of sexual violence

Sprawled on either side of the River Sabarmati, on the western bank of which Mahatma Gandhi built his famous ashram, Ahmedabad city covers a region of well over 460 square kilometres. The fifth largest city in India by population (after Mumbai, Delhi, Bengaluru (earlier Bangalore) and Hyderabad), Ahmedabad is home to over 5.5 million people, or 9.1 per cent of Gujarat's population of around 60.38 million, according to the 2011 census. The city forms part of Ahmedabad district (the eighth largest in India by population), which is spread over an area of 8,107 square kilometres. The district is home to over 7.2 million people and includes rural and rural-urban areas surrounding the metropolis.

Ahmedabad was established in 1411 by the Sunni ruler Ahmed Shah on the eastern bank of the Sabarmati, with its urban core comprising a city enclosed within fort walls. The fort city is still called the walled city or the old city, even though most of the fortifications have disappeared. Nevertheless, Ahmedabad's Islamic legacy is still evidenced by the continued existence of 12 gates that allowed people to enter the boundaries of the walled city. Since the fifteenth century, Ahmedabad has been an important political, cultural and economic centre of Gujarat. The city's world-renowned textile mills had famously earned it the title 'Manchester of India' towards the end of the nineteenth century, while the legendary civic engagement of Ahmedabad's economic and political elite had transformed the city into an epicentre of the national movement by the 1920s (Spodek 2011). After independence, following a strong movement for provincial autonomy in the 1950s, Gujarat was carved out of Bombay Presidency in 1960 and established as a separate state. The inorganically created city of Gandhinagar was named Gujarat's capital, but Ahmedabad remained the state's most politically eminent and economically dynamic city.

The city's population is characterised by significant diversity and socio-cultural stratification. In 2001, Ahmedabad district was home to 5.8 million people, including 4.9 million (84.6 per cent) Hindus and 662,799 (11.3 per cent) Muslims (Gayer and Jaffrelot 2012: 52). Both Hindus and Muslims in Gujarat are stratified into sub-groups, each of which lays claim to a distinct history, lineage, culture and tradition. Although a detailed description of these sub-cultures is beyond the scope of this book, a broad overview would be useful. Hindus are primarily divided along caste lines. The upper-caste layer is composed of Brahmins, Baniyas and Rajputs, who together account for an estimated 12 per cent of Gujarat's population (Shani 2007: 27). These communities dominate white-collar jobs. At the bottom of the upper-caste hierarchy are Kolis or Kshatriyas, a backward-caste group constituting an estimated 24 per cent of the population; and land-owning Patels, who account for about 12 per cent of the population. Scheduled Castes (former untouchables or Harijans) are considered to lie outside the caste hierarchy. They comprise about 13 per cent of the population. Like Hindus, Scheduled Castes are internally divided into

Vankars (traditionally weavers), Chamars (leather tanners), Bhangis (sweepers) and Garodas (Scheduled Caste priests) (ibid.: 28).

The Muslims of Gujarat are equally heterogeneous and form distinct communities. These include Shaikhs, Pathans, Bohras, Khojas and Memons (Gayer and Jaffrelot 2012: 28–9). Shaikhs and Pathans work as cultivators or low-skilled labourers, but Bohras, Khojas and Memons have white-collar jobs or own private businesses. Gujarat is also home to a number of other religious minorities, particularly Jains (who comprise around 1 per cent of the population) and Christians (about 0.5 per cent).

Since 1969, however, Ahmedabad has failed to ensure the peaceful coexistence of its diverse population. In fact, Ahmedabad has now earned the unfortunate distinction of being India's most communally violent city (Varshney 2002: 220). This distinction is attributable to the fact that the city has been the epicentre of some of the deadliest episodes of communal violence anywhere in post-colonial India. For two weeks in September 1969, Ahmedabad saw widespread communal rioting, which left at least 660 people dead (Reddy Commission 1971: 179–82). Even when communal violence reached unprecedented levels across the country in the early 1990s, no single riot and no city recorded as many fatalities (Varshney 2002: 220). In 1985, large-scale communal violence erupted again, claiming the lives of an estimated 220 people, of whom at least 100 were Muslims (S. Patel 1985: 8–9; Shani 2007: 88; see also Dave Commission 1990: 227). In the summer of 2002, the city unfortunately surpassed its own record by becoming the epicentre of the worst anti-Muslim massacre in the history of India, with fatalities of up to 2,000.

With regard to the incidence of sexual violence against minority women during organised communal conflicts, no other region in India has fared as poorly as Ahmedabad. The worst episode involving such violence was the 2002 massacre, during which an estimated 150–200 Muslim women were raped, gang-raped and mutilated in Ahmedabad and two other districts of Gujarat (CCT 2002, 1:226). Less well known is the fact that Ahmedabad had witnessed brutal sexual violence against Muslim women during Hindu–Muslim conflict in 1969 as well. In several neighbourhoods of Ahmedabad, an unknown number of Muslim women were raped, possibly even gang-raped, their breasts were cut, and they were paraded naked on the streets (see Chapter 1). Communal Hindu activists perpetrated these atrocities with a view to inflicting not just deadly bodily harm, but also the maximum humiliation on the victims and their families. Women were sexually brutalised before their husbands, fathers and other family members, and then killed after they had been made to witness the brutal murders of their families.

The city makes an important study for one more reason: Ahmedabad has witnessed another major communal riot during which extreme physical sexual violence, such as rape and genital mutilation, was avoided. This riot occurred between March and July 1985. During this period, sexual violence against Muslim women appears to have been limited to verbal abuse and sexually intimidating behaviour. Moreover, unlike in 1969 and 2002, when almost exclusively Muslim women were targeted, in 1985 a few upper-caste Hindu women were also subjected to sexual violence in the form of verbal abuse and being stripped of their clothing.

This variation in the form and scale of sexual violence enables us to examine the processes involved in the infliction, as well as in the avoidance, of such violence during communal conflict in Ahmedabad. This examination turns on key questions: How are Hindu nationalist organisations or their activists implicated in the occurrence of sexual violence against Muslim women during communal conflicts? Was militant Hindu nationalist ideology, which much of the existing historiography holds responsible for such crimes, absent during the 1985 riot? If it was present, what prevented the incidence of brutal sexual violence against Muslim women? Since extreme forms of sexual violence occurred in 1969 as well, what makes the incidence of such violence in 2002 exceptional, which many scholars claim that it was? What is the role of the state apparatus in handling the occurrence of such violence? By addressing such critical questions, this book provides a comprehensive and nuanced account of the troubled and complex history of sexual violence during communal conflicts in Ahmedabad over the five decades since independence.

The production of sexual violence

The incidence of sexual atrocities against Muslim women during large-scale sectarian violence in 1969, 1985 and 2002 in Ahmedabad was governed by the interaction between Hindu nationalist ideology and local economic, social and political dynamics. This interaction created the conditions for the rape, gang-rape and mutilation of minority women during communal clashes in 1969 and 2002, as well as for the avoidance of such extreme sexual violence during the 1985 riot. By foregrounding the centrality of local specificities to the modalities of sexual violence during communal conflict, this book challenges the predominant scholarly consensus, which has tended to understand these occurrences almost exclusively in relation to elite ideology.

Extreme and less extreme forms of sexual violence against Muslim women during the 1969 Hindu–Muslim riot and the 2002 carnage did not occur incidentally. Rather, these acts were actively produced by a diverse group of actors, especially those affiliated with and sympathetic to the gendered, anti-minority agenda of Hindu nationalist organisations. This violence was employed to achieve both collective and individual objectives: subversion or affirmation of the contemporary political-economic order, destruction of the Muslim minority, assertion of Hindu masculinity, and individual sexual gratification through violent, even savage, 'sex'. In so arguing, I endorse the prevailing view that sexual violence against Muslim women is motivated by a desire among Hindu activists to violate and destroy the 'honour', 'property' and 'procreators' of the Muslim community, and that these motivations draw on Hindu nationalist ideology. I also concur with the explanations advanced by such scholars as Veena Das and Tanika Sarkar, that the manipulation and rehearsal of collective memories of Partition, especially its association with the humiliation of the Hindu male and the virulence of Muslim men, lent potency and salience to these ideological motivations in both 1969 and 2002.

However, I further argue that sexual violence during these episodes was also motivated by prevalent notions that normalise sexual violence as a 'natural' expression of male desire, and that conflate sexual violence with 'sex' (Baxi 2004; Das 1996; Kannabiran and Kannabiran 2002). This made sexual violence simultaneously a tool for publicly and ritualistically violating the political enemy, and a way of seeking opportunistic 'sex' during a major breakdown of law and order.[27] The 'successful' commission of such violence both constituted a collective political victory, and advanced individual desires to have 'sex' with otherwise unavailable women, with both objectives mutually reinforcing one another. Understanding the role of Hindu nationalist ideology in relation to ideas that have become quotidian and are part of everyday patriarchal power structures is key to understanding why Hindu nationalist ideas have gained widespread traction, and, relatedly, why it is so difficult to dislodge them from the fabric of Ahmedabad.

The production of extreme forms of sexual violence against minority women in Ahmedabad is tracked at various levels throughout this book. The first level is that of active communal mobilisation by Hindu nationalist groups through the manipulation and alleviation of the political, economic and social anxieties of various caste, class and professional groups in Ahmedabad.[28] The purview of this communal mobilisation agenda has broadened incrementally since the 1960s. It has extended beyond lower- and middle-class, upper-caste Hindu men to include poor men from backward-caste, Scheduled Caste[29] and Scheduled Tribe[30] backgrounds, as well as middle-class professionals. The scope of mobilisation widened further from the late 1980s and early 1990s onwards to capture Scheduled Caste and upper-caste women from various class backgrounds. During the same period, the focus of Hindu nationalist activities and propaganda changed from protecting Hindu lives in the 1960s and 1970s, to aggressive self-assertion in the 1980s and 1990s, and arguably to the brutal victimisation of minorities in the early 2000s.

The vertical and horizontal expansion in the caste- and class-based support base of the Hindu nationalist movement, the involvement of both men and women, and the rise in the virulence of its propaganda occurred in response to changes in the local, regional and national political economy. The decline of the textile mill industry in Ahmedabad, the demise of the electoral hegemony of the Congress across the country, the replacement of a conservative Gujarat Congress with an overtly politically illiberal BJP as the dominant political force in Gujarat, and the shift from a state-led development model towards economic liberalisation were particularly salient changes. Following the demolition of the Babri Mosque in 1992, organisations comprising the Sangh Parivar (the 'family network' of Hindu nationalist organisations) paid specific attention to occupying power in Gujarat, and were successful in 1995. However, this government lasted barely eight months. After the appointment of the first stable BJP government in 1998, Gujarat began its march towards transforming into a Hindu nationalist 'laboratory' (Dayal 2002; Shani 2007: 15; Spodek 2010) where, compared with other regions in India, the movement's political, social and cultural goals faced the least resistance from the state apparatus. Between 1998 and 2002, the absence of state resistance evolved into the more or less active facilitation of anti-minority activities, paving the way for what many have argued was the complicity of large segments of the state apparatus in the massacre of summer 2002.

The second stage in the production of sexual violence was that of its orchestration. This was accomplished in the riots discussed here through the organisation of mass propaganda campaigns instigating Hindus to inflict 'retributive' rapes against Muslim women, and through the provision of ideological and logistical support to the rioters. In both 1969 and 2002, the campaign was organised by the Hindu right-leaning vernacular print media,[31] Hindu nationalist organisations, and their ad-hoc affiliates that had been established immediately prior to and during the conflict.[32] Promptly after communal tensions started to intensify, these actors circulated false stories about sexual assaults against Hindu women by Muslim men, providing inflammatory fodder via slogans, pamphlets and leaflets that incited men to 'avenge' these crimes through similar actions. Then, leaders of organisations such as the RSS and its affiliates such as the Vishwa Hindu Parishad (World Hindu Council, hereafter VHP) and the Bajrang Dal ('the army of monkey deity Bajrang') allegedly took active part in enabling Hindu activists to attack Muslim women and men, for example, by arming the rioters and identifying Muslim properties with the help of voters' lists.[33] By 2002, Hindu activists were so emboldened by the apparent support of the state apparatus that they made few attempts to conceal their identity, openly publishing the addresses of their offices on propaganda materials, and in some cases attacking Muslims while wearing the RSS uniform (tan-coloured shorts).[34] Consequently, one of the aspects that made the incidence of sexual violence in 2002 exceptional is the failure of the state in preventing such violence, rather than the nature of the violence, since savage sexual violence was perpetrated against Muslim women during the 1969 riot as well.

The third level is that of the actual infliction of such violence. It is at this stage that decades of vigorous communal mobilisation of men and women against Muslims, and the provision of ideological direction and organisational support to rioters, culminated in the rape, gang-rape and genital mutilation of Muslim women and girls at the neighbourhood level. In several cases in 1969 and 2002, men perpetrated these acts against their neighbours, the violence marking an abrupt termination of social ties based on everyday interactions in the locality or at work, as will be illustrated in the following chapters. The rioters sought to inflict maximum humiliation on their victims, often raping and killing Muslim women in the presence of their families. The incremental segregation of neighbourhoods across Ahmedabad along class, caste and religious lines due to communal mobilisation facilitated the abrupt termination of social ties during the violence, reconstituting the neighbourhood into a gendered communal space where nationalist and sexual objectives were achieved on the bodies of women.

The fourth and final stage in the organisation of sexual violence was that of the response of a wide array of actors to the threat and infliction of violence. These actors included police officers, government officials at the state and national levels, the heads of government-appointed independent commissions of inquiry, the judiciary, politicians and Hindu nationalist leaders. A mention of the dominant trends would be illustrative. Between 1969 and 2002, the rise of hard-line Hindu nationalists in the government, the bureaucracy and the police in Gujarat led to a gradual degeneration of their response to the violence. From being partial towards Hindus but nonetheless keen to prevent violence against Muslims in 1969, the state apparatus (especially the police) in 2002 has been criticised for acts of omission, and has been widely accused of acts of commission.[35]

With regard to police actions, it would be illustrative to quote the judgement of a special fast-track sessions court established in Ahmedabad for 'Conducting Speedy Trial of Riot Cases' relating to the 2002 massacre. In her judgement, the presiding judge Jyotsna Yagnik not only criticised the police in strong words for its failure to prevent violence in Ahmedabad's Naroda constituency, but also suggested that the police might have indirectly facilitated the violence:

> It seems very clearly [sic] that the police has not resisted, opposed or hindered the violent mobs and that way, indirectly the men of mob were facilitated because in humble understanding of this Court, the entry point of Muslim chawls near Gate of S.T. Workshop is such where if the police would have made chain then the mob could not have entered inside. To that extent the heart burning of the victims for the police to have ignored the activities of mobs seems to be not wrong.[36]

The court came down particularly heavily on Police Inspector K. K. Mysorewala, who was the senior police officer at the Naroda police station and first investigating officer when the 2002 violence occurred. The court ruled that Mysorewala had failed to take 'even elementary and routine steps' to prevent violence against Muslims in Naroda between 28 February and 8 March 2002, and had 'totally avoided' investigations against the accused. Mysorewala was acquitted since, in the court's view, in 'all such cases of neglect or may be inefficiency one cannot [be] labelled to have malice or any criminality'.[37] Thus, it is not surprising that, whereas in 1969 the Congress-led Gujarat government had appointed an independent commission of inquiry to probe the state's handling of the violence (Reddy Commission 1971), in 2002 the Gujarat administration appears to have obstructed and manipulated the workings of the inquiry commission and may even have sought to subvert the course of justice.[38]

Moreover, despite the occurrence of aggravated sexual assault in 1969 and 2002, neither the state government nor its national counterpart has thus far published any official account of these forms of violence: the commission of inquiry that probed the 1969 riot contained no mention of sexual violence, and the report of the one tasked with probing the anti-Muslim massacre of 2002 has yet to be made public by the Gujarat government (Reddy Commission 1971; Government of Gujarat 2008).[39] Meanwhile, the judiciary has failed to deliver justice to victims: only two cases (from 2002) of sexual violence committed during any communal conflict in India have thus far resulted in conviction, with the possibility of further convictions shrinking with the passage of time.[40]

Whereas most Hindu nationalist leaders have publicly and consistently denied their involvement in any violence, the rhetoric of Hindu nationalist ideology transformed from pleading Hindu victimisation in 1969 to justifying, condoning and even extolling sexual violence in 2002. For example, during the 1969 riot, a pamphlet published by the Hindu Sangram Samiti (Committee for Hindu Struggle), an affiliate of the Jana Sangh, had instigated 'retributive' violence by Hindus against Muslims, warning that if they did not respond to Muslim aggression, 'Hindu religion and Hinduism will be uprooted, their sisters and daughters will be forced to become prostitutes'.[41] By 2002, appeals for the defence of Hindus had been replaced in some instances by crude celebrations of sexual violence against Muslim women. Consider the text of an anonymous pamphlet, entitled 'Jehad', that was circulated in Ahmedabad during the 2002 massacre:

The people of Baroda and Ahmedabad have gone berserk
Narendra Modi you have f****d the mother of miyas [Muslim men]
The volcano which was inactive for years has erupted [...]
We have widened the tight vaginas of the 'bibis' [Muslim women]
She was f****d standing while she kept shouting
She enjoyed the uncircumcised penis.
With a Hindu government the Hindus have the power to annihilate miyas [...][42]

Such celebrations were accompanied by more general calls for violent Hindu assertion: 'Now the Hindus of the villages should join the Hindus of the cities and complete the work of annihilation of Muslims'.[43] This transformation of rhetoric reflects the rise in the assertiveness of the Hindu right in the context of a state apparatus that remained largely apathetic towards the incidence of sexual violence. Yet the unwillingness of Hindu activists to publicly accept responsibility does reflect their continued fear of legal reprisal.

This book also argues that the incidence of rape, gang-rape and other extreme forms of sexual violence is not inevitable in large-scale, organised communal conflict. As in the case of the production of sexual violence, the absence of rape is also a product of the interaction between elite ideology and the social, economic and political triggers of conflict. During the 1985 riot, extreme forms of sexual violence seem to have been avoided despite the active involvement of Hindu nationalist outfits and leaders in the orchestration of communal violence. This avoidance is attributable to the unique orientation of the riot itself. In 1985, unlike in 1969 and 2002, violence arising from caste-based hostilities preceded the emergence of communal conflict, and later continued to occur alongside Hindu–Muslim violence. As a result, the targets of violence included government buildings, police officers, and members of the backward castes and low castes as well as Muslims. In 1969 and 2002, on the other hand, the violence was almost exclusively targeted at Muslims.

This altered the focus of the 1985 riot: it created new forms of mobilisation, an alternative rhetoric and competing networks of violence, thereby diffusing the focus and diluting the potency of the Hindu right's efforts to produce aggravated sexual violence against Muslim women. Upper-caste Hindus instigated and perpetrated violence against backward castes, Scheduled Castes and Muslims, but their rhetoric did not instigate sexual attacks against those identified as 'enemy' women. Acts of sexual harassment in the form of verbal abuse and intimidation were committed by new actors (police officers) against unexpected victims (upper-caste Hindu women) (Women's Research Group 1985: 1730; Dave Commission 1990, 1:237), and by familiar actors (Hindu activists) against familiar targets (Muslim women) (Women's Research Group 1985: 1727–8), but aggravated sexual violence was avoided. Since backward castes and low castes found themselves at the receiving end of some of the violence, they forged neighbourhood-level alliances with Muslims, thereby preventing rapes. By 2002, however, the scope for neighbourhood alliances had shrunk considerably, creating the conditions for the worst forms of sexual brutality inflicted by backward-caste, low-caste and upper-caste men against their Muslim neighbours in Ahmedabad. The analysis of 1985, in sum, foregrounds the complex relationship between elite ideology and the specific, local politics of every individual riot in determining the incidence or absence of rape and other violent sexual acts. This approach suggests that extreme sexual violence is more likely to occur during riots where religious minorities constitute exclusive targets of propaganda and organised attack than in incidents where alternative forms of rhetoric and mobilisation are equally robust.

Why should ideological and organisational plurality have the effect of preventing extreme sexual violence? Even in the pandemonium of a riot, 'mobs' make conscious decisions with regard to perpetrating or refraining from sexual violence against the 'enemy'. Rioters have seldom attacked Muslim women in neighbourhoods where Muslims comprise the majority or a sizeable proportion of the population. A case in point is the absence of violence against Muslim men and women in the Muslim-majority neighbourhood of Juhapura during the 2002 massacre. On the other hand, in both 1969 and 2002, Muslim women were subjected to sexual violence in neighbourhoods where Muslims comprised a small proportion of the local population. For example, the neighbourhoods of

Khokhara-Mahemdabad, Amraiwadi and Bapunagar in the industrial belt were sites of brutal sexual violence against Muslim women during the 1969 riot. In all these neighbourhoods, Muslims comprised a minority: the total non-Muslim population of the region exceeded 158,000 whereas Muslims numbered only 60,000 (Reddy Commission 1971: 29). Due to the force and focus of the riot's anti-Muslim agenda, ties between Muslims and their backward-caste and low-caste neighbours were broken, opening the way for the brutal victimisation of Muslim women. By contrast, in 1985, the local orientation of the riot resulted in the formation of alliances between Muslims and their backward-caste and low-caste neighbours in intermixed localities. This was particularly true of Gomtipur. Such alliances enabled these groups to protect each other's lives and property from upper-caste Hindu rioters and prevent the occurrence of sexual violence against women. This finding has potential implications for feminists and activists working for communal harmony, since it illuminates the positive impact of the political mobilisation of non-upper-caste communities in reining in the destruction wrought by communal violence.

The fact that 'mobs' make deliberate decisions in regard to violence is further evidenced by the apparent absence of sexual violence against affluent Muslim women. In both 1969 and 2002, Hindu activists physically attacked the homes and property of upper- and middle-class Muslims in the affluent, Hindu-majority enclaves of western Ahmedabad. Yet, it seems that such attacks were not accompanied by sexual violence against the women of such families. Lower-class men rarely gain legitimate sexual access to wealthier women, with social networks such as marriage almost exclusively forged among members of a similar or superior class. During episodes of communal violence, men appear not to have ruptured this pervasive sexual boundary between the different classes. Even amid the chaos, crowds appeared to be functioning within definite limits (Das 2006). This claim cannot be made with certainty due to the absence of the testimonies of affluent Muslim women in the existing records. Yet it is likely that the economic and political marginalisation of poorer Muslim women compounded their vulnerability to rape and other sexual attacks in intermixed neighbourhoods.

My explanation for the avoidance of rape is different from the one advanced by cultural theorist Sudhir Kakar in his study of the 1990 communal riot in Hyderabad (the capital of Andhra Pradesh). Kakar (1995: 110) argues that the absence of sexual violence during the Hindu–Muslim conflict in Hyderabad can be explained by the fact that both communities were aware that they still had to inhabit the same geographical space after the riot, and engage in a degree of social and considerable economic interaction in their day-to-day lives. Kakar implicitly suggests that were it not for this everyday interaction and socio-economic interdependence, sexual violence against women would occur during communal riots. This explanation may well be true in the light of the particular political and economic topography of Hyderabad. However, the experience of Ahmedabad shows that what prevents the incidence of sexual violence during certain episodes of large-scale communal conflict is the formation of strategic alliances between different religious communities due to the unique political orientation of the riot, rather than the compulsions of post-violence cohabitation.

In important respects, my argument also differs from the one advanced by political scientist Ashutosh Varshney in his *Ethnic Conflict and Civic Life* (2002). Varshney argues that the eruption or avoidance of communal violence has significant links to the erosion or strength of inter-community engagements forged at the workplace and in other politicised, but non-state, civic settings such as sports clubs and neighbourhood playgrounds. I partly endorse this thesis: as Chapters I, II and III argue, the gradual erosion of inter-community interactions since the 1960s has certainly contributed to the intensification of communal polarisation in Ahmedabad. However, my investigation also foregrounds the presence or absence of transient riot-time alliances between neighbours in creating conditions for the perpetration or avoidance of rape. By contrast, Varshney emphasises the significance of peace-time, civic engagements in preventing or fomenting communal violence. Moreover, as the following chapters will show, not all civic associations endure the onslaught of communal mobilisation during communal riots; longstanding ties between friends, neighbours and colleagues are sometimes terminated abruptly. The infliction or avoidance of aggravated sexual violence then comes to hinge on the formation or lack of temporary alliances during the course of the riot itself.

By foregrounding inter-conflict variations, this book also argues that the incidence of sexual violence during communal riots cannot be understood by means of a linear narrative. Each successive episode of communal riots was not accompanied by an incremental intensification of the nature of sexual atrocities inflicted against Muslim women. The episodes of 1969 and 2002 saw aggravated sexual violence in the form of rape and genital mutilation, but there is no evidence of such extreme violence in 1985. Moreover, this variation is true even though the political power and social purchase of Hindu nationalism has risen consistently since the 1960s, and its rhetoric has become increasingly belligerent and militant. It is also true despite the dislocation of an inconsistently secular state apparatus by an overtly, but not entirely, Hindu nationalist polity between 1969 and 2002. By highlighting the non-linear trajectory of the incidence of sexualised communal violence, I argue that such violence must be understood in close relation with the specific, local context within which a riot occurs, and not just its broader national context, as most studies have done thus far. Relatedly, I seek to emphasise the significance of understanding the modalities of sexual violence by examining episodes where extreme atrocities have not occurred.[44] Probing cases where such acts occur is essential, but an exclusive focus on them risks obfuscating some important nuances of violence, and, equally importantly, possible solutions for preventing it.

Additionally, this book sheds light on the sexual exploitation of women during the transitory phase of relief that follows large-scale, organised conflict. It does this through an examination of the sexual coercion of Muslim women survivors in relief camps in the aftermath of the 2002 massacre. That such incidents occurred is not altogether surprising. Instances of sexual exploitation of women by peacekeepers have been recorded in the aftermath of large-scale violence and civil wars in many others parts of the world, including Cambodia, East Timor, Nepal, the Democratic Republic of Congo (DRC), Mozambique, Liberia, Somalia, Eritrea and Haiti (Bastick et al. 2007). In these various cases, 'peacekeepers' – including but not limited to soldiers, military officers, police officials, development specialists, humanitarian workers and other civilians – used the vulnerability of some female refugees to coerce them sexually. For example, during the five-year civil war in the DRC between 1998 and 2003, mass rapes were inflicted upon Congolese women by the Rwandan rebel group, the Democratic Forces for the Liberation of Rwanda, and the DRC's Mai-Mai Cheka rebels in the eastern part of the country. The UN intervened in 1999 through its various subsidiaries and stationed over 19,000 peacekeepers in the region. In 2005, the UN Office of Internal Oversight Services recorded 72 allegations of sexual violence committed by UN peacekeepers against girls and women. Of these 72 cases, 20 were substantiated. Some of these females were as young as 12 years old and had been sexually victimised 'in return for a glass of milk or a dollar' (ibid.: 21–2).[45]

Returning to India, in 2007 similar incidents were reported in the aftermath of political (but non-communal) violence in Nandigram district of West Bengal. One young female survivor testified to the People's Tribunal, established to probe the Nandigram violence, that she was afraid of the 'bad men' in the relief camps, and that 'some mothers tried to send daughters away at night to sleep with village women instead of sleeping in the camps among men' (All India Citizens' Initiative 2007: 33).

Yet this issue of sexual coercion of Muslim women in the relief camps has thus far been absent in the public discourses on sexual violence during 'Gujarat 2002', making it impossible to determine the scale and, to some extent, the nature of the exploitation. Nonetheless, on the basis of the testimony of a survivor-victim, the work of some civil society activists involved in relief and rehabilitation, and the response of Muslims leaders affiliated to Islamic organisations, it is possible to reflect on its occurrence. My analysis suggests that some Muslim women were coerced by certain relief camp organisers to exchange sexual services for basic aid in the form of books, clothes and money. From the point of view of the victim-survivor, this exchange constituted not only sexual exploitation but also betrayal by members of her 'own community'. At the same time, the possibility of exchanging 'sex' for relief also presented an opportunity, albeit within an intensely restricted context, to improve her family's life-chances in the wake of the destruction wrought by the massacre. This reality illuminates the concurrence of agency and victimisation even in the context of a massacre that radically disempowered Muslim men and women.

From the point of view of civil society activists, the occurrence of such exploitation raises profound dilemmas, since the pressing need to rehabilitate Ahmedabad's besieged Muslim community appeared partially to conflict with the desire to ensure that women's rights were protected. The project of seeking relief and justice for the victims of sexual and other forms of violence in the massacre, and that of preventing and addressing sexual exploitation in the camps, were not fully congruent and compatible. Hence, efforts to achieve justice for and provide relief to the survivors of the massacre appear not to have been accompanied by (and may well have been incompatible with) efforts to secure justice for women who suffered in the camps. Some male and female religious leaders, however, have viewed the situation differently, construing the sexual exploitation of women in the camps as unfortunate and undesirable, but an inevitable expression of natural male sexual instincts. Although these leaders unequivocally condemned the sexual victimisation of Muslim women by Hindu rioters as a political and communal act, their views illuminate the ideological traffic between the popular understanding of sexual violence during 'peace-time' and the production of such violence during conflict.

Structure of the book

This book first examines Hindu nationalist ideology with respect to sexual violence. While placing considerable emphasis on the significance of Hindu right-wing ideology in motivating such violence, scholars have seldom examined this explanation in relation to the founding texts of the Hindu nationalist movement.[46] I address this gap by undertaking an analysis of the writings of all three founding ideologues of the Hindu nationalist movement – Savarkar, Hedgewar and Golwalkar. By examining a broad range of their texts and speeches, I argue that the intricately crafted ideological framework of Hindu nationalism contains an implicit justification of sexual violence against 'enemy' women at its very core. This discussion constitutes the final part of this Introduction.

Chapters I, II and III are dedicated to granular analyses of the Hindu–Muslim riot in 1969, the inter-caste and communal violence of 1985, and the anti-Muslim massacre of 2002, respectively. Each episode of conflict is situated within its local, regional, national and, wherever relevant, international contexts, and the activities of Hindu nationalist organisations in each instance are interrogated. I then disassemble events that occurred during each conflict to investigate how sexual violence was instigated, orchestrated and inflicted, in what form, where and by whom. I trace such violence all the way to the survivors, the eyewitnesses and, wherever possible, the perpetrators. I also probe the responses of

Hindu nationalist leaders, the state, the political class, the Muslim community and civil society to Muslim women's sexual victimisation. Chapter 4 delves into the aftermath of 'Gujarat 2002', examining the nature and scale of relief work, the incidence of sexual coercion in the relief camps, efforts by the Muslim community to rebuild itself in the city, and the responses of the government, national authorities and the judiciary to the sexual violence committed during 2002.

A note on method

This study is based on a wide variety of sources that I collected in the course of fieldwork undertaken during October 2006–January 2007 and September 2007–January 2008. Much of this time was spent in Ahmedabad, although I also visited archives, academic institutions and human rights organisations in Surat, Vadodara, Delhi and Mumbai. For any complex and rich qualitative study, a diverse range of methods is considered essential (Harding 1997). I adopted a documents-based method, which entailed consulting a wide variety of documents (government reports, Hindu nationalist publications, civil society commentaries, academic analyses, etc.) and media reports. Besides this, I used interview-based and observation-based methods.

During fieldwork, I focused on interviewing people from broadly five backgrounds: human rights activists and academics; leaders of Islamic organisations active in Ahmedabad; Hindu nationalist activists and politicians; men who participated in the riots; and riot survivors. In total, I conducted 85 interviews during my fieldwork. Owing to the sensitive and confidential nature of the issues discussed in this book, pseudonyms have been used for all but one of the respondents. Rashida Bano, whom we will encounter in Chapter 1, explicitly requested that I use her real name.

Since my interviewees came from diverse backgrounds, and spoke to me about various events and occasionally about emotionally disturbing issues, I adopted a flexible approach to interviews. For example, I often allowed my interviewees, especially the survivors, to set the pace of the discussion and to choose the location, and did not stick to a planned set of questions. In most instances, discussions were held over several days in the offices or homes of interviewees. Moreover, I consciously chose to interview both men and women from each set.

Among activists, I focused on individuals working on communal harmony, engaged in preventing and addressing violence against women, or involved in the rehabilitation of Muslim families affected during the riots. In addition to prominent activists and academics, I also conducted interviews with a second tier of activists who were mobilised from among disadvantaged Muslims. Together, their testimonies provide insights into the growth of Hindu nationalism in the state, the scale of everyday and episodic violence against women, the avenues of justice available to survivors, and issues involved in their rehabilitation, especially in the aftermath of the 2002 massacre. Interviews with academics and political commentators helped supplement the information provided by rights activists.

I also interviewed leaders of the Jamaat-e-Islami and Jamiat-Ulema-e-Hind who have been active in the rehabilitation of survivors since 2002. Their interviews provided insights into the response of the elite leadership to the incidence of sexual violence during the 2002 carnage, and their reflections on the everyday lives of Muslim women who were displaced in the aftermath of the violence.

Although most Hindu nationalist leaders and sympathisers were unwilling to speak to researchers, I did succeed in coordinating interviews with a few leaders of the BJP, the RSS and the Rashtriya Sevika Samiti. I also conducted discussions with heads of the RSS's publications and media centre and their education wing. Despite initial hesitations, they agreed to share not only their insights but also some of their documentation with me. With the assistance of Muslim activists and some organisations working with Dalit (Scheduled Caste) and Muslim youth, I conducted interviews with members of the VHP and the Bajrang Dal who had participated in the 2002 violence.

Speaking with Muslim women and men who had experienced the riots as adults or youths was an important part of my fieldwork. Since official records have largely obscured the voices of those who experienced the riots, and reports by non-governmental organisations (NGOs) have recorded only a limited number of testimonies, it was important to interview the survivors. Similarly, since the experiences of those who inflicted the violence are also largely absent from official records and NGO reports, direct interviews with participants was the only way to gain insight into their motivations.

In order to make interviews manageable and representative, I concentrated on three areas in Ahmedabad during my fieldwork: Behrampura, Vatva and Juhapura. Behrampura and Vatva are located in the south-eastern part of the city, while Juhapura is located in the south-west. In Behrampura and Vatva, I interviewed lower-income Muslim and Dalit families who depended on the city's textile mills for their livelihoods until the closure of these mills in the mid-1980s and 1990s. These two neighbourhoods were affected repeatedly by communal violence between 1969 and 2002. Moreover, Vatva has become home to a large number of Muslim families who were displaced during the 2002 violence. These families could not go back to their homes for fear of being attacked. Juhapura, which has the largest concentration of Muslims anywhere in India, has all the characteristics of a 'ghetto' (Jaffrelot and Thomas 2012: 70). The area is home primarily to lower-income Muslim families who have survived repeated bouts of communal violence. In the aftermath of the 2002 violence, however, several middle-class Muslim families have also moved into the neighbourhood to ensure their safety. In Juhapura, I conducted interviews with both lower-income groups and the more affluent families. I also conducted several interviews among low-income Muslim families who live in Ekta Nagar, which is a relief colony in Juhapura that exclusively houses the survivors of 2002.

Initial introductions to interviewees were secured through the good offices of some NGOs that are active in these neighbourhoods. Over time, I established independent connections through people I encountered during my long stay in Ahmedabad, and via my interviewees, especially local Muslim leaders who live in these neighbourhoods. The interviews were mostly conducted in the homes of the interviewees and in the absence of other members of the family. Their testimonies were collected through repeated in-depth interviews, usually over several days.

I asked questions about the background of the locality, its history, caste, class and religious composition, the nature of social and economic interactions before and after riots, political views and means of livelihood. A second set of questions related to the everyday lives of residents, their experiences of domestic violence, how they coped, whether they sought help from the police or NGOs, and their impressions about the incidence of similar violence within their neighbourhoods. A third set of questions focused on their experiences of the riots: when and why the violence began, who was involved in inflicting the violence, how they defended themselves or engaged in violence, whether they or any members of their family were injured, whether they faced a threat of sexual violence, or witnessed such crimes being committed upon someone else, and what the impact of curfew had been on their daily routines and sources of income.

These interviews often left me dealing with ethical questions. I was concerned that by asking people to share their experiences of surviving or witnessing violence, I might inadvertently undermine their coping mechanisms. In order to assuage this persistent worry, I confessed to my respondents that our discussion might stir painful memories and could have severe emotional repercussions. A lot of people, however, generously agreed to be interviewed. Moreover, I refrained from contacting survivors of sexual violence. I also did not resist when my (male and female) interviewees asked me personal questions, not all of which were welcome.

Some group discussions were also conducted in the house of one of the interviewees in which members of the immediate and extended family and next-door neighbours participated. Another group discussion was organised in the office of a local civil rights organisation in which young Dalit and Muslim men and women participated. Some of the Dalits in the group had participated in the 2002 violence, while some of the Muslim participants had witnessed their families being coerced into exchanging sexual favours for aid in the relief camps after the 2002 massacre. In contrast to what I had expected, men and women in each group discussion were remarkably frank about their everyday lives and their experiences during communal violence. Although my questions kept the discussions focused, the participants commented on each other's remarks as well. This dynamic brought out some important ideas that may not have emerged had the interviews been conducted individually.

Apart from group discussions in which I participated partially, observation-based methods that did not involve any direct participation on my part also remained important throughout the fieldwork. In Delhi and Ahmedabad, I observed several meetings and events organised by members of different rights groups, academics and journalists, addressing the social and political situation of Gujarat. I also attended two meetings organised in Ahmedabad by an NGO on Muslim women's issues and India's domestic violence laws, particularly the Protection of Women from

Domestic Violence Act of 2005. These meetings brought together a diverse group of actors who had witnessed the various riots in Ahmedabad.

Working on sexual violence and the limitations of sources

Research on sexual violence against women during conflict is confronted with unique difficulties. Notions of honour routinely prevent women from speaking out about their personal experiences. The picture is complicated by contemporary socio-political discourses in Gujarat that constrain the creation of archives of information relevant to the issue. The following discussion describes how these notions and discourses impose limitations on the sources available. This poses unsurpassable constraints on what can and cannot be known about instances of such violence during large-scale conflict.

One major limitation is the unavailability of authoritative statistics on the rates of sexual violence during episodes of communal conflict. In many instances of brutal sexual violence, especially those that occurred during the 2002 massacre, the victims did not survive. Moreover, as discussed earlier, in 2002, the police failed to prevent sexual and other forms of violence against Muslims, omitted details about rapes from complaints filed by survivors, and has been criticised by the judiciary for indirectly facilitating the violence.[47]

A more local reason for the obliteration of data on the true scale of such crimes from the records is that Gujarat has consistently maintained a façade of being a non-violent region as compared to other states in India. When I asked my (middle-class, upper-caste) respondents about the incidence of violence against women in Gujarat, they almost invariably had one of two main responses. First, Gujarat is a safer place for women because they can travel alone without need of a male escort and with no fear of violence. Second, riots are temporary events with no long-term implications for women's lives. The conversation I had with a mathematics professor at Gujarat University, who also heads the media cell of the BJP in Gujarat, is illustrative:

SY: Women in Gujarat are very safe and independent, they drive their own kinetic scooters, they go everywhere alone, they are studying on merit in universities, they wear modern dress [...] they are out to capture the world.

MK: If women are so safe and independent why is there so much violence against Muslim women during the riots?

SY: Riots are a different thing [...] In any case riots don't make much of a difference to women's lives [...] I don't think [...] they start and then they come to an end. In general Gujarat is a very safe place for women. (Interview, Ahmedabad, 10 December 2007)

In such descriptions, the purported safety of women 'in general' serves to make invisible the gendered violence that occurs during riots. Since riots are considered momentary aberrations that 'start' and then 'come to an end', their long-term implications for the lives of women who survive sexual violence get obscured.

The difficulties of creating comprehensive descriptions of the events that occur during riots are compounded by the lack of legal documentation. In Gujarat – in fact, all over India – only two cases of sexual violence that occurred during Hindu–Muslim strife have thus far led to convictions. This points to the extent to which such crimes have gone unaccounted for since India's independence in 1947. As a result, affidavits, verbatim transcripts of legal proceedings and official testimonies of the accused and the victims do not exist.

In order to compensate for the lacunae in police records and for the partiality of contemporary socio-political and judicial discourses, I approached the oldest Ahmedabad-based women's organisation, Jyoti Sangh, for their records. Significantly, however, the counsellors at the organisation informed me that due to the stigma associated with sexual violence, most survivors register their complaints under 'kidnapping and abduction' charges. As a result, their records do not provide any indication of the rate of sexual violence. As a last resort, I approached three prominent women's organisations in Ahmedabad, and one each in Surat and Vadodara. I had hoped that their records would provide an indication of the rate of such crimes during the riots. However, I was not allowed to access their materials. It seems that the heads of these organisations did not wish to aid research that would be critical of the incumbent BJP government out of fear of reprisal. Their refusal could also, perhaps, be motivated by the desire to maintain control over the data they had collected so that they could claim national and international funding. This NGO politics limited my access to records that may exist on the rate of such crimes during communal riots in Ahmedabad.

Consequently, I had to rely on non-official publications by civil society organisations and academics to provide some indication of the nature and scale of gendered violence. I also had to rely on the testimonies of my respondents to provide this information, while being cautious of the fractured and selective nature of memory, especially traumatic memories. Since the survivors were recollecting events that had happened several years or decades previously, their memories were sometimes fragmentary or inaccurate. During my fieldwork, the narratives of some survivors, especially those who had been witness to more than one episode of communal violence, confused the events of different riots. Other survivors who had suffered utter devastation during the 2002 violence understandably found it difficult to talk about their experiences coherently. Pain, suffering and loss overwhelmed their narratives. Although these two sets of testimonies uncover the toll that frequent and ghoulish violence takes on human lives, they do not retain the coherence that would be necessary for reconstructing the past.

Significantly, however, I also came across people who remembered previous riots quite vividly; or, as one survivor described it, 'like it was yesterday'. These survivors remembered the riots down to the most mundane details: the day on which the violence began and where, what they were wearing, what they were doing, how they responded when their neighbourhoods were attacked, what they were cooking at the time and whether the radio was on. It is this last set of testimonies that appears throughout this book. Even though these narratives were not immune to the selective processes of memory, their relative coherence made it possible to triangulate information.

Moreover, engaging members of Hindu nationalist organisations who participated in the riots in conversations about sexual violence in particular, and communal violence in general, has been difficult. First, most Scheduled Caste men (except two) whom I interviewed explicitly denied having participated in any violence, even when their Muslim neighbours insisted that they 'saw them with their own eyes'. The unwillingness of people to discuss their political affiliations, their views on communal and sexual violence, and their reasons for participation, seems to have grown particularly acute in the aftermath of the 2002 massacre. Since the gaze of human rights organisations, academics (myself included) and legal practitioners continues to be firmly set on Gujarat, people deny any knowledge of violence out of fear of legal reprisal. This denial has made it impossible to access their interpretations first-hand.

Hindu nationalist ideology and the instigation of sexual violence

An articulate, exclusionary Hindu nationalist movement emerged in the 1920s, when Indian politics was undergoing decisive shifts.[48] At the time, a mass anti-colonial struggle was gathering pace under the leadership of Gandhi, who envisioned a non-violent, principled agitation against British colonisation and the creation of an inclusive Indian nation (Brown 1989). Under the influence of religious reform movements in regions such as Punjab and Bengal, religious identities were becoming increasingly politicised, and Hindu–Muslim riots were on the rise (T. Basu et al. 1993: 12–13). Formidable anti-caste movements were developing in western India, especially in Bombay Presidency, threatening the hegemony of upper-caste Hindus (S. Sarkar 1996). In response to these shifts in national politics, three Brahmin men from Bombay Presidency first articulated the ideology of the Hindu nationalist movement (C. Bhatt 2001).

Vinayak Damodar Savarkar (1883–1966), Keshav Baliram Hedgewar (1889–1940) and Madhav Sadashiv Golwalkar (1906–73) believed that a glorious Hindu *rashtra* (nation-state) had existed in antiquity, but had fallen from grace due to the corruption of Hindu civilisation, the dilution of people's faith in scriptural Hinduism, the loss of Hindu male vigour, and repeated invasions by physically more powerful but morally degenerate enemies, especially Muslims. They wished to restore the magnificent and powerful imaginary Hindu nation-state (Andersen and Damle 1987; T. Basu et al. 1993; Jaffrelot 2005). This Hindu rashtra would be a majoritarian state, wherein the rights of religious minorities would be limited, if not non-existent, and subject to the wishes of the Hindu majority. In terms of its socio-cultural order, the Hindu rashtra would adhere to an orthodox scriptural interpretation of Hinduism, at the expense of other interpretative and syncretic traditions within Hinduism. The caste system and patriarchal structures would be reinforced, consolidating the supremacy of the upper-caste Hindu male.

To create such a nation-state, these ideologues believed that it was imperative to cultivate a martial spirit among Hindu men (which would allow them to suppress Muslims) and to bring lower castes into the 'Hindu fold' (so as to pre-empt any challenges to the caste hierarchy).

The lynchpin of the emerging Hindu nationalist movement was the RSS, an all-male paramilitary organisation formed by Hedgewar in 1924–26 under the ideological tutelage of Savarkar. After Hedgewar's death in 1940, Golwalkar took over as sarsanghchalak of the RSS, a position he retained, in line with RSS custom, until his own death in 1973.

The RSS seeks to reinvest the Hindu male with martial vigour, reaffirm Hindu cultural values, and 'purify' the civilisation (Andersen and Damle 1987). To that end, it organises *shakha*s (neighbourhood branches) where volunteers meet regularly (daily, weekly or monthly) and receive military-style training in the use of weapons such as sticks, batons, swords and firearms. They follow a strict regimen of physical exercises to inculcate discipline and bodily vigour. In ideological training sessions, volunteers receive instruction in the RSS's warped version of South Asian history, with an emphasis on stories about the 'demonic' Muslim enemy. The aim of this training is to instil in volunteers an unquestioning devotion to militant Hindu revivalism, to the removal of the purported Muslim threat, and to the project of national reinvigoration. Up to this day, Hindu nationalism in India owes its success and strength to the RSS and its shakha model. The RSS requires its *pracharak*s (preachers), who are tasked with generating support for the organisation across different parts of India, to take a vow of celibacy and lead an austere life in order to establish their probity. (The current Prime Minister of India and former Chief Minister of Gujarat, Narendra Modi, is a former RSS pracharak.)

Since fascist groups that emerged in Europe between the 1920s and 1940s promoted similar notions of racial supremacy and xenophobic nationalism, and also mobilised paramilitary forces, numerous commentators have described the RSS as a fascist organisation (T. Basu et al. 1993; Jaffrelot 2005). Indeed, the founding ideologues of the RSS had links with European fascist outfits and exalted Hitler's leadership (Casolari 2000). Inspired by the uniforms of Italy's fascist Voluntary Militia for National Security and the Nazi paramilitary wing, Sturmabteilung (Storm Detachment), RSS volunteers wear tan-brown ('khaki') shorts and black caps, and the RSS salute is a variant of its Nazi counterpart. Golwalkar was also an ardent admirer of Hitler's anti-Semitic views (see Golwalkar 1947).

In order to make an ideological case for an armed, anti-Muslim, Hindu nationalist movement, Savarkar, Hedgewar and Golwalkar carefully constructed in their writings and speeches a narrative around the ferocity of Muslim men and women, the weaknesses of the Hindu male, and an ever-present Muslim threat to Hindus and Hinduism. Together, these three elements of the narrative formed a powerful incitement to commit retaliatory and pre-emptive sexual violence against Muslim women.

The construction of self and other

The question of how the 'we' of a possible Indian nationhood might be constituted was deeply contested from late nineteenth century onwards, as articulate critiques of colonisation and political demands for independence began to emerge. The debate became particularly intense and divisive in the 1920s, when proponents of Hindu and Muslim communalism sought to conflate religious and national identity (Gilmartin 1998; Pandey 1991). Savarkar, by far the most articulate proponent of an exclusive Hindu nationalism, made the most explicit attempts to provide a comprehensive definition of Hindu identity. He rejected the idea that a Hindu is a person who believes in the tenets of Hinduism and practises its rituals. Instead, he defined a Hindu as a 'person who regards the land of Bharatvarsha from the Indus to the Seas as his Fatherland [*pitribhumi*], as well as his Holyland [*punyabhumi*] – that is the cradle of his religion' (Savarkar 1949: 3–4). With this definition, Savarkar sought to submerge caste-based, regional, linguistic as well as religious differences among people who could identify their 'Holyland' with the 'Fatherland'. Ideological and customary differences among Jains, Buddhists and Sikhs, for instance, were submerged under the overarching rubric of 'Hindu', on the grounds that Jainism, Buddhism and Sikhism had emerged in India. Muslims and Christians were the only ones excluded, because their 'Holylands' are situated outside the country.

Having provided an easily accessible definition of 'Hindu', Savarkar attempted to define Hindu male and female sexuality, which for him was closely intertwined with nationalism. He was not alone in trying to redefine sexuality through the lens of nationalism and vice versa. Many colonial critics stereotyped colonised Indians as sexually degenerate, effete and passive, and such descriptions were used to justify continued colonisation (Mosse 1982; Sinha 1995). In response, Indian leaders, including Gandhi, attempted to redefine the sexuality of the colonised race and to reform masculine and feminine behaviour, with a view to achieving national independence (Kishwar 1985; Parekh 1989).

Savarkar did not have a clear conception of a positive ideal of Hindu sexuality. So he adopted a more reactionary approach, which entailed the careful construction of a historical description of the 'enemy' so that a Hindu self could be forged as an inverted, mirror image of the adversary. In his *Six Glorious Epochs of Indian History* (1970), Savarkar describes the 'essence' of Muslim identity. He describes Muslim men as invaders, iconoclasts, fanatic proselytisers and rapists. A typical passage in Savarkar's writings on the alleged 'sexual immorality' of Muslims reads:

> With this same religious fanaticism the highly aggressive Muslim of those times considered it their highly religious duty to carry away forcibly the women of the enemy side, as if they were commonplace property, to ravish them, to pollute them, and to distribute them to all and sundry, from the Sultan to the common soldier [. . .] almost every Muslim kept at least three or four such forcibly polluted women. (Ibid.: 176–7)

Having described Muslim men as repellent, aggressive rapists and Islam as a 'demonic faith', Savarkar characterises Hindu men as civilised, non-violent and mild. In fact, he thought Hindus were excessively virtuous, an excess bordering on perversion. In one chapter of *Six Glorious Epochs of Indian History* titled 'Perverted Conception of Virtues', Savarkar blames this excessive virtuosity of Hindus for the degeneration of the Hindu race: 'Far greater than the Muslim could ever attempt were the defeats inflicted on themselves by these morbidly virtuous Hindus! If a comparatively mild term is to be used for this infatuation, this mental imbalance of the Hindus, which caused disastrous losses for themselves, we have to call it a perverted sense of Hindu virtue' (ibid.: 167).

While he continued to speak of the relevance and desirability of virtues, Savarkar sought to encourage Hindus not to be virtuous towards Muslims by narrating the adverse impact of inappropriate and misapplied ethics:

Having only learnt by rote the maxim [that] to give food to the hungry and water to the thirsty is a virtue, the Hindus went on giving milk to the vile poisonous cobras and vipers. Even while the Muslim demons were demolishing Hindu temples and breaking to pieces their holiest of idols like Somnath, they never wreaked vengeance upon those wicked Muslims, even when they had the golden opportunities to do so, nor did they ever take out a single brick from the walls of the Mosques, because their religious teachers and priests preached the virtue of not inflicting pain on the offender. (Savarkar 1970: 168–9)

By describing the violence supposedly perpetrated by Muslims against the Hindu community, the Hindu nation and the Hindu religion, Savarkar could formulate a provocative repertoire of images about Muslim men.

Female sexuality was as important to nationalist projects as notions of masculinity. Colonial critics often portrayed the 'brown woman' as a victim of the tyranny of the 'brown man', and as being in need of the benevolence and protection of white men and colonial institutions (Burton 1994). In response to this criticism, Indian reformers from the nineteenth century onwards promoted reforms of patriarchal and religious traditions that affected women (Mani 1989; T. Sarkar 1992). By the twentieth century, the nationalist worldview had shifted. Indian leaders projected both Hindu and Muslim women as the custodians of tradition, paragons of devotion, and symbols of (non-sexual) love and sacrifice. Women were seen as responsible for the preservation of the sanctity of their own homes and the superiority of their male relations (Devji 1991: 151; Ghosh 1994: 80; Kishwar 1985: 1691; T. Sarkar 2001: 198). There was a striking similarity between the discourses on Hindu women and those on Muslim women in much nationalist and even colonial politics.

In the writings of the founding ideologues of the RSS, however, stereotypes about Muslim women contrasted sharply with those about Hindu women. The former were portrayed as immoral, vicious and complicit in the sexual and non-sexual crimes of Muslim men, whereas the latter were projected as gullible, virtuous, honourable and devoted to preserving their chastity. Savarkar, for instance, wrote:

No Muslim woman whether a Begum or a beggar, ever protested against the atrocities committed by their male compatriots; on the contrary they encouraged them to do so and honoured them for it [...] Not only in the troubled times of war but even in the intervening periods of peace [...] they enticed and carried away young Hindu girls, locked them up in their own houses, or conveyed them to the Muslim centres – in Masjids and Mosques. The Muslim women all over India considered it their holy duty to do so. (Savarkar 1970: 178)

By contrast, in his account of Akbar's attack on the kingdom of Gondwana in medieval India, Savarkar describes Hindu women in a sharply different light:

The dowager Queen Durgawati, decided not to surrender but to fight the well-equipped imperial army of Akbar, and offered such a tough resistance that for a while the invaders were astounded. She bravely defended the cause of Hinduism till she was overwhelmed by the vastly superior numbers of the Muslim emperor [...] Knowing full well from hundreds of such cases how these Muslim wolves ill-treated and molested the royal Hindu ladies who fell captives in their hands, Rani Durgawati offered her body, along with many other ladies of the court, to the sacred fire of the battle. She left strict orders to her attendant to burn her dead body and not to let the Muslim infidels touch it. (Ibid.: 381)

By suggesting that Hindu women have historically prized the preservation of their religious identity and sexual chastity over their own lives, Savarkar's intention was also to prescribe these 'virtues' to Hindu women in the future. However, he advocated these 'virtues' not because they were essential to self-realisation among women, but because of the impact that errant behaviour would have on Hindu men. For Savarkar, women were the symbols of honour of the family, the community and the nation. In his story about the daughter of a Hindu Rajput king, Savarkar made explicit the connection between the female body and the honour of the Hindu race and religion. He lamented that the Hindu woman chose to marry the Muslim king who attacked her kingdom, wishing she had instead committed suicide and preserved Hindu honour. Savarkar wrote, 'Had she swallowed fire like some [other Hindu queens and princesses] [. . .] and followed the path of martyrdom for the sake of religion, her life and her family tradition would both have been forever glorified!' (1970: 327).

This description completed the image of the enemy and the self: the Muslim male was portrayed as a violent iconoclast, a proselytiser and a sexually promiscuous rapist, and the Muslim female was stereotyped as immoral, perverse and violent. By contrast, the Hindu male was described as being peaceful, sexually abstinent, monogamous and civilised, and the Hindu female as a chaste, devout mother and wife.

Female bodies and male weakness

In addition to these characterisations of male and female sexuality, the Hindu nationalist narrative portrayed the violence allegedly inflicted against Hindu women by Muslim conquerors as responsible for a purported decline in the Hindu population, and as a product of the weaknesses of the Hindu male.

In most of his writings, Savarkar expressed deep remorse about imaginary Muslim efforts to abduct, rape and forcefully convert Hindu women. He was not, however, primarily concerned with women's experience of violation, but rather with the decrease in the number of women capable of producing Hindu progeny. Lamenting the alleged forced abductions of Hindu women, he said, 'Our woman-world [. . .] suffered such a tremendous numerical loss, which means their future progeny [has] been lost permanently to Hinduism [. . .] Without any increase in their womenfolk the Muslim population would have dwindled into a negligible minority' (Savarkar 1970: 180–1). In lamenting the loss of 'Hindu wombs', Savarkar was echoing the concerns of other nationalist leaders of his time who were equally paranoid about a relative reduction in the Hindu population and rise in the Muslim population (C. Gupta 2004: 4303). Consequently, Muslim men were projected as a threat to the future of the Hindu race.

The ideologues of the RSS construed what was seen as the continued appropriation by Muslims of the biological reproducers of Hindu men as a 'challenge to their manhood' and as a sign of Hindu weakness. According to Hedgewar, it was because of this weakness that Hindu men failed to prevent the degeneration and colonisation of the Hindu race and the violation of Hindu women:

If I start describing the atrocities committed against Hindus and the rapes perpetrated against our daughters and daughters-in-law to forcefully convert them to Islam, then I will not be able to control my emotions. The Christians also regularly perpetrate similar kinds of violence against us [...] [Such] innumerable difficulties have befallen us. Even then we continue to remain weak. *We can neither protect our women, nor save our daughters from being humiliated.*[49] They have come to believe that Hindu wives-daughters are *their* property. It is because of *our weakness* that they don't feel the need to be scared of us [...] From now on we shall not commit this sin. *It is because of this sin that our body parts have been cut.* (Hedgewar 1972: 9–12; emphasis added)

Here, women are construed as the symbols of honour and property of the male members of the community, and the bodily violation of a woman is viewed as evidence of masculine weakness. With the sexual humiliation of women impinging on masculinity in this way, Hedgewar felt able to call on Hindu men to cultivate an alternative sexuality – one that would 'scare' the enemy and prevent their own 'property' from being forcefully appropriated by Muslims.

Threat of further violation

The RSS ideologues wished to project the 'Muslim threat' as a contemporary reality rather than as an aspect of history. The idea that the threat of Muslim aggression was very much a part of current affairs stemmed primarily from two worries: the presence of a Muslim minority within India, and the creation of Pakistan in 1947 as a separate Islamic state with a large Muslim population. According to these ideologues, the former factor represented an internal and the latter an external threat to the future of Hindus and their nation.

In order to make the internal threat posed by the Muslim minority seem significant enough to warrant concern, Hindu nationalist ideologues equated their presence in India with a disease present in the body of the nation. Consider the following lines penned by Golwalkar in this context: 'If the blood-stream in the body is infected with germs, boils will erupt all over the body. If you treat and bandage them at one spot it will appear at another place. The basic remedy would be to purify the blood-stream itself. So also is the case with the body-politic of society' (1996: 230). The metaphor of disease makes the 'Muslim threat' appear invasive, intimate and dangerous. It effectively conveys the magnitude of the danger ostensibly posed to Hindus by India's religious minorities.

The persuasive power of such metaphors assumed increased significance when Hindu nationalist ideologues repeatedly drew parallels between the body of the nation and the body of a mother. In his 1905 pamphlet *Vande Mataram*, Savarkar explained his conception of the nation:

> Brothers we are, being the children of Mother Bharat [Mother India]. Our memorable ancestors were the sons of Mother Bharat. The children to be born in this land in the future would be Mother Bharat's sucklings, nestling in her arms [...] Does not Mother Bharat strike you as the granary of all grace and beauty [...] To this land made fertile by these sacred rivers we bow, O Mother [...] Like the swelling breasts of Parvati, the mangoes of India are. Like the sweet unkissed lips of the heavenly damsels, the grapes here are. And the grape-vines bend like a loving mother bending to suckle her baby. (1983: 1–4)

Like many other writers of his time, Savarkar conceived of India as a 'motherland' that took the form of a woman's body – one that was young, fertile, graceful, beautiful, compassionate and sensual.[50] The 'motherland' was imagined as a woman who gave life to brave men and provided nourishment on the one hand; on the other hand, the subtle sensuality of this figure was pleasing to a heterosexual male sensibility. The presence of an infection in the graceful body of the mother could lead to the loss of her beauty as well as her life. The fear and pain associated with the death of one's mother could thus be transferred on to the nation. Thus, the nexus between a feminised nation and a bodily disease served to represent the Muslim presence in the 'body-politic' of India as still more repulsive and provocative.

This strategy depended on a displacement of the idea of the 'fatherland' by that of the 'motherland' in describing the Hindu nation. As mentioned earlier, in his work *Hindutva*, Savarkar (1949 [1923]) had defined a Hindu as one who regards the land of Bharatvarsha as his 'Fatherland' and his 'Holyland'. Here, the 'fatherland' (*pitribhumi*) was understood as an entity to which one owed allegiance, in contrast to the feminine 'motherland' (*matrubhumi*) that needed to be protected. The ancient, unconquered, powerful nation assumed the body of a man as pitribhumi, while the colonised, weak, helpless, present-day Hindu nation was imagined as a woman and became matrubhumi.[51] The ideologues of Hindutva propagated this idea not only in their writings and speeches but even in RSS prayers. One such prayer reads as follows:

Affectionate Motherland, I eternally bow to you
O Land of Hindus, you have reared me in comfort
O Sacred Land, the Great Creator of Good, may this body of mine
be dedicated to you
I again and again bow before You
O God Almighty, we the integral part of the Hindu Rashtra salute
you in reverence
For Your cause have we girded up our loins
Give us Your Blessings for its accomplishment.
(Quoted in Islam 2000: 13)

Several complementary tasks were successfully accomplished through this rhetorical reference to the 'motherland'. First, it reinforced patriarchal notions of men as powerful and heroic, and women as weak and in need of male protection. Second, the conflation of the motherland with the body of a Hindu woman would make it possible for the very presence of Muslims in the country to be seen as a form of sexual violation of the motherland. Hence, the expulsion of Muslims from the body-politic of the nation-state would protect the motherland as well as Hindu women from further sexual violation. Third, through the image of a vulnerable, helpless woman, these ideologues could advocate the inculcation of a martial spirit as mandatory for the preservation and redemption of masculine pride. Last, they could argue that the presence of a supposedly aggressive, and therefore masculine, Pakistan, which could further ravage the vulnerable Hindu motherland, should be a matter of concern for Hindu men. It was now up to Hindu men to 'dedicate' themselves to neutralising the 'Muslim threat'.

Golwalkar often reminded his readers that the existence of Pakistan as a separate state ought to be a source of anger for Hindu men, because the nation, or the body of the mother, had been cut into pieces and her sons had been unable to prevent it. He incited them to exact retribution in the following words:

> There are some who tell us, 'Bygones are bygones. What is the use of raking up old dead issues? After all, Partition is now a settled fact'. How is this ever possible? How can a son forget and sit idle when the sight of his mutilated mother stares him in the face every day? Forget? No true son can ever forget or rest till she becomes once again her complete whole [. . .]
>
> The tearing away of the limbs of our mother and the gory blood-bath of millions and millions of our kith and kin is the price that we have paid for that ignoble attitude. (Golwalkar 1996: 93)

The invocation of a wounded, mutilated mother was again intended to provoke Hindu men and incite hatred against Muslims living in India and in Pakistan. Factual descriptions of territorial division, no matter how detailed, can scarcely exercise the same psychological influence on the mind of the reader as a description of the mutilated body of one's mother. It is also worth noting that the call here was only to the 'sons' of the motherland, suggesting that the protection of territorial borders was a male affair, and that failure to protect the mother/nation would be construed as a sign of their weakness.

Golwalkar also projected Pakistan as a potential future threat to the masculine pride of Hindus because of its alleged expansionist designs. He claimed that the 'Muslim menace has increased a hundredfold by the creation of Pakistan which has become a springboard for all their future aggressive designs on our country' (1996: 178). A constant sense of emergency and threat was thus relayed, necessitating the control of women and the protection of the mother/nation so that the honour of Hindu men would not be threatened.

Instigating sexual violence

The RSS ideologues believed that to create a powerful Hindu nation, Hindu men would need to avenge past crimes allegedly committed by Muslims, humiliate the Muslim community, and pre-empt future enemy aggression.

Retribution for past 'Muslim crimes', according to both Savarkar and Golwalkar, would be possible only if Hindus committed the same crimes against Muslims. For this, detailed description of the forms of violence perpetrated by Muslims against Hindus was useful. Just as Muslims had purportedly done in the past, Hindus would desecrate mosques and shrines, loot and destroy their property and humiliate Muslim women. Savarkar, for example, argued that 'in order to reward the meritorious services of the choicest [Hindu] warriors in this Hindu–Muslim war at least as many young and beautiful Muslim girls should be captured, converted to Hinduism and presented to them' (1970: 245).

While thus legitimising violence against women, RSS ideologues were nevertheless mindful of the implications of their instigation of violence. Hence, they sought to counter any ethical constraint a Hindu man might feel in inflicting such violence against Muslims. They argued that *ahimsa* (non-violence), kindness or chivalry towards enemy women, mercy towards the enemy and religious tolerance were all virtues, but inapplicable and inappropriate in the Hindu struggle against the Muslim enemy. Savarkar stated:

> It is blind and slovenly – even impotent – adoption of all these very virtues irrespective of any consideration given to the propriety of time, place or persons, that so horribly vanquished the Hindus in the millennial Hindu–Muslim war on the religious front. For every virtuous act done without the least regard to the propriety of the persons concerned – without the least thought whether the other person concerned deserves such noble treatment or not – becomes a glaring vice most harmful to the true religion. (1970: 187)

According to Savarkar, the decision regarding whether to adopt a given set of virtues depended on the nature of the enemy. Through the scathing portrayals of Muslim men and women in the works of these ideologues, readers could be encouraged to view the infliction of sexual violence as immoral in all contexts, except in the struggle against 'demonic' Muslims, where such acts would be justifiable, even necessary.

As if to remove all vestiges of ethical doubt, the ideologues employed religious imagery borrowed from the mythological epic *Ramayana* to instil this idea of the relativity of virtues in the minds of readers.

Describing the mythic episode of the abduction of the Hindu princess and goddess Sita, wife of Rama, by the demon-king Ravana, Golwalkar declared:

> Sri Rama was aware of his ultimate duty of establishing the rule of righteousness by destroying the wicked. The slaying of an innocent woman is sinful but the same principle cannot be applied to a demon. The technique of fighting also varies according to the nature of the enemy. This is the right understanding of warrior dharma [religious/ethical duty] and Sri Rama followed it. (1996: 286)

By invoking episodes from the *Ramayana*, a text revered by most believing (upper-caste) Hindus at least in northern India, Savarkar and Golwalkar provided a powerful moral sanction to the use of rape as a justifiable tool in the struggle between Hindus and Muslims. Sexual violence against Muslim women, in the Hindu nationalist worldview, was implicitly construed as a religious duty of righteous Hindu men, and a justifiable tool in communal conflict.

Apart from avenging the supposed past sexual crimes of Muslims, these ideologues believed that the rape of Muslim women would deter Muslim men from attacking Hindu women in the future. Savarkar, for instance, stated: 'in the event of a Hindu victory our molestation and detestable lot shall be avenged on the Muslim women. Once they are haunted with this dreadful apprehension, that the Muslim women, too, stand in the same predicament in the case the Hindus win, the future Muslim conquerors will never dare to think of such molestation of Hindu women' (1970: 179). Whereas the 'retributive' rape of Muslim women would soothe Hindu wounds, this 'pre-emptive' sexual violence was advocated as a deterrent to future Muslim aggression. This instigation to rape and molest Muslim women was effectively predicated on the idea that women's bodies are the carriers of community history, constituting the site on which past historical wrongs (imaginary or otherwise) can be corrected.

The sexual violation of the Muslim female body was seen by these ideologues as a way to redeem the Hindus' lost masculine pride. Descriptions of the weaknesses of the Hindu male facilitated this prescription. From as early as the 1930s, Savarkar and Hedgewar started advocating the militarisation of Hindus. They asked Hindu men to join body-building gymnasiums and obtain training in the use of arms and swords to cultivate a martial spirit among local shakhas of the RSS. They firmly believed that 'he wins half the war who takes the offensive – who is aggressive' (Savarkar n.d., quoted in C. Bhatt 2001: 103). According to them, the Gandhian idea of non-violence was leading to the 'emasculation of the Hindu community', rendering it incapable of defending Hinduism and Hindu women or creating a glorious Hindu nation-state (T. Basu et al. 1993: 23). Since non-violence was equated with weakness and impotence, and violence with power and male honour, attacks against Muslims and sexual violence against Muslim women were seen as tools to redeem and boost the pride of Hindu men.

The rape and slaughter of Muslim women, to these ideologues, may also have seemed like an effective way of neutralising the 'threat' posed by the Muslim minority to the future of the Hindu people and the Hindu nation. By destroying or appropriating the reproductive capabilities of Muslim women, Hindu nationalist activists could disrupt the production of Muslim progeny. The anxiety with regard to the supposedly ever-increasing Muslim population and decreasing Hindu numbers could be assuaged by the occupation of the Muslim womb. Raping Muslim women would result in their impregnation by the seed of the 'superior and pure Hindu race' and eventually help increase the Hindu population.[52] This would result in a diminution of the Muslim population and, by implication, a reduction in the infection in the body of the 'diseased' mother/nation.

Restoration of the Hindu nation to its lost glory required more than increasing the Hindu population and decreasing Muslim numbers, according to Golwalkar. He contended that revitalising Hindu masculinity was key:

> Real national regeneration should start with the moulding of 'man', by instilling in him the strength to overcome human frailties and to stand up as a shining symbol of Hindu manhood [. . .] We should unfailingly keep this vision, this real essence of our glorious nationhood, before our eyes so that we can again rise to our original pedestal of the world preceptor. (Golwalkar 1996: 47–8)

From Golwalkar's perspective, the 'regeneration' of Hindu men was integral to realising the essence of the Hindu nationalist project of eliminating the internal and external Muslim threat. This regeneration, as discussed previously, required the cultivation of a martial spirit and willingness to vanquish the Muslim enemy through violence, including the rape of Muslim women.

To conclude, this section has argued that Savarkar, Hedgewar and Golwalkar carefully constructed a historical narrative about the ferocity of the masculine and feminine actors of the enemy community, the weaknesses of the Hindu male, and the ever-present Muslim threat; these ideas contributed to an instigation of sexual violence against Muslim women. In providing this ideological justification, these founding ideologues also created a powerful language in which the need for the cultivation of an aggressive Hindu male sexuality could be articulated. Pre-emptive and retaliatory sexual violence against Muslim women could then appear as a way to redeem injured Hindu male pride, and assert Hindu power and virility. Since the distinctions between past and present, history and the future, were so creatively blurred in these texts, the insertion of an alternative moral code for current application was also made possible. Under this new moral code, sexual violence against one's perceived enemy could be regarded as a necessary, justifiable and even commendable act.

Although insensitivity and injustice towards women is implicitly condoned by many political and religious worldviews, rarely is the sexual violation of women overtly rationalised. Hindu nationalist ideology, however, since its formulation, as I have argued, has contained an implicit encouragement of sexual violence against 'enemy' women at its very core. This ideology, as the ensuing chapters will show, has gained widespread traction since independence, and has played an important role in aggravating and sexualising communal divisions. Yet there is no simplistic causal relationship between the degree of acceptance of the ideology of the Hindu right and the actual perpetration of sexual violence against Muslim women during communal conflict. Rather, as the following chapters will explore, the production of such acts is shaped by the interaction between these belligerent ideas and the economic, political and social dynamics in operation at the local level, with the interplay resulting in the infliction, or in some cases the avoidance, of sexual violence.

CHAPTER 1

1969

Many Muslim women were subjected to severe sexual violence during the 1969 Hindu–Muslim riot in Ahmedabad.[1] This violence was similar to that which occurred during Partition in 1947, and during the anti-Muslim massacre in 2002 – the two most devastating episodes of communal violence in India's modern history. In 1947, 1969 as well as 2002, women were stripped, paraded naked on streets, raped in fields, on roads and in their homes, sometimes in the presence of their husbands, siblings, parents and children. Their breasts were scratched and cut off, and their genitals mutilated. Some of the victims were left for dead, some murdered. Yet in significant ways, the 1969 riot was different from the episodes that preceded and followed it.

The foremost difference is in the scale of the violence. During 1947 and 1948, thousands of Hindu, Sikh and Muslim women were raped, at least one million people were killed and up to 15 million people were displaced (Khan 2007). Punjab and Bengal, the two regions that were partitioned, were the epicentres of the violence, but several other parts of India were affected as well. Since Partition, India has mercifully never witnessed a human tragedy of comparable magnitude. However, those it has witnessed are by no means negligible. Whereas Gujarat escaped Partition violence largely unscathed,[2] it has since witnessed recurring communal violence. The worst such episode in the state occurred in the summer of 2002. Between February and April 2002, up to 2,000 people were killed in 19 of the total of 26 districts in Gujarat. An estimated 150–200

Muslim women were subjected to brutal sexual violence in Ahmedabad (the worst-affected region) and at least two other districts (CCT 2002, 1:226). Some 2,500 Muslims were reported 'missing' and 113,000 others were forced to flee their homes and seek refuge in 103 relief camps across the state.[3]

In contrast to 1947–48 and 2002, the overall toll taken by the 1969 riot was relatively smaller: according to official estimates, 660 people were killed, 1,074 grievously injured and over 48,000 rendered homeless in sporadic rioting across Gujarat between 18 and 30 September 1969 (Reddy Commission 1971: 179–82). Informal estimates put the number of fatalities at 1,000–2,000 (Spodek 2011: 172). No other state apart from Gujarat was affected by the riot. In 1969, Ahmedabad was the epicentre of the violence; seven of Gujarat's 19 districts were affected.[4] These were Banaskantha, Mehsana, Sabarkantha and Gandhinagar in the north; Kheda and Anand in the east; and Vadodara in the south. Sexual violence was perpetrated against Muslim women in several neighbourhoods across Ahmedabad, as will be shown in the course of this chapter.

Although relatively smaller in scale compared with 1947–48 and 2002, the 1969 riot in Ahmedabad was the deadliest episode of communal conflict India had witnessed between 1950 and 1995. Even when communal violence reached unprecedented levels across the country in the early 1990s, no single riot and no city recorded as many fatalities (Varshney 2002: 220). In Gujarat, Hindu and Islamic festivals and mass religious processions had frequently resulted in inter-community scuffles since at least the eighteenth century (Dave Commission 1990, 1:67–9). Just prior to independence, communal riots occurred in the state in 1941 and 1946 as well. Between 1956 and 1968, the government had also recorded numerous 'minor incidents' of rioting involving Hindus and Muslims (Reddy Commission 1971: 46). The 1969 riot, however, surpassed all these episodes.

The religious background of those involved in the violence also sets the 1969 conflict apart from the events of 1947 and 2002. During Partition, Sikhs, Hindus and Muslims were perpetrators as well as victims of sexual and other forms of violence. During 2002, on the other hand, the overwhelming majority of the victims were Muslims, and almost all the perpetrators of the post-Godhra massacre were Hindus. The 1969 riot lay somewhere in between these extremes: both Hindus and Muslims were targeted for violence, but the latter comprised the majority of the victims and incurred disproportionate losses. According to official statistics, of the 660 people killed, 430 were Muslims and 230 Hindus; of the 1,074 injured, 592 were Muslims and 482 were Hindus. Out of the Rs 42 million worth of property destroyed or looted in Ahmedabad alone, property worth Rs 32 million belonged to Muslims (Reddy Commission 1971: 179–82). Unofficial statistics put the death toll at up to 2,000, which if true would make the 1969 riot as deadly as the 2002 massacre. Yet there is an important distinction between these two episodes: the marked widening of the gap between the casualties suffered by Muslims and Hindus. In 1969, Muslim fatalities would have comprised about half to two-thirds of the overall death toll, unlike in 2002, when the overwhelming majority of those killed were Muslims. This shift reflects the intensification of communal divisions across large parts of Gujarat, particularly from the mid-1980s.[5]

Another crucial difference among the three episodes has to do with the role of the state apparatus, especially the government, individual politicians and the police. In 1947–8, the Indian subcontinent was undergoing a tough and bloody transition from colonial rule to democratic self-governance. Both the newly created Indian and Pakistani administrations were overwhelmed as over 10 million people crossed the Radcliffe Line in Punjab and Bengal in the largest mass migration of people in the twentieth century. Neither the Indian administration nor its Pakistani counterpart was directly implicated in perpetrating sexual and other forms of violence against Hindu or Muslim women and men. On the contrary, the government led by India's first Prime Minister Jawaharlal Nehru took an overtly paternalistic attitude towards women who had been raped, abducted or converted to Islam during Partition, and were still in Pakistan. In 1948, it launched a 'Recovery Operation' to ensure that such women were returned to their rightful 'owners' (their country and their families), even if that meant disregarding the wishes of those women who did not want to return to India or to their families (Butalia 1998; Daiya 2008; R. Menon and Bhasin 1998).

Since Partition, however, the role of the state in inter-religious riots has undergone a significant shift, which culminated in 2002 when several senior politicians, members of the Gujarat legislative assembly and police officials condoned the violence against Muslims, and in some instances even actively facilitated it.[6] At the time, the BJP was in power in Gujarat as well as in the national government in Delhi. By contrast, in 1969, the Congress Party–led regional government was neither overwhelmed by external contingencies (as the Indian government had been in 1947–48), nor overtly Hindu nationalist in ways that the BJP government in 2002 certainly was. Yet, as will be argued in what follows, it was overwhelmed by the riot and was not completely impartial in its handling of the violence.

While journalists, writers, academics, commentators and activists have done much to restore the events that occurred in 1947–48 to the archives, and have prevented the horrors of 'Gujarat 2002' from being forgotten or concealed, relatively little is known about the sexual violence that occurred during the 1969 riot. This lacuna is conspicuous in both official records and academic commentaries. On 13 October 1969, less than two weeks after the 1969 riot was brought under control, the Home Department of the Gujarat government appointed a three-member official commission of inquiry and tasked it with investigating the causes of the riot, the efficacy and adequacy of the administration's preventive and control measures, and proposing recommendations that might be adopted to prevent such riots from recurring. Supreme Court Justice P. Jaganmohan Reddy was appointed the commission's chair, and Gujarat High Court justices Nusservanji K. Vakil and Akbar S. Sarela were its other members.

In just over a year, on 24 October 1970, the Reddy Commission submitted a two-volume report to the government, which in turn published it for public perusal on 9 March 1971.[7] The report contained invaluable information on areas affected by the violence across Gujarat, notes on some major incidents, testimonies of government officials, the police, politicians, social activists, Hindu nationalist leaders, propaganda material seized by the authorities, details of injuries caused, etc. However, it made not a single reference to the sexual violence that had occurred in September 1969. In fact, the Reddy Commission made no attempt to disaggregate fatalities or injuries on the basis of gender or age, occupation and caste. In the context of a communal riot, it assumed that religious identities – 'Hindu' and 'Muslim' – alone qualified as categories of analysis, with the result that violence inflicted against women because of their gender was omitted from the investigation.

The lacuna is also present in all but one academic commentary on the issue. Sociologist Ghanshyam Shah has provided the only scholarly account that I am aware of.[8] In his 1970 article, Shah records the most gruesome aspects of the violence:

> Atrocities multiplied by the 20th (September) evening when several poor labourers were either burnt alive or murdered. In some places they were thrown into fires. Scythes, axes, knives and spears were used for killing people. Women were raped or ripped bare and forced to walk naked on the road: children were beaten against stones or their legs were torn apart. Limbs were cut out of dead bodies, women's breasts were cut and sex organs were mutilated or torn apart. (G. Shah 1970: 195)

However, Shah's article does not analyse this violence. It contains no investigation of how sexual violence against women was instigated, orchestrated or inflicted. This chapter is an attempt to fill that gap.

Expecting present-day sensitivity to gendered violence from local, regional and national institutions of the 1960s would perhaps be anachronistic. After all, modern feminism emerged in India only around the early 1970s, and it was only from the late 1980s and early 1990s that feminist activists, gender-sensitive academics and other scholars raised our awareness about sexual violence and other gendered crimes. Even so, the gaps in the official documents on the 1969 riot with regard to sexual violence are glaring, and compound the already acute difficulty in establishing the precise scale of sexual violence against women, specifically during any large-scale conflict. As a result, it is impossible to gauge, for example, how many Muslim women were sexually victimised during the 1969 riot in Ahmedabad; whether Hindu women, or some men, were also subjected to similar brutality; and whether rapes occurred beyond Ahmedabad in the other affected parts of Gujarat as well.

This chapter endeavours to recover fragments of this lost history. Here, I examine the context in which the 1969 riot occurred, the specific events that catalysed the violence, and how sexual violence against women was instigated, orchestrated and inflicted across Ahmedabad, with particular reference to the experience of Muslim women during the riot. An exploration of events that occurred outside the city is beyond the purview of this book.

Decline of the textile industry and Ahmedabad's industrial workers

The textile industry is the oldest manufacturing industry in India. At the dawn of independence in 1947, it was also the largest organised domestic industry, with the cities of Bombay, Ahmedabad, Coimbatore and Kanpur as its main centres. From the 1960s, the industry was heading towards terminal decline as composite mills (i.e., mills where spinning, weaving and processing were carried out in the same plant) struggled to preserve competitiveness vis-à-vis the burgeoning small-scale industrial units. Ahmedabad was desperately vulnerable: the composite textile mills had been the backbone of the city's economy since at least the early twentieth century, as well as its largest employer. At the start of the decade, some 141,347 workers, well over a quarter of the 433,000-strong urban workforce, depended directly on the mills for their livelihood, while a substantial number worked in sectors ancillary to the mills such as construction, chemicals and mining (Government of India 1971: 24–5).

In the mid-1960s, as economic stagnation set in, hundreds of mill workers were made redundant or temporary, and work was increasingly outsourced to cheaper, contracted labour. The total number of workers employed in the mills fell in 1970 to 132,803 (which was equivalent to about one-third of the city's adult male population) (Government of India 1971: 24). Up to 10 per cent of these workers were hired on temporary contracts, which offered only about a quarter of the pay of full-time employees and no benefits (Spodek 2011: 158). Yet even as the textile industry declined and avenues of employment shrank, thousands of unemployed migrants from rural Gujarat, UP, Maharashtra and Rajasthan continued to pour into Ahmedabad in search of livelihoods and better futures. Consequently, the population of Ahmedabad district rose from over 2.2 million in 1961 to 2.9 million in 1971 (Government of India 1961: 20; 1971: 80). During the same period, the population of Ahmedabad city increased 38.25 per cent from 1.1 million to 1.7 million (Gayer and Jaffrelot 2012: 49). This created a shortage of both jobs and housing.

Scheduled Castes and Muslims were disproportionately affected by these changes: they comprised a mere 10.8 per cent and 7.9 per cent, respectively, of Ahmedabad city's population in 1961, but formed the bulk of the mills' labour. Even though the mill workforce comprised people from UP, Maharashtra, Rajasthan and rural Gujarat, the work was determined by their caste and religious identities. Muslims and upper-caste Hindus (especially Patels) dominated the weaving departments, while Scheduled Caste communities such as Vankars and Chamars ran the spinning shops (Gillion 1968). Moreover, since Scheduled Castes were considered ritually impure, they were prohibited from entering the premises of weaving shops to prevent them from 'contaminating' the textiles (Breman 2004: 17). This spatial segregation had been an enduring source of animosity between the different caste and religious groups in the city.

Yet, despite caste-based discrimination and spatial segregation, employment in the mills was invaluable to the Schedule Castes. Mills offered job security, insurance against disability and illness, higher wages compared to those in the informal economy, social facilities and political representation through Ahmedabad's Textile Labour Association (TLA), which was formed under Gandhi's guidance in 1919 (Breman 2004). Redundancy took all this away from them.

Muslims, for their part, had been gradually pushed out of the mill workforce from the 1940s because of the prejudiced hiring preferences of mill owners, most of whom were orthodox Hindus who desired cultural homogeneity in the mills (Breman 2004: 134). Yet, as with their Scheduled Caste counterparts, the mills were dear to Muslim workers as well: besides considerations of economic and social security, communal hostility beyond the compounds of the mills was worse, and other employers were deeply reluctant to hire Muslims to permanent posts.

As the economic situation worsened for male workers previously employed in the mills, so also working-class women were affected adversely. Already from the 1940s, Scheduled Caste and Muslim women had been pushed out of the mill labour force – partly to create employment opportunities for men, and partly because of patriarchal notions that women's 'proper place' was in the house (Breman 2004: 24). Women comprised only 5,487 (or under 4 per cent) of mill workers in 1960 (ibid.: 82). In other sectors of Ahmedabad's formal economy, such as the non-household manufacturing, processing, services and repairs industry, there was only one female worker for every 20 male workers (9,759 women to 197,725 men) in 1961. By 1971, this ratio had deteriorated to 1:27.6 (8,622 women to 238,101 men). In the household manufacturing sector, where women have traditionally constituted a larger proportion of the workforce, the decline was even more dramatic: there was one female worker for every 1.4 male workers in 1961 (20,972 women to 29,901 men), and one female worker for every 5.7 male workers in 1971 (2,892 women to 16,491 men) (Government of India 1961: 20; 1971: 80–1).

Indeed, nationwide industrial stagnation had made women across India more vulnerable than men to unemployment and under-employment and to expulsion from the organised labour market. At the pan-Indian level, the participation of women in the paid labour force (including middle-class workers and industrial labourers) had fallen to 17.4 per cent in 1971 from 31.5 per cent in 1961 (census data quoted in Roy 2005: 138). Between 1961 and 1971, women's participation in the formal economy of Gujarat plummeted from 491 per 1,000 male workers to 231 (Women's Studies Research Centre 2003: 77).

Failure to find secure employment and reasonable wages, and the need to supplement family incomes, also led more women into sex work. According to the records of Jyoti Sangh, the oldest women's organisation in Ahmedabad, at least 192 women were involved in sex work between 1960 and 1970, as opposed to 142 in 1950–59 and 161 in 1940–49.[9] Interviews conducted by the present author and by sociologist Jan Breman with industrial labourers in Ahmedabad (many of whom were formerly employed in the textile mills) also suggest that the decline of the textile industry, and overall economic stagnation from the mid-1960s, forced more women into this trade, further undermining women's social standing.

Ahmedabad's burgeoning informal economy offered relief, but only barely. Laid-off, underemployed and unemployed male and female workers increasingly sought employment in semi-skilled or unskilled sectors, such as wood and paper manufacturing and small repair and alteration workshops. However, this employment offered lower pay, minimum or no benefits, longer hours, a diminished social standing and a sharp decline in living standards (Breman 2004: 113–15). Moreover, entrenched caste and religious prejudices blocked the access of Scheduled Caste and Muslim workers to better-paid and more secure jobs. This left upper-caste Hindu (both migrant and Gujarati), Scheduled Caste and Muslim industrial labourers increasingly competing with one another for jobs and social respectability. The housing crisis that paralleled the economic decline of the textile industry made matters worse.

The industrial belt, the walled city and the western enclave

In the 1960s, the majority of Ahmedabadis lived east of the River Sabarmati. A significant proportion of the labour class, which constituted almost a quarter of the population, lived here in dilapidated *chawl*s and slums close to the factories and mills. Built on either side of dead-end alley-ways, chawls were one- or two-room tenements that lacked even the most basic civic amenities such as water, electricity and sanitation. Most of the chawls were built by mill owners in the 1930s and 1940s and made available to the workers at subsidised rents.

However, in the 1960s, the stagnation in the textile industry slowed down the construction of new chawls. The rising demand for housing due to the continued influx of migrant labour exacerbated shortages of chawl housing, forcing ever-growing numbers of people to live in slums. Located around the chawls, slums offered dismal living conditions. In both the slums and the chawls, caste- and religion-based spatial segregation was strictly observed, low castes and Muslims living separately but in close proximity to one another. Housing shortages in the industrial areas became another source of pernicious rivalry between these groups, already in competition with each other over jobs.

Outside the industrial region, industrial workers and lower-income groups were housed in *pol*s in the walled city, which was founded in 1411 by Ahmed Shah on the eastern bank of the Sabarmati river. Pols, an architectural style unique to Ahmedabad, are dense, elongated housing areas in which multi-storey wooden buildings surround a quadrangular courtyard with common water and sanitation facilities. In the pols, as in the chawls and slums, residential space was ordered along caste and community lines. Upper castes, Muslims and Scheduled Castes lived in separate pols located in close proximity to one another. Like the different caste communities, Muslims were not a homogeneous, monolithic community either; they too were divided internally along occupational, sectarian and regional lines. For example, in Muslim-dominated pols, the residents were divided into sect- and occupation-based groups, each dominated by a specific *jamaat*. Jamaats are religious and occupation-based associations, which adjudicate religious and everyday disputes between their members. Different jamaats dominated each Muslim pol. For instance, the Qureshi jamaat, members of which worked as butchers, dominated the Mirzapur pol.[10] Remarkably, economic status was not a basis for segregation: relatively better-off upper-caste, Scheduled Caste and Muslim residents lived alongside poorer families in the pols.

The pols of the walled city were also home to the majority of Ahmedabad's middle class, whose members hailed predominantly from upper-caste Hindu communities such as Brahmins, Patels and Baniyas. Scheduled Castes and Muslim middle-class families were a small minority. The caste- and religion-based biases of middle-class Hindus were acute, and were most visibly manifested in their spatial segregation in different pols and in the mills. According to Ghanshyam Shah, middle-class Hindus harboured strong suspicion and latent hostility towards Muslims, who were viewed as anti-national (or pro-Pakistan), unwilling to modernise their traditions, as insular, non-secular, and as recipients of unjustified special privileges from the Congress for the sake of their votes (G. Shah 1970: 189). Scheduled Caste men and women faced similar discrimination, not least due to their engagement in 'impure' tasks such as leather tanning and manual scavenging.

Although better off compared with the inhabitants of the squalor-ridden chawls and slums in the industrial area, middle-class Hindus of the walled city were suffering a palpable deterioration in the quality of their life. Pols across the walled city were dilapidated and overcrowded, with population density exceeding 300,000 per square mile by 1974 (Spodek 2011: 136). The demand for necessary civic amenities far outpaced supply. For example, an underground sewage system had been established for the entire walled city in the 1930s. However, its extension to the industrial area and to the western part of the city between 1939 and 1958 overstretched the capacity of the sewage drains, causing regular blockages (ibid.: 133–4). Meanwhile, the cost of living soared, especially due to food inflation. The consumer price index for urban, non-manual workers in Ahmedabad rose 25 per cent from 140 in 1966 to 175 in 1971. The rising cost of several essential food items such as vegetable oil, milk and vegetables was becoming a source of deep discontent (G. Shah 1974a: 233).

Those who could afford to purchase property in the western part of the city moved out of the pols, especially to the predominantly middle-class Ellisbridge area. Consequently, the population of Ellisbridge rose to

223,954 in 1971 from 110,825 in 1961 (Spodek 2011: 134). However, as affluent families moved out, migrant upper-caste Hindus from lower-income groups moved into the vacated houses. From the mid-1960s, economic and social competition escalated between older Muslim residents of the pols and new Hindu entrants (Gillion 1968).

As economic conditions in eastern Ahmedabad deteriorated, the western part of the city was rapidly developing into an affluent enclave where residential buildings were interspersed with educational institutions, offices and university buildings. An overwhelming majority of the residents were middle-class, upper-caste Hindus who lived in apartments and bungalows, although the region was also home to wealthy mill owners of the city, such as the Sarabhai family, which owned the Calico Mill. Spatial segregation along caste, religious and regional lines, which characterised residential patterns in the pols, chawls and slums, was replicated here. Upper-caste Hindu communities of Brahmins, Patels and Baniyas dominated the area, living in separate buildings or on separate floors within the same building. They shared the caste- and religion-based prejudices of the middle-class residents of the walled city. A small number of affluent Scheduled Caste and Muslim families also resided in western Ahmedabad, living separately from each other and from upper-caste Hindus. A majority of these residents worked in the services industry, while others ran their own businesses (Shani 2007: 34).

Unlike the vast majority of the residents of eastern Ahmedabad, people living west of the Sabarmati had access to civic amenities, educational opportunities and well-paid, secure jobs. Women were allowed school-level education, although their access to university and professional colleges was severely restricted.[11] In contrast to their poorer counterparts, women living in western Ahmedabad usually did not work outside the house (Shani 2007: 34). In fact, upper-caste, middle-class Hindu families in the walled city and in the western part of Ahmedabad actively discouraged women from working outside the confines of the regulated domestic space. Two notions guided this practice. First, middle-class women were provided for by their male family members, and so did not need to earn a living. This rationale was widely reproduced and repeated in the vernacular media during the 1960s. For example, *Gujarat Samachar*, the daily newspaper with one of the highest circulations in Gujarat, carried numerous articles that stated that women were only 'forced' to work outside the home when the male members of the family were unable to earn enough to meet the family's needs and fulfil its aspirations. So women joined the paid labour force in order to 'support the parents', or to 'provide for the education of their younger siblings'.

Second, when middle-class women worked beyond the ostensibly safe confines of the home, the argument went, they faced 'sexual dangers'. Numerous articles on this theme filled the pages of popular vernacular newspapers throughout the 1960s, constructing an image of the 'outside world' as (sexually) unsafe for (upper-caste, urban, middle-class) women. A typical article published in *Gujarat Samachar* at the time stated: 'To the outside world, lives of working women seem emancipated and independent. However, these girls are forced to continue working even though they have to face countless inappropriate questions and problems because of it. A job is not a straight-forward and simple path of service, it is a path full of thorns'.[12]

Yet home itself was 'full of thorns' for a lot of women in Ahmedabad. Between 1960 and 1970, reported incidents of gender-specific crimes within the domestic space rose rapidly in Ahmedabad. This assessment is based on the annual records of Jyoti Sangh, which was established under Gandhi's guidance in 1934 and worked with women from all backgrounds. Its records, although not disaggregated on the basis of the complainant's caste, religious or class affiliation, show that the total number of reported crimes against women increased significantly in the 1960s. The rise may represent greater reporting or increased levels of violence. Some 14,289 women came to Jyoti Sangh between 1961 and 1970, compared with 12,142 between 1950 and 1960, to report crimes ranging from domestic abuse and physical violence to child marriage and adultery. Between 1961 and 1970, reported incidents of 'domestic abuse' by family members increased 91 per cent to 8,325, from 4,359 between 1950 and 1960.

Yet, during the same period, there was a marked decline in reported incidents of certain forms of victimisation, such as 'domestic violence'. This could reflect a reduction in the incidence of such crimes, a decline in the reporting of specific crimes, or the manner in which certain complaints were categorised by the staff of Jyoti Sangh. For instance, reported incidents under the category 'domestic violence' declined to 2,228 from 3,283 between 1950 and 1960, while complaints categorised as 'domestic abuse' rose 91 per cent during this period. Jyoti Sangh counsellors informed me that rape cases have historically been recorded under the category 'kidnapping and abductions' because of the stigma and shame associated with sexual violence. Indeed, the organisation recorded its first case under the category 'rape' only in 1981. Hence, it is impossible to track the number of rape cases reported to Jyoti Sangh between 1960 and 1981. What we do know is that cases under the category 'kidnapping and abductions' decreased to 134 from 167 between 1961 and 1970.

This high incidence of crimes against women remained relatively below the radar of the state apparatus. For example, the National Crime Records Bureau did not start collecting data on the total incidents of rape per year in India until 1971 (that year, 2,487 such cases were reported[13]), and also did not record gender-specific crimes against women – for instance, under categories such as 'dowry deaths', 'sexual harassment', 'molestation' and 'cruelty by husbands and relatives' – until 1995. Before 1995, the bureau recorded crimes under broader categories, most of which concealed the extent to which women were targeted because of their gender. These categories included 'criminal breach of trust', 'murder', 'kidnapping and abduction', 'cheating', 'arson' and 'hurt'.

The state's blind spots with regard to violence against women were reproduced by women's organisations such as Jyoti Sangh, since they were inspired by Gandhian views on ideal feminine and masculine behaviour.[14] For Gandhi, women embodied the virtues of (non-sexual) love, self-sacrifice and selfless service, and their primary arena of activity was the domestic sphere. Yet he also saw them as potential agents in the struggle to create a new, harmonious social order wherein each individual would endeavour to imbibe the best 'masculine' and 'feminine' virtues. Strongly opposed to violence against women, Gandhi's emphasis was on reforming the domestic arrangement rather than disintegrating it.

In line with this view, Jyoti Sangh's aim was – and still is – to bring about reconciliation between aggrieved women and their kin, by offering counselling to both parties, facilitating compromise and admonishing the perpetrators (Pathak 2006: 7). The organisation believes that police intervention is necessary only when violence reaches extreme levels and repeated counselling fails. This is why, out of the total of 833 cases the organisation received in 1950, Ahmedabad's police was involved in only 74. In 1960, when the total number of complaints nearly doubled to 1,580, only 290 cases were reported to the authorities. In 1970, police intervention was sought in 226 – or less than 16 per cent – of the total number of 1,445 cases. The focus was always on negotiations and preserving relationships, on compromise rather than revolt. Irrespective of the merits of this approach to engendering social reform, it did restrict accountability for crimes committed against citizens to the familial sphere, defusing pressure for legal compliance.

Over the course of the 1960s, two vastly different cities developed within Ahmedabad. One, on the east of the River Sabarmati, was marked by declining social respectability and deepening economic insecurity, while in the other, west of the river, caste and religious privileges sat comfortably with affluence and prospects of upward mobility. Social injustice and insecurity suffered by those lower in the economic order increased. Political ruptures, as we will see later, both exacerbated and reflected the social and economic strain on marginalised groups. Violence against women in both extreme and less extreme forms was imbricated with the daily life of Ahmedabad in the 1960s. Yet the crime of rape and other forms of sexual violence were concealed under misleading categories due to patriarchal notions of shame, and consequently local authorities were often not involved. The brutalities perpetrated during the communal riot in September 1969 were built on this structural political, social, economic and patriarchal violence (Kleinman 2001: 237). What occurred was less a sharp departure from the 'normal', and more a targeted and aggravated manifestation of the mundane and concealed violence of day-to-day life.

Disintegration of the Congress

India's political leadership in the 1960s had neither the vision nor the legitimacy of the first generation. Nonetheless, the Congress Party, an institution that Gandhi had shaped and Jawaharlal Nehru had led until his demise in 1964, remained the most entrenched political force in the country. It was in power in the central government in Delhi, in the state government in Gujarat, and in the Ahmedabad Municipal Corporation (AMC) when the 1969 riot occurred. However, Nehru's death marked the beginning of the end of the Congress's political dominance.

This was true across the country, but particularly in Gujarat. Nehru died in 1964, leaving no obvious successor. After two years of bitter intra-party debates, his left-leaning daughter Indira Gandhi was handed the reins of the Congress in 1966. Her rise to power increased the gulf between the national Congress leadership and its Gujarat counterpart.

The Congress leadership of Gujarat was always significantly more socially and politically conservative, and economically more liberal, than its counterpart at the national level. Most Gujarati Congress leaders hailed from upper-caste Hindu backgrounds, especially land-owning Patel communities, the dominant caste group of Gujarat. Under their leadership, the Gujarat government was historically apathetic to the grievances of Scheduled Castes, Muslims and women.[15] These leaders endorsed limited intervention of the state in the economy, and favoured a business-friendly (but not necessarily a level-playing, market-friendly) policy environment. As social conservatives, they found the entrenched caste and patriarchal order not just acceptable but desirable. Gujarati Congress leaders staunchly opposed what Indira Gandhi promoted: a socialist growth model, pro-poor economic policies and heavy state regulation of the economy. (In 1969 her administration, for example, nationalised 14 banks.) In order to preserve the Congress's political stronghold, Prime Minister Indira Gandhi also began promoting backward-caste and Scheduled Caste candidates in elections. Further-more, her authoritarian leadership style was in sharp contrast to the strategy of negotiation and compromise preferred by Nehru, and did much to alienate veteran Congress leaders.

Indira Gandhi's approach was unacceptable to the Gujarati old guard of the Congress. Consequently, veteran Gujarati Congress leader Morarji Desai split from the Congress to form his own party, the Congress (Other), in 1969. Factionalism within the Congress in the state created a political vacuum for the first time since independence. Right-wing political parties (such as the Swatantra Party) and the Hindu nationalist Bharatiya Jana Sangh (hereafter the Jana Sangh) stepped in to fill this vacuum. Subsequently, some disgruntled Congress members threw their weight behind the Swatantra Party or the Jana Sangh. The Jana Sangh had been set up in 1951 with the blessings of supreme leader-philosopher of the RSS Madhav Sadashiv Golwalkar. The Jana Sangh represented Hindu nationalism in electoral politics until 1980, when the party was dissolved and one of its factions formed a new party, the BJP (Graham 2005).

Internal ruptures at the elite political level accompanied the erosion of Congress's popularity among middle-class voters, who were also predominantly upper-caste Hindus. Repeated accusations that the Congress had historically 'appeased' Muslims at the expense of the Hindu majority – most notably by acceding to the demand for the creation of Pakistan – had already alienated many Hindus from the party. India's war with China in 1962 and with Pakistan in 1965 generated widespread criticism about the Congress-led national government's ability to secure Indian borders and protect Indian citizens. Affluent upper-caste Hindus in Gujarat and Ahmedabad also rejected the Congress's attempts to alter the caste status quo.

Economic decline from the mid-1960s further eroded popular confidence in the Congress's ability to govern. Although Indira Gandhi had sought to legitimise her populist policies under the famous slogan of 'Garibi Hatao' ('Eradicate Poverty'), the living conditions of people at the bottom of the economic hierarchy had in fact worsened, as discussed earlier. Despite constitutional guarantees against discrimination based on religion, caste and gender, prejudices of all hues were rife. Yet the party's decision to promote backward-caste and Scheduled Caste candidates in elections, and to prioritise (at least at the level of rhetoric) the economic security of the poor, alienated the middle class, whose caste-based power was being undermined and whose economic woes were being ignored. The party came to be viewed as excessively left-leaning by industrialists and land-owners, even though it was insufficiently sensitive to the concerns of the middle class and the working poor. Its policies were threatening the caste-based patronage structure of Gujarati politics, while not doing enough to protect low-caste groups from everyday discrimination. Traditional Hindus identified the party with Muslim minority appeasement, whereas Muslims viewed it as a Hindu-leaning organisation.

These religion-, caste- and class-based anxieties were reflected in the electoral choices of Gujarati voters. In the 1962 Gujarat assembly elections, the Congress won 50.8 per cent of the popular vote, mainly due to the support of low-caste and Muslim voters who were despondent but not defiant. However, the middle class began to shun the Congress in favour of smaller parties, such as the conservative Swatantra Party (which received 24.3 per cent of the vote) and the anti-Muslim Jana Sangh, which won 1.8 per cent (Yagnik and Sheth 2011: 253). By the 1967 regional polls, the Congress had been reduced to 45.8 per cent of the vote compared with the Swatantra Party's 34.7 per cent. The Jana Sangh's share remained at 1.8 per cent, partly because some voters found its communal image repulsive (ibid.). However, soon after the 1969 riots, in the 1972 Gujarat elections, the Jana Sangh massively increased its vote share to 9.2 per cent. In Ahmedabad also, the party's membership rose from 18,000 in 1970 to 22,000 in 1972–73 (G. Shah 1974a: 237).

The rise in electoral support for the Jana Sangh within Gujarat was not a region-specific phenomenon. The erosion of the Congress's stronghold in electoral politics and government was turning people across India towards alternatives such as the Jana Sangh. The latter's appeal was growing nationwide: whereas in 1954, the party claimed a membership of over 143,000 members, by 1960 the number had nearly doubled to 274,907, rising further to 1.3 million by 1966 (Graham 2005: 247–9).

Nonetheless, the Congress remained the most well-organised, well-funded and entrenched political force in the country. In Gujarat, it was not until the late 1980s and early 1990s that any political party felt able to pose a sustained electoral challenge to it. However, the seeds of the Congress's decline in the state were sown in the mid-to-late 1960s, when political disillusionment, economic hardship and social fragmentation increased simultaneously. The occurrence of the 1969 riot, and the lack of a clear response by the Congress-led government to the violence, has to be understood in the context of the class-, caste- and religion-based gridlock of the time.

The Congress's weakened position within Ahmedabad itself was another factor. Within the city, the legitimacy of the party had begun to erode from the late 1950s, well before its decline in the rest of the state. This occurred in the wake of the formation of the Maha Gujarat Janata Parishad (MGJP), or the Grand Gujarat People's Council, in 1956. The MGJP was a loose coalition of left-leaning political parties and citizens' groups, whose singular aim was the territorial reorganisation of the Bombay Presidency (of which Gujarat was a part) into three separate states: Bombay city (India's commercial capital), Gujarat and Maharashtra. The MGJP championed this demand at public protests and meetings, emerging as the primary electoral competitor of the Congress from 1957. The national Congress leadership initially accepted this three-state demand, but, following an outbreak of violence in Bombay, decided to include Bombay city in Maharashtra. The Gujarat Congress acquiesced to this decision, but middle-class and elite voters in Ahmedabad were deeply shocked and aggrieved (Spodek 2011: 142–8). Although the majority of the residents of Bombay city spoke Marathi and therefore had more in common with the majority Marathi-speaking population of Maharashtra, Gujaratis dominated Bombay's economy and wanted to retain control over its commercial enterprises (ibid.: 143).

In May 1960, Gujarat was carved out as a separate state, with Gandhinagar as its capital, and Bombay became the capital of Maharashtra. Having at least partially fulfilled its raison d'être, the MGJP was dissolved. However, seeking to sustain the anti-Congress political momentum, its left-leaning and communist constituents in July the same year formed the Nutan MGJP (New MGJP), appointing the charismatic, left-minded Gujarati Indulal Yagnik as its president. Between 1960 and 1965, the Nutan MGJP mostly mobilised middle-class Ahmedabadi voters against issues such as rising socio-economic inequality under the Congress, winning the AMC elections in 1965. However, soon after its election victory, cracks began to emerge. The strain of intense factionalism and infighting over leadership was compounded by the MGJP's lack of governance experience and a narrow electoral base that did not include working-class voters and the urban poor. The MGJP lost the 1969 AMC elections to the Congress (Spodek 2011: 162–4). However, despite the Congress's return to power, it could no longer take Ahmedabad's electoral endorsement for granted. The MGJP had proved a failure as a party of governance, but achieved remarkable success as a temporary political force that shattered the Congress's support among Ahmedabad's middle class.

Politicisation of religious identity

For many Hindu men seeking political direction, economic relief and social belonging, the RSS became an attractive platform. At the receiving end of considerable economic and social discrimination, Muslims too became more receptive to communal mobilisation, thereby intensifying the politicisation of religious identity.

The RSS had begun establishing its shakhas in Gujarat from the early 1940s, when the state was still part of Bombay Presidency. Between 1943 and 1948, its membership trebled from an estimated 20,000 to 60,000 in the Presidency alone (Jaffrelot 2005: 3). When a former RSS member Nathuram Godse assassinated Gandhi in 1948, RSS volunteers were seen distributing sweets and celebrating on the streets of Gujarat (A. M. Shah 2002: 59).

From the 1960s, as economic insecurity and social marginalisation fuelled hostility against Muslims, and created anxiety among Hindu men about their ability to provide for their families, many of them found the RSS's focus on the cultivation of an aggressive masculinity, the creation of a united Hindu social community and the project of combating the 'Muslim problem' both appealing and empowering. They actively participated in daily or weekly shakhas of the RSS in the walled city and the industrial belt. In the shakhas, volunteers met regularly to take part in the organisation's regimen: physical exercise, drills, marching, games, and training in the use of weapons such as sticks and swords. They engaged in intellectual discussions and listened to commentaries on the 'history' of the 'glorious Hindu nation', including accounts of Muslim atrocities allegedly committed against Hindu women (see C. Bhatt 2001: 119–20; T. Sarkar 1991: 2057). The RSS shakhas also constituted a social network whereby volunteers could rely on one another for succour and material resources in times of need.

In providing this training to volunteers, the core objective of the RSS was – and continues to be – to establish a cadre of 'ideal' Hindu men devoted entirely (in 'body, mind and wealth') to the protection of Hindus, to the glory of the Hindu nation-state, and to combating every Muslim aggression with a 'fitting reply' (Deshpande and Ramaswamy 1981: 94–9). As Bacchubhai Thakkar, a longstanding RSS and Jana Sangh member from Gujarat, put it:

In Gujarat and everywhere else in India the RSS has always worked towards a single aim – *purush nirman* [creation of an ideal man]. Once a visiting foreign journalist asked Guruji Golwalkar, 'For how long do you intend to run RSS shakhas in India?' Guruji replied, 'Until all of Bharat becomes an RSS shakha and every man becomes an ideal man'. So, when that happens, the RSS will not be needed. (Interview, Ahmedabad, 26 November 2007 and 5 December 2007)

This 'ideal man', as will be argued, was implicitly encouraged to inflict sexual violence against Muslim women so as to avenge or pre-empt similar crimes allegedly committed or planned by Muslim men.

As economic and social conditions worsened in the late 1960s, the RSS stepped up its campaign to mobilise support and produce such 'ideal' Hindu men. It organised a mass rally (its largest ever in the city) and a three-day camp in December 1968. Organised in the industrial area of Maninagar, the rally was presided over by Golwalkar himself (Reddy Commission 1971: 51). Over 1,600 RSS volunteers from across the state participated, as did the top brass of the Jana Sangh, including RSS activists and senior party workers Balraj Madhok and Atal Bihari Vajpayee (ibid.). (Vajpayee later led the national coalition as Prime Minister when the anti-Muslim massacre occurred in 2002.) Such mobilisation activities paid off: before the 1969 riot began, the RSS had successfully recruited at least 8,600 men in Gujarat for its nationalist cause.[16] In Ahmedabad, the RSS had an estimated 900 regular volunteers and at least 2,400 'sympathisers' by 1974. The number of its shakhas in the city increased from 42 in 1971 to 45 in 1973 (G. Shah 1974a: 237).

Activities carried out in RSS neighbourhood branches were popularised by *Sadhana*, a weekly vernacular news magazine established in Ahmedabad in 1956. It was the unofficial local counterpart of the RSS's national, English-language mouthpiece *Organiser* (established in 1947 in Delhi). By 1968, *Sadhana* claimed a circulation of over 2,500 copies every week (Government of India 1969, 1:101). Its readership would have been considerably larger because, across India (as in many other parts of the world), periodicals are read not just by the family members of subscribers but also by neighbours, friends and colleagues. This publication was such a valuable purveyor of Hindu nationalist ideas that in the late 1990s, the Gujarat administration, then led by the BJP, attempted to make its subscription compulsory for all schools in the state.

India's war with Pakistan in 1965 rekindled collective memories of Partition and sharpened religion-based hostilities in the city, giving *Sadhana* an excellent opportunity to popularise the work of the RSS. When, in September 1965, the Pakistan Air Force shot down an aircraft carrying former Gujarat Chief Minister Balwant Rai Mehta, who died in the crash, communal hostilities in the city increased even further – and alongside, opportunities for communal mobilisation. An article published in *Sadhana* in January 1968 illustrates this point:

> Enemies have surrounded the motherland on all four sides and are threatening to attack [...] Twenty years ago this land was partitioned and we were unable to stop it [...] do we see ordinary people hurting over any of this? [...]
>
> It is because of the lack of self-belief and self-respect that this country is facing so many dangers and will continue to face more in the future [...] Therefore it is important to raise awareness and build self-belief in the country. In order to accomplish this goal the people of this country should assess the primary activities of the Rashtriya Swayamsevak Sangh.[17]

Even though religious identities were hardening, mobilising support for Hindu nationalism in Ahmedabad was not easy. While Gujarati and non-Gujarati upper castes, Scheduled Castes and Muslims did not live in intermixed neighbourhoods in the walled city or in the industrial areas, they still lived in close proximity to one another in these regions. This geographical proximity afforded them opportunities to interact with each other on a daily basis. Although religion- and caste-based discrimination was rife within and beyond the compounds of the textile mills, years of working together in the mills and interacting outside them had also created a sense of familiarity. As Vinod Parmar, a Scheduled Caste man who worked as a temporary labourer in the Calico Mill, said:

> I used to work in the automatic cell of the mill. In our mill, 80 per cent of the workers were either Dalits [Scheduled Castes] or Muslims. Only 20 per cent of the workers were people of other castes. In the mills we Dalits had to face lots of discrimination. Work that involved hard manual labour was always given to us. But, whatever the problems in the mills everyone worked together. (Interview, Ahmedabad, 19 January 2007)

Despite the inability of the TLA to prevent the informalisation of the textile labour force, it nonetheless facilitated inter-community interaction. It propagated Gandhian discipline and ran facilities such as film clubs and sports clubs where people from different religious groups met on a regular basis. Civic engagement between members of different religious communities, as political scientist Ashutosh Varshney (2002) has pointed out, impedes communal mobilisation. By the 1960s, Golwalkar had recognised the need to mobilise Scheduled Castes along with upper-caste men. Hence, during the three-day camp in 1968, he advised RSS volunteers 'not to misbehave' with Scheduled Tribes and Scheduled Castes, 'but to treat them on par with other civilized people' (Reddy Commission 1971: 51). However, rooting out deep-seated caste prejudices is easier said than done and, up to this day, the bulk of the RSS's leadership and membership is upper-caste. Moreover, even though Golwalkar wished to mobilise low-caste men for the Hindu nationalist cause, the RSS eventually decided in 1964 to create a separate organisation for them, namely, the VHP.

Another reason why support for Hindu nationalism was limited in the 1960s was the movement's focus on mobilising men. Harnessing the potential of women in leading and shaping Hindu nationalism was not on the RSS's agenda at the time. Women appeared frequently in Hindu nationalist ideology as helpless victims of Muslim aggression against the Hindu community; or as heroic defenders of their chastity and the Hindu tradition; or as metaphors for the Indian motherland purportedly under threat from Muslim-majority Pakistan. However, only 'disciplined', 'virile' and 'strong' Hindu men were seen as capable of securing the future of the Hindu race, Hindu traditions and the Hindu nation. Women, in the Hindu nationalist imagination of the time, were best suited for domesticity, and were incapable of being self-determined political agents. An article entitled 'Women rulers are disastrous' published in the *Organiser*, the national mouthpiece of the RSS, in July 1969 is particularly revealing in this regard. The article partly aimed to show that Prime Minister Indira Gandhi was unfit for the office because she was a woman; in doing so it also betrays the gendered stereotypes that guided Hindu nationalist mobilisation activities at the time:

> It is a characteristic of all women that they think with their hearts. Their reasoning, except in the cases of highly gifted and intellectual women is based on a logical category which is different from one generally employed by men [...] in every country and in every age, wise men have never burdened

women with responsibilities which concern the well-being of many men and women. Most women think in terms of themselves or at most of their families and their immediate surroundings. They are almost always incapable of looking at problems in broader terms and when they do they always do it wrongly.[18]

This lack of confidence in women's ability to shape or lead a political movement pervaded Hindu nationalist thinking. The RSS founder Hedgewar had agreed to the establishment of a women's wing for middle-class women, called the Rashtriya Sevika Samiti, as early as 1936. However, the RSS made no attempt to popularise or develop the Samiti's activities as an extension of its own work, even though the Samiti's projects in neighbourhood branches (for example, self-defence training and intellectual discussions) mirrored those of the RSS (T. Sarkar 1991). The RSS's emphasis on preserving the gender-based status quo – whereby limits were placed on women's activities beyond the household and their contribution to society and the nation was considered inherently inferior to that of their male counterparts – was for many volunteers and sympathisers one of the main attractions of the organisation. As a result, the Samiti was relatively obscure in the 1960s. Furthermore, due to entrenched caste and gender biases, Scheduled Caste women were peripheral to Hindu nationalist interests in the 1960s. Indeed, it was only in 1984–85 that a special organisation called Durga Vahini was established to mobilise women from low-caste backgrounds (see Chapter 3).

Just as in the case of the RSS, the appeal of the Jana Sangh as a platform for political activism was far from universal. The party's main support base was the urban lower middle class, small traders and businessmen (Graham 2005). Women's membership in the party was also limited, as gauged from the degree of their participation in the national conventions of the party. Out of the 2,000 delegates who attended the 1959 annual Jana Sangh convention in the city of Bangalore, 300 were women.[19] At the 1969 convention, a quarter of the total of 2,000 participants were women.[20]

Besides having a narrow mobilisation focus, the rhetoric of Hindu nationalism was much less belligerent before the 1969 riot began than it became from the late 1980s, as will be discussed in Chapter 3. It is true that *Sadhana* regularly sought to manipulate and capitalise on religious hostilities fuelled by the 1965 India–Pakistan war by publishing provocative articles, such as the one cited earlier. However, while it questioned the loyalty of Muslims to India, it always stopped short of overtly demanding their expulsion to Pakistan: 'Muslims of India have frequently demonstrated their love for their religion. However, they have yet to prove their love for this country'.[21] The national leadership of the Jana Sangh, too, espoused a moderate Hindu nationalism, which favoured the cultural assimilation of Muslims rather than their expulsion from India on the grounds that their loyalty was suspect. In fact, this moderation was consciously projected, because the party's close association with the RSS was seen as the main reason behind voters' hesitation throughout the 1960s (Graham 2005).

For example, when Balraj Madhok, senior Jana Sangh leader and RSS activist, addressed a gathering at the Rifle Club, Military and Rifle Training Association, Ahmedabad, on 14 September 1969, he stressed the need for cultivating a martial spirit among Hindus. Blaming Gandhian ideals of non-violence for the India–Pakistan war, he claimed:

No country in the world which is not aware of self-defence and is indifferent to the military power can remain alive. It cannot even achieve peace [. . .] This is the reason why in the last 23 years our country was attacked four times. Had we prepared our country and youth for war instead of the shibboleth of peace and flying pigeons of peace, we would have achieved peace [. . .] The road to achieve peace in the world is the road to power. (Reddy Commission 1971: Appendix VIII, p. 214)

Keep a correct model before yourself. Let Sardar Patel, Netaji Bose and Shivaji be our models. We have talked much about peace and non-violence; now we should try to learn to talk about war. (Ibid.: 226)

Yet, like *Sadhana*, Madhok felt able to publicly question the loyalties of Muslims, but not their right to remain in India. To counter the political threat ostensibly posed by Pakistan, he argued:

The first step would be to Bharatiyakaran [indianise (*sic*)] Indian Muslims. We nationalise Banks, we nationalise others – we say this also that the Indian people – Indian Muslims should be [. . .] 'nationalised'. They are our brothers. I say at the outset that they are not aliens. Their blood is our blood – nationalise them – explain to them. You worship Mohamed Saheb you worship the mosque but the culture of this country is that of yours. Rama belongs to you as well as to me, similarly Krishna – your blood is the same as mine. (Ibid.: 225)

By the 1990s, as later chapters will argue, this relatively moderate Hindu nationalism had been replaced by a more strident, violent variant.

As the RSS, the Jana Sangh and the VHP mobilised upper castes and low castes along communal lines, political and religious Muslim organisations, such as the Jamiat-Ulema-e-Hind (hereafter the Jamiat), sought to mobilise Muslims. However, the scale of Muslim mobilisation was considerably smaller than Hindu communal mobilisation in Ahmedabad, because Muslims comprised less than 11 per cent of the city's population of 1.7 million in 1971. The Jamiat had been established in Ahmedabad in 1945, and was seen as having 'a good influence over the poor Muslim class' (Reddy Commission 1971: 47). The economic and social marginalisation of Muslims during the 1960s paralleled that of their non-Muslim counterparts, so a similar response to communal mobilisation could be expected.

In June 1968, the Jamiat organised a major conference, which the Reddy Commission (1971: 52) described as the 'biggest [of its kind] in Ahmedabad'. According to several police witnesses to the commission, many provocative speeches were made during the conference and inflammatory books and pamphlets were distributed. Reportedly, senior Muslim leaders also accused Golwalkar, the RSS and the Jana Sangh of orchestrating violence against Muslims and imparting 'training for murders, dacoities and robberies; and asked who could deny that the training of today might not be used in the disputes between different communities' (ibid.: 47). The deputy commissioner of police (special branch) of Ahmedabad, M. J. Chinoy, in his testimony to the Reddy Commission, took special note of the speech delivered by the president of the conference, A. R. Palanpuri. According to Chinoy, Palanpuri expressed the following sentiments at the conference:

During the past five years numerous communal riots took place in the country, such as Calcutta, Roorkela, Allahabad and U.P. where the Muslims had lost their lives and property. The modesty of their wives and daughters was outraged and their property looted and houses set on fire and all this resulted due to the weak policy of the Government which allowed a free hand to the parties such as Jan Sangh and other *Goonda* [thug] elements. (Ibid.)

Remarkably, the only portion of this speech that Chinoy found objectionable was the allegation regarding the incidence of sexual violence against Muslim women. According to Chinoy, 'the reports regarding communal riots at Calcutta, Rourkela received from the Government of India confidentially showed casualties of both the communities, they did not show that modesty of wives and daughters was outraged [. . .] such exaggerated statements narrated before a big gathering are likely to create enmity between the communities' (ibid.: 48).

This refutation reveals important characteristics of the role of sexual violence in communal conflict before the 1969 riot began. First, among both Hindus and Muslims, there seems to have been an implicit acceptance of the potential that news of sexual violence contained to 'create enmity' between the two communities. Second, reports of actual or alleged sexual violence against Muslim women by Hindu men was believed to have the potential to generate solidarity among Muslims, irrespective of the geographical location or the time in which such violence was supposed to have occurred. (This has parallels with the way in which the RSS mobilised support in its neighbourhood branches by recounting real and imagined stories about similar violence 'historically' perpetrated by Muslim men.[22]) Thus, the rape of a Muslim woman anywhere in the country could be construed as a symbolic attack against all Muslims.

Third, women were invoked only in terms of the relationships they had with men (husbands and fathers), so that violence against *their* women could be interpreted as a symbolic violation of the men of the community. In effect, the seemingly gender-neutral categories of 'Muslims' (as used by Palanpuri) and 'communities' (as used by Chinoy) were in actuality imagined as male-only collectives. Fourth, while women's organisations such as Jyoti Sangh recorded cases of rape under 'kidnapping and abductions' to protect women from the shame and dishonour commonly associated with such violence, communal organisations cited such violence with a view to invoking the very same sentiments among men – shame for failing to protect their women, and dishonour for allowing their sexual property to be violated. Last, since Ahmedabad's police held strong views about the inflammatory potential of news about sexual violence, it seems fair to speculate that they had an interest in suppressing not only rumours but possibly actual occurrences as well. Besides the disavowal of such violence due to the notions of shame associated with it, this may be another reason why none of the police witnesses mentioned a single case of sexual violence that occurred during the 1969 riot to the Reddy Commission.

Communalisation of trivial events

Immediately before the 1969 riot, several events served to sharpen communal sentiments among both Hindus and Muslims across the city. The local police responded in a relatively even-handed manner (in sharp contrast to their response from the late 1990s forward). On 10 March 1969, in the Kalupur locality of the walled city, a police officer moved aside a handcart stacked with books, which was obstructing the road. In the process the cart, which was owned by a Muslim, toppled over and a Qur'an fell to the ground. The owner started protesting and a mob of about 2,000 gradually gathered. Senior police officers alleged that during the protest, Muslims shouted pro-Pakistan slogans such as, 'Even Pakistan would be better than this. What if a Hindu's temple had been burnt?' (Reddy Commission 1971: 53). Keen not to allow this incident to blow out of proportion, the police department promptly issued a public apology on loudspeakers on behalf of the commissioner of police for inadvertently hurting the religious feelings of Muslims. However, these measures to placate the mob proved futile. According to *Gujarat Samachar*, the protest led to minor clashes in Kalupur, which left at least 25 people injured, including some police personnel, and the destruction of property worth Rs 3,000 to Rs 5,000.[23] The police resorted to a cane-charge and fired tear-gas shells, finally restoring normalcy around midnight.

Communal tensions intensified on 31 August when Gujarati Muslims organised a large protest in the walled city against the desecration of the Al Aqsa Mosque in Jerusalem by Israel. Some police officers charged that during the protest march, Muslims had shouted inflammatory slogans such as, 'Anyone who clashes with Islam will be obliterated', 'We cannot tolerate the insult of the Mosque', and 'Long live Muslim unity' (Reddy Commission 1971: 54). The commissioner of police E. F. Deboo denied that the protesters had shouted any anti-national slogans such as 'Long live Pakistan'. He added, however, that Jana Sangh leaders saw this protest as a 'show of Muslim force', which created 'resentment amongst the Hindus' (ibid.: 55). The Gujarati press aggravated this feeling of 'Hindu resentment' by unhinging the Al Aqsa protest from its local context and inserting it into an imagined history of Muslim atrocities:

> Feelings of Muslims [were] wounded by Al Aqsa mosque incident; Hindus understood it and sympathized. Muslims would remove historical injustice by handing over to the Hindus that portion of Kashi Vishwanath Temple which is being used under the name of Aurangzeb Mosque and that portion of Shiv Temple Rudramal at Sidhipur which has been converted into a mosque. Shiva Linga made into pieces by Mohmed Gazni which are under threshold of mosque should be returned from being trampled.[24]

Claiming a daily circulation of over 63,000 copies and a readership of over a million, the *Gujarat Samachar* acted as a mass vehicle for the dissemination of stereotypes about Muslims and Hindus.[25] These portrayals identified Muslims who had come out in protest against the destruction of the Al Aqsa Mosque with the 'violent', 'iconoclastic' Muslim 'invader', and identified Hindus as the 'historically tolerant' victims of 'Muslim aggression'. However, a significant difference between past and present Hindu generations was also publicised. Unlike their predecessors, contemporary Hindus were demanding 'justice' and claiming that what was rightfully theirs 'should be returned'.

The idea that Hindus were unwilling to acquiesce to Muslims gained further traction following an incident in Behrampura in the industrial area of Ahmedabad on 4 September 1969. On that day, a police officer, while trying to disperse a Ramlila audience,[26] accidentally dropped a copy of the *Ramayana*. This trivial incident was transformed into a communally charged situation because the officer involved happened to be a Muslim. Immediately after the incident, RSS and Jana Sangh leaders redoubled their efforts to interpret the accident as a calculated Muslim affront to the Hindu religion. Along with members of the Hindu Mahasabha and religious priests, they formed the Hindu Dharma Raksha Samiti (HDRS), or Committee for the Protection of the Hindu Religion, on 11 September. An old RSS worker convened the HDRS.

The HDRS organised several processions during which its leaders delivered anti-Muslim speeches and distributed inflammatory pamphlets (Reddy Commission 1971: 59). Police witnesses reported that during these processions participants shouted slogans that closely mirrored those shouted by Muslims during the Al Aqsa protests, such as 'Anyone who clashes with Hindus will be obliterated' (ibid.: 58–9). The Reddy Commission noted that these processions aimed to warn Muslims that Hindus would not tolerate any insult to their religion and community: 'It has also to be noticed from the police report that the Bharatiya Jan Sangh workers had said that it was not the Muslims alone who could show strength by taking out processions etc., but the Hindus also can take out similar processions and show their unity and strength' (ibid.: 66).

Subsequently, vernacular newspapers began circulating the HDRS's version of the 'Ramayana incident' along with the notion that the Hindu community was not prepared to suffer 'Muslim atrocities' silently. For example, on 12 September 1969, Jai Hind, a Gujarati afternoon daily, demanded that the Muslim officer who had 'insulted' the Ramayana should be promptly expelled because, 'if this demand is not accepted, the offended feelings of the Hindu community will result in agitation and the Government alone will be responsible for its consequences' (Reddy Commission 1971: 61).

The deadly riot of September 1969

'There was no issue whatsoever', 71-year-old Rashida Bano, a Muslim woman and a mother of 10 from Vatva, insisted when I asked her what had sparked the Hindu–Muslim riot in September 1969. Looking both bemused and pained, she continued, 'Still, Hindus started killing Muslims and Muslims started killing Hindus' (interview, Ahmedabad, 29–30 November 2007). She was right: the event that catalysed what was until then the worst episode of communal conflict since 1947 was indeed relatively trivial.

Trouble began around 3.30 p.m. on 18 September. A few cows from the Hindu Jagannath Temple, situated near Jamalpur gate in the walled city, disrupted the Muslim Urs procession, injuring some men, women and children. Some Muslims entered the temple premises to complain to the priests. As news of the incident spread, about 100 to 200 people gathered around the temple. In an attempt to prevent an escalation of tensions into violence, the police issued special press notes to inform the public about the reality of the temple scuffle. Meanwhile, prominent Hindu and Muslim religious and political leaders formed a peace committee and appealed to the public to maintain communal harmony. Arrangements were made to broadcast the appeals through special radio bulletins, and to publish an extra edition of *Sandesh* with appeals for peace. Muslim leaders also went to the temple priests to apologise expressly on behalf of the community and offered to publish that apology formally in the vernacular press.

In the meantime, Hindu nationalist organisations and their sympathisers had sprung into action. The priests of the Jagannath Temple, and members of the Jana Sangh, the RSS and the HDRS, disregarded these pleas for peace, and attempted to give the incident a communal colour. In the evening of 18 September, they called a public meeting to protest against the 'insult' of Hindus by Muslims (Reddy Commission 1971: 87–93). Some 400 to 500 people gathered around the temple, where they declared that the 'attack' against the temple must be avenged. The riot had begun. The trivial incident at the Jagannath Temple became a lightning rod for all the social, political, economic and communal stresses that had been building up throughout the 1960s, bringing these multiple antagonisms to a violent head.[27]

During the riot, hundreds of Muslims were killed, thousands of their homes and shops were destroyed and many Muslim women were raped and mutilated. Hindus also suffered serious casualties and losses, although to a comparatively lesser degree.[28] The violence against Muslims was clearly inflicted intentionally; as will be argued in what follows, leaders and supporters of Hindu nationalist outfits such as the RSS and Jana Sangh appear to have played a key role in instigating and mobilising their supporters to inflict sexual and other forms of violence against Muslim residents of the city. These agents contributed to the infliction of sexual violence in two ways: first, by organising a mass propaganda campaign that incited Hindu men to inflict such violence against Muslim women; and second, by orchestrating the violence in individual neighbourhoods across the city.

Communal propaganda and sexual violence

The propaganda campaign of Hindu nationalist agents began on the morning of 20 September. Its primary aim, as will be shown, was to instigate Hindu men to sexually victimise Muslim women. This was done by manipulating the socio-economic frustrations of people, and by drawing on gendered, communal stereotypes that had been widely circulated by the vernacular media, and further reinforced throughout the 1960s by the RSS in its neighbourhood branches and by communal Muslim organisations such as the Jamiat in public gatherings.

The first element of the Hindu propaganda campaign was to arouse a feeling of violation and insecurity among Hindu men. In order to invoke this sentiment, the *Sevak*, the afternoon edition of the most widely circulated vernacular daily in Gujarat,[29] published an article on 20 September about an alleged incident of sexual violence against Hindu women by Muslim men. Making the connection between female violation and male humiliation was not difficult, because the notion that the sexual violation of women symbolically dishonoured and violated their husbands, brothers and fathers, as previously observed, had traction among both Hindus and Muslims well before the riot started. Entitled 'A shocking event', the article published by the *Sevak* read as follows:

An inhuman and shocking incident has occurred in the Gandhi Park Society situated in Rakhial near Lal Mill to-day in the early hours [...]

About 250 families are residing in this Park. In all there are 40 buildings. The persons residing in the surrounding areas of the Park, not only made an attack with scythes, hockey-sticks and Kabbal etc., but also stripped unmarried and married women naked and outraged their modesty [a euphemism for rape] in early morning.

On account of this deed, the persons residing in the park were highly pained and for the safety of their lives shifted to other societies. The deplorable aspect of this incident as reported is that the police were present when this took place. This incident has occurred because the Park is surrounded by the population of other community. (Reproduced and translated in Reddy Commission 1971: 106)

Although this news report did not specify the religious identity of the alleged assailants, it was hardly necessary to do so: as the Reddy Commission report (1971: 106) observed, the 'public at large is having the knowledge' that Gandhi Park was a Hindu locality that was 'surrounded' by Muslims. Therefore, even without identifying the religious affiliation of the 'other community', this report managed to project Muslim men as the perpetrators of sexual violence. By alleging that the police had failed to protect Hindu women, the report sought to fuel Hindu insecurity.[30]

The *Sevak* appears to be the only major Gujarati newspaper to have published a report on the alleged Gandhi Park incident. Indeed, *Gujarat Samachar*, one of the most widely circulated newspapers in the state besides *Sandesh*, made no mention of any incident of sexual violence against Hindu or Muslim women anywhere in Gujarat in its coverage of the riot. Between 18 and 30 September, it published detailed reports every day on the toll taken by the violence in Ahmedabad and elsewhere in the state: including the numbers of deaths and injuries; the scale of destruction of property; the types of weapons used by rioters; government and police response; areas where curfew had been imposed, lifted or relaxed; and the names of Ahmedabadi neighbourhoods where violence had occurred. Yet, as just pointed out, unlike the *Sevak*, the *Gujarat Samachar* did not mention any incidents of sexual violence committed during the riot.

However, the entrenched religious bias of *Gujarat Samachar* did colour its coverage. On 20 September, when the *Sevak* ran the report on sexual violence in Gandhi Park, *Gujarat Samachar*'s front page carried the following report:

Following yesterday's *attack* on Sri Jagdish temple, tensions were prevailing in different parts of the city. Life began as normal in the morning but after news of the attack on the temple spread the city's markets, hotels, shops, schools and colleges etc began to shut down. By the afternoon the city's main market, shops on Relief Road and Gandhi Road, and the markets in Raipur, Khadia, Shahpur, Dariapur and other areas also shut down. That is when some senior leaders of the Muslim community expressed sorrow and regret over the attacks on Shri Jagdhish temple.[31]

Despite the absence of any mention of sexual violence, such reports were nonetheless inflammatory. By describing the misunderstanding at the Jagannath Temple as an 'attack', and foregrounding regrets expressed by senior Muslim leaders, they implicitly attributed responsibility for the riot to Muslims, justifying a Hindu 'reaction'. Moreover, given Ahmedabad's extensive segregation along religious lines in this period, reports carrying details of affected neighbourhoods would have enabled readers to decipher the religious identity of the rioters as well as the primary victims. This is why, in its report, the Reddy Commission admonished *Gujarat Samachar* and other vernacular dailies such as *Jan Satta*, *Sandesh* and *Jai Hind* for instigating violence. The commission claimed that these newspapers had violated the national Code of Ethics for Press in Reporting and Commenting on Communal Incidents, which was formulated in 1957 and refined in 1963. The press code, among other things, prohibits newspapers from publishing reports that could 'arouse communal passions', and from publishing the names of religious communities (Reddy Commission 1971: 102–3). The commission concluded:

It will be observed that almost all the Gujarati newspapers did not conform to the press code in that they not only gave the news in a sensational manner, but referred to the temple as a temple and the mosque as a mosque instead of referring them as religious places. They also referred to names of the areas which can indicate the community which lives in it, and have mentioned the names of the community. (Ibid.: 105)

The police promptly conducted an inquiry into the Gandhi Park incident and announced that the the *Sevak* report was baseless. The government was also proactive: the Director of Information circulated a special notification on 20 September itself, denying that Hindu women had been raped.[32] Subsequently, the *Sevak* retracted the story and issued an apology for misleading its readers.

However, the apology, and the fact that the *Sevak* appears to be the only major vernacular newspaper to have carried a report on the occurrence of sexual violence, did nothing to dilute the impact of the report. By the time the story was retracted, it had acquired a life of its own. Communal pamphlets published immediately after the release of the *Sevak* story not only ensured that the latter remained in circulation, but also reinforced Hindu nationalist ideology on the basis of this story. These pamphlets projected the Gandhi Park 'incident' as exemplifying the sexual atrocities 'historically' committed by Muslim men against Hindu women. A pamphlet entitled 'Awake, Oh Hindus: Awake, Oh Youths', published by the Hindu Sangram Samiti (Committee for Hindu Struggle), an affiliate of the Jana Sangh, came into circulation from 26 September. According to the Reddy Commission, this pamphlet claimed that

> Muslims have made a heinous attack on the well-known temple of Jagannathji and have broken the idols of the temples and that Muslims have been repeating the history and that their main object is not only to destroy as many Hindu temples as possible but also to abolish Hindu religion and Hinduism and to convert Hindu community into Muslim community, to pollute Hindus and to molest Hindu women and that when India was partitioned, lakhs of Hindus were converted into Muslims and harems were formed of their wives, mothers and daughters. They were raped and converted into Muslims. [The pamphlet] refers to the atrocities said to have been committed against Hindus, *viz.* in the Gandhi Park – a Hindu Society – Muslims rushed into houses and made Hindu girls and women naked and raped them in broad-day light. Even in Kalupur, houses of Hindus surrounded by Muslims were also set ablaze. Males were massacred, children were kept in burning houses and women were made naked and raped. Hindu women, men and children surrounded in a lane near Jamalpur Pagathiya were burnt alive in houses. It then goes on to say that if Hindus do not wake by the above incidents, Hindu religion and Hinduism will be uprooted, their sisters and daughters will be forced to become prostitutes. (Reddy Commission 1971: 108–9)

By dislodging particular events, whether real or fictitious, from their specific contexts, such pamphlets relayed the message that sexual violence against Hindu women by Muslim men had followed a historical continuum. The distinction between events that occurred during

Partition in 1947 and the events of 1969 was blurred. The pamphlets played on entrenched anxieties that the survival of the 'Hindu community' was at risk due to forced conversions of Hindus to Islam and violent appropriations of Hindu women by Muslim men. They circulated sexual stereotypes about Muslims as iconoclasts, rapists and butchers, warning that the 'enemy' posed a threat to the future security and purity of Hindus and their religion: 'if Hindus do not wake by the above incidents, Hindu religion and Hinduism will be uprooted, their sisters and daughters will be forced to become prostitutes'. At the same time, such pamphlets played on the anxieties of working-class men, whose 'sisters and daughters' had indeed been forced into sex work due to the economic downturn of the 1960s, as described previously in this chapter.

The third component of anti-Muslim propaganda then followed seamlessly. The aim here was to project the 'historical' sexual atrocities committed by 'Muslims' as a symbolic humiliation of Hindu men, and to instigate the latter into 'retaliatory' and pre-emptive violence against Muslims as a way of redeeming their lost masculine pride: 'Hindus get organized, be bold. Take weapons in your hands and attack the Muslims who are out to destroy Hindu religion and Hindu temples [...] Every Hindu to save his religion, caste, sisters, and daughters must awaken and learn how to attack and learn the policy of defence not cowardice' (anonymous pamphlet, reproduced in G. Shah 1991: 192). Differences among the historical and local contexts of the incidence of sexual violence were thus blurred in this pamphlet, just as they had been blurred in the context of the Al Aqsa protest on 31 August (described earlier in this chapter), when propaganda materials had elided the historical aggressions allegedly committed by Muslims against Hindus with the purported actions of Muslims in Ahmedabad in 1969. All Hindu men were expected to view themselves as victims of Muslim aggression, and see every Muslim man as the 'enemy' of Hindu religion, Hindu temples and Hindu women.

However, in order to incite Hindus to violent 'defensive' action against Muslim men and women, these pamphlets had to remove the moral constraints posed by Gandhian ideals, which were still popular in Ahmedabad during the 1960s. They did so by describing non-violence as tantamount to the emasculation of the Hindu male, and encouraging Hindu men to display their masculine potency by inflicting violence. The pamphlet 'Awake, Oh Hindus', for example, called on Hindus

> to prepare hand bombs, keep 'dhariyas' [knives] and sticks, prepare
> bows and arrows to throw flaming cotton rags [...]
>
> to give up defence policy and attack and assault, gird up their
> loins to take revenge for the desecration of the temples and the
> molestation of their women.
>
> Let each Hindu take a vow to take revenge for the insult of
> Hindu religion and molestation of Hindu women [...] Tell
> preceptors of peace that Gandhiji had never taught to defend
> Muslims who insult religion and molest women. Gandhiji never
> taught non-violence of cowards and impotents [...] Drive out
> cowards and impotents from your areas. (Reproduced and
> translated in Reddy Commission 1971: 109)

This pamphlet faithfully reproduced the core tenets of Hindu nationalist ideology as articulated by its founding ideologues (see the discussion in the Introduction, this volume), signalling how salient this ideology was in Ahmedabad in the 1960s. It equated violence with power, non-violence with cowardice, the infliction of sexual violence with masculine self-assertion, and the unwillingness to assault with impotence.

'Nearly 10,000' such pamphlets had come into circulation from 20 September, according to the Reddy Commission. Most of these pamphlets were issued by the HDRS, the organisation founded by members of the RSS, Jana Sangh, Hindu Mahasabha and some religious priests in the wake of the 'Ramayana incident' on 11 September (Reddy Commission 1971: 107). Some of them were published, photocopied and distributed by the Hindu Sangram Samiti; others were published anonymously by 'lovers of Hindu religion'. Some of them boldly carried the names of the publishers: 'Ratanlal Gupta, Ward Convenor, Hindu Dharma Raksha Samiti', or 'Sheth Brothers Printing Press, Hathikhai, Ahmedabad' (ibid.). They were circulated by hand, or surreptitiously pasted on walls and billboards. The HDRS, Ghanshyam Shah (1991: 193) notes, received emotional, moral, and material and intellectual support from Ahmedabad's increasingly disgruntled middle class. Its members wrote articles, published pamphlets, coined slogans and formed the Hindu Sangram Samiti, which was also affiliated to the Jana Sangh.

Inflammatory pamphlets were complemented by rumours, such as those published by the *Sevak* on 20 September, and anti-Muslim slogans, which were handwritten on blackboards in different localities.[33] The Reddy Commission noted that some messages written on blackboards 'in effect, challenge those who consider themselves Hindus to take severe steps, as [they call] upon them to take law into their own hands' (Reddy Commission 1971: 107). The commission added: 'These rumours, some of them at any rate, which were current between 19th and 22nd, coming as they do immediately after the inciting and inflammatory pamphlets and "patrikas" [booklets] and exaggerated reports in the newspapers, must have contributed to the spread of the riots' (ibid.: 113).

Several eminent personalities, politicians and religious leaders blamed this propaganda for inciting violence. These included representatives from a civil society organisation called the Citizens' Council, the Congress, the Sumyukta Socialist Party, the Communist Party of India (CPI) and the Jamiat-Ulema-e-Hind (Reddy Commission 1971: Appendix III, pp. 21–31). Harubhai Mehta from the Communist Party of India (Marxist) (CPI-M) stressed a direct connection between the publication of the Gandhi Park report in the *Sevak* and attacks against women. Referring to the news report, Mehta testified that until its publication, the 'Hindu crowd did not touch the Muslim ladies and children. They were allowed to go. They were given shelter. On hearing the rumour Muslim ladies and children were beaten up' (ibid.: 31).[34]

The claim that propaganda instigating sexual violence against Muslim women influenced rioters in 1969 (and in subsequent riots) is plausible in the light of research on organised ethnic violence in other parts of the world. For example, research on the genocide in Rwanda in 1994 and in the former Yugoslavia in 1995 has found that the circulation of ideas, facts or allegations against ethnic minorities via media such as newspapers, pamphlets and radio played an important role in facilitating the coordination of violence, and directly affected the behaviour of the perpetrators. Indeed, a recent paper has established a statistical correlation, suggesting that of the 51,000 people who killed Tutsi men and raped and murdered Tutsi women during the Rwandan genocide, at least 10 per cent were mobilised by anti-Tutsi radio broadcasts (Yanagizawa-Drott 2012).

While Hindus were consistently incited against Muslims through belligerent speeches, pamphlets and rumours from the evening of 18 September, 'there is no evidence of any incitement of that nature by Muslims against Hindus. No patrikas were issued by Muslims and the Inspector General of Police admits that he did not come across any rumours spread by Muslims against Hindus' (Reddy Commission 1971: 149).

Large parts of the state machinery sought to quell the circulation of Hindu nationalist propaganda, just as the police had done in the immediate aftermath of the the *Sevak* report on 20 September. The police arrested at least ten people for writing, publishing or distributing virulent pamphlets (Reddy Commission 1971: 110). The Congress-led Gujarat government tried to counteract these pamphlets through radio broadcasts, announcements on loudspeakers and by issuing press notes. It even set up a special telephone line to inform the public about the truth of the Gandhi Park incident (ibid.: 112–13). Although the state administration, especially the police and the government, was ineffective in controlling the circulation of Hindu nationalist propaganda, its efforts did signal its commitment to preventing communal violence and protecting Muslim life.

Thus far, we have seen that immediately after the riot began on 18 September, Hindu nationalist organisations and their affiliates actively indulged in spreading propaganda that may have provided ideological encouragement for sexual violence against Muslim women. By projecting Hindu men as victims of symbolic violations by Muslim men, Hindu nationalist propaganda was inciting them to inflict 'retaliatory' and pre-emptive violence. These calls had force because they carefully manipulated the socio-economic anxieties of Hindu men. According to witnesses testifying before the Reddy Commission, this instigation seems to have then been given organisational direction by some RSS and Jana Sangh leaders, as described in the following section.

Organisation of violence

Leaders and workers of Hindu nationalist organisations and their affiliates appear to have taken an active part in orchestrating the riots of 1969 and leading the marauding mobs. Several witnesses charged that they saw Jana Sangh and RSS members leading the crowds, pointing out Muslim properties to the attackers with the help of voters' lists, and otherwise instigating violence (Reddy Commission 1971: 162, 216, 218). Although the Reddy Commission concluded that there was no evidence to confirm that the Jana Sangh and RSS were involved as organisations, it added: 'the evidence on the whole indicates that the police had reason to believe that some local Jan Sangh leaders and workers were actively participating in the riots' (ibid.: 218). Testimonies of district magistrates on the course of riots outside Ahmedabad also indicate that some local Jana Sangh and Hindu Mahasabha leaders may have participated in or incited violence, although they denied culpability (ibid.).

Violence gathered pace on 19 September when 'communally minded Hindu elements' in the city started circulating rumours about the deaths of Hindu priests and attacks on temples, as discussed previously. From then on, the size of the rioting mobs grew to between 500 and 1,000, and the number of incidents and the extent of damage to life and property rose sharply (Reddy Commission 1971: 144). On that day, at least 152 shops and homes were destroyed, eleven religious places desecrated and three people killed (ibid.: 145). Attempting to quell the violence, the police imposed a curfew in the affected parts of the walled city. Although the curfew was extended to the whole of Ahmedabad the following day, the violence continued sporadically until 30 September.

Mobs of 200 to 2,000 men armed with knives, sticks, iron pipes, torches, stones, swords, kerosene-soaked rags, acid bulbs, stones and firearms, were transported in lorries from one locality to another. On reaching each locality, these mobs often divided themselves into groups and attacked from different directions simultaneously. 'Some times one group kept the local inhabitants who were resisting engaged while other came from another place and attacked' (Reddy Commission 1971: 215). According to Brigadier Sukhwant Singh, who led army deployments in the affected parts of Ahmedabad, 'small pockets of minority communities in area of larger communities were wiped out or stood to be wiped out' (ibid.: 217). Attackers barricaded the roads to prevent the police and the army from entering the neighbourhood and dispersing the crowds. 'Inside the barriers the houses and shops were looted, inmates killed and household goods were dragged outside the house in the street and set ablaze throwing kerosene soaked rags therein' (ibid.). This violence was probably facilitated by a measure of support from the police machinery, which in some cases may have played a partisan role: 'We have, however, an impression that though the whole of the police force may not be communally involved, there may be some instances where the police were affected by the Jagannath temple incident' (ibid.: 193).

Between 19 and 30 September, violence spread east and west of the River Sabarmati. Since the overwhelming majority of the residents of western Ahmedabad were upper-caste Hindus, violence there was relatively limited; the posh enclaves of Ellisbridge and Navrangpura saw the destruction of 431 commercial and residential establishments and the deaths of 49 people. The toll was higher in the walled city, where Scheduled Castes, upper castes and Muslims lived in close proximity to each other. Muslim-dominated pols in several parts of the walled city – Dariapur, Shahpur, Mirzapur, Kalupur, Khadia, Raipur, Gheekanta and Khanpur – were singled out for attack. At least 1,979 shops were looted or destroyed, and 118 people killed (ibid: 151, 155, 159).[35]

However, the toll in the industrial belt was higher than in the walled city and western Ahmedabad put together. Here, communal mobilisation and the economic and social stresses of the 1960s manifested themselves in gory violence. Much of this violence was concentrated in the mill districts. The industrial regions of Maninagar (where the RSS had organised a mass rally in 1968), Behrampura, Rakhial, Chamanpura, Sarangpur, Vatva, Bapunagar, Naroda, Asarwa, Amraiwadi, Narol, Sardar Nagar, Jamalpur and Khokhara-Mahemdabad saw the destruction of 3,891 properties and 712 killings.[36] Of the casualties among Muslims, at least 100 were identified as Muslim workers employed in the city's textile mills, manifesting rising tensions between industrial labourers competing for jobs.

According to survivor testimonies recorded in the next section, during the riot, Muslim women were subjected to various forms of sexual violence, including rape, genital mutilation and sexualised verbal abuse in several neighbourhoods in the industrial region of Ahmedabad. These areas were Khokhara-Mahemdabad, Amraiwadi, Bapunagar and Bhilwada.[37] According to Ghanshyam Shah (1970: 195), New Mental Bombay Housing Colony and Chamanpura saw similar violence. In all these neighbourhoods, Hindus vastly outnumbered Muslims, allowing rioters (a number of whom hailed from the surrounding Hindu localities) to overwhelm the minority community and inflict sexual and other forms of violence upon Muslim residents. Khokhara-Mahemdabad,

Amraiwadi and Bapunagar were all Muslim localities in a Hindu-majority area. These three localities fell under the jurisdiction of the Gomtipur police station. According to the records of this police station, the total population of Hindus here was over 158,000 and that of Muslims only 60,000 (Reddy Commission 1971: 29). The same was true of the New Mental Bombay Housing Colony and Chamanpura, which were under the jurisdiction of the Madhupura police station. The Hindu population in the remit of this police station stood at 120,421, whereas Muslims numbered only 16,000 (ibid.: 26).

In the industrial neighbourhood of Khokhara-Mahemdabad, violence began in the evening of 19 September when a crowd of 500 people burned a shop owned by a Muslim man (Reddy Commission 1971: Appendix V, p. 122). Before the day was over, numerous houses belonging to Muslims had been incinerated by mobs of 50 to up to 300 men armed with sticks, knives, pickaxes and iron pipes. In many instances, houses belonging to Muslims were broken into, Muslim men and women were attacked, and their property was looted, destroyed or set alight. According to the testimony of Amina Sheikh, a 57-year-old Muslim resident of Gomtipur and the daughter of a former mill worker, Muslim women were subjected to sexual violence in this neighbourhood: 'My maternal uncle and aunt used to live in Amraiwadi Khokhara. During the riot, they killed my uncle and raped my aunt in their own house. When she came to our house my aunt was in a very bad shape' (interview, Ahmedabad, 16 November 2007). Due to ineffective police intervention, similar attacks occurred sporadically all day on 20 September in areas that contained small Muslim pockets. Even though a curfew was imposed at 7 p.m. on 20 September, attacks against Muslims and their property continued until 22 September (Reddy Commission 1971: Appendix V, pp. 122–30). Two attacks occurred on 23 and 25 September as well, but by that time the size of the mobs had reduced to 10–25 men.

In the working-class neighbourhood of Bapunagar, violence began in the early hours of 20 September, when '5 houses, 6 shops, and a flour mill of Muslims were attacked and the articles set on fire' by a 'Hindu crowd' of 25 (Reddy Commission 1971: 134). Violence gathered pace as the day went on: crowds of up to 500 men, armed with sticks, daggers and spears, went on a rampage, looting or destroying shops, shrines and homes belonging to Muslims, and killing or injuring Muslim men and women (ibid.: 133–42). According to Jamila, a Muslim community worker and currently a resident of Jamalpur, during these attacks Muslim women were subjected to brutal forms of sexual violence:

> I came to Gujarat in 1969. I was 21 years old at the time. Since I was educated I was called to do community work in the area. I have seen horrid scenes in Bapunagar [...] there I saw women in such a state that I can never forget. [...]
>
> When they raped women, they first made their husbands stand there and asked them do you have any courage [to stop us]? See your father-in-law, see this, see that. Then they beat everyone one by one and then in front of them they raped their women, cut their breasts [...] meaning they tortured them. I brought these dead bodies myself.[38]

As in the case of Khokhara-Mahemdabad, a curfew was imposed in Bapunagar in the evening of 20 September. However, in the early hours of 21 September, violence escalated when a 'Hindu crowd of 1,000 persons armed with [knives], pipes and sticks' looted and burnt 77 residential properties and two houses (Reddy Commission 1971: Appendix V, p. 139). Targeted attacks against Muslims continued sporadically until around 3 p.m. on 22 September, with the size of the crowds fluctuating between 500 and 1,000.

In sharp contrast to such attacks by Hindu men against Muslim men and women, counter-attacks by Muslims were considerably smaller in scale and significantly less organised. Even though divisive religious organisations had been mobilising Muslims along communal lines, Hindu nationalist activists were far more organised and had a much wider support base. In its report, the Reddy Commission took a rather sympathetic stance with respect to the sporadic and uncoordinated attacks by Muslims:

> It is true that there were also Muslim mobs in the initial stages which had caused damage to property and person in the walled area, but that was a consequence of the reaction of the attack by the Hindus o[n] their person and property. It is not as if the Muslims could be expected to be docile and remain idle when properties and persons of their co-religionists were being attacked. The incident

of Jagannath temple therefore had its chain reactions both on the Hindu and Muslim mobs. Though this was the position in the initial stage and later in some areas, there were attacks on some individual Hindus in the suburban area and firing by Muslims from Soneria blocks, the action of the Hindu crowds had no relation to some of these incidents and was massive and became organized as the course of the riots continued. (Reddy Commission 1971: 213)

It is possible that during some of these attacks, Muslim men raped Hindu women. However, it is impossible to confirm or reject this; the Reddy Commission contains no reference to sexual violence against women from any religious community, and none of my interviewees mentioned cases in which such violence was inflicted on Hindu women.

The police failed to inform the Gujarat government about the seriousness of the Jagannath Temple incident in a timely and effective fashion, make more preventive arrests, disperse mobs effectively and call on the army to restore order. The Reddy Commission came down heavily on the police: 'The police, in our opinion, were caught napping and became confused and had misappreciated and mis-judged the seriousness of the situation' (1971: 214). The police were also unwilling to submit evidence about the modus operandi of the rioters: 'The impression we got was that the police was not prepared to place any evidence before us or speak about any circumstance which will show that crowds had rampaged in a systematic manner or that they were being supplied with weapons, or that the targets were being traced with the help of the electoral lists and some lists' (ibid.: 216). Yet, the state apparatus was not blatantly anti-Muslim in 1969, as many have accused it of being in 2002. While describing the administration's response as 'tardy', 'ineffective', 'weak' and 'timid', the Reddy Commission added: 'we cannot also countenance the suggestion that all this was permitted to be done either by the Government or the police deliberately to enable the decimation or genocide of Muslims' (ibid.: 214). This assessment appears correct in the light of the various preventive actions taken by the police prior to and during the course of the 1969 riot, especially with regard to preventing sexual violence, as discussed previously in this chapter.

In organising propaganda that contributed to inciting violence against Muslims, Hindu nationalist groups had received support from the various communities they had painstakingly mobilised throughout the 1960s. Middle-class, upper-caste families (especially Patels) provided financial support to these groups, wrote anti-Muslim articles for the vernacular press, and published handbills (G. Shah 1991: 193). The men who actively looted Muslim homes and participated in inflicting physical violence against Muslims included migrant workers from UP, Rajasthan, Maharashtra and other parts of the country; Scheduled Castes (such as Vagharis, Harijans and Bhois); backward-caste Kolis; and upper castes, particularly Patels and Rajputs (Reddy Commission 1971: 193, 195).

Hindu nationalist calls for violence against Muslims inspired this heterogeneous group of participants and channelled their religious prejudices and socio-economic grievances. For upper-caste rioters, Hindu nationalist ideology became a vehicle of protest against the Congress government, which seemingly threatened their caste privileges, showed scant regard for their economic interests, and appeased Muslims at the expense of the Hindu majority. By physically attacking or condoning violence against Muslims, upper-caste men could symbolically subvert the Congress's authority and simultaneously overcome their sexual-religious anxiety about the 'Muslim threat'. For backward castes, lower castes and migrants, the sexual violation of Muslims in line with the retaliatory violence espoused by Hindu nationalist ideology seems to have accomplished multiple aims. First, as with upper-caste Hindus, it was a means of symbolically subverting what seemed to them the excessively secular ideology of the Congress, by egregiously asserting their Hindu identity. Second, it served to carve an important and respectable role for them in Hinduism by enabling them to present themselves as virile and vigorous defenders of Hindus and their temples. Third, amid their deepening economic vulnerability and consequent loss of social standing, the infliction of violence on the minority community served to reclaim their self-esteem through violent assertions of masculine vigour. At the individual level, as we will see in the following section, male rioters also saw Hindu nationalist ideology as a justification for obtaining sexual gratification through the violation of (otherwise unavailable) Muslim women.

Infliction of sexual violence: The experience of Bhilwada neighbourhood

Thus far we have examined how Hindu nationalist propaganda incited various forms of violence against Muslims in the 1969 riot. We have also discussed the involvement of Hindu nationalist leaders and workers in orchestrating anti-Muslim attacks. In order to understand how such violence was actually inflicted during the riot, this section focuses on an episode that occurred in the Bhilwada neighbourhood of Gomtipur's mill district. Bhilwada was home to migrants from UP, Maharashtra and rural Gujarat, who lived in chawls and adjoining slums in close proximity to Muslims. These migrants, according to Ghanshyam Shah, usually lived in Ahmedabad without their families, were deeply religious, and harboured deep-seated animosity towards Muslims. Moreover, they lacked cultural roots and familial bonds in the city, which made them 'available for mob action' (G. Shah 1991: 196).

On 20 September, a group of 200 to 1,000 men attacked the Muslim residents of Gomtipur.[39] Before the end of the day, at least 100 Muslims were dead, and 1,198 homes and shops had been destroyed (Reddy Commission 1971: 141, 155, Appendix V, pp. 144–5). According to Rashida Bano and her younger sister Khurshida Bano, two Muslim survivors of the 1969 riot, several Muslim women were subjected to sexual violence in Bhilwada on 21 September.

On that day, Rashida's father, Rafiq Khan Pathan, was brutally beaten, repeatedly stabbed, and ultimately killed in front of Rashida's five-year-old daughter, her sister Khurshida and their mother. Rafiq, a Communist Party worker, had been actively involved in the progressive Indian People's Theatre Association and welfare work in the industrial belt. He was one of the thousands of Muslim workers who had been pushed out of the textile workforce from the 1940s, and earned a living running a cycle repair shop. A day after his murder, a major English-language broadsheet newspaper carried his obituary on the front page describing him as the 'grand old man of the left in Gujarat'.[40]

Rashida's mother was beaten mercilessly as she tried to protect her family. According to the sisters, their mother never really recovered from the trauma: 'the scene of our father's murder kept replaying in her head over and over again'. Khurshida, who was aged around 19 at the time, was physically assaulted and narrowly escaped gang-rape. Although Rashida's neighbourhood, Rakhial, was relatively peaceful, surviving the riot was extremely difficult for her too. She was expecting her fourth child and was beginning to feel labour pains. Her husband, a Scheduled Caste man who had converted to Islam, had been made redundant from the Lal textile mill, forcing her family into abject poverty. Rashida relied on her parents to raise her five-year-old daughter, to bring her food, and for the kind of support that usually only family provides. The sisters remember the events of the day vividly. 'I long for the day when someone will tell my story', Rashida told me. I promised her I would, as best as I could. So let us hear what she and Khurshida have to say.

Rashida Bano's account runs as follows:

In our locality there were only 20 to 25 Muslim families and their houses were in one row. My father used to repair cycles. The shop was owned by a Hindu man from UP but my father had taken the contract to run it. Ram Bhai [the shop owner] lived with other people from UP in a separate colony, but my father ran the shop. My father had good relations with these people and was especially respected among the Rabaris.[41] They were all very friendly with my father [. . .] they would get together at his shop every day and chatted for hours. He had lots of friends. He had filed lots of petitions with the Corporation [Ahmedabad Municipal Corporation] and got a road built and had water taps installed. He had earned a lot of respect even though he was very poor, wore rags and barely managed to eat a square meal. Occasionally, there were some scuffles between Hindus and Muslims either over money or during some festival or over some other small issue but we still talked to each other and were part of each other's daily life.

On Saturday night [20 September 1969] rumours started circulating that riots were going to start in our locality. In our area, where my parents used to live, there were lots of UP *ke bhaiyas*.[42] These people were quite orthodox and active in the RSS. My father had close ties with them so he was sure that no harm would come to us. But our Rabari neighbours told him to escape with his family and children. They said *chacha* [uncle] run away [. . .] this time they will not leave any Muslim alive. But my father was still sure that nothing would happen.

On the morning of the 21st my father decided to escape to Rakhial with everyone else. He had barely walked a hundred metres when those people spotted him. Before the riot, these people used to spend the whole day chatting with him at his shop. When those people spotted him they said, 'See chacha is coming, he has his daughter with him'. They said to each other, '*Gira do Mussalman ko*' ['Kill the Muslim']. They came out with their sticks and shouted, '*Eh budhe, eh budhe, idhar aa*' ['You, old man, come here']. People who had grown up calling him chacha every day, were calling him *budha* ['old man'] that day. My father thought that these people just wanted to take whatever little money and possessions he had on him. God knows what had come over my father, he walked back towards them [...] that is when [...] they attacked him with swords and sticks. My mother started screaming. When she tried to protect him, they started beating her too.

These people, who killed my father, and attacked my mother and sister, were *ghar ke hi log* [members of the family], they were not strangers.

When they attacked my sister, one of them saved her. There are good people in this world too. He confronted the other men so they let her run away. The same people, for whose rights my father dedicated all his life, killed him in 1969. (Interview, Ahmedabad, 29 November 2007 and 30 January 2008)

Khurshida Bano narrated the story as follows:

They first attacked my father with swords and sticks. My mother started screaming. When she tried to protect him, they started beating her too. They said to me, 'We will not kill you here, we will take you inside'. They tried to drag me inside the house. They said to each other, 'She is *bade kaam ki cheez* [very useful object] [...] we won't kill you here, we will kill you inside'. [...] They were pulling me towards them. They said that they would rape me [*beizzati karenge*]. I screamed at them and said, 'You should be ashamed of yourself. Don't you have mothers and sisters in your house?' But they pinned me with knives between them [...] they warned me that if I tried to escape they would stab me from all sides. Then one of them came to my rescue. He was also a UP ka bhaiya. He scolded the others and made all those men leave me [...]

I ran towards the open fields near Bhilwada. Women and children were hiding in those fields for a whole day. During the riot so many women and girls were raped [...] These women [...] would tell me how their husbands were killed [...] and how they [the attackers] raped them [...] and raped their daughters [...] Half of them came naked. All their clothes were torn. They had come in a very bad state. Rabaris wear *safa*s [turbans]. On seeing these naked women Rabaris gave them their safas to cover themselves. (Interview, Ahmedabad, 29 November 2007)

Rashida's and Khurshida's words describe the everyday life of ordinary people in the mill districts of Ahmedabad in the 1960s, and how the stresses and strains of that life led Hindu men to inflict sexual violence against Muslim women. Their accounts point to the extent to which poverty and governmental neglect had marred the lives of workers who inhabited the dilapidated chawls and slums in the industrial belt, which lacked even the most basic amenities such as roads and water. Deprivation was so extreme that eating a square meal was 'barely' possible. However, despite having much in common, migrant workers privileged differences of religion and regional background when it came to housing. Hindu and Muslim workers lived close to, but not with, each other, and tensions between them flared up periodically over issues such as money and festivals. Yet their close proximity and everyday interaction had also enabled them to forge friendships, or, as Rashida stressed, this proximity enabled Hindus and Muslims to still be part of each other's lives.

However, the riot abruptly shattered neighbourhood ties based on everyday interactions. Communal mobilisation by organisations such as the RSS not only led Hindu labourers to arm themselves with swords and sticks, but also to use them; indeed, to use them against people they had interacted with every day, and against someone they endearingly called 'chacha' and at whose shop they would all get together and 'chat for hours'. Once communal hostility had replaced respect and friendship, all that remained were sharp divisions based on religion. The neighbourhood was reconstituted as a gendered communal space where Hindus were transformed into defenders of the 'victimised' Hindu community, and neighbours who happened to be Muslims into embodiments of the imaginary Muslim 'enemy'.

Rashida's and Khurshida's narratives also shed light on how the breakdown of neighbourhood ties created space for the conflation of sexual violence with sex. Once ethical-moral codes, whose function is to deter violence, were dispelled, Khurshida could be viewed not as a neighbour or as a person, but only as a 'kaam ki cheez' – a useful sexual object. This sexual object could then be forcefully appropriated and used for the purposes of sexual gratification. Khurshida resisted her objectification by invoking the familial responsibilities accorded to men within patriarchal structures. She tried to make her attackers view her as their own 'mother' or 'sister' in the hope that her appeal would humanise her for them. She hoped such pleas would remind the men of their patriarchal obligation to protect the sexual chastity of their mothers and sisters. However, her attackers, on the contrary, seemed to derive pleasure out of her pleading. Why else would they declare their intentions to Khurshida? The declaration that she was going to be raped, the fear it invoked in her, her powerlessness, and her frantic efforts to escape, appear to have been for them a kind of sexual foreplay. Her resistance and fear seem not to have served as a deterrent to violence, but rather heightened the state of sexual arousal and the anticipation of sexual gratification that would come out of raping her. The aggressors felt able to act on such motivations because communal mobilisation, high levels of everyday gender-specific violence, and the breakdown of law and order during the riot created a permissive environment where women could be victimised with impunity.

To conclude, the combination of communal hostility against Muslims and everyday patriarchal sanctions for gendered violence broke down neighbourhood ties forged on the basis of everyday interactions among different communities during the 1969 riot. The neighbourhood was reconstituted into an arena where sexual violence could be inflicted against Muslim women without any regard to social ties. The expulsion of moral hesitation, the absence of fear of punishment, and the disappearance of empathy for neighbours enabled Hindu aggressors to view Muslim women as their communal enemies and as dehumanised sexual objects. Sexual violence was seen as a way of asserting Hindu masculinity and gratifying sexual desires. Yet, as demonstrated by the Hindu man who helped Khurshida escape, a modicum of moral revulsion to sexually violating women remained intact at least in some cases during the 1969 riot.

Diffusing responsibility, denying culpability

Various actors involved in the riot were obliged to depose before the Reddy Commission during its inquiry. Prominent among them were representatives of Hindu nationalist organisations, the HDRS and the Jana Sangh; officials from the police and government; politicians from the Congress, the CPI and the CPI-M; and members of organisations involved in relief and rehabilitation work such as the Jamiat, the Ahmedabad Relief Committee and the Central Relief Committee. Depositions were also made by the representatives of the Hullad Pidit Sahayta Samiti (HPSS) (Relief Committee for Riot Victims), which was set up on 8 October 1969 by the Jana Sangh to offer relief to Hindu survivors. In their deposition, all these actors were questioned about the role they had played in instigating or quelling violence, and asked to reflect on the causes of the riot.

The statements of the HPSS and the testimonies of Jana Sangh leaders, and the articles published by propaganda vehicles such as *Sadhana* and *Organiser*, reveal that at the time of the 1969 riot, Hindu nationalist leaders already felt able to publicly justify communal violence, describe it as understandable, and lay the responsibility squarely on Muslims. For example, organisations such as the HPSS sought to portray Muslims as the aggressors and Hindus as helpless victims who acted only in self-defence and in retaliation against Muslim attacks. Their denial of facts was vehement:

> The Samiti begs to point out that it is the Muslims who had launched the first murderous attack on Hindu that it was the Muslim who had started assault on persons who were Hindus and it was the Muslims who had first caused the major damage to the whole shopping centres in which the goods worth Rs. 1 crore were being destroyed and it was the Muslim who had first started attack on the police party and which has led Hindus to act in defence and retaliation. (Reddy Commission 1971: 149)

The Reddy Commission rejected this submission unequivocally, saying that the statement was baseless and 'inconsistent with the whole course of events' (ibid.).

National-level Hindu nationalist leaders also sought to apportion blame for the riots to Muslims and describe the Hindu 'reaction' to the 'attack' on the Jagannath Temple as understandable. For example, in an article in the *Organiser* on 3 January 1970, RSS worker and senior Jana Sangh leader Atal Bihari Vajpayee described the riots as an understandable Hindu reaction to the Jagannath Temple incident, implicitly holding Muslims responsible for triggering the violence:

It needs to be considered as to why such a terrible holocaust should have taken place in a State whose population is relatively mild-tempered and law-abiding, and that too in the Birth Centenary Year of Mahatma Gandhi [...] I do not propose to make any detailed comments on the Ahmedabad happenings. Nevertheless, this much is beyond doubt that the riots were touched off by an attack on the Jagannath Temple.

If Muslims can feel angry and excited about the desecration of Al-Aqsa thousands of miles away from India, why should any one feel surprised about the indignation expressed by Hindus when a temple within the city itself is attacked.

When I say this, I do not in any way wish to justify what has happened in Ahmedabad. I would, however, request my Muslim friends to ponder as to what exactly is the reason that in 99.9 percent cases the riots originate with members of the Muslim community.[43]

However, even though the HPSS and leaders like Atal Bihari Vajpayee apportioned blame for the riots to Muslims, Hindu nationalist organisations did not extol the violence explicitly, nor clearly did they feel bold enough to confirm openly that Hindus had launched the attacks against Muslims. For example, two days before the violence was brought to a halt, on 28 September 1969, the HDRS and the VHP issued a joint statement in the national newspaper *Jansatta* 'denying that they had anything to do with the "Hindu Sangram Samiti"' – the organisation which published several of the inflammatory pamphlets that had incited Hindus to attack Muslims (Reddy Commission 1971: 108). Jana Sangh and RSS leaders also denied their involvement in orchestrating the riots. In some cases they did this by claiming that the Jana Sangh lacked the organisational capacity to foment violence. 'So far as the Jan Sangh and other parties are apportioned blame, there is no organisation of Jan Sangh so powerful in this State so as to cause trouble'.[44]

In other cases, the explanations offered were complete fabrications: 'There were about 500 Pakistani citizens staying in Gujarat and it was this foreign network that had organized the present disturbances'.[45] Representatives of the HDRS also blamed 'Pakistani agents' for organising the riots: 'The immediate cause of the riots is the attack on the Jagannath Temple. The attack on the Jagannath temple was pre-planned. Pak national involved in this attack'.[46] These defences, denials and divergences demonstrate the inability of Hindu nationalist leaders to take on the Congress-led state apparatus in 1969. They form a contrast to Hindu nationalist responses to sexual and other forms of violence against Muslims from the early 1990s, and especially to corresponding discourses around the 2002 massacre. By then, Hindu communal forces were no longer denying attacks by Hindus against Muslims; on the contrary, they often condoned such attacks. Some later Hindu nationalist propaganda pamphlets went still further, publicly accepting, even celebrating, violence as a sign of Hindu assertiveness and aggressive masculinity, as will be discussed later in this book.

Rebuilding life

As mentioned at the outset, the report of the Reddy Commission contained no reference to sexual violence. It took detailed notes of the inflammatory propaganda material circulated by Hindu nationalist organisations and their affiliates (materials which often raised the issue of sexual violence explicitly) and of the state's efforts to prevent 'retributive' attacks against women.[47] However, the experiences of women such as Khurshida and Rashida found no place in the official records of the riot, most likely reinforcing the sense of marginalisation and disenfranchisement felt by them and other Muslim victims.

The Gujarat government did provide some relief. It housed between 15,000 and 18,000 refugees in three temporary relief camps until 23 September, and after 28 September in a central relief camp in the Malek Sabhan stadium. However, the number rendered homeless was around 48,000. The government offered subsidies for rebuilding and reconstructing households, cash compensation to people whose family

members had been killed or left permanently disabled, and grants to
artisans and small traders to re-establish their businesses. Together with
expenses incurred in relief and reconstruction and on loans, the
administration committed itself to spending Rs 3.4 million on its relief
and rehabilitation efforts. However, the damage caused by the
destruction of residential places, religious sites, shops, factories, goods
and materials was worth over 12 times as much (Rs 42.3 million) (Reddy
Commission 1971: 210–11). The Reddy Commission recognised this:
'If we take all these figures into account large though is the amount
expended by the Government in giving relief, it fades into insignificance
when compared with the huge damage done and suffering undergone'
(ibid.: 211).

The inadequacy of the government's arrangements, and the closure of
the central relief camp on 15 October (two and a half months ahead of
schedule), meant that refugees had to rely on private charity or restart
their lives on their own. Religious Muslim organisations such as the
Jamiat-Ulema-e-Hind offered some relief to Muslims, while the HPSS,
set up by the Jana Sangh, did the same for Hindus. The vacuum left by
the government's withdrawal from relief efforts was filled by religious
organisations, deepening the wedge between members of different
religious communities.

Boundaries between Hindu and Muslim neighbourhoods became less
porous over time. When many textile mills closed down in the mid-
1980s, Hindus and Muslims lost the associations they had developed by
virtue of working together in the mills. As economic insecurity
deepened and opportunities for social interaction shrank between the
late 1960s and the mid-1980s, as the following chapter will argue, it
became easier to dehumanise and demonise the 'Muslim enemy'.

However, as the discussion of the 1985 riot in the next chapter will
show, the correlation between hostility among Hindus and Muslims and
sexual violence against Muslim women during communal conflict in
Ahmedabad has been neither linear nor predictable. The widening of
rifts between members of different religious communities does not
necessarily result in the infliction of extreme sexual violence by one
community against the other; much depends on the overall orientation
of every individual riot.

CHAPTER 2

1985

The 1985 riot probably did not involve extreme forms of sexual violence against Muslim women. This is not to suggest that sexual violence did not occur at all. It did, but its modalities were notably different from those observed during the other episodes of conflict examined in this book. First, sexual violence in 1985 took the form of the stripping of women, verbal abuse and sexually intimidating behaviour; violence in this form also occurred in 1969 and 2002, but alongside more extreme brutalities. Second, in 1985, the profiles of perpetrators and victims were different: perpetrators included not only upper-caste and Scheduled Caste men but also some police officers; victims included both Muslim and upper-caste Hindu women. Whereas upper-caste and Scheduled Caste men targeted Muslim women, police officers targeted women of upper-caste Hindu households. By contrast, there is little evidence to suggest the involvement of the police in inflicting sexual violence during the 1969 riot. In 2002, several police officers allegedly inflicted physical and verbal sexual abuse, but the violence was directed exclusively at Muslim women.[1]

Sexual violence during the 1985 riot occurred in four separate incidents. On 4 and 5 April, the police hurled verbal obscenities at upper-caste women in Ahmedabad's eastern industrial area of Asarwa, and the clothes of two women were torn off. Similar violence was perpetrated against upper-caste Hindu women on 16 and 17 April in the Raipur region of the walled city. In the third instance, upper-caste women were sexually intimidated and verbally abused in the mill district of Gomtipur in industrial Ahmedabad on 18 April. Violence against Muslim women occurred on 20 July, the day the annual *rath yatra* (Hindu religious procession) was organised in the walled city. Some upper-caste and Scheduled Caste men who participated in the procession stripped before Muslim women, waved sticks held to their groins and used sexually abusive language.

All the three incidents involving the police are recorded in the report of the official one-man commission of inquiry set up under Justice Vinod Shanker Dave of the High Court of Rajasthan. As in the case of the Reddy Commission that probed the 1969 riot, the aim of the Dave Commission was to investigate the causes and modus operandi of the 1985 riot and the role of the state apparatus in preventing and quelling it. The Dave Commission was quite thorough: its three-volume report published in April 1990 contained media reports, pamphlets, and affidavits and statements of government officials, police officers, top bureaucrats, representatives of Islamic and Hindu religious organisations, Scheduled Caste leaders, civil society activists, some survivors, and politicians from all the major parties active in Gujarat. The commission reported: 'there are several police officers who committed excesses and atrocities, their [behaviour] was inhuman and indecent and unbecoming of members of the police force. Some of them had gone to the extent of misbehaving, maltreating and women handling' (Dave Commission 1990, 1:268).

The inventory of violence during the 1985 riot in Ahmedabad most likely did not include rape, gang-rape and genital mutilation. This is a plausible claim for several reasons, though it cannot be made with absolute certainty. During my fieldwork, Hindu and Muslim survivors of the 1985 riot did not mention a single specific case of extreme sexual violence, whereas the testimonies I obtained regarding 1969 and 2002 refer to various such instances. For example, Amina, who told me that her maternal aunt was raped during the 1969 riot, stated: 'In 1985 we used to live in Gomtipur [. . .] The whole chawl was burnt, lots of people were killed, but in our neighbourhood I did not hear about any rape case' (interview, Ahmedabad, 16 November 2007). When asked whether she had heard about such incidents elsewhere in the city, she said, 'In 1985, I did not hear about rape cases [. . .] I remember distinctly [. . .] by that time I was older and sensible. In 2002, I heard a lot'. Rashida, who had informed me about her sister's experience of escaping gang-rape in 1969 (see Chapter 1), also said that she had not heard of any incident of extreme sexual violence during the 1985 riot. Given that both Amina and Rashida had had first-hand experience of the 1985 riot as well as 1969 – Amina's chawl in Gomtipur was incinerated and Rashida's husband was killed in 1985 – it is highly unlikely that they would withhold such information exclusively with respect to the riot of 1985.

My own interpretation of the absence of any reference to extreme sexual violence in academic studies and civil society reports on the 1985 riot is similar: probably, the references are absent because such violence did not occur. Unlike the 1969 riot, the 1985 riot has been the subject of several detailed ethnographic studies. Notably, longstanding historian of Ahmedabad Howard Spodek (1989) has written an article on the 1985 riot. More recently, in an insightful book on Ahmedabad's twentieth-century history, Spodek (2011) devotes a chapter to the turmoil of 1985. Sociologist Ornit Shani's (2007) book is dedicated almost exclusively to an examination of the 1985 riot, based on a detailed study of some of the worst-affected areas (Dariapur, Vadigam and Naginapol) of the walled city.

None of these studies reports incidents of severe sexual violence in 1985. This cannot be attributed to academic blind spots with regard to women or to gender-insensitive analysis, since the studies just mentioned raise (albeit briefly) the issue of rape and genital mutilations in 2002. Spodek (2011) also cites Ghanshyam Shah's (1970) description of sexual violence during the 1969 riot. Likewise, there is no mention of extreme sexual violence in reports published on the 1985 riots by activists. In October 1985, less than three months after the violence was brought to an end, the Ahmedabad-based Women's Research Group conducted a special inquiry into the impact of the riot on women. In the report, the group diligently documented instances of verbal abuse and sexual intimidation during the riot. It would be very surprising if it had failed to document more extreme forms of sexual violence had they occurred (Women's Research Group 1985).

Could the absence of reports of rape and gang-rape be attributed to the lack of public attention to this issue in the mid-1980s? After all, at the international level, it was only in 1998 that the UN International Criminal Tribunal for the Rwandan genocide recognised rape as an act of genocide under international law, even though information about the widespread occurrence of such crimes during large-scale conflict has been in the public domain since at least World War I

(Harris 1993). At the national level, India's National Crimes Records Bureau did not record cases of rape until 1971. Locally, it was only in 1981 that one of the most prominent women's organisations in Ahmedabad, Jyoti Sangh, decided to record incidents of sexual violence under the category 'rape'.[2] Moreover, even when the Dave Commission reported sexual violence committed against Hindu women during the 1985 riot, it considered the 'excesses and atrocities' committed by police officials as a matter of 'indecent behaviour', not as cognisable crimes that were punishable by law.

Together, this state of affairs suggests that public sensitivity towards sexual violence in 1985 was low. However, this still seems insufficient to explain the absence of reports of such acts as rapes, gang-rapes and genital mutilation in 1985. This is not least because awareness about gender-specific issues has risen gradually since at least the 1970s, when the Indian feminist movement began to emerge (Omvedt 1975). Moreover, in 1974, the Indian government established a special commission of inquiry to investigate the political, economic and social status of women after nearly three decades of independence, with a view to addressing their constraints (Government of India 1974). In light of this growing awareness, it seems unlikely that incidents of extreme sexual violence would have gone unreported in 1985.

Given the absence of information about extreme sexual violence in the oral testimonies, official records, and academic and civil society reports pertaining to the 1985 riot, it therefore seems safe to claim that sexual violence in the form of rape, gang-rape or genital mutilation most likely did not occur. The apparent absence of such sexual violence is striking, because the 1985 riot resembled those of 1969 and 2002 in terms of the location, the geographical spread and the profile of victims of non-sexual forms of violence. Ahmedabad city was the epicentre of each of these three episodes, but communal violence spread to several neighbouring districts in Gujarat in each case: seven of a total of 19 districts in 1969; 19 of a total of 26 districts in 2002; and 11 out of 25 districts between 1 March and 18 July 1985 (Dave Commission 1990, 3:440, Annexure 38). Although the Dave Commission did not provide the total numbers of fatalities, unofficial estimates suggest that Muslims were badly affected in the riot: of the 220 estimated fatalities, 100 were Muslims (compared with 430 out of 660 in 1969).[3] Some 2,500 Muslim homes were destroyed, 1,500 shops belonging to members of the community were incinerated or looted, and about 12,000 Muslims were left homeless while 900 were arrested (ibid., 1:227; see also S. Patel 1985: 8–9; Shani 2007: 88). Despite being less deadly than the 1969 and 2002 conflicts – when the death toll ran into thousands, according to informal estimates – the 1985 riot also saw targeted violence against Muslims. Moreover, murders, destruction of property, beatings, stabbings, bombings and shootings were common features of all three conflicts.

Yet extreme sexual violence was most likely not a shared feature across these riots, as the 1985 conflict testifies. How can this be explained? The answer appears to lie in the unique ideological orientation of the violence in 1985, which in turn shaped the nature of violence during the riot. Violence in 1969 and 2002 was inflicted primarily along religious lines from the very outset. However, the 1985 riot had two different phases: between January and February, violence was inflicted along caste lines, and it was only in March that the violence turned communal. This ideological characteristic affected the actions of those involved in the violence. Moreover, whereas large parts of the state machinery, especially the government and the police, acted as arbiters between religious communities in the 1969 riot, and allegedly as allies of rioters in 2002, in 1985 they were the primary antagonists. This influenced the way in which the violence of 1985 was prevented, inflicted and controlled.

The main perpetrators of sexual and other forms of violence in 1969 and 2002 were the upper-caste, backward-caste and low-caste supporters of Hindu nationalist organisations. Their anger was targeted almost exclusively at Muslims in these conflicts. By contrast, in 1985, the focus of communal Hindu outfits was multi-dimensional. In the first phase, rioters instigated and orchestrated violence against the Congress-led Gujarat government and the backward-caste and low-caste groups who supported the government's proposed reservation policies. These policies entailed setting aside or reserving a certain percentage of public sector jobs and seats in government-financed educational institutions for members of disadvantaged caste groups, especially Scheduled Castes and Scheduled Tribes (Adivasis, or indigenous people). In the second phase, the focus of rioters turned towards Muslims, although violence against backward castes, low castes and state targets also continued. Unlike in 1969 (when backward castes and low castes were pitted against

Muslims), and in 2002 (by which time Hindu nationalism commanded strong loyalty across the caste spectrum), in 1985 Scheduled Castes and backward castes were made targets of attacks by upper-caste Hindus alongside Muslims. This multi-dimensional focus shaped Hindu nationalist propaganda, mobilisation strategies and the ways in which its supporters orchestrated the violence. These differences among the conflicts help to explain the profiles and responses of victims, and the nature of the sexual violence inflicted on women.

In order to understand how these processes unfolded, this chapter examines the nature and modus operandi of the 1985 riot, and how it differed from the other episodes studied in this book. To this end, I first explore the economic, social and political setting in which the riot occurred.

Closure of textile mills and the predicament of mill workers

A day after Prime Minister Indira Gandhi's assassination on 31 October 1984, the national leadership of the Congress appointed her son Rajiv Gandhi as her political successor. In the December 1984 parliamentary elections, the Rajiv Gandhi–led Congress returned to power with a thumping majority, winning 79 per cent of the 545 Lok Sabha seats and 49 per cent of the vote. With 415 seats in the lower house, Rajiv Gandhi's government had the numerical strength to implement policies that furthered liberal economic reforms.

In June 1985, the recently installed central government introduced a new textile policy, which prioritised, among other things, labour market flexibility and small-scale production in powerlooms over large-scale composite mills (Breman 2004: 144; Shani 2007: 44). This policy accelerated the decline of large-scale textile industries across India, a process that had begun around the early 1960s (see the discussion in Chapter 1). By the mid-1980s, the backbone of the organised textile industry had been broken, not only in Ahmedabad but also in other key textiles-oriented cities such as Bombay (Heitzman 2008: 206) and Kanpur (Joshi 2003: 314–15). The adverse impact of national policy on Ahmedabad's textile mills was compounded by several other factors: the unwillingness of mill owners to invest in new technology; attempts to boost profits by outsourcing weaving to smaller powerlooms where wages were lower; the mill owners' desire to rid themselves of the social obligations associated with running large mills; and their desire to reduce the power of the TLA.[4] It was not in the mill owners' interests to save the composite textile mill industry.

By 1985, the composite mill industry was close to disappearing. Ahmedabad had up to 75 textile mills in the late 1970s (Mahadevia and D'Costa 1997: 23). Between 1979 and 1984, at least 19 of them shut down, leaving over 50,000 workers unemployed. This constituted approximately a fifth of the estimated 250,000 workers who depended on the mills for employment in the early 1980s (Shani 2007: 37). Although Scheduled Caste workers constituted only 14 per cent of the city's population of 1.7 million in 1971, and Muslims less than 15 per cent, these groups formed over two-thirds of the workers made redundant by the decline of the textile industry (Spodek 1989: 773). However, upper-caste and Other Backward Class (OBC) communities who worked in the mills were also left unemployed. Since women had been gradually eliminated from the textile mills over the previous three decades, the overwhelming majority of those rendered jobless were men.

The closure of several textile mills took labour insecurity to an altogether new level. Already forced into unskilled or semi-skilled and poorly paid jobs from the mid-1960s, ever-greater numbers of workers sought jobs in small-scale industries (especially powerlooms) from the early 1980s onwards. They also found jobs in small-scale factories in the three industrial estates established between 1963 and 1965 along the periphery of eastern Ahmedabad, in Naroda, Vatva and Odhav (Spodek 2011: 198). This shift was reflected in a rise in the number of registered small-scale industries in the city, and the size of their labour force. While, in 1970, some 1,910 small-scale units employed 35,497 workers, by 1975 the total number of such units had risen to 2,282 and the total strength of their workforce to 43,467. By 1985, the city hosted 3,221 small-scale industries, which together employed over 55,000 workers (Government of Gujarat 1995, 1:77, Statement No. 1). Labour laws pertaining to protection and welfare did not apply to factories with small workforces (10–100 workers), where wages were considerably lower than in the mills and the working conditions significantly poorer. Workers, especially from the Scheduled Castes, lost access to the influence of the TLA, which, despite its faults, had provided them with numerous welfare benefits such as affordable mortgages (Breman 2004: 88, 124). The TLA also negotiated with the mill owners for better working conditions and inflation-indexed pay (Hirway and Terhal 2002: 18–20).

A sharp rise in living costs exacerbated the economic difficulties of the thousands of laid-off mill workers. Between 1960 and 1980, the rise in the cost of essential commodities outpaced the increase in wages.[5] Redundant mill workers lost their daily average wage of around Rs 50, and had to contend with the Rs 10–12 per day that they earned in small-scale industries (Jani 1984: 13). To compensate for the drop in their wages, and to cope with rising prices, more working-class women and children were led into poorly paid, menial work. The decline in the quality of work done by women is reflected in the fact that the number of female workers per 1,000 males in the organised sector in Gujarat fell to 368 in 1981 from 491 in 1961 (Women's Studies Research Centre 2003: 77). Moreover, many workers were no longer able to educate their children or secure good jobs for them – options that had been previously available to them due to the support of the TLA.

Nonetheless, since women had been expelled from the mill workforce from the early 1940s, they had more experience than their male counterparts in navigating the informal labour market. This experience, coupled with the pressure of household responsibilities that routinely and disproportionately fall on women, enabled them to cope better with the harshness of the changing reality (Breman 2004: 212). However, men found this adjustment much more difficult; perhaps understandably so. After all, they lived in a country where universal social security was non-existent (as it still is), and employment was the only way out of poverty; and where entrenched patriarchal systems frequently deemed a man's failure to provide for his family a sign of emasculation.

Intensification of economic strife was paralleled by a housing crisis in Ahmedabad's eastern industrial belt and the walled city. Ahmedabad district's population had increased from 2.2 million in 1961 to 3.8 million by 1981 (Government of India 1981: 4). Meanwhile, the population of Ahmedabad city had more than doubled, rising from 1.1 million in 1961 to 2.3 million by 1981 (Gayer and Jaffrelot 2012: 49). However, the significant rise in population was accompanied by a decline in the availability of affordable housing. The construction of new chawls to house industrial workers was suspended with the closure of the textile mills, forcing workers to seek shelter in the slums burgeoning along the periphery of the mill districts in eastern Ahmedabad. In the 1980s, nearly a quarter of the city's population was housed in the slums. About 15 per cent of slum residents were Muslims, and 83 per cent belonged to low-caste groups. Of these 83 per cent, some 21 per cent were Scheduled Caste (AMC 1976: 5).

Most of these slums were constructed illegally on expensive and increasingly rare urban land. Workers would pay large sums of money to local slum builders in exchange for a scrap of land, in addition to the monthly rent. Since the AMC had long outsourced the responsibility for maintaining and providing basic civic facilities in the slums to these local slum builders, the working poor were faced with the problem of overcrowding, deplorable living conditions and rising living costs all at once.

The continued existence of these slums was itself subject to the builders' relations with corporators (elected representatives) of the AMC and other politicians. Through their connections with corporators and politicians, slumlords provided basic amenities to slum residents. In exchange, they offered politicians support during elections (Shani 2007: 50). However, the rising prices of land in Ahmedabad provided local builders and slum developers with more lucrative options than simply renting out slum dwellings to labourers. With the growing commercial value of slum lands, the trend of evacuating the land and 'selling' it to the highest bidders set in (Nandy et al. 1995: 112–13). According to Shani (2007: 51), slumlords terrorised slum dwellers – sometimes even orchestrating riots – in order to force them to evacuate the land.

Hindu nationalist groups sought to capitalise on the various stresses created by the closure of the mills. As competition between retrenched mill workers gathered pace, outfits such as the VHP and RSS offered to find them employment. The VHP mobilised Scheduled Caste men, whereas the RSS focused on the upper castes, and to some extent on backward castes. As survival became precarious due to declining real wages and lack of affordable housing, these organisations promised emergency rations, medicines and monetary help during religious festivals. When the TLA failed to help Scheduled Caste workers get unpaid wages from closed mills, or to put pressure on mill owners not to close their mills, avenues for the redress of grievances also closed (Spodek 2011: 199–200). Hindu nationalist leaders lent a sympathetic ear to the grievances of laid-off workers, and offered them space to voice anger and frustration with the TLA and the Congress (with which party the TLA was closely aligned). To Scheduled Castes, specifically, the VHP promised the possibility of a united Hindu society, free of everyday caste-based violence and discrimination.

Owing to the secretive nature of these organisations, accurate estimates for their membership in Gujarat are unavailable. However, it is remarkable that between 1981 and 1985, when deindustrialisation was under way in large parts of India, the total number of RSS neighbourhood branches increased from 17,000 to 20,000, and RSS membership grew to over a million from 600,000 in 1951 (Jaffrelot 2005: 4). In Ahmedabad, my interviews with former mill workers confirmed the link between the closure of the textile mills, the rise in unemployment and the intensification of support for Hindu nationalist organisations among young, unemployed men. Satish Parmar, a Scheduled Caste casual worker at Calico Mill[6] in Behrampura, described how the difficulties wrought by the closure of textile mills created scope for Hindu mobilisation:

In our locality 98 per cent of the people used to work in the mills, but after the mills closed down in 1984–85, most of the workers started doing menial labour work. Some started working in small workshops or garages and some started selling vegetables on handcarts. Children's education had to be stopped. Even women and children had to be sent to work. Women who stayed at home also found some work to do. Some women, who were literate, found work in women's organisations [...] more and more people were left unemployed. So the standard of education also went down. Would people think about food or education of their children? The first necessity was *roti* [bread]. But then our children would find work at times and at other times nothing would work out. Then these RSS, VHP people started coming to our locality. They would collect young boys and hold meetings with them and brainwash them. Once I went and fought with these people and said to them that you are putting our youngsters on the wrong path [*gumraha kar rahe ho*]. But [...] they didn't listen to me. (Interview, Ahmedabad, 21 January 2007)

Besides jobs, medicines and other material support, Hindu nationalist organisations offered these men the opportunity of a degree of upward social mobility otherwise unavailable to them because of their low-caste status. During the early 1980s, for example, the VHP organised several rath yatras in which Scheduled Castes were encouraged to participate (Nandy et al. 1995: 107). Since members of this caste group are considered ritually impure and usually prohibited from entering temples and joining religious processions, participation in the rath yatra offered them social respectability and an opportunity to feel part of the Hindu mainstream.

To be sure, the rise in economic insecurity and growth in the social purchase of Hindutva ideology were not inexorably linked. There are several ways in which disgruntled workers might have expressed their genuine anger and deep despair – non-violent strikes and fasts (methods of resistance popularised by Gandhi across Gujarat), mass street protests, or possibly even violent rebellion. Yet a large number of them turned to communal politics. Shani (2007: 41) explains why this was the case:

> The structure and mechanisms of industrial relations that had emerged in the Ahmedabad textile mill industry were impediments to a labour struggle. An industrial relations act created institutional and legal constraints on workers' range of responses to industrial disputes. The division of labour within the mills and the labour union formed an additional barrier for workers' consolidation. Finally, the shift in the structure of the economy and the new policies, which enhanced economic deregulation, further reduced the power of the workers.

When the mills closed down, laid-off workers lost access to an important marker of their identity: that of the mill *mazdoor*, or mill worker. They were now members of disparate (and potentially hostile) religious and caste communities, which competed internally and with each other over the essentials of living. Over the next two decades they forged a new collective, one that was based on a crude religious identity, not on shared class-based experiences; it was this new collective which asserted itself in 2002.

Since pols, chawls and slums were spatially segregated along religious and caste lines, and the closure of the mills further diminished the scope for everyday interactions among different communities, it became that much easier for these groups to accept the Hindu nationalist rhetoric about Muslims. The Dave Commission's report on the 1985 riot was astute in capturing the risk of communalisation posed by the ordering of social space along community lines:

> There is positive evidence to suggest that some of the localities which have come up after 1969 riots in Ahmedabad have 90 per cent population believing in a particular ideology, may be Hindu or Muslim. This has also contributed to the recurrence of communal conflicts. However, till now in isolated forms. It is also established that the groupwise settlements or communitywise housing societies are profit [sic] fertile grounds for cementing and strengthening communal loyalties which are being used [by] communal organisation to spread communalism; and such living is delimiting social interaction and exposure to diversity of culture, and is likely to make people less mobile and prevent them from competing in various vo[c]ations; yet another danger is uneven lop sided and slow development in some of the localities which will deprive people from proper development. (Dave Commission 1990, 2:15)

While thousands of low-caste, upper-caste and Muslim workers were facing downward social mobility in eastern Ahmedabad, residents of western Ahmedabad – who were predominantly upper-caste Hindus but included a small Scheduled Caste and Muslim population as well – were moving up the socio-economic hierarchy. The everyday reality of their lives was far removed from the congested, dilapidated pols in the walled city and the squalor-ridden slums in the industrial belt. The primary worry of middle-class families in the 1980s, as the following section will show, stemmed from changes in the political order.

Congress and the KHAM alliance

The increased popularity of Hindu nationalist organisations up and down the caste hierarchy was paralleled by the rise in electoral support for their political wing, the Jana Sangh. (The Jana Sangh was dissolved in 1980, and one of its factions formed the BJP.) This rise in support was primarily due to the institutional decay and ideological disarray of the Congress. Under Indira Gandhi (Prime Minister during 1966–77 and 1980–84), politics had become more personalised, governance more authoritarian, and rhetoric more populist. Loyalty to Indira Gandhi took precedence over ideology and discipline within the party, and the writ of the central leadership was abrasively and arbitrarily enforced over regional leaders (Rudolph and Rudolph 1987: 155). Simultaneously, the party's populist rhetoric of alleviating poverty brought the harsh economic realities of soaring unemployment and declining purchasing power into sharper focus, alienating voters from the Congress.

The impact of these shifts on support for the Jana Sangh and later the BJP was clearly visible in Gujarat between 1970 and 1985 – first in the wake of the Nav Nirman (or social reconstruction) movement in 1970s, then following the imposition of a nationwide Emergency in 1975, and later after the formation of a political alliance in 1980 between Kshatriyas (a backward caste), Harijans (Scheduled Castes), Adivasis (Scheduled Tribes) and Muslims. Kshatriyas (also called Rajputs) were an upper-caste Hindu community who had held political power during ancient and medieval times. In order to increase their electoral clout, the Kshatriya Sabha (Kshatriya Association) in the 1940s accepted into the Kshatriya fold the backward-caste Koli community, which comprised an estimated 20–4 per cent of Gujarat's population (Shani 2007: 26–7). Since then, Kshatriyas have been seen as a backward-caste group in Gujarat.

In the 1970s, the Congress-led Gujarat government under Chief Minister Chimanbhai Patel came under attack from the middle class over allegations of widespread political corruption and skyrocketing inflation. In 1973, rising prices of essential items such as rice and oil (due to a food shortage in Gujarat and the first international oil shock) led to violent protests across Ahmedabad, in which the urban middle classes, especially university students, participated actively (Jones and Jones 1976: 1018; G. Shah 1974b: 1429). In 1974, protest against the Congress turned into a movement for the 'Nav Nirman' (reconstruction) of Gujarat. This movement received critical impetus from the on-going movement against corruption and social injustice in Bihar led by Gandhian socialist Jayaprakash Narayan.

In Gujarat, students and teachers of Gujarat University in Ahmedabad took the lead in organising the movement, receiving support from the urban middle and lower middle classes. White-collar employees of private and public sector enterprises, professionals including journalists, lawyers and doctors, and students strongly supported the movement (Jones and Jones 1976). The RSS, Jana Sangh and the Akhil Bharatiya Vidyarthi Parishad (ABVP; the student wing of the Jana Sangh) also threw their weight behind this movement, with a view to increasing their social credibility among middle-class groups and weaning voters away from the Congress towards the Jana Sangh. The rise in the membership of the RSS between 1981 and 1985 has to be understood in the context of this rising anti-Congress sentiment.

By February 1974, popular disaffection with the Congress government had intensified so much that Chimanbhai Patel was forced to resign. The Gujarat legislative assembly was dissolved, and the state was placed under president's rule (i.e., under the direct control of the federal government). The first non-Congress Gujarat Chief Minister, Babubhai Patel of the Janata Front, was sworn in for seven months, and fresh elections were called. The Congress paid a heavy price in the 1975 Gujarat assembly elections. It won only 75 of 181 seats, and was consigned to the opposition benches. When Prime Minister Indira Gandhi imposed Emergency on 25 June 1975 to pre-empt the further spread of the anti-Congress/anti-corruption movement led by Jayaprakash Narayan, the Gujarati elite moved further away from the party.

During the Emergency, several Hindu nationalist leaders, Muslim religious leaders, and labour and left-wing activists across India were incarcerated, and a ban was placed on their organisations. Proscribed organisations included the RSS, and one of the leaders arrested for opposing the Emergency was socialist trade unionist George Fernandes. The persecution that the RSS faced during the Emergency helped it gain wider social traction, while the incarceration of leaders such as Fernandes solidified their opposition to the Congress. Within the next two decades, Fernandes's anti-Congress stance hardened to such an extent that his Samata Party joined the BJP-led national coalition in 1998. He was in charge of the Ministry of Defence when the 2002 massacre occurred, and became infamous for condoning brutal sexual violence against Muslim women (Dutt 2002: 214).

The Emergency, which lasted 21 months until 21 March 1977, dealt a major blow to Congress popularity nationwide. In the parliamentary elections held between 16 and 21 March 1977, Indira Gandhi's Congress lost to the Janata Party, a coalition of socialist and left-leaning parties, the Jana Sangh, breakaway factions of the Congress and other small anti-corruption parties. The unwieldy coalition, marred by deep factional rifts, ideological incompatibilities and contests over leadership, lasted less than two years, leaving voters little choice but to re-elect the Congress in the 1980 parliamentary elections. Yet the Janata Party did interrupt the Congress's continuous control of the national government for the first time since independence.

The Congress needed to regain its popularity after the Emergency and the widespread anti-corruption protests, and to curb challenges to its political survival. To that end, Gujarat's Congress leadership, with Indira Gandhi's blessings, fronted a populist KHAM strategy from the mid-1970s. The strategy prioritised advancement of the economically and politically marginalised backward castes, low castes and minorities, at the expense of concerns raised by upper-caste, middle-class groups. It proposed a political alliance of Kshatriyas (a backward caste), Harijans (Scheduled Castes), Adivasis (Scheduled Tribes) and Muslims, who together accounted for approximately 55 per cent of the population of Gujarat (Shani 2007: 70; Wood 1984: 210). Gujarat Chief Minister Madhavsinh Solanki himself hailed from a backward-caste community. Hoping that this strategy would give them political clout and social respectability, communities belonging to the KHAM alliance voted for the Congress en masse in the 1980 Gujarat assembly elections. The party won with a thumping majority, claiming 141 of 182 seats, and the KHAM communities came to dominate the assembly formed in 1980 (Government of Gujarat 1982: 10–11).

However, the KHAM alliance benefited no-one (except a few ambitious politicians from Scheduled Caste and backward-caste communities), and alienated affluent upper castes. The social conditions of marginalised groups did not change (Shani 2007: 72–3). The police continued to humiliate members of the Scheduled Castes in day-to-day interactions (Sheth 1998), and, just like Muslims, they remained at the receiving end of the discriminatory hiring practices of employers. In fact, the rise in socio-economic insecurity, especially among the bulk of Ahmedabad's Scheduled Castes and Muslims, only increased cynicism about Indira Gandhi's rhetoric about eradicating poverty, Rajiv Gandhi's economic revitalisation plans, and the promises of the KHAM alliance. Since the Congress was in power in the national government as well as in

Gujarat, these groups held the party responsible for their poor social and economic situation. The Congress's 1980 election slogan in Gujarat – 'power to the poor' – had proved vacuous.

While the Congress's political strategy did little to bring about social transformation for the marginalised, it did everything to alienate the hegemons: upper-caste, middle-class communities such as Patels, Baniyas and Brahmins. These groups strongly criticised the Congress for appointing a backward-caste person as Gujarat Chief Minister, and for its KHAM alliance strategy, which portended a transfer of control over political patronage and social influence from them to low-caste communities (Scheduled Castes and Scheduled Tribes), backward-caste Kshatriyas (who chose to align themselves with low castes rather than upper castes) and religious minorities (Muslims). The emergence of political support for reservation policies in other parts of India, especially UP and Bihar, only intensified the fears of upper-caste, middle-class communities. In several instances, this fear resulted in violence inflicted by upper castes against low-caste communities (Shani 2007: 65).

Upper-caste anger against the Congress government increased when, in 1980, it announced reservations in post-graduate medical colleges. The policy involved reservations for Scheduled Castes and Scheduled Tribes in promotions, and the option of carrying forward unfilled reserved seats to the following year. Students from Ahmedabad's B. J. Medical College agitated strongly against the move, pressuring the government into nullifying the carry-forward scheme. Even though the government acquiesced, large-scale violence erupted across the city for 102 days in which Scheduled Castes were the main targets. They were killed (at least 15 in Ahmedabad alone) and their property damaged or looted in at least 19 villages in Ahmedabad, Kheda and Mehsana districts (Shani 2007: 65; Spodek 2011: 210). The KHAM strategy and the reservation policy engendered a deep disdain for the Congress among Ahmedabad's upper-caste, middle-class voters, including teachers, students, police officials, judges and other professionals – a distrust that transformed into votes for the BJP from the 1980s, vocal support for Hindu nationalism's violent communal agenda in the 1990s, and justification of and participation in the anti-Muslim massacre in 2002.

Large sections of middle-class Hindus were unwilling to tolerate threats to their political and social privileges, and were ready to defend these privileges with violence if necessary. In 1985, they amply demonstrated how far they were prepared to go to neutralise any challenge to the status quo. They also had a stronger hand in this fight, since the police routinely failed to intervene to protect Scheduled Castes from caste-based discrimination and violence. During the 1981 anti-reservation riots in Gujarat, the police had been accused of failing to protect Scheduled Castes from violent attacks by upper castes. Moreover, the TLA neither expressed support for Scheduled Castes nor for the reservation policy, depriving Scheduled Castes of an important and influential political platform. Scheduled Caste organisations established to support reservations and curb casteism in society, such as the Dalit Panthers, were small and could not compete with better-organised anti-reservation rivals such as the RSS, the BJP and the ABVP.

So far, we have seen how spatial segregation along community lines, the closure of the textile mills, and the concomitant intensification of socio-economic insecurity among the urban poor opened an ever-greater number of young upper-caste and low-caste men to Hindu nationalist mobilisation. Abrogation of democratic rule during the Emergency, high inflation and malfeasance fuelled public cynicism towards politics, especially among the educated urban middle class, and exposed the contradictions between the Congress's rhetoric and practice. In such a context, government efforts to alleviate caste-based inequality through reservation policies proved too radical for upper-caste communities in Ahmedabad, in Gujarat as a whole, and beyond. This augured the end of the Congress's status as the dominant political force in Gujarat as well as in other parts of India.

These developments opened up multiple fault lines in Ahmedabad's socio-political landscape: between Muslims and non-Muslims; upper and low castes; the poor and the affluent; political parties and voters; government and the governed. Everyone in Ahmedabad was a member of more than one of these groups, and hence affected along multiple axes. For example, everyone, irrespective of their caste, class and religious identity, was (at least in principle if not practice) a citizen and had the right to good, democratic governance. Most low castes and Muslims were also poor, and upper castes disproportionately constituted the affluent strata of society. During the 1985 riot, these multiple memberships gave rise to and manifested themselves in multiple conflicts. People came together – to protect themselves and their families or to attack others – in some instances as upper castes, in others as disaffected voters, as poor neighbours, or as Hindu nationalists, rather like shards of glass in a rotating kaleidoscope.

Anti-reservation to anti-Muslim: January–October 1985

The event that triggered the 1985 riot had little to do with religion or religious identity. The catalyst was the Congress-led central government's decision in January 1985 to increase the reservation quota in government jobs and in medical and technical educational institutions for 'socially and educationally backward' OBCs to 28 per cent of all vacancies from 5–10 per cent (Dave Commission 1990, 1:193). Since the reservation quota for Scheduled Castes and Scheduled Tribes in the same areas was 14 per cent and 7 per cent, respectively, this move took the overall number of seats unavailable to upper-caste students and job-seekers to 49 per cent. The federal cabinet made the decision on 10 January and officially announced it a couple of days later (ibid.: 202). Since the policy did not aim to benefit Muslims or any other religious minorities, the media debate (which started around 15 January) focused on caste rather than religious issues.

Already unhappy with the KHAM strategy and the Gujarat government's efforts in the early 1980s to expand the purview of the reservation policy, upper castes were not willing to allow the government to implement the move. For them, reservations were anti-meritocratic and threatened traditional caste hierarchies. They did not, however, turn to violence instantly. In the first two weeks of February, middle-class Hindu professionals and students along with their parents organised peaceful protests in the affluent enclaves of western Ahmedabad. On 6 February, students of engineering colleges in Rajkot and Bhavnagar districts joined in, launching a strike against the government's move. Students of L. D. Engineering College in Ahmedabad followed suit: they held their first meeting on that day and decided to agitate against increasing reservations in engineering and medical colleges. Yet no violence occurred anywhere in Gujarat until 17 February.

What had been a peaceful protest turned into a violent agitation on 17 February soon after the BJP's student wing, the ABVP, took 'command of [the] agitation' (Dave Commission 1990, 1:268).

According to the police deposition to the Dave Commission, ABVP activists 'master-minded' the planning and execution of the agitation, and started damaging public property across Gujarat (ibid.: 269).[7] From then onwards, 'rallies and processions became the order of the day, [Ahmedabad and state transport] buses in particular were the targets of the student's fury' (ibid.: 202). On 17 February, two Gujarat state transport buses were set alight in the city of Nadiad (Kheda district), an incident in which two people were killed. In the same week, two buses were hijacked by agitators in the cities of Rajpipla (in Narmada district) and Surat (in Surat district). Between 19 and 28 February, agitators damaged government property, stoned the houses of some state officials, burnt municipal and transport buses, and even attacked some policemen. On 25 February, agitators called an Ahmedabad *bandh* (strike), demanding the closure of businesses, shops and offices in protest against the reservation policy. The call was supported by several bar and medical associations across Gujarat, including those in the cities of Vadodara, Rajpipla and Nadiad, with many resident doctors and surgeons in Ahmedabad going on strike.

Yet even as the agitation spread within the urban areas, and from urban areas to rural districts, government property remained the primary target of violence, rather than the person or property of Muslims. Due to this particular focus of the unrest, moreover, no vernacular newspaper instigated sexual violence against Muslim women by publishing inflammatory rumours about rapes of Hindu women by Muslim men. As noted in the previous and the following chapters, such reports were published within two days of the scuffle at the Jagannath Temple on 20 September 1969, and a day after the train accident in Godhra on 28 February 2002. Such reports contributed to the infliction of brutal sexual violence against Muslim women in both these cases.

There was a temporary lull in the agitation during the Gujarat legislative assembly elections, which were scheduled for 5 March. Even though the KHAM alliance had done little to alleviate everyday discrimination and violence based on caste, the concept held out hope for a new kind of politics among Kshatriyas, Harijans, Adivasis and Muslims. This hope manifested itself in voter behaviour. Votes from KHAM communities, and the fear of instability generated after Prime Minister Indira Gandhi's assassination in October 1984, led the Congress to a strong majority. Whereas it had won 141 of 182 seats in the 1980 elections, in 1985 it won 149 of 182 seats, and 55.5 per cent of the vote. Nevertheless, the tide was shifting decisively against the Congress. Although the Jana Sangh had won only three seats and 8.8 per cent of the vote in the 1972 legislative assembly election, in 1985 its successor, the BJP, managed to win 11 of the 124 seats it contested, and 14.9 per cent of the vote (Government of Gujarat 1985b: 14, 47). The Jana Sangh's electoral performance was still weak, because its vote base was confined primarily to urban upper castes. However, within two years, the BJP had managed to woo low-caste voters. By 1987 it had succeeded in ousting the Congress from Ahmedabad's municipal corporation; by 1990, from the Gujarat government; and by 1998, from the central government in Delhi. What happened in Ahmedabad from March 1985 onwards must be seen in the light of this shift.

Immediately after coming to power in the Gujarat legislative assembly, the Congress on 11 March allotted 14 of 20 state cabinet posts to members of the KHAM alliance. For the first time since the formation of Gujarat in 1960, upper-caste communities, especially Patels, did not dominate the government. With this move, as far as upper castes were concerned, the Congress had gone too far: it had not only expanded the purview of reservation policies favouring OBCs, but directly threatened upper-caste political and social hegemony by appointing KHAM members to top government offices. Violence re-erupted, and students once again took the lead. On 11 March, students from Ahmedabad, Vadodara, Surat and Jamnagar established the Akhil Gujarat Navrachna Samiti (All Gujarat Committee for Reconstruction; henceforth AGRS), calling for a statewide bandh on 18 March. Parents of these students formed a similar body.

Notably, up until 18 March, public mobilisation in Ahmedabad had focused primarily on galvanising upper-caste, middle-class professional groups against the government and its reservation policy. These organisations were notably different in character and intent from those that had emerged in 1969 during the months prior to the riot. Unlike organisations such as the HRDS, which had played an active role in instigating anti-minority violence during the 1969 riot, the raison d'être of agitators such as the AGRS and the Acharya Mandal (Teachers' Group) was to oppose reservations, not to forge a Hindu community or defend Hindus and Hinduism against an imaginary Muslim enemy.

On 15 March, the Gujarat government acquiesced to demands by educationists and social workers in Ahmedabad that implementation of the reservation policy be delayed until after the 1985–86 academic year (Dave Commission 1990, 1:203). However, rather than mollifying the agitators, this concession reinvigorated the anti-reservation agitation. A Gujarat-wide bandh was successfully observed on 18 March, and the police recorded over 50 incidents of stone throwing and destruction of government property on that day alone (ibid., 3:178–87, Annexure 35). On the evening of 18 March, a *mrityughant*[8] (death knell) was sounded in Vadigam, a Hindu-majority neighbourhood in the walled city, to symbolise the death of the reservation policy. While this death knell rang out, a stone, allegedly thrown by a resident of Vadigam, hit a Muslim boy from the neighbouring Muslim-majority locality of Naginapol. Before the end of the day, the 'anti-reservation agitation took a sudden and sharp turn in the shape of communal riots' (ibid., 1:27).

Between 18 and 19 March, upper castes and Muslims clashed in Vadigam, Naginapol, Dariapur, Dabgarwad and Kalupur in the walled city (Dave Commission 1990, 1:226): 'The whole night of March 18, 1985 till morning of the 19th March, 1985 was the beginning of communal riots followed by arson and looting and killing of the people by private firing, shrieking voices of the male, female and children were heard from all around the area of Wadigam, Naginapole, Dariapur and Kalupur'. Before the violence could spiral out of control, the government on 19 March called in the army and imposed a curfew in the walled city. Consequently, the last two weeks of March remained relatively peaceful. From April onwards, however, the anti-reservation agitation and communal riots took place simultaneously. During that month, the anti-reservation agitation spread to Saraspur and Gomtipur in the industrial belt; Astodia, Shahpur, Gheekanta and Dariapur in the walled city; and Naranpura, Paldi and Ellisbridge in western Ahmedabad (ibid., 1:236, 234, 260, 261).[9] By the time violence abated in mid-July, the 1985 riots had affected an estimated 500,000 people in the walled city and 150,000 people outside it (ibid., 1:57).

The transformation of the anti-reservation riots into communal violence was unexpected: 'Neither the intelligence of the police nor the regular police either suspected or had the information that communal riots would be started' (Dave Commission 1990, 1:226). The occurrence of communal violence was particularly perplexing for the Dave

Commission because 'Muslims had not participated in any [anti-reservation] demonstration from 18th February to 18th March, 1985 the day on which a Bandh call was given and death knell was sounded. They had not shown any resentment against increase in quota hence they too were not spared and possibly the agitationists wanted to chastise them' (ibid., 2:10). Yet for the commission the occurrence was not inexplicable. It pointed to the history of communal violence in Gujarat, which made the state 'prone to riots' (ibid., 1:226), and held Hindu nationalist organisations responsible for orchestrating the anti-reservation riots and communal violence in order to dislodge the Congress government:

> To conclude, motives of the agitation, initially started in Morbi was opposing the anti-reservation policy but courses of events show that once the planning came in the hands of the ABVP supported by BJP and VHP, further joined by Congress dissidents, and some other persons and more particularly after induction of Shri Madhavsinh Solanki as Chief Minister of Gujarat, the motive for continuance of the agitation and spreading communal disturbances became the ouster of Shri Madhavsinh Solanki. (Ibid., 2:11)

This explanation for communal rioting has found favour among certain political commentators (Engineer 1985b), and seems plausible. Several Hindu nationalist organisations – first the ABVP, and then the BJP, VHP and the Bharatiya Mazdoor Sangh (Indian Labour Union, the labour union of the BJP) – had thrown their weight behind the anti-reservation agitation, and they fiercely opposed the Congress (Dave Commission 1990, 2:11, 191). They had publicly opposed the Congress and its policies in Gujarat, especially during the Nav Nirman agitation and the Emergency in the 1970s.

However, for other commentators, the root causes lay elsewhere. Some hold the Congress responsible, arguing that the communal riot was a ploy by Congress politicians to deflect attention from caste issues and the anti-reservation agitation, and to unite Hindus.[10] Others have held various criminal elements responsible for instigating and orchestrating the violence. For some observers, it was land speculators and real estate developers who engineered communal riots in order to force people to

evacuate their homes, thereby enabling the local strongmen to either grab
the vacated properties or sell them on the open market (Engineer 1985a).
Considering that the shortfall of affordable housing had intensified
steadily between the 1960s and mid-1980s, the demand for urban
housing was indeed burgeoning, and, alongside, the illicit economy in real
estate. Another view blames bootleggers for fomenting the communal
violence. Gujarat is one of the four states in India where trade and
consumption of alcohol are prohibited by law.[11] Consumption of
contaminated alcohol had led to some 22 fatalities on 13 March, leading
to demands for a clampdown on bootlegging (ibid.: 629).

While there is little consensus on why the anti-reservation riots
turned communal, there is no doubt that from 18 March, reservation
riots occurred alongside communal violence, particularly in Ahmedabad,
but also in other districts of Gujarat. Between 1 February and 18 July, a
total of 2,632 incidents and offences related to the anti-reservation
agitation were reported from across Gujarat, out of which 662 took place
in Ahmedabad city, 634 in Vadodara city and 493 in Surat city. Over the
course of these five and a half months, reservation riots also spread to
rural areas, especially Mehsana (where 222 incidents were reported) and
Patan (112) (Dave Commission 1990, 3:439, Annexure 37). Out of 25
districts in Gujarat, 11 were affected. Incidents of communal violence
were geographically more concentrated. Although 11 districts were
affected, well over half (743) of the 1,234 incidents recorded between
1 March and 18 July were reported from Ahmedabad city, 78 from rural
Ahmedabad, and 328 from Vadodara city. Compared with the
reservation riots, rural districts outside Ahmedabad were hardly affected
by communal riots: notably, Mehsana reported only 24 incidents, and
there was no communal violence in Patan, even though these districts
were seriously affected by reservation riots (ibid., 3:440, Annexure 38).

Between March and July, the simultaneity of reservation-related and
communal violence shaped the rhetoric and orchestration of gendered
violence. On the one hand, the circulation of anti-reservation, casteist
propaganda diluted the potency of Hindu nationalist rhetoric against
Muslim men and women. On the other, widespread hostility among
upper castes against the Congress government, Kshatriyas and
Scheduled Castes introduced multiple antagonists and protagonists
into the theatre of violence, undermining efforts to forge a 'Hindu'
community unified against 'Muslims', and to inflict violence on this

basis. This complexity also created new victims – Kshatriyas, Scheduled Castes and upper castes – and deflected the focus of violence away from Muslim women.

Militant rhetoric, plural focus

On 13 May, some Muslims allegedly slaughtered a cow belonging to the Saryudas Temple in the walled city (Dave Commission 1990, 3:374–5, Annexure 36). Although the Dave Commission in its report described this as an 'incident of a rumour' (ibid., 1:229), one senior police officer insisted in his deposition that the incident did indeed occur (ibid., 1:93–4). From the following day, the Hindu Yuvak Mandal (Hindu Youth Group) and the Navrachna Nirman Samiti (Committee for the Creation of a New Order), outfits affiliated to the ABVP and the VHP, began a massive anti-Muslim propaganda campaign. Their aim was to 'avenge' the alleged attack against one of Hinduism's most sacred symbols, and pre-empt violence against Hindus by forging unity among them. While in 1969 Hindu nationalist propaganda had largely projected anti-Muslim violence as a mode of Hindu self-defence, by 1985 the rhetoric had become markedly emboldened: it now portrayed such violence as a sacred duty. Consider a pamphlet published by the Hindu Yuvak Mandal entitled 'The Cow of the Temple Decapitated: Its Head Thrown in the Temple at Dariapur':

> This horrifying act of desecration was committed by Muslims on 13 of May 1985. The Saryudas Temple is situated in Prem Darwaza, and one of the cows of the temple, named Jasodha, was beheaded by the Muslims from Jijiwada who left its bleeding head lying at the Temple Gate. They also wrote a message in its blood, 'the Hindus are Kafirs [infidels] and Pigs' [. . .]
>
> We Hindus worship cows as mothers. Muslims have killed one such cow. Now it is the time to awaken, and to take revenge for this cruel deed of the Muslims by beating them to death. To kill the demons in the guise of Muslims who perform such cruel deeds to behead a sacred cow, is our Dharma [religion and sacred duty]. There is no sin in killing people like them, even the sacred Gita vouchsafes.
>
> Forget your differences and all Hindus unite.[12]

This pamphlet employed familiar Hindu nationalist tropes, but encouraged its readers to draw new conclusions. As the founding ideologues of Hindu nationalism had done in their writings since the 1920s (see the discussion in the Introduction to this volume), it conflated the veneration of cows among Hindus with the respect and love children traditionally have for their mothers, thereby giving the call for revenge a human touch and a personal resonance. Claims that Muslims considered Hindus infidels revived longstanding Hindu nationalist ideas about the alleged intolerance of Muslims towards other religions. However, this time the call was not to 'defend' the Hindu religion or Hindu men and women, but to beat Muslims 'to death' and 'kill the demons', the acts variously described as a 'sacred duty' and the opposite of 'sin'. As the founding ideologues had done in their writings, and Hindu nationalist propaganda had sought to do in 1969, this pamphlet also provided a moral sanction for violence by invoking the *Bhagavad Gita*,[13] an ancient mythological text revered by most religious north Indian Hindus. The pamphlet stated that the scripture does not deem sinful the killing of a cruel enemy; rather it deems the commission of such acts part of a Hindu's religious and sacred duty. The pamphlet sought to unite Hindus against the 'demonic Muslim enemy' by modifying the rhetoric of vengeance into appeals for the collective fulfilment of the sacred duty of Hindus.

Other pamphlets sought to cement this message by questioning the national loyalty of Muslims and by conflating non-violence – a virtue popularised by Gandhi as essential to an ethical political struggle – with cowardice, and violence with bravery:

How long will the tolerant Hindu community continue to accept the empty slogan of 'Hindu–Muslim Bhai-Bhai' [Hindu–Muslim Brotherhood]? The blood on Hindu dead bodies expects you to arise and show bravery. That Muslims attack Hindu Temples to desecrate idols is a well-known blot in history.

How can such a Muslim be considered a citizen of India? Have we Hindus become so cowardly?

Brave Hindus, arise to protect religion and culture and to teach the enemy a bitter lesson that if they want to live in India, they must first become Indians and then Muslims. Come to save the Hindu community! One hundred to two hundred sacrifices will be sufficient.

Arise and awake and give reply to every brick with a stone.
(Reproduced and translated in S. Patel 1985: 142, Appendix 2)

This pamphlet blurred the boundaries between past and present by reminding Hindus of the 'well-known' history of Muslim atrocities. In order to incite Hindus to abandon their 'cowardice', it forged imaginary blood ties between the readers and the previous generation, and sought to create a Hindu brotherhood based on a shared need for vengeance: 'The blood on Hindu dead bodies expects you to arise and show bravery'. Hindus of the past, present and future would be tied together by their commitment to avenging imaginary crimes. Upon taking this revenge and 'sacrificing' 'one hundred to two hundred' Muslims, this Hindu brotherhood would 'sufficiently' prove its 'bravery' and neutralise the Muslim threat.

Yet forging a Hindu brotherhood in the mid-1980s was a particularly difficult task. The KHAM strategy promised to unite Kshatriyas (OBCs), Harijans (Scheduled Castes), Adivasis (Scheduled Tribes) with Muslims, not with upper-caste Hindus. Moreover, anti-reservation riots in the early 1980s and since February 1985 had brought upper castes in direct and violent conflict with Scheduled Castes; forging fraternity among these groups would be challenging. A pamphlet widely circulated across Ahmedabad between May and June 1985, and published anonymously under the title 'Hindus Awaken, Wage the Holy War', delineated a solution to this problem. It called on all (non-Muslim) men to ignore their caste, religious and regional differences to unite as 'Hindus' and boycott the Muslim community:

We remember Shivaji Chattrapati's and Maharana Pratap's sacrifices [...] Have the Hindus who are now indulging in luxuries forgotten these sacrifices? [...] Hindus awake! Declare social and economic boycott of the bigot Muslim community. You should not buy any material from their shops. The rupee that is paid by us is used in destroying our Hindu religion [...] They have arranged to murder Hindus or create arson and theft.[14]

Claims that Muslims had perpetrated sexual violence against Hindu women were central to this call for unity:

Many a helpless Hindu women have been raped by these barbarous people. Will you forget the torture perpetrated on your mothers and sisters?

This licentious, treacherous community has captured daughters of two Harijan brothers from Gomtipur and the daughter of one Harijan brother from Mirzapur for satiating their ferocious sexual appetites.

Come, Hindu, Harijan, Sikh, Marathi, Punjabi, forget the differences between lower and higher castes, the rich and poor and unite. We must solemnly pledge that 'all Hindu [are] One' [. . .]

For a Kshatriya (Hindu) there is no greater duty than to wage a war over religion [. . .] this war is like an entry to heaven.[15]

In this pamphlet, it is clear that the Hindu brotherhood was to include communities in the Congress's KHAM alliance. The pamphlet sought to suppress the caste-based differences of Kshatriyas through the careful insertion of the word 'Hindu' after 'Kshatriya', with the brackets being used to impose religious unity among the different caste groups. Subsumed under the broader category of a 'Hindu' community, Kshatriyas were called on to wage the holy war of religion. The pamphlet insisted on calling Harijans 'brothers' in a rhetorical attempt to forge imaginary familial ties between them and Hindus, and thus create a 'brotherhood' that would jointly avenge sexual violence committed against the 'daughters' of the family. Put differently, the pamphlet was seeking to inspire the very same groups that had sexually violated Muslim women during the 1969 riot: Gujarati and migrant upper-caste, low-caste and Kshatriya men.

Yet appeals for the creation of this brotherhood did not entail an endorsement of the reservation policy. None of the aforementioned pamphlets refers to reservations and, as noted earlier, the ABVP and BJP had actively supported the anti-reservation agitators. The brotherhood would emerge from, and be based on, a shared hatred of Muslims, and from jointly taking revenge; not from taking measures that challenged the caste status quo.[16]

Moreover, the membership of this brotherhood was not restricted to the different caste groups, such as Kshatriyas and Harijans, which were imagined to be part of a large 'Hindu family'. Rather, it was extended to members of all castes and classes, disparate linguistic and regional groups, and other religions besides Hinduism. These included non-Muslim migrant men with cultural roots in different regions in India (Marathis from Maharashtra and Punjabis from Punjab), those with diverse linguistic backgrounds (e.g., Marathi, Punjabi), and followers of other religions that originated in India (such as Sikhs). In this, the pamphlet was reiterating the expansive definition of 'Hindu' devised in the early 1920s by Savarkar, the most articulate ideologue of Hindu nationalism. Savarkar envisioned that people who traced their paternal lineage within India and whose religion had also emerged in India were 'Hindus' (see the discussion in the Introduction, this volume). The only people thus left out were Muslims and Christians, since they could not identify their 'holy land' with the 'fatherland'. Since Sikhism originated in India, Sikhs would make natural allies of Hindus in their holy war against Muslims. Indeed, the only feature uniting this cross-caste, cross-class, religiously diverse Hindu brotherhood would be a shared hatred of Muslims and a collective commitment to avenging all sexual and other atrocities allegedly committed by the 'enemy'. The brotherhood was defined not by those it included and united, but rather by those it excluded, opposed and sought to violate.

Emotive pleas for the creation of a Hindu community by projecting Muslims as violent iconoclasts and rapists contributed to the infliction of violence against Muslim men and women during the 1969 riot and in the 2002 massacre. As the pamphlet just cited illustrates, similar pleas were in circulation during 1985. Yet, in all likelihood, as discussed earlier, extreme sexual violence did not occur, even though at least 100 Muslims were killed during this riot. Why? One factor here appears to be the circulation of equally articulate counter-rhetoric that diminished the impact of anti-Muslim mobilisation. Explicitly anti-reservation and anti-low-caste in orientation, this counter-rhetoric undermined efforts to engineer Hindu unity on the basis of a shared hatred for one enemy: Muslims. This rhetoric sought to create an alternative brotherhood, which was united in its opposition to the KHAM alliance and in its contempt for Kshatriyas and Scheduled Castes as well as for Muslims. This blunted the effectiveness of Hindu nationalist appeals for the infliction of violence on Muslim men and women.

This alternative brotherhood was composed of, and forged by, upper-caste Hindus, themselves a key constituency of Hindu nationalists.

The ABVP supported upper castes during the anti-reservation agitation; the BJP pandered to them as voters; and the RSS sought to mobilise upper-caste men as volunteers in its neighbourhood branches. Already in the early phase of the anti-reservation riot (January–February), upper-caste students, their parents and professionals had formed public committees such as the AGRS and the Akhil Gujarat Vaali Maha Mandal (All Gujarat Teachers' Group). However, even after communal rioting started occurring alongside reservation-related violence, such committees continued their efforts to mobilise opposition to the government and its reservation policy. They claimed that the anti-reservation movement was 'not against any particular caste or class, but it [was] against the thoughtless policies of the government' (pamphlet quoted in Shani 2007: 129).

To this end, these groups established alternative, reactionary public platforms, whose aims differed markedly from those of Hindu nationalist organisations and their affiliates such as the Hindu Yuvak Mandal. Organisations such as the Nagrik Sangathan (Citizens' Association) were secular in orientation and dedicated to relief, whereas others such as the Naranpura Patel Yuvak Mandal (Naranpura Patel Youth Committee; henceforth NPYC) formed in May 1985 were vocal anti-reservationists. The challenge to Hindu nationalist rhetoric came from this latter group. While Hindu nationalists called on men to ignore their caste, religious and cultural differences for the sake of countering the Muslim threat, the propaganda of outfits such as the NPYC was dedicated to sharpening the divisions between upper castes, on the one hand, and Kshatriyas, Harijans and Muslims on the other.

Consider the contents of a pamphlet circulated by NPYC entitled 'Patels of Gujarat Awake':

Now the time has come. The frequent and fatal attacks of the Muslims, Harijans, and Thakors [Kshatriyas] on our community are to be tolerated no longer. It is now a dire necessity that each Patel is awakened to this humiliation and a befitting reply be given. We are not going to tolerate the challenge thrown by the Kshatriyas who publicly worship the 'bow and arrow'. Now, in its reply, we too are going to unite and equip ourselves [...] The Patel community is ready to answer them any time, and are never afraid of damage to our goods and bodies when fighting for

honour, have you forgotten? Have you also forgotten that these
people [Harijans] belong to the low community, which used to
pick up the night soil from our homes? Those who used to do this
work for ages are now seated in huge offices of the bank due to the
Reservation policies, and have become our senior officers! We
cannot tolerate this any longer. Then, these non-vegetarian
Muslims! We have already paid them by creating Pakistan as
compensation. We must now exile them from India. The nation
is now only for the Hindus. Just because the Harijans and
Muslims have united in these days of riots, they should be
boycotted by us, and that is our request to the entire community
of Patels.[17]

This pamphlet exposes the anxieties and prejudices of the upper-caste
Patel community that the NPYC claimed to represent. They opposed
reservation policies, which gave socio-economic mobility to low castes
and threatened the caste order and the political power of the Patels. They
rejected the Indian citizenship of Muslims, and condemned their
culture. Along the lines of Hindu nationalist rhetoric, such propaganda
also projected violent action against, and the boycott of, the enemy as a
matter of honour and pride. However, unlike the RSS, the VHP and the
ABVP, which called for united action against Muslims alone, the NPYC
preached violence against Kshatriyas and Harijans as well as Muslims.
Its version of a Hindu brotherhood was more exclusive, being confined
to 'the entire community of Patels'. Moreover, this brotherhood of Patels
was driven by the desire to neutralise challenges to the socio-political
order, not to avenge sexual crimes committed against 'their mothers and
sisters' (a central leitmotif of Hindu nationalist propaganda).
Accordingly, this pamphlet was not overtly gendered and did not
encourage sexual violence against Kshatriya, Scheduled Caste or Muslim
women. Such ideological alternatives were absent in both 1969 and
2002, particularly in the latter conflict.

Rhetoric to counter Hindu nationalist encouragement of the
infliction of sexual violence against Muslims also emerged from the
vernacular media. Between February and July 1985, the coverage of
the Gujarati print media (also dominated by upper-caste Hindus) had a
twin purpose: generating enmity towards Muslims *and* opposing
reservations. As the Dave Commission recorded:

From 17 February to 18 March newspapers played a very important role in creating an atmosphere of hatred against backward communities (Dalits and Muslims) with false news and exaggerated reports, and after 18th March they tried to give communal colour to this so-called agitation in which the Muslims became direct targets. In these riots the houses and shops of Muslim were burnt. They were also burnt alive, even Muslim women were not left alone. They were also attacked with knives and acid. The documented report of these riots is shocking in terms of the loss incurred by the Muslim community. (Dave Commission 1990, 3:18, Annexure 7)

On the other hand, the vernacular media sought to mobilise public opinion against the Congress and its reservation policy. The coverage of *Gujarat Samachar*, the most widely circulated newspaper in Gujarat besides *Sandesh*, provides the best example. Between February and July, apart from reporting on communal violence, the newspaper extended generous moral support to urban middle-class opponents of the reservation policy. It proudly reported the establishment of anti-reservation forums by students, teachers and parents in various parts of Gujarat, criticised the police for arresting student protesters, and published innumerable editorials describing the shortcomings of the policy. It also lent logistical support to the organisers of protest meetings, strikes, closures and rallies by notifying readers about the timing and location of such events in Ahmedabad, Surat, Bhavnagar, Vadodara and Nadiad. Following these events, the newspaper faithfully reported on their success and outcome, taking special care to mention that the anti-reservation agitation commanded support among large swathes of the middle class, including professionals, small and large businesses and government employees. A typical front-page report from the period reads as follows:

Reports are coming in from various parts of the State that the 'Gujarat Bandh' called by the Akhil Gujarat Maha Mandal and the Akhil Gujarat Navrachna Samiti has been largely successful. The residents of the State's metropolis, Ahmedabad, have observed what one might call a complete 'bandh'. The city's various businesses, big and small markets, hotels and restaurants, shops, handcarts and roadside vendors have all stayed shut. Even the employees of the city's nationalised and cooperative banks stayed away from work completely today in support of the 'bandh'.[18]

This coverage demonstrates that during the 1985 riot, the focus of the vernacular media was not exclusively on publishing anti-Muslim reports, but also on ridiculing the government and its policies, and supporters of the reservation policy. The Dave Commission put it succinctly: 'Instead of playing a creative role for the benefit of the society, a section of the press in Gujarat has played a negative role for its own benefit to the detriment of pro-reservationists *and* for aggravating communal tensions *and* creating hatred against the police force as whole' (Dave Commission 1990, 1:286; emphasis added).

The plurality of inflammatory media rhetoric mirrored the multiplicity of conflicts that manifested themselves in violent conflict during the 1985 riot. This was in sharp contrast to 1969, when news reports on events during the riots focused primarily on the communal angle, and 2002, when the Gujarati-language media was reluctant to criticise the government's failure to prevent and quell the violence, often taking a blatantly anti-Muslim line. Due to the unique ideological orientation of the 1985 riot, the local press did not publish 'reports' about rapes of Hindu women by Muslim men. Such reports had had devastating consequences for Muslim women in September 1969 and later in February–March 2002. In 1985, however, the vernacular print media was deeply embroiled in the anti-reservation movement, and purveyed both anti-Muslim and anti-low-caste messages. In fact, their rhetoric was so powerful and inflammatory, and their involvement so deep, that the building of *Gujarat Samachar* was set on fire by a mob on 22 April. The unique orientation of the vernacular media appears to have reduced its ability to foment violence along exclusively religious lines, including sexual violence against Muslim women.

Thus far, we have seen how diffused the focus of violent rhetoric was during the 1985 riots. Hindu nationalists attempted to incite 'Hindu' men to avenge past sexual and non-sexual crimes inflicted by the 'demonic' Muslim enemy. However, anti-reservationists and the media propagated anti-low-caste, anti-government rhetoric alongside communal hatred, making not just Muslims but also Kshatriyas, Harijans and the government targets of hostility. There were multiple active antagonists and protagonists. As a result, as we will see in what follows, the methods and motivations with regard to the infliction of sexual violence also varied considerably.

The infliction of sexual violence

Two primary agents inflicted sexual violence during the 1985 riot: established and prospective supporters of Hindu nationalist organisations, and the police. The main targets of the former were Muslim women, and of the latter, lower-to-middle-class, upper-caste Hindu women. Sexual violence took the form of verbal abuse, obscene gestures and a degree of bodily harm, which did not include rape or gang-rape. A different dynamic emerged during 1985 at the neighbourhood level, which is where these extreme crimes were perpetrated in 1969 and 2002 in Ahmedabad. The parallel, anti-reservation focus of the riot aligned the interests of neighbours from disparate religious and caste communities, mitigating the occurrence of extreme sexual violence.

Rath Yatra

The scheduled date for the annual rath yatra was 20 June 1985. The procession traditionally commences at the Jagannath Temple in the Jamalpur region of the walled city, meanders through several Hindu- and Muslim-dominated pols, and, at the end of the day, culminates back at the temple. Coincidentally, in 1985, 20 June was also the day of the Islamic festival of Id-ul-Fitr. Initially, the police had appealed to the priests of the temple to abstain from organising the yatra because the walled city was under curfew, and the communal situation in the city was tense. The police was concerned about intensifying tensions, since the Jagannath rath yatra had historically been used as an occasion to display the 'might and strength of Hindus [. . .] in the shape of Akhadas [gymnasiums] and acrobats' (Dave Commission 1990, 1:262). However, the organisers of the yatra carried out the procession as scheduled and took pride in defying the police. The army tried to stop the procession from taking its traditional route through the walled city via Prem Darwaza, since large parts of the walled city were under military curfew and declared 'communally sensitive'. However, under pressure from a crowd of thousands of participants who were chanting religious slogans, the army ultimately relented.[19] It was during this yatra that male participants in the procession inflicted sexual violence against Muslim women in the form of verbal abuse and obscene gestures.

As is customary in Hindu religious festivals, upper-caste Hindu men participated in the yatra along with priests and sadhus (religious mendicants). Scheduled Castes, considered ritually impure, have historically been barred from participating in this procession. In 1985, however, for the first time, the BJP and the VHP encouraged young Scheduled Caste men to participate. At the beginning of the procession, devotees shouted slogans against Madhavsinh Solanki and his government along with their traditional chants, such as 'Hail Lord Krishna, the thief of buttermilk'. When the procession entered the walled city, its traditional route through Muslim-majority pols, the slogans suddenly transformed. The one just mentioned was modified to 'Hail Lord Krishna, Muslims are thieves', and others shouted slogans such as 'Muslims have only one place, either Pakistan or the graveyard'. Stone throwing and looting started on both sides and the army resorted to firing shots that led to at least six fatalities (Dave Commission 1990, 1:266).

For the upper-caste organisers of the yatra, sexual violence against Muslim women was a way of creating and asserting Hindu unity. For Scheduled Caste participants, the spectacle became a means of gaining social acceptance by reinventing themselves as virile and martial defenders of Hinduism (Gooptu 2001: 242–3). Several Muslim women complained that when the procession passed through Dariapur, a mixed locality, men made obscene sexual gestures: 'holding the lathis they carried at their groin and waving them at the women, and even pulling down their trousers (a tactic which seems to have been used also by the police and the [State Reserve Police Force])' (Women's Research Group 1985: 1727). Other people from Kalupur and Dariapur stated that Scheduled Caste and upper-caste Hindu men pelted stones at Muslims and shouted sexually derogatory slogans at Muslim women.[20] In doing so, some Scheduled Caste men 'felt part of the Hindu community' (Shani 2007: 118). Others justified their actions by stating that 'we are in a majority in Ahmedabad, and we must show this' (Women's Research Group 1985: 1728).

Police criminality

Sexual violence against upper-caste Hindu women occurred in April after the Congress government ordered the police to suppress the anti-reservation agitation with whatever force was necessary from around late March. The police came down heavily on the anti-reservation protestors: it dispersed protests by firing tear-gas shells; entered the homes of agitators, beat them and destroyed their property; and arrested agitators, some of whom were young students. Complaints from parents about police brutality against their children were also met with brute force (Dave Commission 1990, 1:234). It was during this crackdown that police inflicted sexual violence upon Hindu women in at least three separate incidents.

The first incident occurred on 4 and 5 April in the Asarwa industrial region of Ahmedabad, following the arrest of some upper-caste Hindu students who were protesting against reservations. When Pramila Patel, an upper-caste Hindu woman, complained of the illegal arrest and harassment of her son by the police, senior police officers beat her mercilessly, humiliated her with abusive language and tore off her clothes. Similar treatment was then meted out to several other women of the area who had expressed their sympathy with Pramila Patel and accompanied her to the office of the governor of Gujarat to lodge a complaint (Dave Commission 1990, 1:234).

The second incident occurred between 16 and 17 April in Raipur, an upper-caste-dominated neighbourhood in the walled city, which was under curfew. On 16 April, a contingent of the State Reserve Police Force (hereafter the SRPF) forcefully established a watch-point in the house of an upper-caste family. The house owner's wife, Sudha Bhat, was intimidated, and asked the men to leave, saying that her husband was out of town. The policemen not only stayed put, but also made lewd suggestions to her, saying that 'they were there to substitute her husband' (Women's Research Group 1985: 1730). The following morning, 25 women from the neighbourhood defied the curfew to come to Bhat's aid and forced the policemen to vacate her house. However, the policemen locked the house from the outside and detained all the women for several hours. Later, senior SRPF officer R. K. Vashisht arrived with more policemen, who beat the women as they came out of the house and removed the sari of one of these women (ibid.; Dave Commission 1990, 1:237).

The third incident occurred on 18 April in the industrial area of Gomtipur. On that day, under the authority of Additional Commissioner of Police A. K. Bhargava, a parade of 30 naked policemen was organised in the neighbourhood. This parade was enacted periodically between 6.30 and 9.30 p.m. Policemen also made lewd comments and obscene gestures at women in order to pressure the residents into stopping their anti-reservation agitation. Although in his deposition to the Dave Commission, Bhargava denied the allegation (Dave Commission 1990, 1:137), one of Ahmedabad's most respected women's organisations, the Ahmedabad Women's Action Group (AWAG), recorded statements of women who claimed that such a parade had indeed taken place.[21]

These episodes demonstrate the extent to which the police resorted to sexualised crimes during the 1985 riot to intimidate women who (as in the first two incidents) dared to challenge their abuse of power. They also signal how some police officers viewed women's participation in the anti-reservation agitation as a transgression of gendered social boundaries. By protesting against the establishment and its policies, women had asserted their agency and threatened the authority of the state, violating traditional patriarchal boundaries that relegated women to the household. Sexual violence served to punish this transgression. It functioned as a warning (as in the third incident) about the sexual risks women might face when they chose to defy authority and step outside their homes.

The reassertion of the patriarchal norm, whereby women are expected to be passive recipients of change rather than active agents of it, did not end with the infliction of violence. In the aftermath of the harassment of Pramila Patel and the other women who came out to support her, the police department sought to further reassert the gendered status quo by casting aspersions on their sexual chastity and invoking the gendered boundaries imposed by their high caste. When a women's group approached Ahmedabad's deputy commissioner of police, Deepak Swaroop, over the Asarwa incident, he replied that these women were of 'easy virtue' and that 'they may have been lower caste women with their customarily different set of values hired for the specific purpose of embarrassing the police [. . .] since upper caste women would not take off their blouses and show their injuries' (quoted in Women's Research Group 1985: 1730).

On the one hand, such comments served as a warning to upper-caste Hindu women that if they stepped out of the protected confines of the domestic space, their chastity would be questioned, and result in justifiable sexual violence against them. On the other, they betrayed the gender/caste biases of senior police officials. According to Swaroop, low-caste women allegedly did not have any qualms about removing their clothes in front of strangers (who in this case was the Gujarat governor B. K. Nehru, an upper-caste Hindu man). Their violent disrobing by the police could not be interpreted as criminal. Should upper-caste women expose themselves to their male counterparts, they ran the risk of being viewed and treated as low-caste women.

Given such caste biases of the state apparatus, it is not hard to understand why, from the mid-1980s onwards, Scheduled Caste men and women turned increasingly to the BJP and lost confidence in the Congress. The Congress's KHAM strategy had promised political representation and social acceptance, and yet there was a major disconnect between its rhetoric and practice.

Compulsions of survival and ideological alliances

The 'darkest period' of the anti-reservation and communal riots occurred between 16 and 23 April, when over 100 incidents of rioting occurred, including 92 cases of arson and 14 murders (Dave Commission 1990, 1:215). Even though OBCs were intended as the main beneficiaries of the reservation policy, Scheduled Castes and Muslims were the main targets of violence by upper-caste Hindus across Ahmedabad (ibid., 3:158–291, Annexure 35). Western Ahmedabad was relatively peaceful, although sporadic instances of stone throwing and arson did occur, especially in the mixed localities of Ellisbridge, Paldi, Naranpura and Navrangpura situated adjacent to the River Sabarmati. Organised violence (in the form of killings, arson and looting) took place in large parts of the walled city, and in the industrial belt where Scheduled Castes, Muslims and upper-caste Hindus lived separately but in close proximity to each other. In the walled city, upper-caste Hindus attacked Muslims and their homes in Naginapol, Dariapur and Kalupur between 18 and 19 March (ibid., 1:226). Similar attacks occurred against Scheduled Castes in the walled city, especially in several pols in Karanj on 18 April (ibid., 1:224, Annexure 35).

The industrial area was by far the worst affected. Scheduled Castes and Muslims were attacked in Asarwa, Saraspur, Bapunagar (and its surrounding locality Indira Garibnagar), Gomtipur and Odhav (Dave Commission 1990, 1:251–60, 215–16). The worst episodes were reported from Bapunagar–Indira Garibnagar between 21 and 25 April, where at least 13 people lost their lives (ibid.: 260). According to an eyewitness, a mob of 8,000 to 10,000 Patel men attacked on the morning of 21 April. The mob was armed with knives, iron rods and pipes, and was led by the police. The mob, in connivance with the police, first pelted stones at the locality, and then attacked the property of Muslims and Scheduled Castes, looting and incinerating their shops and homes with petrol and diesel from police vehicles (ibid.: 253–5). Similar attacks took place on 22 and 23 April (ibid.: 251). Several witnesses claimed that the police did not come to their aid, or that they actively helped the mobs attack Muslims (ibid.: 252). By the time the violence was brought under control, nearly two-thirds of all houses belonging to Scheduled Castes had been burnt down in Bapunagar, and more than 6,000 Muslims had been rendered homeless in Indira Garibnagar (ibid.: 215–16).

Indeed, violence by upper-caste Hindus and the police against Scheduled Castes was so widespread and brutal that several of my respondents remembered the 1985 riot as having been sparked by reservations for Scheduled Castes, rather than OBCs. Kishen Parmar, who worked as a *badli* (casual worker) in Calico Mills in Behrampura, had this to say about the suffering of Scheduled Castes during the riot:

The 1985 riots started over the reservation issue. Whatever happened was not so much between Hindus and Muslims. During that riot, Dalits[22] [Scheduled Castes] were badly beaten by the police. In front of me in my locality men, even women and 10–11 year old children were beaten up. We [Dalits] suffered a lot during the riot. One of the boys [. . .] was beaten so badly that he died after six months. We filed a case also but that time everyone was afraid of the police [. . .] Upper-caste people did not want Dalits to get educated and reach good high posts or become government officers. They just wanted us to do small menial jobs for them in their houses. (Interview, Ahmedabad, 15 January 2007)

Muslims echoed similar sentiments. Shamsulbhai, a Muslim and a former employee of Calico Mills in Behrampura, explained:

> The 1985 riot started because Dalits were being given reservations by the government. Upper castes did not want Dalits to get reservations. Once the riot started the military came and it imposed a curfew in our area. But the police used to come and beat up Dalits in our locality. I saw with my own eyes that the police mercilessly beat Dalits who were fighting for their rights. (Interview, Ahmedabad, 20 January 2007)

These testimonies point to the tragedy that the KHAM strategy and the reservation policy had become. These policies had raised hopes of political representation, economic betterment, social dignity and upper-caste acceptance for Scheduled Castes and backward-caste groups. This hope was particularly precious in the 1980s, when the closure of the textile mills, rising living costs and the lack of affordable housing had already made existence precarious for them. Identifying the potential of these policies, these caste groups rewarded the Congress by bringing it back to power in 1985. However, the 'suffering' of low castes recalled by Kishen Parmar had scarcely begun. Once the riot commenced, the systemic caste biases of the state apparatus were exposed, most palpably in the violent and abusive behaviour of the police. In some ways, the KHAM strategy had actually led to violence against low-caste groups.

Yet it did have some positive impact as well. During the 1985 riot, the alliance enlarged the scope for cross-caste, cross-religion solidarity at the neighbourhood level. Muslims were largely indifferent to reservation policies, yet their membership of the KHAM alliance, and their religion, placed them at the receiving end of violence by upper-caste Hindus. Moreover, the perception that the Congress 'appeased' minorities, especially Muslims, to win their votes was widespread (Shani 2007: 150–1). As a result, during the riot, the survival of Muslims was threatened just as much as that of their Scheduled Caste neighbours. Survival depended on cooperation.

Several alliances were formed between Muslims, Scheduled Castes and migrants from UP, Maharashtra, Kerala and rural Gujarat, and backward castes (for example, Rabaris, who are an OBC community) in parts of the industrial region, where they lived in close proximity to one another. The same was true in several parts of the walled city (Shani 2007: 119). Such alliances not only helped these communities protect their own and each other's lives and properties, but also seem to have prevented extreme forms of sexual violence. Two survivors explained how these alliances were forged. A Muslim survivor from Pannalal Ki Chawli in Gomtipur gave the following testimony to activists in 1985 while living in a relief camp:

On 23 April situation became tense in our area. I used to help in the relief camps during the day and go back home to my chawl at night and tell people to maintain peace. On 10 May, a meeting was conducted at the house of Ibrahim Bhai, who runs a flour-grinding shop. Since violence had erupted in Dariapur and Kalupur people were afraid. I was told that there is a meeting of Muslims, Hindus and the police. From our neighbouring chawls spokesmen and leaders of Harijan brothers, Pathan brothers came to the meeting. Some people who hail from Maharashtra and Kerala also came to the meeting. There was someone from all areas between Raipur and our chawl. It was decided that if someone comes to attack Muslims from your area then you would stop them, and if some Muslims attack or come to loot then we will take responsibility and not let them do anything [...] We also decided that two people from each neighbourhood would stay up at night and make sure everything is okay. At night, around 2 at night, Hindu and Muslim brothers would meet at a nearby cycle shop at an SRP point to update each other on the latest developments. So we used to stay up at night and keep watch [...] some people sent their women and children and some of their other belongings to their relatives or here and there [...]

There are lots of instances where Harijans have helped Muslims. If you see Harijan brothers, Sikh brothers, brothers from UP, and Rabaris who participated in the 1969 riot have not joined the majority [upper-caste Hindus] this time.[23]

Mumtaz Bano lived in Rakhial, a mixed neighbourhood in the mill district of Gomtipur. Her neighbourhood was attacked by a mob of upper-caste men and the police on 21 April. She spoke of similar alliances:

The 1985 riot started over the reservation issue, but later became a
Hindu–Muslim riot. In our locality, Muslims and Harijans used
to live side by side. In one row people from UP lived, in one there
were Rabaris. I think there were some people from Maharashtra
also. We had good relations with those people. All of us were poor
– *dal roti khane wale log* [people who eat bread and lentils]. When
the fight over reservations started Hindus and Muslims in our
slum reached a settlement: Muslims will not attack and Hindus
will not react. Peace was declared. When my husband went to buy
milk, suddenly a mob appeared. They burnt houses, and looted
shops. Police was firing so many bullets it was like rainfall. But
then Harijans and Muslims together fought the mob.
We defended ourselves with whatever we could find. (Interview,
Ahmedabad, 22 November 2007)

When read together, these testimonies reveal how neighbourhood ties
crossing caste, regional and religious boundaries were forged during the
1985 riot. Faced with armed and organised mobs, neighbours from
different communities organised all-night vigils to prevent violent
confrontations, and kept each other informed about local developments.
When their localities were attacked, they protected one another from
marauding crowds. Even though migrants from UP and Maharashtra
had participated directly in the 1969 violence, during the 1985 riot they
forged a different form of community, one based on everyday interaction,
a shared sense of persecution, and existential necessity. They created a
new 'brotherhood', which not only rejected Hindu nationalism's anti-
Muslim brotherhood based on revenge and the sexual violation of
Muslim women, but actively subverted it. Instead of taking advantage of
the prevailing chaos to inflict opportunistic rape, they formed alliances
of self-defence with their Muslim neighbours.

Significantly, shared fears about violence were not the only driver of
such alliances. Muslims had helped their Scheduled Caste neighbours
during the 1981 reservation riot, and concerted efforts had been made by
politically engaged Scheduled Castes to forge a social brotherhood with
Muslims along class lines (Shani 2007: 150). Hence, their solidarity had
a recent historical precedent and some ideological basis.

These alliances are particularly noteworthy because Hindu nationalist
organisations had firmly established themselves in these industrial

regions of the city from the 1960s, and actively recruited Scheduled Caste and backward-caste communities between 1970 and 1985. Yet during the riot, a significant section of these groups chose to remain loyal to their Muslim neighbours, highlighting the fluidity of support for Hindu nationalism in the mid-1980s. The memories of these alliances outlived the riot. As we will see in the next chapter, some Scheduled Caste survivors of the 1985 riot pleaded with their children and grandchildren during the 2002 massacre not to attack Muslims. However, these appeals amounted to very little: later generations grew up in a more religiously polarised environment ridden with communal violence. This was partly because the 1985 riot triggered an intense wave of spatial segregation in Ahmedabad, which accelerated in the wake of the demolition of the Babri Mosque in December 1992. This issue is discussed in detail in the following chapter, which deals with the period after 1985.

Defensive Hindu nationalism

The Dave Commission, as part of its inquiry, summoned representatives of various organisations involved in the violence or in relief efforts to depose before it. These included the VHP and the BJP; the Central Relief Committee, which was led by local Muslims; the All India Muslim Majlis-e-Musawarat; and a couple of civil society groups.

In their depositions, both the VHP and the BJP gave predictable responses: they accused the police of failing to protect the lives of Hindus and their property, and apportioned blame for the violence to Muslims more or less directly. Vishwa Nath Ananth Vanikar, vice-president of the VHP in Gujarat, stated that Muslims had organised deadly attacks against Hindus across Ahmedabad and elsewhere in Gujarat, including Vadodara, Palanpur, Broach (or Bharuch) and Nadiad (Dave Commission 1990, 1:55). Referring to 18 March, when violence began in the Vadigam area of the walled city, he said: 'A call for Bandh was given and at 8.00 p.m. students had a programme of sounding death knell but with this programme simultaneously the Muslims made a violent assault on Hindu localities which were preplanned and systematised [...] where-ever the police went, Muslims attacked police parties also. They were shouting "Kill Hindus"' (ibid.: 54).

The BJP representative, the party's state secretary Dattatreya Narain Chirandas, was more politically savvy. He stated that the '1985 anti-reservation agitation was not against any community. It was neither anti-Harijans, nor anti-backward classes, nor anti-Muslim' (Dave Commission 1990, 1:61). He nonetheless implied that Muslims were the main culprits of the violence when he informed the commission that 'Muslims staying in Naginapole climbed up their roofs and threw burning rags and cement bowls with nails on Hindu locality' (ibid.).

Neither the VHP nor the BJP felt able to accept that they had had any involvement in the violence orchestrated during the anti-reservation agitation and the communal riot, even though their popularity and social legitimacy had increased in the 1970s and 1980s, and even in the course of the protracted riot itself. In fact, the BJP explicitly denied involvement: 'No worker of the BJP has participated in any incident' (Dave Commission 1990, 1:62), and sought to generate political capital by holding the Solanki administration responsible (ibid.). The state, howsoever partial in its handling of communal violence, was still a deterrent to Hindu nationalist mobilisations of violence. The VHP and the BJP could justify violence against Muslims and blame the minorities for sparking riots, but they had to stop short of accepting that they had had any role in fomenting this violence.

Developments between 1985 and 2002 brought about a marked change in the attitude of the various Hindu nationalist organisations to communal violence in general, and sexual violence against minority women in particular. During this period, Hindu nationalism transformed completely: its rhetoric became more belligerent, its social support grew many fold, its electoral fortunes turned such that a party espousing its ideology could form its first government in Gujarat in 1995, and then a more stable administration in 1998. Sexual violence against Muslim women became a routine and spectacular part of the activities of cadres of the Hindu right.

CHAPTER 3

2002

In the summer of 2002, Gujarat witnessed the worst anti-Muslim massacre in the history of independent India. The violence started on 28 February, and did not subside until April, affecting 19 of 26 districts in the state. Although Ahmedabad was the region affected worst, the districts of Banaskantha, Patan, Mehsana, Sabarkantha and Gandhinagar in the north; Kheda, Anand, Panch Mahals and Dahod in the east; Vadodara, Bharuch, Narmada and Surat in the south; and Kachchh, Surendranagar, Rajkot, Junagadh and Bhavnagar in the west also witnessed violence. According to statistics released by the national government, the violence claimed 1,169 lives and left at least 2,548 people injured.[1] The Gujarat government put the total number of fatalities at 1,044.[2] However, the vast majority of investigative reports have disputed these figures, placing the number of fatalities at close to 2,000 and the number of people 'missing' at around 2,500. Over 75,000 homes were damaged and 1,024 were completely destroyed. Some 10,429 shops were incinerated and another 1,278 ransacked. Property worth an estimated Rs 30 billion is said to have been destroyed.[3] The majority of the victims of the violence were Muslims. According to the statistics of the Gujarat government, of the 1,044 people killed, 790 were Muslims and 254 were Hindus.[4]

Sexual violence against Muslim women and girls (0–16 years of age) was a widespread feature of the massacre, according to reports published by civil rights groups, academics and the National Women's Commission. Brutal sexual violence in the form of rape, gang-rape and genital mutilation was reported from the industrial areas of Naroda

Patiya, Naroda Gaon and Chamanpura in Ahmedabad. Verbal abuse and sexual intimidation were reported from the labour regions of Bapunagar, Danilimda, Behrampura and Vatva. Outside Ahmedabad, Muslim women were subjected to rape, gang-rape and mutilation in Kalol, Dailol, Godhra and Lunavada in the rural Panch Mahals district, and in Randhikpur village in Dahod district.[5] In many cases, women were first sexually victimised and then killed with swords and knives or by burning. Some of the victims were as young as three, although the majority were between 20 and 45 years of age.

Despite extensive documentation of this violence, there are no authoritative records on its exact scale. According to the human rights activist who has carried out the most extensive documentation and rehabilitation work in the state, at least 150–200 women were subjected to sexual violence in 2002.[6] When I documented the testimonies of victims of sexual violence in the relief camps in Panch Mahals, Ahmedabad and Dahod districts in May 2002, I came across at least 16 cross-verified cases of women who had been subjected to sexual violence. Significantly, most surviving victims mentioned the rapes of at least 25–35 women in their respective neighbourhoods and villages.[7] Reports by other investigative teams have published similar details (Citizens' Initiative 2002; International Initiative for Justice 2003). The sheer brutality of the sexual violence inflicted during the massacre, and the dismal response of Gujarat's state authorities to this violence, has led political and legal theorist Upendra Baxi (2005) to warn of the emergence of a 'democidal rape culture' wherein sexual violence has become a key method of destroying religious minorities and bankrupting India's democracy.

The origins of the 2002 massacre lie in the socio-economic, political and communal developments that occurred between 1985 and 2002, and the manner in which these developments paved the way for the transformation of the Hindu nationalist movement. This transformation had several distinctive features. A mass movement for the liberation of the Ramjanmabhoomi (the birthplace of the mythological prince Rama) in Ayodhya (a religious pilgrimage town located in the northern Indian state of Uttar Pradesh), along with the orchestration of communal violence, emerged as the central mobilisation tool of the Hindu nationalist movement from the late 1980s to the early 1990s. This drive culminated in the destruction of the Babri Mosque in December 1992 and a sharp escalation in the number of communal riots in the country. In 1993, there were 2,292 Hindu–Muslim riots in India, more than in any other year between 1950 and 2009 (Gayer and Jaffrelot 2012: 327–8).[8] Sexual violence against Muslim women, ranging from sexual intimidation and verbal abuse to stripping and gang-rape, became a recurrent feature of several such episodes of rioting, including those in Bombay (Patwardhan 1994; Srikrishna 1998), Surat (Chandra 1993; Lobo and D'Souza 1993) and Ahmedabad (AIDWA et al. 1996; Engineer 1992; Mehta and Shah 1992).

The rise in communal violence against Muslims, including the infliction of sexual violence against Muslim women, was both a product and a facilitator of profound political shifts in India, Gujarat and Ahmedabad. In the last two decades of the twentieth century, the Congress's hegemony over politics and government at the national level in Delhi, at the state level in Gujarat, and at the municipal level in Ahmedabad, was overturned, as voters revolted against corruption, ideological disarray and the adverse impact of some of the party's economic policies, such as rising living costs. The BJP and smaller regional parties stepped in to fill the vacuum across the country; the BJP did so largely by politicising religious identities, whereas regional parties, especially in UP and Bihar, mobilised low- and middle-caste voters to counter upper-caste dominance. Even though the Congress remained the most influential force in national politics, it had to swallow being voted out of the national government by a BJP-led coalition in the 1998 parliamentary elections. The party also lost the Gujarat assembly elections to a Janata Dal–BJP coalition in 1990, and later to the BJP in every consecutive state election since 1998. It was also ousted in 1987 by the BJP in Ahmedabad's municipal corporation polls, for the first time since the corporation's establishment in 1950. The Congress was re-elected to the central government with the help of leftist and regional parties in 2004 and then again in 2009, but the BJP retained Gujarat in 2002, 2007 as well as 2012.

From 1998 onwards, Gujarat became a strong base for the Hindu nationalist movement, even as the latter's appeal moderated elsewhere in the country. Communal riots in the state turned into one-sided offensives against Muslims and Christians;[9] and the Gujarat administration became complicit in anti-minority violence through acts of omission and, in 2002, allegedly even commission (as will be documented in the course of this chapter and the next). The administration also specifically embraced the Hindu right's gendered agenda, for example, by establishing a special police cell to monitor marriages between Hindus and Muslims.[10] Strong support from the Gujarat administration, in turn, emboldened the Hindu right, whose rhetoric from the late 1990s began to call for total economic and social segregation between Hindus and Muslims.[11]

Profound economic shifts in India between 1985 and 2002 facilitated the Hindu right's efforts to mobilise support for its more militant agenda. From 1991, the central government began systematically implementing liberal economic reforms across the country. The Gujarat government embraced the new regime, which was in line with policies favoured by successive state governments since the late 1960s (Breman 2004: 236–7). Ahmedabad was deeply affected by this shift; its historically dominant organised textile industry began to make way for new industries such as chemicals, pharmaceuticals, petrochemicals, agro-processing and metallurgy (Government of Gujarat n.d.: 12). These new industries, and smaller-scale household industries in areas such as manufacturing, processing, servicing and repairs, offered employment to some re-trenched mill workers, as well as to the city's burgeoning workforce. Consequently, the number of workers employed in household industries in Ahmedabad district nearly doubled from 29,726 in 1981 to 56,715 in 2001 (Government of India 1981: 6; 2001, Part XII A & B, p. xviii).

However, these industries did not offer regular employment. Moreover, in these enterprises wages were lower than in the textile mills, working conditions poorer and union representation non-existent. Low-skilled and unskilled working-class men and women fared still worse as the labour market became increasingly devoid of government regulation and competition over jobs increased with the rise in Ahmedabad city's population, from 2.3 million in 1981 to 3.6 million in 2001 (Gayer and Jaffrelot 2012: 49). Ahmedabad district's total population expanded to 5.8 million in 2001 (of which 80.2 per cent was urban) from 3.8 million in 1981 (of which 71.5 per cent was urban) (Government of India 1981: 4; 2001: xvii). By contrast, the wealthy elite prospered as the expanding liberal economic regime created new and more lucrative investment opportunities, and the middle classes flourished due to increased demand in the expanding tertiary sector for professional skills and educational qualifications.

These far-reaching economic changes had the effect of boosting grassroots-level support for the Hindu right. As the dignity and economic standing of Ahmedabad's working-class population declined, cadre-based organisations such as the VHP provided political direction, psychological support and material benefits to this stratum. At the same time, with rapid urbanisation and increased consumerism eroding traditional ways of life, organisations such as the RSS and the Rashtriya Sevika Samiti addressed the alienation and existential void felt by the middle classes by organising social programmes that created a sense of community belonging. In mobilising such broad-based support, a key goal of the Hindu nationalist movement was to encourage Hindu men to cultivate a militant masculinity,[12] and to motivate Hindu women to develop an equally fierce nationalist spirit, tempered only by a servile devotion to patriarchal domestic structures (T. Sarkar 2005; Sethi 2002).

By the dawn of the twenty-first century, the increasingly assertive Hindu nationalist project, having achieved new heights of popular support, had precipitated unprecedented changes in the fabric of social relations. New restrictions were imposed on sexual relations between Muslim boys and Hindu women,[13] and public attacks were launched by the ABVP against women wearing non-traditional clothing in universities (Engineer 2003: 16; Ghatwai 1998). Among the most striking of these new trends was the recourse taken by hundreds of Hindu families to the Navchetan Group (Organisation for a New Awakening), established in 1998 by Bajrang Dal leader Babu Bajrangi, for the forcible return to the family home of daughters who had eloped with men from a different caste or religion.[14] These and other changes in the scope, agenda and influence of the Hindu nationalist movement between the mid-1980s and early 2000s became manifest in the events that followed the burning of a train compartment in Godhra (a small town located nearly 50 kilometres from Ahmedabad) on 27 February 2002. This tragedy triggered a massacre of Muslims, involving brutal sexual violence against Muslim women.

This chapter interrogates the various developments between 1985 and 2002. It is divided into three sections. The first section focuses on the period between 1985 and 1992, during which time the Hindu nationalist movement came to dominate the national scene. The second section examines the period between 1993 and 2002, when Gujarat became a Hindu nationalist stronghold following the BJP's decisive rise to power in 1998. These sections foreground the broader trends that form a backdrop to the occurrence of the massacre in 2002. The final section examines the events that occurred during the massacre itself, focusing particularly on how sexual violence against Muslim women was orchestrated and inflicted by Hindu activists. The chapter ends with an examination of the response of Hindu nationalist leaders to such occurrences of violence. (Responses of BJP politicians and government officials are included in the section on state responses in Chapter 4.)

National ascent of the Hindu right

The period between the mid-1980s and 1992 was a transformative phase for the Hindu nationalist movement across India. The transformation was apparent in its rhetoric, its support base, its mobilisation strategies and the nature of the violence against religious minorities inflicted by its supporters. No longer merely focused on preparing Hindu men to defend Hindu women, Hinduism and the Hindu community from the imaginary Muslim 'enemy', the movement's rhetoric was now much more overtly sexualised and aggressive,[15] focusing on the creation of martial and virile Hindu men in order to vanquish Muslims. The network of Hindu nationalist organisations was vigorously expanded to bring new members into the fold, in particular Scheduled Caste youth and, to some extent, backward castes. Whereas the RSS stepped up its shakha-based work among upper castes, the VHP began organising religious campaigns and public processions to mobilise support among backward-caste and Scheduled Caste communities. The VHP in the mid-1980s also established two new organisations to mobilise low-caste men and women between the ages of 15 and 35: the Bajrang Dal for men in 1986, and Durga Vahini (Army of Goddess Durga) for women in 1984–85. The launch of the Ramjanmabhoomi movement was the most dramatic and influential component of the Hindu right's new mobilisation strategy.

As the rhetoric of Hindu nationalist organisations became more militant, their popular support expanded and their mobilisation activities became more aggressive. The infliction of verbal abuse and sexual intimidation of Muslim women became a routine part of their activities (AIDWA et al. 1996; Engineer 1992; B. Mehta and Shah 1992). The rising tide of anti-minority sentiment culminated in the destruction of the medieval Babri Mosque by Hindu activists in Ayodhya on 6 December 1992. The demolition sparked an unprecedented wave of communal riots across large parts of northern, central and western India, during which hundreds of Muslims were killed and many more injured. The worst communal riots occurred in the cities of Bombay and Surat, where Muslim women were raped, paraded naked on streets, gang-raped and mutilated (Chandra 1993; Lobo and D'Souza 1993; Patwardhan 1994; Srikrishna 1998). Unlike Bombay and Surat, Ahmedabad did not witness a full-blown riot in the aftermath of the demolition of the mosque. In Ahmedabad, rioting was limited and occurred sporadically between December 1992 and January 1993. Sexual violence against minority women here appears to have taken the form of verbal assault and sexually intimidating behaviour.[16]

The following sub-sections examine why and how Hindu nationalism was transformed between 1985 and 1992 in Ahmedabad. I first examine the wider economic, social and political context that facilitated this transformation, and then the various mobilisation strategies followed by the Hindu right to expand its support base. I then describe how less extreme forms of sexual abuse began to be inflicted regularly during street activities organised by Hindu nationalist organisations. Finally, I track the sporadic violence that occurred in the city in the immediate aftermath of the demolition of the Babri Mosque.

Communalism and the advent of economic liberalism

Under the leadership of Prime Minister P. V. Narasimha Rao, India accelerated its transition from a mixed socialist-capitalist economy towards a market-led liberal economy. Although a few liberal policies had been adopted by the central government from the mid-1970s, they only began to be implemented systematically across the country from 1991. That year, India faced a balance of payments crisis, which led it to seek financial support from the pro-free-market International Monetary Fund (IMF) to avert sovereign default. Partly due to the stringent conditions attached to the loan by the IMF, and partly because the gradual disintegration of the Soviet Union over the 1980s had resulted in the widespread rejection of a state-led economic development model, the Indian government began liberalising the economy. It introduced a plethora of new policies to promote private enterprise, notably currency devaluation and the easing of restrictions on trade and industries (Balakrishnan 2010: 171). As part of this macroeconomic policy reorientation, capital was allowed to move more freely into emerging sectors of the economy, and government intervention in establishing wages was reduced.

The Gujarat government welcomed the liberal policy regime. Successive Congress governments in the state had adopted aspects of liberal reform from the late 1960s, well before the rest of the country. For example, since the 1970s, the Gujarat government had promoted labour market flexibility and reduced government regulation of the economy (Breman 2004: 236–7). The post-1991 liberal regime was in line with the state government's historical policy preferences. Ahmedabad's textile magnates recognised the potential of this regime. Already between 1979 and 1984, as the Gujarat government adopted aspects of economic liberalisation, 19 composite mills out of a total of around 75 were closed down. From 1991, the process of transferring capital from the textile industry to new sectors such as chemicals, petrochemicals and diamond polishing gathered pace. Between 1985 and the late 1990s, another 52 mills were closed or were on the verge of ceasing operations (ibid.: 145).

The incremental closure of mills badly affected mill workers. Whereas in 1960 the number of workers employed in the mills stood at well over 140,000, by 1996 the figure had fallen to 25,000 at most (Breman 2004: 145). Several retrenched mill workers joined the new industries; those that did not took up daily waged jobs as truck drivers, shuttle drivers, petty shopkeepers, construction workers or vegetable vendors. By 1991, out of the 959,073 main industrial workers in Ahmedabad,[17] over 36 per cent worked in small-scale household industries in sectors such as manufacturing, processing, servicing and repairs (Government of India 1991: Part XII A & B, pp. 310–13). This is in contrast to the 1960s, when well over a quarter of the city's workforce depended on the mills (a non-household industry) for their livelihood and a significant number were employed in ancillary industries. Wages in the new sectors were below those offered in the mills, and employment welfare benefits were often non-existent.

Women, owing to the lack of skills and discriminatory hiring practices, found it particularly hard to gain employment in the city's formal economy. The female work participation rate (i.e., the percentage of female workers to total female population) in the formal labour market stood at only 13 per cent in Ahmedabad in 1991. This was in sharp contrast to the predominantly rural district of the Dangs, where 47.5 per cent of all women were employed, and it was also lower than other industrialised districts in Gujarat such as Surat, where the rate stood at 26 per cent (Women's Studies Research Centre 2003: 78).

For both men and women in the working class, the new economic reality was marked by lower wages, few (if any) employment benefits, and the absence of union representation and job security. Within this context, the communal mobilisation of this disaffected population gained renewed vigour. Scheduled Caste and backward-caste men and women were now on the top of Hindu nationalist organisations' recruitment list. Since the RSS continued to be predominantly an upper-caste organisation, the task of mobilising low castes was assigned to two militant outfits established in 1984–86 – the Bajrang Dal (for men) and Durga Vahini (for women) – which were supported by the VHP and the ABVP. The VHP, the Bajrang Dal and Durga Vahini organised several youth conventions in Ahmedabad and elsewhere in Gujarat, appealing to low- and upper-caste youth to dedicate themselves to the 'abolition of untouchability' and to work for the all-round development of their 'economically and socially backward Hindu brothers' (Yagnik and Sheth 2005: 256–7). Meanwhile, the ABVP, which had opposed reservations in the 1985 agitation, started favouring them after the riot of that year in an effort to woo the low castes.

Together, these organisations capitalised on the desire among low- and backward-caste men and women to be active political agents, to be accepted as respectable members of society, and to be economically more secure. Mohan Macwan, a Dalit and the son of a former mill employee, and a resident of the industrial area of Gomtipur, was one of the young men who joined the Bajrang Dal in the late 1980s. He explained why he was drawn to the organisation:

I was into body-building since I was 15 and I used to teach 20–25 boys of my locality. Local VHP leaders had noticed this and approached me to conduct proper classes for all the boys in my locality. They provided me with all the resources and equipment and even bought us an old vacant house and converted it into a gymnasium. They put me in charge, promised to make me a youth leader and paid me a salary for this work. They also trained us in using *lathi*s [canes] in the shakhas they organised in the main cricket grounds.

They also held intellectual classes where they told us about Ambedkar and the work he did to raise the dignity and social standing of Dalits. They said Ambedkar wanted us all to be Hindus and live together. I had not studied very much, so I believed what they said. I knew that it was because of Ambedkar's work that I have respect today, can wear good clothes and sit among you [upper-caste] people. So if Baba Ambedkar wanted us to be with Hindus and live together as brothers, then I must do it. This is why many other Dalit boys like me decided to go with them.

They would tell us that Hindus must forget their old caste problems. Whatever wrongs were inflicted on you by our ancestors are in the past [. . .] today we are all together. We will come and live with you, come to your house, eat with you, sit and talk to you [. . .] and they did. They would come home when someone at home was ill and give us money for medicines. If they found out that a family is too poor to afford an evening meal then these VHP people collected money and gave it to that family. They said you must come to our temples and worship there, like the rest of us. In the neighbourhood, we are all Hindu brothers and we have to work together to protect the Hindu community from Muslims. (Interview, Ahmedabad, 20 October 2007)

Mohan's experience reveals why he and others like him were drawn to the Hindu right. The VHP and Bajrang Dal gave them a sense of political purpose; by joining these outfits, Mohan could be not only a part of a wider political movement ostensibly against the caste system, but also one of its leaders. These organisations harnessed the loyalty of Scheduled Caste communities to Ambedkar, a leader who had fought tirelessly for the abolition of the caste system. They manipulated the knowledge they imparted to Scheduled Caste youth about Ambedkar to mobilise them against Muslims. In the absence of a strong anti-caste movement in Gujarat, and the lack of commitment on the part of the Congress to reducing caste-based discrimination following the failure of its KHAM policy, the Hindu right's efforts to co-opt Ambedkar's legacy faced few challenges. The co-optation of Ambedkar helped the VHP and the Bajrang Dal shrink the scope for a genuine subversion of the caste system.

Moreover, these organisations held out the prospect of greater social respectability for Scheduled Castes by at least theoretically calling for the abolition of untouchability. The practice of untouchability has for centuries prohibited low castes from sharing food with upper castes, coming into close physical proximity to them and entering temples. By interacting closely with Scheduled Caste families, visiting their homes and inviting them into temples, Hindu nationalist organisations at least partly removed a longstanding source of everyday humiliation for low castes.

Furthermore, they ameliorated economic hardship and showed compassion at a time when the closure of the textile mills had pushed thousands of workers, such as Mohan's father, into a life of uncertainty. In a context where the Congress government in Gujarat and in Delhi was promoting economic policies that resulted in the incremental closure of textile mills, thereby also eroding the system of social welfare that workers had access to within the mills, the Hindu right forged an alternative welfare system that was responsive and sympathetic to the deprivation of retrenched workers and their families. Hindu nationalist organisations offered them an opportunity to cultivate their masculine pride, which had been hurt due to their low-caste status and economic hardship. Mohan could continue his body-building regime, utilise his skills to train other boys in the locality, while being gainfully employed and receiving training in the use of weapons by shakhas organised by the VHP. In exchange for recognising, rewarding and honing the political potential of men such as Mohan, the Hindu right mobilised militant foot soldiers against Muslims.

Through its work in Ahmedabad, Durga Vahini harnessed similar desires among low-caste women, especially from Scheduled Caste backgrounds, to be politically engaged, socially respected and economically secure. However, the purpose assigned to these women as Hindu right activists was not free of gender-based stereotyping. Whereas low-caste men were entrusted with the task of 'protecting the Hindu community against Muslims', as Mohan put it, and encouraged to cultivate a militant masculinity, female recruits were called on to cultivate a militant nationalist spirit while simultaneously observing the traditional feminine virtues of selfless, loving devotion to the family and the nation. Mohan explained:

> Durga Vahini used to do similar work with Dalit girls of our locality. Its leaders would tell them that they should work for the country, for their religion and come and participate in Durga Vahini programmes. They would tell girls that today, a woman is not afraid of anyone; she is strong like Jhansi ki Rani. She can fight and is on a par with men. They started a crèche in my neighbourhood and one of my neighbours, a college graduate, was put in charge of that. She was asked to teach other girls and got 3,000–4,000 rupees for it. They told her to teach them whatever you want but tell them stories of Rama, sing religious Hindu prayers and start the classes with Vande Mataram. (Interview, Ahmedabad, 20 October 2007)

By offering monetary security to such women, and by drawing comparisons between contemporary women and the valiant nineteenth-century warrior-queen of Jhansi, Durga Vahini sought to instil a sense of political and social independence among its recruits. However, it carefully manipulated the purpose of this independence. Rani Laxmibai, the queen of Jhansi, is said to have lost her life in battle defending her kingdom from colonial occupation. Hence, the adulation of this figure was not designed to empower women to promote social reform or subvert patriarchal practices such as dowry. Rather, this iconography aimed at instilling militant religious and nationalist devotion among low-caste women and mobilising them against the Muslim 'enemy'.

Simultaneously, Durga Vahini sought to encourage women to adopt the ideals of upper-caste womanhood. Religious Hindu prayers, the *Ramayana* and the famous nineteenth-century poem 'Vande Mataram' are replete with Hindu imagery and rituals historically associated with upper-caste beliefs and practices, and with the valorisation of women as nurturing mothers and obedient wives. By insisting that low-caste activists make these texts central to their daily routine, Durga Vahini sought to propagate such upper-caste norms at the expense of the cultural traditions of other caste groups. Indeed, the decision to name the organisation after Durga, a Brahminical goddess who embodies the virtues of motherhood but slays demons in moments of crisis, succinctly reflects the Hindu right's ideal of partial, regulated, and ultimately regressive women's empowerment (Sethi 2002).

For the first time from the late 1980s, the Hindu right also put special emphasis on mobilising upper-caste, middle-class women who were pursuing higher education and even paid employment and political engagement (T. Sarkar 2005: 179). In the electoral arena, the BJP promoted its Mahila Morcha (Women's Forum), whereas the Rashtriya Sevika Samiti sought to harness women's potential to be active political agents through their neighbourhood shakhas. Historian Tanika Sarkar (ibid.) and sociologist Paola Bacchetta (2005) have pointed out that in mobilising women, the primary goal of the Samiti in particular, and the Hindu nationalist movement more broadly, remained that of promoting domesticity and religious devotion, entrenching Brahminical patriarchy and encouraging Hindu women to cultivate *samskara*s (good virtues) within the family. In the Hindu nationalist worldview, women would be devoted mothers and wives, prioritising their families over all else, while men would be breadwinners and protectors of their own and their families' honour and well-being.

However, from the late 1980s onwards, these organisations realised that women from conservative upper-caste, middle-class families too had the potential to advance their political agenda of preserving the gender- and caste-based status quo (T. Sarkar 2005: 180). These issues had risen up the agenda of the Hindu right as economic liberalisation and globalisation disrupted the traditional ways of life and the gendered order of society. Moreover, strong caste-based regional parties were emerging in states such as UP and Bihar, challenging upper-caste hegemony. Threats to the caste system became particularly acute in August 1990, when the central government announced its intention to implement the recommendations of the Mandal Commission, which (among other things) proposed the reservation of 27 per cent of all public sector jobs for backward-caste communities. This policy threatened to increase the number of reserved jobs – including those for Scheduled Castes and Scheduled Tribes – to 50 per cent. The announcement vexed the majority of upper-caste Hindus, especially in northern and western India, and led some upper-caste students, who feared that the policy would limit their career options, to stage disturbing protests by immolating themselves and committing suicide (Brass 2004: 252).

Amid such threats to patriarchal and caste structures, the Rashtriya Sevika Samiti sought to mobilise upper-caste Hindu women who would dedicate themselves selflessly to the renewal of Hindu nationalism's vision of India, albeit within more flexible domestic structures (T. Sarkar 2005: 179–80). Some Samiti members' 'activism' remained confined to collecting dowries for other women in the shakha, offering advice on marital disputes, finding suitors for members' daughters, and, as Sarkar points out, 'writing to newspapers about oppression of Hindus and about sex and violence in Western movies and TV shows' (ibid.: 185). However, others used the opportunity to circumvent, but not challenge, traditional restrictions on their mobility, marital arrangements and activities, while simultaneously working for the preservation of a conservative national social ethos. One such woman is Sandhya Tipre, an upper-caste, middle-class Ahmedabadi who was in her early 40s in 2007. Tipre hails from a conservative Hindu family. Her male relations are actively involved in the RSS in the city. She joined the Samiti as a *pracharika* (female propagandist) in 1991, after finishing her bachelor's degree. Since pracharaks (male propagandists) and pracharikas have to be celibate, Tipre is unmarried, a choice unavailable to most women in traditional families. When I met her in 2007, I found her to be soft-spoken and articulate. She had this to say about why she enjoys working with the Samiti:

> I like this work because it is among women. There is no self-interest in this; we have to work with selfless devotion. And with this we join people, which is the best work. Women have to be empowered to ensure their own protection and we need to instil rashtra *bhavna* [feelings for the nation] among them. This is very good work. This is why I am working with the Samiti. Samiti's goal is to make women self-sufficient in terms of their own protection, and awaken rashtra bhavna among them. The medium for this work is the shakha. Each shakha lasts an hour. Although we organise daily shakhas, but sometimes due to time constraints everyone can't come every day. (Interview, Ahmedabad, 8 December 2007)

When asked why it is more difficult to organise a daily shakha for women, Tipre added that women's participation in the Samiti is harder than men's involvement in the RSS, because 'women have to work for the Samiti, while fulfilling all their domestic responsibilities. Men also have domestic responsibilities, but fewer'. Tipre's unwillingness to challenge the skewed allocation of domestic responsibilities sits comfortably with her commitment to the Hindutva cause of preserving the traditional gendered, caste- and class-based status quo:

> Samiti says women should increase their own strength and competence, and with that they should attain their rightful position in the world. We have to do this according to our own potential [. . .] we don't need reservations [. . .] If someone has the ability to excel and the potential he will succeed himself. We don't need to bring him forward today. You don't need to help someone to succeed; he will flourish automatically. By taking advantage of reservations you create a wrong mentality that it doesn't matter whether we work hard or not, because reservations are available to us. So even a hardworking person will not put in the effort and will not became a hardworking person. He will continue to rely on reservations [. . .] Reservations not only corrupt your mentality, but also stop more capable people from excelling. People should flourish on the basis of their intellectual capability, bodily strength and economic standing. That is better. It is the ideal situation.
> (Interview, Ahmedabad, 8 December 2007)

Although Tipre insisted that the Samiti, the RSS and she herself supported reservations for Scheduled Castes and OBCs, her testimony betrayed her deeper ideological leanings. Like many other upper-caste, middle-class people, she saw reservations as inherently non-meritocratic and a source of mental corruption. This attitude results from the failure to recognise the structural discrimination that impedes the ability of those lower in the caste hierarchy to gain access to the socio-economic opportunities that upper castes take for granted.

Moreover, while she claimed to be committed to enhancing women's stature in society, Tipre remained unwilling to question the traditional constraints on their choices, thereby advancing the Hindu right's goal of partially modifying while not subverting patriarchy. She seemed unable to envision a world where women might choose to prioritise their careers over domestic responsibilities, and men might choose not to be career-driven. This may be why she unconsciously switched to the male pronoun when referring to people's careers and material success: 'If someone has the ability to excel and the potential *he* will succeed himself'. Moreover, Tipre revealed a deep commitment to a non-egalitarian social order in proposing that the 'ideal' society would favour only people who are intellectually capable, physically strong and wealthy. People whose intellectual growth is hampered by restrictions on their access to knowledge and resources, and those who are weaker, physically disabled and economically disadvantaged, would constitute this 'ideal' society's underclass. By working with the Samiti, therefore, Tipre works to create an order in which the existing status quo, wherein women, low castes and the poor are disproportionately marginalised, would stay firmly intact. This would constitute a step towards creating what she described as the 'correct mentality' of the 'glorious Hindu nation'.

The rise in social support for the VHP, Bajrang Dal, the Samiti and Durga Vahini among poorer and low-caste communities was paralleled by an increase in the popularity of cadre-based organisations such as the RSS and ABVP that mainly mobilised upper-caste Hindus. According to one estimate, in 1986 the all-male RSS ran over 1,099 full shakhas and sub-branches in Gujarat and had 25,320 volunteers (Shukla 1991: 46, 233). By 1990, it had 1,289 full branches and sub-branches and 28,956 volunteers. The membership of the ABVP more than doubled from 5,037 in 1986 to 10,972 in 1990. The rise in popular support for the BJP was even more dramatic. The number of ordinary members of the party increased from 55,000 in 1980–83 to 140,000 in 1984–87. By 1990, the membership had reached 200,000 (ibid.).

Partitioning space, segregating lives

As the membership of Hindu nationalist organisations grew across Ahmedabad, religious identities sharpened and the support for communal politics increased. To advance their project and demonstrate their increased assertiveness, Hindu nationalist organisations started physically inscribing divisions between different religious communities on the city. Billboards proclaiming Hindu-dominated areas as 'Hindu Rashtras', usually erected by local chapters of the VHP, began appearing across Ahmedabad. These boards typically read, 'Hindu Rashtra's Gomtipur Village Welcomes You', or 'You Are Now Entering Saraspur

Village of Hindu Rashtra' (interview with human rights activist G. Shah, Ahmedabad, 5 January 2007). Similar boards were erected on roadsides in other districts of Gujarat as well.[18] One such board was situated on the road that leads to Vadodara (called Baroda before 1974). It read: 'You are now entering Vadodara Pradesh of Hindu Rashtra'. These boards were physical manifestations of the growing assertiveness of Hindu nationalism in Gujarat.

Communal mobilisation accelerated physical and demographic changes in neighbourhoods across Ahmedabad. For the first time, Muslims were expelled from mixed neighbourhoods in various parts of the industrial belt, and boundaries were drawn between the Hindu- and Muslim-dominated parts. For example, Bapunagar had witnessed horrific anti-Muslim violence during the 1969 riot, but its internal spatial order was left unaltered. However, the locality was partitioned soon after the 1985 riot: Muslims were evicted and forced to sell their property in the Hindu-dominated area of Indira Garibnagar. The Muslim-dominated part came to be known by local residents as 'Pakistan', while the other, dominated by Scheduled Castes, came to be known as 'Hindustan'. The road dividing the two was called 'the border', physically inscribing the animosity between India and Pakistan, and between Hindus and Muslims, onto the geography of the city (Shani 2007: 127).

In regions where Muslims were not evicted, many of them moved out of Hindu-dominated areas out of fear for their safety. Indeed, in the immediate aftermath of the 1985 riot, both Hindus and Muslims were so anxious about their safety that they sold their houses in mixed neighbourhoods at throw-away prices. The steep rise in such 'distress sales' compelled the government to issue a special ordinance to cancel them with retrospective effect. The fear engendered by the riot was articulated by a Muslim survivor from Saraspur in the following words: 'Hindus say that they don't want Miyan bhai [Muslims] in the chawli. This time we barely managed to save our lives. What if they attack us again? Now I will accept living on the streets, but will never go back'.[19] This led several Muslim families to move to the city's largest Muslim-dominated region, Juhapura, which was fast developing into a Muslim ghetto and came to be known locally as 'mini-Pakistan'.[20] The road dividing Juhapura from the nearby Hindu-dominated locality of Gupta Nagar came to be known as the 'India–Pakistan border'.

In the walled city, a similar process of spatial segregation unfolded. Here, however, the evacuees were upper-caste, middle-class Hindus, not Muslims. For example, the better-off upper-caste residents of Vadigam sold their property and moved to the affluent Paldi area west of the River Sabarmati. At the same time, some backward-caste families from the industrial regions moved into the Hindu-dominated pols in the walled city to seek safety in numbers. This intra-city migration sharpened the lines between Muslims and non-Muslims, while concealing the internal heterogeneity of these groups. Even though the cultural and social practices of backward castes and upper castes varied significantly, the former too came to be identified as 'Hindus'. Similarly, sectarian, cultural and religious heterogeneity among Muslims became less publicly apparent as they started moving into 'Muslim-dominated' areas.

As in the walled city and the industrial belt, spatial shifts also occurred west of the river. Although western Ahmedabad was primarily an upper-caste Hindu enclave, there were some affluent Muslim families in the Paldi area. In 1989–90, the VHP started harassing these families. It circulated a map with saffron and green markers (the former signifying Hindu and the latter Muslim areas), and pressured these families into relocating to Muslim-majority areas.[21]

Slums on the periphery of western Ahmedabad underwent the same process. These slums were home to Scheduled Caste, backward-caste and Muslim daily wage labourers working as vegetable vendors, menial workers, shopkeepers or domestic helps in middle-class homes. As in the industrial belt and the walled city, the VHP once again erected boards, welcoming visitors, for example, to 'Hindu Rashtra's Thaltej Village' (interview with human rights activist G. Shah, Ahmedabad, 5 January 2007).

Political rise of the BJP

The rise in membership of Hindu nationalist organisations was reflected in the political ascent of the BJP. Its popularity was boosted by separatist militancy in the north (especially Punjab) and in the north-east (particularly Assam) in the 1980s, since the party continued to place strong emphasis on the preservation of India's territorial integrity. The BJP also benefited from the political decline of the Congress in large parts of the country, including Gujarat. In the 1984 parliamentary elections, a nationwide sympathy 'wave' triggered by the assassination of Prime Minister Indira Gandhi had delivered the Congress its most resounding victory since 1952. However, Indira Gandhi's successor, Prime Minister Rajiv Gandhi, purged oppositionists and competitors from Congress ranks during his tenure between 1985 and 1989 (he was assassinated in 1991 by Liberation Tigers of Tamil Eelam militants while campaigning for the forthcoming elections). As a result of all these developments, the Congress lost the temporary gains it had made in 1984, and its old guard began to splinter (Rudolph and Rudolph 1987: 152–4). Indeed, Gujarat Chief Minister Chimanbhai Patel defected to the Janata Dal, another ascendant political party. Moreover, the Congress could no longer take for granted votes from Muslims, Scheduled Castes and tribals in the state, especially following the failure of the KHAM alliance in Gujarat.

The party had also further alienated middle-class, upper-caste Hindu voters, who had been shifting towards right-wing politics from the 1960s. Disillusionment with a corrupt and factionalised Congress had brought them out on the streets during the Nav Nirman movement in the mid-1970s. When the Congress introduced the KHAM alliance and then the reservation policy in the 1980s, middle-class Hindus had waged violent protests in 1981 and again in 1985. In 1986, the national Congress government used its parliamentary majority to pass the Muslim Women (Protection of Rights on Divorce) Act, acquiescing to the demands of the Islamic clergy and orthodox Muslim men that Muslim women be denied the right to alimony following a divorce. The Act overturned a Supreme Court ruling that had granted the right to a monthly alimony to Shah Bano, a Muslim woman who had appealed to the court to seek maintenance following her divorce in 1978. Whereas women's organisations and secular political parties protested against the denial of alimony to Muslim women, the BJP portrayed the act as the Congress's effort to appease Muslim voters.[22]

The ensuing public debate turned many Hindus away from the Congress. Disappointed with the Congress, its reservation policy, and its so-called 'minority appeasement' efforts, upper-caste students from middle-class families joined the ABVP in greater numbers. Affluent land-owning communities, especially Patels, who were disgruntled by the Congress's KHAM policy, also threw their weight behind the BJP. Government officials, many of whom had also opposed reservations for low and backward castes in public sector jobs, did the same. Their support brought Hindutva ideology to the heart of the state administrative machinery in Gujarat, with bureaucrats, police officers, municipal and district officers, and other government officials openly espousing Hindu nationalist ideas (Sud 2007: 269).

Due to this phenomenal rise in its popularity, the BJP recorded its first major election victory in 1987, winning the AMC elections with a convincing majority. By 1990, the BJP seemed to be the only party in the state with political purpose and ideological direction. In the Gujarat assembly elections held that year, the party secured 67 of 182 seats. This electoral success propelled the BJP to the corridors of power in the state, enabling the party to form a coalition government under the leadership of the Janata Dal leader Chimanbhai Patel. This replacement of the Congress with the BJP and Janata Dal was part of a broader trend across central and northern India. In the February 1990 assembly elections, the BJP won an outright majority in Madhya Pradesh and Himachal Pradesh, and formed a coalition government with the Janata Dal in Rajasthan. In 1991, the BJP also won the UP state elections.

The Ramjanmabhoomi movement and normalisation of sexual violence

Parallel to the grassroots work undertaken individually by organisations such as the RSS, VHP, Bajrang Dal and Durga Vahini, the Hindu nationalist network launched the nationwide Ramjanmabhoomi movement in the mid-1980s. This movement remains the most successful and the most pernicious mobilisation drive in the history of the Hindu right. It communalised the everyday social fabric of large parts of India, helped spread a new, militant Hindutva ideology, and sparked numerous communal riots that left thousands of Muslims dead in their wake. The sexual intimidation of Muslim women through verbal abuse and physical gestures became a regular activity for Hindu nationalist volunteers, as will be discussed shortly.

The Ramjanmabhoomi movement aimed at reclaiming the *janmabhoomi* (birthplace) of the mythological Lord Rama in Ayodhya. This reclamation involved building a magnificent Hindu temple at the site where the medieval Babri Mosque had stood. The site had been under dispute since 1947. The gates to the Babri Mosque were locked and people were barred from entering the structure from that time.

However, when these locks were removed in 1986, Hindu nationalist organisations claimed that this was the first step towards 'liberating' the janmabhoomi and building a Rama temple.

Gujarat was one of the states where the Ramjanmabhoomi campaign was pursued most aggressively. Led by the then BJP president Lal Krishna Advani, the party organised a major rath yatra on 25 September 1990. The procession began at the Hindu pilgrimage site of Somnath in Gujarat's Saurashtra district, and was to traverse 10,000 kilometres across India, culminating at Ayodhya on 30 October the same year. As the rath yatra progressed through Gujarat, hundreds of propaganda pamphlets warning Muslims to relinquish their claim over the Babri Mosque were circulated widely across the state. A pamphlet entitled 'The Story of the Ramjanmabhoomi', circulated by the VHP in Ahmedabad, is notable in this regard:

> Till date, 76 battles have been fought to free the janmabhoomi. 300,000 Hindus have lost their lives fighting for this space. Today, the Ramjanmabhoomi Trust has resurrected the call for handing over this space to Hindus [. . .]
>
> An appeal to our Muslim brothers [. . .]
>
> [. . .] some fundamentalist Muslims and Maulvis are being encouraged by the current government to instigate ordinary Muslims on the janmabhoomi issue. The seeds of poison are being sown [. . .] Muslims are advised to [. . .] hand over the birthplace of Ram to Hindus [. . .] If Muslims do not, Hindu society is equipped to sacrifice the path of the Constitution.[23]

Besides circulating such propaganda materials, the VHP organised a number of religious processions with a view to mobilising support for the Ramjanmabhoomi campaign and generating communal sentiment against Muslims. These processions were organised in remote rural areas of Gujarat as well as in urban centres such as Ahmedabad and Surat. In Ahmedabad, the VHP took the lead in organising the Jagannath procession in the walled city and a Ram–Janki Shobha Yatra (procession of Lord Rama and his consort) in 1987. Both old and new supporters of Hindu nationalism – middle-class Hindus, Scheduled Castes, backward castes and women – generously donated money for such processions, joined as participants, or cheered them on from the roadside (Yagnik and

Sheth 2005: 258). Such processions involved cavalcades of vehicles, each carrying dozens of men shouting slogans and frequently wielding arms; they often left a trail of communal riots behind them. Between 1986 and 1987, there were no fewer than 95 riots in the state. The areas most affected were Ahmedabad and the neighbouring districts of Kheda, Panch Mahals, Sabarkantha, Banaskantha, Mehsana and Bharuch (Nandy et al. 1995: 108, 121–2). By 1987, communal rifts in Gujarat had grown so deep that even trivial issues such as cricket matches and rickshaw fares led to inter-religious violence. Since the BJP could always count on its cadre-based affiliates to convert Hindu nationalist supporters into voters, these processions also helped the party win the AMC elections in 1987.

Alongside such local mobilisation and the associated violence, an important media event changed the face of Hindu nationalism – and with it the course and tenor of the Ramjanmabhoomi movement. This event was the telecast of a series based on the mythological epic *Ramayana* on national television in 78 weekly episodes between 1987 and 1988. The telecast was produced to coincide with the Ramjanmabhoomi movement. The serial standardised a textbook version of the great epic at the expense of other, vastly different interpretative traditions. The televised version denuded the text's characters of their richness and trivialised its more abstract ethical pronouncements, drawing simplistic distinctions between 'right-eousness' and 'evil'. Yet it was precisely this oversimplification that made the *Ramayana* widely accessible and helped consolidate a national Hindu identity on an unprecedented scale (Rudolph 1992: 92). In turn, this new national Hindu identity enabled the Ramjanmabhoomi movement to garner support from a broader constituency (Rajagopal 2001: 118–19).

The programme's portrayal of desirable and repulsive male and female sexuality was also co-opted by the Hindu right. The television series transformed the image of Rama from a virtuous prince – who in traditional iconography personified 'tranquillity, compassion, and benevolence' – into an angry, heavily armed, militant warrior (Kapur 1993: 74–5). For example, in traditional iconography, Rama usually carries his bow but is rarely shown using it. In Hindu nationalist imagery, however, he is depicted as pulling the bowstring, with 'the arrow poised to annihilate' (ibid.: 74). This image presented the Hindu right with a well-articulated and widely recognisable ideal of militant Hindu manhood.[24] The main antagonist in the *Ramayana*, Ravana, was presented as the antithesis of the ideal Hindu man: as evil, powerful and lascivious. These were characteristics that Hindu nationalist propaganda routinely ascribed to Muslim men. The goddess Sita, portrayed on the programme as the chaste, docile, self-sacrificing wife of Rama, personified Hindu nationalism's image of the ideal Hindu woman. In the *Ramayana*, after her rescue from captivity, Sita underwent a trial by fire on Rama's insistence to prove her piety, chastity and purity. The act is sometimes seen as the first *sati* (self-immolation by a woman on the pyre of her deceased husband). When Roop Kanwar, an 18-year-old Rajput woman, committed sati in Deorala village in Rajasthan in September 1987, Hindu nationalism's image of the ideal Hindu woman became anchored in a real event.

Yet the story of Rama and Sita, as narrated in the television serial, was to serve as much as a warning as an ideal. Sita's experiences were meant to warn Hindu women about the dangers they faced from the imaginary Muslim enemy. In the televised story, Ravana, masquerading as a mendicant in need of charity, abducts the large-hearted but gullible Sita, imprisons her in his castle in Lanka, and makes sexual advances towards her. She is saved only when Rama attacks Lanka with his army led by the monkey god Hanuman, and slays Ravana. Muslim men, in the Hindu nationalist imagination, presented the same dangers to Hindu women as Ravana did to Sita. Therefore, it was the responsibility of Hindu men to protect Hindu women from their own gullibility, by cultivating a martial masculinity and protecting Hindu women's sexual purity.

The telecast of *Ramayana* thus invigorated the Ramjanmabhoomi agitation, and circulated notions of ideal Hindu male and female sexuality that resonated with and gave impetus to Hindu nationalist ideals of desirable masculine and feminine behaviour. This sharpened Hindu nationalist rhetoric from the early 1990s, making it more bellicose, graphic and overtly sexualised. The speeches of the firebrand female leader of the VHP, Sadhvi Rithambara, reflect this transformation:

Young [Hindu] men came to me and asked for arms. I asked them, 'Why do you need arms?'
They said, 'To kill the enemies of Hinduism'.

I responded, 'Why would you want to waste bullets to kill eunuchs?' [...]

Let no one forget [...] whoever challenges Hindus will die a dog's death.

Say with pride, we are Hindus! Victory to Lord Ram![25]

This new militancy in Hindu nationalism's anti-Muslim rhetoric increasingly found expression in the locally distributed propaganda materials of the VHP. Descriptions of the sexual atrocities allegedly suffered by Hindu women were now more graphic, and acts such as gang-rape received their first mention. Simultaneously, these materials rehearsed historical stereotypes about Muslims as killers and rapists with the aim of mobilising support for the Ramjanmabhoomi movement. One such pamphlet, entitled 'Terrorism Attacks India', circulated widely in Ahmedabad in 1990, is illustrative:

In the Doda district of Jammu and Kashmir, two Hindu children were murdered and their flesh was stuffed into the mouths of their mother and father. In Pakistan and in Bangladesh Hindu women were stripped on the streets and then they were gang raped.

What happened in Kashmir could happen in India as well [...] Today when Hindus protect the country then it is considered communal but when Muslims support terrorism then that is considered secular.

What is the solution? There is only one solution to this problem: The construction of a Ram Temple at the Ramjanmabhoomi. This is a holy task. This will unite the whole Hindu society.[26]

As propaganda material became more lurid and inflammatory, the infliction of verbal and visual sexual violence upon Muslim women became a routine aspect of religious processions organised by the VHP in Ahmedabad. For example, when the VHP organised the annual Jagannath yatra on 2 July 1992, some participants stripped in front of Muslim women. When the procession passed through Muslim neighbourhoods in the walled city, VHP volunteers shouted slogans such as 'Children of Tipu Sultan bring your Ruqayyas[27] [...] our Ram and Laxman are coming to f**k them' (Engineer 1992: 1643). Similar verbal abuse and sexual intimidation were perpetrated during religious processions elsewhere in Gujarat, such as in the city of Vadodara (B. Mehta and Shah 1992: 2253).

The rise in communal violence across Gujarat polarised the state's electorate along religious lines, helping the BJP perform strongly in the 1990 Gujarat assembly elections and form a coalition government. Increasingly, the state government and large sections of Gujarat's administration – the bureaucracy, police and municipal corporations – were filled with Hindu nationalist supporters. Under the stewardship of such an administration, the police and other government officials in Ahmedabad were both unwilling and unable to stop the VHP's religious processions, to arrest people who published and circulated incendiary propaganda or who blatantly inflicted the forms of sexual violence just mentioned upon Muslim women.

This lack of intervention on the part of the authorities was in contrast to the late 1960s, when the police and local government officials took steps to quell rumours about rapes and arrest propagandists and miscreants. Many of these steps were half-hearted, woefully ineffective and inadequate even during the 1969 riot. However, it is significant that from the early 1990s, when Hindu nationalism was considerably more belligerent and sexual abuse on the streets had become routine, large parts of the administration were not even trying to prevent such clear violations of the law.

Demolition of the Babri Mosque and its aftermath

Ayodhya maa Ram, pachi aaram
[We will rest after Rama has been seated in Ayodhya]
                    – a slogan painted on walls across Ahmedabad
                                              in December 1992
         (Interview with S. Pathan, Ahmedabad, 15 January 2007)

On 1 December 1992, BJP president Lal Krishna Advani issued an ominous warning to India: '*Karseva* [religious service] does not mean singing religious songs and saying religious prayers. We will perform karseva with shovels and bricks'.[28] Five days later, *karsevak*s (Hindu religious activists) armed with tools such as bricks, shovels and iron rods demolished the Babri Mosque in Ayodhya. For karsevaks, the demolition was the first step towards 'liberating' Rama's birthplace, identified as the area where the mosque had stood. Retired army officers had trained some of these karsevaks in demolition, combat and the use of weapons in special camps near Ahmedabad (A. Bhatt 1991: 106). The demolition triggered an unprecedented wave of Hindu–Muslim riots. In addition to UP (where Ayodhya is located), communal rioting erupted in at least nine other states – Gujarat, Rajasthan, Madhya Pradesh, Bihar, Maharashtra, West Bengal, Andhra Pradesh, Karnataka and Kerala. Sexual violence against Muslim women in the form of rape, gang-rape and genital mutilation were reported from Bombay and Surat. In Gujarat, violence broke out on 6 December itself, and continued sporadically until 11 January 1993. The district of Bharuch, especially the city of Jambusar, and Khambhat in Anand district were affected, as was the city of Ahmedabad.[29] By the time rioting was brought to a halt, at least 305 people had been killed and several hundreds injured or rendered homeless.[30] Although disaggregated data are unavailable, media reports suggest that the overwhelming majority of those killed were Muslims.[31]

In Ahmedabad, each outburst of violence was quickly brought under control by the government with the help of the military. The city was thus saved from witnessing a full-blown communal riot, as it had done in 1969 and 1985. Violence began on the morning of 6 December in the walled city, especially Kalupur, Dariapur and Jamalpur, and in the industrial areas of Rakhial, Gomtipur, Danilimda and Behrampura. Organised groups of 200 to 1,000 men, armed with sticks, tridents, swords, spears, stones and crude petrol bombs, rampaged through the streets. Identified by witnesses as VHP, RSS and Bajrang Dal activists, these men shouted slogans such as 'Cut and kill the Muslims', 'Victory to Lord Ram' and 'Victory to monkey deity, Bajrang', the slogan of the Bajrang Dal (AIDWA et al. 1996: 305, 320). They singled out Muslims, their mosques, shops and homes for attack, but left untouched the property of Hindus, marked with signs such as 'This is a Hindu house', 'This is Ram's shop', and 'Victory to Lord Ram' (ibid.: 304–5). Several Muslim women reported that the attackers shouted sexually abusive language, made obscene gestures and sometimes unzipped their trousers before them (ibid.: 321).

However, the government did not allow the violence to escalate. On 7 December, it called in the army, which imposed an indefinite curfew in Shahpur, Karanj, Haveli, Kagadpith and Vejalpur in the walled city and in the working-class neighbourhood of Maninagar. Between 8 and 10 December, minor incidents of looting, arson and destruction of mosques were reported from Shahpur, Haveli and Kagadpith, Bapunagar and Vejalpur, and the semi-urban industrial area of Naroda. To quell the violence, curfew was extended to these areas, and the army was asked to organise flag marches to ensure peace.[32] This brought the violence to a halt, and relative peace prevailed until 24 December. On 25 December, violence erupted in the industrial area of Gomtipur. The army was again promptly called in, after police attempts to disperse clashing groups with 40 rounds of bullets and 30 tear-gas shells failed to deter the rioters. Extensive patrolling by army personnel and a strict curfew once again brought the violence to a halt.

On 6 January, exactly a month after the destruction of the Babri Mosque, Muslims in Ahmedabad organised a procession to mourn the demolition, while Hindu activists celebrated the day on the streets by bursting firecrackers, lighting lamps and shouting slogans such as 'Victory to Lord Ram'. The processions led to some street violence, but this was promptly brought under control. On the same evening, the VHP and the Bajrang Dal organised a *maha arti* (a grand Hindu religious ceremony) in the Scheduled Caste-dominated area of Behrampura to celebrate the demolition. According to several witnesses, in the evening, a mob of 8,000 men gathered near the Meladi Mata Temple (the temple of a local deity) to attend the ceremony.[33] Sporting saffron headbands and in some cases even khaki shorts (the uniform of RSS volunteers), these men carried tridents, spears and swords.

After the ceremony was over, the men attacked a Muslim-dominated chawl of the area where nearly 200 Muslim families resided. According to Sakina Pathan, a Muslim resident of the chawl, these mobs were 'shouting such filthy slogans and swear-words about Muslim women that if you heard them you would just shut your ears' (interview, Ahmedabad, 15 January 2007). First, the mob pelted stones at Muslim houses. In order to defend themselves and prevent the attacking mob from entering the chawl, Muslim men and women also threw stones. Asiya Rafiq was one such woman who helped in warding off the marauding crowd. She told me:

When these people came to attend that arti, they all had weapons in their hands. Some had tridents and spears, and others had swords. We did not have anything except stones. We still managed to defend ourselves for one hour. I also went with my son to the corner of the road and threw stones at them. Then they burnt down Muslim houses in the back row. I recognised some of the people who attacked our basti but there were also others whom I did not know by face. But I did see that the police was for Hindus. They fired at us and arrested so many of our boys but they did not arrest any Hindu. So many of our shops were looted but the police did not do anything. (Interview, Ahmedabad, 18 January 2007)

While the police thus apparently connived with the mobs, several Muslim houses in the chawl were burnt down, and grain shops and transport depots owned by them were looted and incinerated. However, once again the army was called in and the violence in Behrampura was brought to a halt.

On 8 January a fresh round of violence began, following a canard that a mosque had been demolished on Relief Road. Hindu–Muslim clashes rocked the eastern industrial suburbs of the city, leaving 12 dead, including a police constable, and a hundred injured before the end of the day. Fearing an escalation of violence, the army was called in yet again, and an indefinite curfew was imposed on the walled city and the industrial areas. On 10 January, more instances of stone throwing, stabbings, and firing of kerosene bombs and acid bulbs took place, claiming another 18 lives. Biscuit Galli, Kalupur, Relief Road, Shahpur, Astodia and Gomtipur were the worst-affected areas in which Muslim and Hindu mobs attacked one another. The violence was brought under control by 11 January, and the army started relaxing the curfew in some areas. However, by then, 134 people were dead in Ahmedabad, and a total of 305 dead in the entire state.

In the aftermath of the 1992–93 violence in Ahmedabad and Surat, an official commission of inquiry was appointed under Justice Chauhan of the Gujarat High Court. However, Gujarat's government, then led by Chief Minister Shankersinh Vaghela, disbanded the commission without justification in 1996 before its report could be finalised and made public. Despite its many failings, during the 1969 and 1985 riots, the state government had been willing to subject its handling of communal rioting to independent judicial scrutiny. However, by 1992, this willingness had diminished markedly. This may have been because of the extensive presence of Hindu nationalist supporters in the state administration and their reluctance to accept a probe into their own actions and those of the organisations they endorsed. Over the next decade, this reluctance to allow independent probes into communal riots transformed into what has been widely described as the active and widespread complicity of large sections of the state apparatus in orchestrating and inflicting violence against minorities.

The making of a Hindu nationalist 'laboratory'

Between 1985 and 1992, the development of the Hindu nationalist movement in Gujarat occurred in line with a wider, indeed nationwide, trend. As we have seen, violence against religious minorities during religious processions was not unique to Gujarat in the late 1980s and early 1990s. The creation of a broad Hindu constituency, which embraced to varying degrees the goals and ideology of the Hindu right, was also by no means a Gujarat-specific phenomenon. Although the demarcation of neighbourhoods with signs declaring them to be parts of an imaginary Hindu nation was unique to the state, the segregation of urban space along religious lines was not singular to Gujarat.[34] Moreover, Hindu nationalism's anti-minority ideology had acquired such nationwide popularity that the destruction of the Babri Mosque in the northern state of UP sparked riots in Rajasthan to the west, as far south as Kerala, and in an otherwise communally peaceful West Bengal in the east. That the demolition of the Babri Mosque, and all the mobilisation campaigns that preceded it, was allowed to proceed at all, also suggests that infiltration of the state apparatus by Hindu nationalist sympathisers and active supporters was not limited to Gujarat.

The period between 1993 and 2001, however, saw a complete transformation of this trend. Gujarat became a 'laboratory' of Hindu nationalism. The limits of the state's tolerance of organised, one-sided attacks against religious minorities, particularly Muslims but also Christians, were pushed farthest in Gujarat. The extent to which the authorities and the society at large endorsed Hindutva's primary objectives – the physical and economic destruction of Muslims and their spatial and sexual segregation from non-Muslims – was also unparalleled elsewhere in India. Ahmedabad was one of the places where Gujarat's experiments with the Hindu right's political, social and cultural goals were most actively pursued. The success of these experiments ultimately paved the way for the worst anti-Muslim massacre in the history of independent India, and bestial sexual violence against Muslim women during the deadly summer months of 2002. The following sections examine how Ahmedabad came to be identified locally, nationally and internationally with horrific violence and minority persecution at the dawn of the twenty-first century.

Removing secular impediments

Since the late 1980s, one of the most important goals of the Hindutva network had been to enable the BJP to come to power in Delhi and in as many states as possible. The Ramjanmabhoomi agitation, the involvement of Hindu cadres and senior BJP leaders in the destruction of the Babri Mosque, and the wave of communal violence across India were supposed to help the BJP gain nationwide electoral appeal. In fact, however, these events had just the opposite effect. On the advice of Prime Minister P. V. Narasimha Rao, the president dismissed all four BJP state governments in India for their involvement in the events, and called fresh elections in 1993. These were the governments of Madhya Pradesh, Himachal Pradesh, UP and Rajasthan. Since the BJP was a coalition partner in the Gujarat government, it was not dismissed. The national government did not stop at these dismissals: on 17 December it imposed a ban on the RSS, VHP and Bajrang Dal, and two Islamic parties, the Islamic Sevak Sangh and the Jamaat-e-Islami Hind, for their roles in the destruction of the mosque and the riots that ensued. The Ministry of Home Affairs published notifications declaring the bans in all the main national newspapers.[35] Although these organisations remained active at the grassroots level, the ban forced them to soften their rhetoric and refrain from activities that might result in violence.

The national electorate also came down equally heavily against the BJP for inappropriately politicising Rama and religious devotion during the Ramjanmabhoomi agitation (Udaykumar 2005: 165). Compared with the 1990 assembly elections, in 1993 the party's tally declined from 219 to 116 seats out of a total of 320 in Madhya Pradesh, and from 44 to 8 seats out of 68 in Himachal Pradesh. In UP, where Hindutva's very aggressive posture had left numerous riots in its trail, the electorate voted for the party in only 176 of 422 constituencies, as opposed to 211 in 1991. The party retained power in Rajasthan, albeit with a narrow margin, due to the 'moderate, relatively secular leadership of Chief Minister Bhairon Singh Shekavat' (A. Basu 1996: 68).

Constrained by the bans and bruised by the electoral rejections, Hindutva leaders redoubled their efforts to capture state power. Gujarat was one of the states where their pursuit of state power was successful. The BJP had managed to win the AMC elections in 1987, and had become a coalition partner in Chief Minister Chimanbhai Patel's Janata Dal government in 1990. However, the party struggled to remain in power. In under a year, the coalition split, but the Janata Dal managed to retain its hold on government by securing the support of the Congress in the Gujarat legislative assembly. The government lasted until Chimanbhai Patel's sudden death in 1994, which left Gujarat without clear leadership (Spodek 2011: 236). Extensive corruption and criminalisation marred state politics, with the death of Chimanbhai Patel plunging the Janata Dal–Congress coalition into chaos. The lack of an effective opposition, and extensive communal mobilisation, however, reaped spectacular electoral rewards for the BJP. Further, inter-party defections had weakened the ideological differences between the Congress and the BJP, the former wavering between a 'softer' version of Hindu nationalism on the one hand, and secularism on the other.

Amid this political vacuum, the BJP seemed to be the only party with an ideological focus. In the 1995 Gujarat elections, the BJP received 43 per cent of the vote share, and doubled its seat tally between 1990 and 1995 to 121 of 182 seats, reducing Congress to a mere 45 seats. The party also swept the sub-assembly polls. In the 1995 district panchayat elections, the BJP won 599 of 772 seats (up from 62 out of 683 seats in 1987), leaving the Congress with only 111 (down from 492 seats in 1987) (Yagnik and Sheth 2005: 270). It also prevailed in the six municipal corporations of the state with 395 seats, leaving the Congress to settle for a mere 37. In March 1995, Keshubhai Patel, an RSS volunteer, was appointed Chief Minister of the first independent BJP government in Gujarat. Aggressive pursuit of electoral victory by the Hindutva network had also been partially successful at a pan-Indian level. In the 1996 parliamentary elections, the BJP won 160 of the total 537 contested seats, whereas the Congress won 136.

However, in Gujarat, cracks were beginning to appear within the BJP itself: the party's old guard was beholden to the hard-line ideology of the RSS, whereas those who had joined in the 1980s and 1990s preferred a relatively moderate stance. Moreover, rivalries between ambitious politicians within the party were undermining internal discipline. These tensions came to a head when Shankersinh Vaghela, a former RSS volunteer and veteran Gujarat BJP leader, challenged Keshubhai Patel's leadership, paving the way for the appointment of a compromise candidate, Suresh Mehta, as Chief Minister in October 1995. When the latter failed to prove his majority in the Gujarat legislative assembly, president's rule was imposed on the state between September and October 1996.

In the interim, Shankersinh Vaghela defected from the BJP and established his own Rashtriya Janata Party. With support from the Congress, he was appointed Gujarat Chief Minister between 1996 and 1997. This coalition also collapsed, and Vaghela joined the Congress. Indeed, party politics in Gujarat was in such flux in the 1990s that the state saw as many as seven Chief Ministers between 1990 and 1998. Meanwhile, the Congress's decision to allow former RSS volunteers and BJP leaders such as Shankersinh Vaghela to join its ranks further undermined the party's credibility. Now, in terms of ideology and leadership, little separated the Congress from the BJP. Fed up with the Congress's lack of political focus and direction, Gujarati voters gave a clear mandate to the BJP in the 1998 assembly elections. Since then, the BJP has won every consecutive election in the state.

Hindutva mobilisation in an era of liberalisation

Liberalisation created new economic opportunities for Gujarat in industries such as salt, caustic soda, fertilisers, petrochemicals and diamond polishing, enabling Ahmedabad to recover from the loss of the once all-important textile industry (Government of Gujarat n.d.). However, the new industrial enterprises were unable to absorb the city's burgeoning labour force. Between 1990 and 2001, Ahmedabad's population grew 22 per cent, from 2.9 million in 1991 to 3.6 million in 2001 (Gayer and Jaffrelot 2012: 49). Although the overall poverty rate declined marginally from 33.5 per cent in 1987–88 to 31.7 per cent in 1993–94 (Mahadevia 2002: 4854), a primary survey of 1,000 households in the city revealed that 64.8 per cent of male workers and

70.2 per cent of female workers were employed in the unorganised sector of the economy in 1998–99.[36] Consequently, the overwhelming majority of Ahmedabad's workforce did not have permanent jobs, or access to the minimum wage or employment benefits (ibid.: 4853). The rise in the cost of transportation, amenities, health care and education only heightened economic insecurity (ibid.: 4856).

The opening up of the economy also triggered an expansion of the private sector, where reservation policies did not apply. These policies constitutionally guaranteed Scheduled Castes and Scheduled Tribes 14 per cent and 7 per cent, respectively, of seats in Parliament, state legislative assemblies, public sector jobs and government-funded educational institutions. Since the majority of the members of these socially marginalised communities in Ahmedabad were, like Muslims, working-class or poor, these policies had been an important facilitator of upward mobility for them (Breman 2004: 88, 124). Now this source of opportunity was slipping out of their reach.

Overcrowding and the deterioration of living conditions in large parts of the walled city and the industrial areas in eastern Ahmedabad made life harder still. While in 1976 slums accounted for 30 per cent of the total number of houses in the area covered by the AMC, by the end of the 1990s this number had risen to 44 per cent (AMC 1985, 1: 69).[37] Often devoid of basic amenities, these slums housed low-wage workers and the urban poor. People who worked in small-scale industries or did other menial jobs in suburban industrial areas such as Naroda were accommodated in similar slum housing. Since most of these houses were constructed illegally, workers lived under the constant threat of eviction by the government, and were often forced to acquiesce to the local slum landlord to ensure their protection.

Meanwhile, wealthier upper castes, some affluent Muslims and low and backward castes moved west of the Sabarmati river. While millions of people lived in squalor and without the most basic necessities of life in eastern Ahmedabad, residents of western Ahmedabad availed of world-class educational and vocational institutions interspersed with shopping malls, cinemas, cultural centres and restaurants. However, the rapid accumulation of wealth and urbanisation was accompanied by a sharp rise in conspicuous consumption, alienation, and disengagement from the political and social life of the city (Spodek 2011: 233–4). So when Hindu outfits organised religious festivals and requested donations for their activities, middle-class Ahmedabadis responded enthusiastically and generously. By doing this, they could alleviate the guilt associated with ostentatious consumption, and cope with the loss of the closely knit community life still prevalent in rural areas.

With the trend of rising economic uncertainty and social insecurity now in its fourth decade, Hindu nationalist organisations found ever-greater opportunities to mobilise backward and low-caste communities and Scheduled Tribes against Muslims. The RSS, VHP, Bajrang Dal, Durga Vahini and their educational wings Vidya Bharati (India's Knowledge) and Shishu Mandir (Children's Temple) sought to address the material concerns of Scheduled Castes and other backward communities by providing medical aid, education and jobs. Simultaneously, they offered opportunities for social mobility and inclusion by recruiting and training cadres in shakhas, organising religious festivals and building temples in slums in the industrial areas of Ahmedabad.[38] The Vanvasi Kalyan Ashram (Hermitage for the Well-Being of Forest Dwellers) and the VHP carried out similar work with tribals and low- and backward-caste communities in the northern and southern districts of Gujarat.[39]

Active communal mobilisation was both a product of and a precursor to further spatial segregation along religious lines. Already by the early 1990s, 'borders' had been drawn between Muslim- and non-Muslim-dominated neighbourhoods; the destruction of the Babri Mosque and the 1992 riot further intensified the reordering of social space. Out of fear, ever larger numbers of Muslim families moved to Juhapura, which had already come to be known as 'mini-Pakistan', in the south-western part of the city. Some Muslim families moved to Vatva, which had developed rapidly as a Muslim enclave in the 1990s, in south-eastern Ahmedabad. Rashida Bano and her family, who, despite their experience of the 1969 and 1985 riots, had continued to live in the mixed neighbourhood of Rakhial until 1992, were one such family to relocate to Vatva. According to Rashida, 'After Babri, home, neighbourhood, environment everything was separated. We also moved to a "Muslim area". Hindus also sold their property and bought houses where only Hindus lived' (interview, Ahmedabad, 29 November 2007). Increasingly, VHP-erected boards proclaiming Hindu-dominated areas as Hindu 'rashtras' inscribed religious homogeneity within neighbourhoods.

Rising socio-economic insecurity and spatial segregation in the 1990s translated into a phenomenal rise in the membership of various outfits affiliated to the Hindu right. For example, the national membership of the low-caste-dominated Bajrang Dal grew from approximately 32,000 in 1991 to around 1.5 million by 1999 (Atkins 2004: 39). Indeed, Haresh Bhatt, the central VHP vice-president in Gujarat, boasted that by the late 1990s, the Bajrang Dal had one activist for every 2,000 people in India, as well as offices at the district, taluka (a sub-division of a district) and village levels.[40]

Converting popular support for Hindutva into votes for the BJP was one of the primary goals of the RSS, the VHP and the Bajrang Dal. To that end, the VHP organised several mass rallies across Gujarat between 1993 and 1995. The VHP's hard-line female leader Sadhvi Rithambara led one such rally in Ahmedabad's Bapunagar region in February 1995, where she called on voters to 'throw the anti-Hindu Congress into dustbins' and vote for the BJP (Chaudhary 1995: 145). Over 200,000 people turned up to cheer her. For its part, the BJP, in its 1995 election manifesto, promised to free voters' lives of 'fear' (presumably, at least in part, fear of the imaginary Muslim 'enemy'), 'hunger' (a careful manipulation of the economic insecurity of the urban poor), and 'corruption' (of the Congress) (BJP 1995). To drive home its agenda, the party promised employment to 150,000 retrenched mill workers, and civic amenities for the poor. It also appealed to the social anxieties of low- and backward-caste voters by claiming that the BJP was committed to bringing them into the 'Hindu fold'. The party especially appealed to poor Scheduled Caste, Scheduled Tribe and backward-caste women by promising a gift of Rs 5,000 along with *mangal sutras*,[41] and by pledging to organise religious festivals for them.

Infiltration of the state machinery

Following the appointment of the first BJP government in Gujarat in 1995, the Hindutva network set about appointing committed or at least compliant supporters of its ideology to critical posts in the administration and within the police (Yagnik and Sud 2004). One of the beneficiaries of the network's drive to place supporters in the state machinery was Dr Maya Kodnani. Kodnani came from a staunch RSS family from the Banaskantha district of Gujarat, and had attended two officer training camps of the Rashtriya Sevika Samiti (interview,

Ahmedabad, 10 November 2007). In 1995, she contested and won the election in the Naroda constituency of the AMC – the industrial suburb in which the worst instances of sexual violence took place in 2002.

The infiltration of Hindutva supporters at all levels of government in Gujarat emboldened activists who wanted to pursue their anti-Muslim activities without fear of government, police and judiciary. This renewed confidence manifested itself in the BJP's more explicit embrace of Hindutva as its main political mission in 1996: 'Hindutva is a unifying principle, which alone can preserve the unity and integrity of our nation. It is a collective endeavour to protect and re-energize the soul of India, to take us into the next millennium as a strong and prosperous nation'.[42] The Gujarati mouthpiece of the RSS, *Sadhana*, explained what this reinvigorated Hindutva meant for religious minorities: 'Muslims cannot look to the police for protection anymore. They can live safely only if they maintain amicable relationships with Hindus'.[43]

The confidence of Hindutva activists grew considerably in 1998 when the BJP once again won the assembly elections (winning 117 of 182 seats) and, equally importantly, formed a coalition government in Delhi. Atal Bihari Vajpayee, a staunch RSS supporter and veteran party worker who had attended the 1968 mass rally in Ahmedabad (see Chapter 1), was sworn in as India's Prime Minister. Keshubhai Patel remained Gujarat's Chief Minister. Now the BJP was in power both in Gujarat and in the national capital, and RSS volunteers were at the helm. No longer afraid of the state, the Hindutva movement's bellicosity in Gujarat reached unprecedented heights from 1998 onwards. The events that occurred over the next few years bore intimations of the horrors that the state, especially Ahmedabad, was to witness in the summer of 2002.

One-sided offences against minorities

In 1998, the VHP and Bajrang Dal set up a special Hindu Jagran Morcha (Forum for Hindu Awakening) to organise a mass propaganda campaign. The aim of this campaign was to promote an illiberal political-social order wherein religious minorities (especially Muslims but also Christians) would be expelled from society altogether; the caste hierarchy would be preserved; and the patriarchal familial arrangement would be reinforced. The design of this campaign took into account the different class- and caste-based sensibilities of the 'Hindu majority'.

The propaganda, which was aimed at the affluent upper castes, contained three interrelated ideas: Muslim men were seducing and forcing Hindu women into marriage; these forced alliances threatened to decrease the proportion of Hindus in India's population; and in order to prevent Hindus from becoming a minority in India, it was important to 'protect' Hindu women and destroy the Muslim community through an economic boycott. Familiar Hindutva tropes were used to drive home these messages. Muslim men were depicted as treacherous polygamists, who were supposedly committed to converting Hindu women to Islam and increasing the Muslim population by having numerous children. An illustrated VHP pamphlet entitled 'Warning Campaign' (Figure 3.1), for example, described to its readers how a Muslim man beguiled a Hindu woman by adopting a Hindu name. He married her and converted her to Islam. Later he took a second wife, breaking his promises to the first and threatening to sell her. The pamphlet also warned Hindu women that marriage to a Muslim man would mean having to bear seven children. It called on Hindu women to 'awaken' and be cautious.

Yet simply regurgitating such old Hindu nationalist ideas about the sexual threat ostensibly posed by Muslims would have been a weak ploy. Readers had to be convinced that Muslims posed a realistic and immediate threat to the Hindus of Gujarat and Ahmedabad. To that end, on the reverse of the pamphlet were published fictitious stories about such incidents having occurred all over Gujarat (see Figure A1, Appendix). Characters were given common names, and incidents were anchored in plausible circumstances and real places:

> [...] a Muslim driving instructor seduced a Hindu millionaire's daughter and kidnapped her [...]
>
> [...] a man pretending to be Raju [a common Hindu name] beguiled a young Hindu woman graduate. Only after getting married she realised that she was now trapped in Muslim hands [...]
>
> [...] a Muslim man running a shop of beauty products seduced his customer, a Hindu woman [...]
>
> [...] a Muslim man deceived a Hindu woman, Sonal, that he has a bungalow and a good job. After marrying her, he kept her in a slum in Gomtipur. Sonal managed to escape and returned home.

Figure 3.1 VHP's 'Savadhan Campaign'

(Male labelled as 'Iqbal Bhai, alias Paresh') Female: Hey Ram! He said he was Hindu but he turned out to be a Muslim!!

Male: Keep quiet! You are going to be sold off. Female: First you promised to keep me like a princess. (Arti became Ayesha)

If a Muslim man trapped me, then today this is what my condition would be!!!

Hindu women awaken!! Be cautious!

Source: Vishwa Hindu Parishad, Ahmedabad, 1998.

Such pamphlets sought to increase hostility against Muslims and encouraged Hindus to boycott the community. They also propagated the notion that educated, middle-class Hindu women were incapable of independently maintaining their sexual virtue, and required parental control. Simultaneously, these campaigns discouraged Hindus from purchasing services (such as driving lessons and goods) from Muslims, and discouraged women from seeking physical mobility (through driving, for instance), or making independent choices with regard to their marriage.

Having relayed the nature and extent of the Muslim 'threat', the pamphlets appealed to 'Hindu Mothers-Fathers' to take reparative action. They called on Hindu parents to approach the police or the VHP, Bajrang Dal and Durga Vahini, and to ask them to retrieve the girl in case their daughters fell into the Muslim 'trap'.[44] In fact, in 1998, Bajrang Dal leader Babu Bajrangi set up a special outfit for just this purpose. Called the Navchetan Group (Organisation for a New Awakening), its main mission was to 'recover' women from inter-caste and inter-religious marriages. In its widely circulated publicity material, the group consoled parents that 'in case your daughter forgets your home and society then Navchetan Group will talk some sense into her on your behalf for free' (see Figure A6, Appendix).[45] In exchange for such 'free' services, the group called on Hindu parents to assist in the work carried out by the Hindu right, because 'if one Hindu became a Muslim or a Christian', Hindu numbers would go down, and more importantly the 'Hindu community would have one more enemy'.[46]

This propaganda gained social traction because it manipulated the gender-, caste- and religion-based anxieties of middle-class Hindus. In the alienating urban environment, parents could no longer count on arranging a 'perfect' marriage for their daughters (i.e., one involving a groom from their own religious, class and caste background), or on keeping modern influences (such as 'love marriages') out of their homes. Deviance from the traditional social order was so deeply unacceptable to some families that they complained to women's organisations. The Jyoti Sangh was one such port of call. For the first time since its inception in 1933, the organisation started receiving 'complaints' about love marriages and love affairs; the first such complaints were received in 1998. Jyoti Sangh received five such complaints between April 1998 and March 1999, two the year after, seven between April 2000 and March 2001, and one the following year.[47] Others sought the support of Babu Bajrangi's Navchetan Group. In 2007, the group's founder boasted: 'Nine hundred and fifty-seven – that's how many Hindu girls I have saved. On average, one girl married to a Muslim produces five children. So, in effect, I have killed 5,000 Muslims before they were born'.[48]

Preparing Hindu foot soldiers

While the affluent sections of the population constituted the financial and moral backbone of the Hindutva movement, poorer and lower-income Scheduled Castes, Scheduled Tribes and OBCs comprised its foot soldiers. No longer under state pressure to tone down their rhetoric or to avoid violent activities, the Hindu right aggressively pursued the work of preparing these groups for combating the 'Muslim threat', and defending the Hindu community, Hindu religion and Hindu women. This preparation entailed circulating virulent anti-Muslim propaganda, training foot soldiers and organising special ceremonies for distributing weapons across Gujarat, including the cities of Ahmedabad, Vadodara,[49] Surat,[50] and the Dangs district (Human Rights Watch 1999).[51]

As in the previous three decades, the Hindu right tried to mobilise these communities by manipulating their economic and caste-based insecurity. One set of pamphlets encouraged these groups to boycott Muslims economically. For example, a pamphlet entitled 'Victory to Mother India' encouraged 'Hindutva lovers to awake' and made the following appeal:

> Do not buy anything from Muslims
> Do not sell them anything
> Do not use any thing or item made by them
> The reason for this is that Muslims are merciless, brutal, thankless, and cunning.
> (See Figure A5, Appendix)

The other set of materials called on these communities to stay within the Hindu fold despite their low-caste status, and not to convert to Islam or Christianity. The reason given for this was that a diminution of the Hindu population would result in sexual violence against 'their' women. Circulated by the VHP, Bajrang Dal and the Hindu Jagran Morcha, these pamphlets described how 'Christian men beguile Adivasi "Hindu" women in order to convert them',[52] and warned them about the rise in the Christian and Muslim populations and plummeting Hindu numbers (see Figures 3.1 and A2, Appendix). Citing the case of Muslim-majority Bangladesh, one such pamphlet carried explicit warnings about the risks facing Hindus:

> Do you know what will happen if Hindus become a minority? 15,000 families (1 lakh men and women) will become homeless [. . .]
> 200 mothers-sisters will be raped. Daughters will be raped in front of their mothers [. . .]
> Hindus will be killed and their homes will be looted [. . .]
> Women will be stripped, paraded naked and gang-raped [. . .]
> in Muslim majority nations Hindus cannot live in safety [. . .]
> Hindu community should unite and put an end to these atrocities and protest against such behaviour. Indians awake! Indians awake![53]

The strategic replacement of 'Hindus' with 'Indians' served to project religious minorities as foreigners, and interpret violence against them as the patriotic duty of low-caste and tribal communities. At the same time, the explicit mention of acts such as gang-rape and stripping, absent in the Hindu right's propaganda until the late 1980s, served to instigate pre-emptive actions of a similar kind.

Hindutva activists were also tasked with undertaking the sexual surveillance of women to combat the 'threat' of Muslims. Bajrang Dal members, for example, were asked to keep a watch on Scheduled Caste girls and Muslim boys in their schools and slums. Their task was to ensure that low castes did not convert to Islam or Christianity; to intervene if Muslim boys got 'too close' to Hindu girls; and more generally to ensure sexual-religious segregation, by force if necessary. Mohan Macwan, a youth leader of the Bajrang Dal from Gomtipur, explained:

> VHP people came to the chawl and told people that they should make sure your girls don't speak with Muslim boys [. . .] this used to happen in the school as well. I had a teacher who was in the VHP who used to keep an eye on Hindu girls and Muslim boys of the

school. He used to make sure that Dalits don't convert to Christianity. If he suspected that one of us might convert, he would ask us to talk some sense into him, tell him not to convert, speak with him, and warn him of the dangers of conversion. If a Hindu girl spoke with a Muslim boy, or met him regularly, then he would intervene and say that this should not happen. The girl was given stern warnings. If a Muslim boy spoke with a Hindu girl, or met her or fell in love with her then we would warn him. Even if there was no love, it was bad enough. In one case a Muslim boy was beaten up for talking to Hindu girls. (Interview, Ahmedabad, 20 October 2007)

Indeed, this sexual surveillance is believed to have led one Scheduled Caste family in Naroda to murder their daughter for bearing a Muslim man's child (Qaumi Ekta Trust et al. 2000: 9–10). In western Ahmedabad, the Hindu right's student wing ABVP started attacking women wearing 'western dress', ostensibly to 'protect' them from Muslims (Engineer 2003: 16; Ghatwai 1998).

In addition to preparing Hindutva's foot soldiers ideologically and asking them to perform surveillance at the neighbourhood level, the VHP and Bajrang Dal prepared them physically for their cause. They organised several ceremonies from 1998 onwards to impart training and distribute weapons. One such ceremony was organised in the industrial area of Maninagar on 15 September 1998 (see Figure A4, Appendix). At this ceremony, the VHP and Bajrang Dal presented tridents to the recruits in order to prepare them to

protect the nation and Mother India [. . .]
wage a strong protest against people who insult the Hindu community [. . .]
protect the Hindu religion and Hindu civilisation [. . .]
protect mothers and sisters [. . .]
confront anti-national forces [. . .][54]

State indifference and complicity

The state machinery, extensively infiltrated by Hindutva supporters, did nothing to curb such propaganda or to arrest Hindutva leaders for distributing weapons. On the contrary, it legitimised their activities by changing state policies. For example, the government explicitly endorsed Hindutva rhetoric concerning the supposed threat that Muslim men posed to the sexual chastity of Hindu women, by setting up special police cells to monitor inter-religious marriages. Although this move was unconstitutional, Gujarat home minister and BJP leader Haren Pandya justified it by stating that such marriages were not made out of free choice but were forced on Hindu women for ulterior motives.[55] Moreover, the director general of police (intelligence) sent special circulars to police departments across the state to monitor the activities of Muslims and Christians and collect information about them.[56] The Gujarat administration had become directly involved in maintaining what it believed was the 'correct' sexual order in society.

While the government advanced the ideological agenda of the Hindu right, the police offered impunity. It did not apprehend the producers and circulators of this hate propaganda, even though the VHP, Bajrang Dal and Hindu Jagran Morcha frequently published the names of the printers along with the addresses and phone number of their local offices. Moreover, the government did nothing to reproach the vernacular media when the latter violated the law by occasionally reproducing such pamphlets in full.

Emboldened by the support of the government and the police, Hindu nationalist activists intensified their violent attacks against religious minorities from 1998. Between 1998 and 1999, no less than 40 instances of violence against Christians and Muslims were reported across Gujarat (Forum against Oppression of Women and Awaaz-e-Niswaan 2002). Unlike in previous decades, incidents of communal violence during this period were one-sided offensives against Muslims and Christians.[57] In December 1998, VHP and Bajrang Dal activists led brutal attacks on Christians in the south-eastern Dangs district (Human Rights Watch 1999). The violence continued unabated for over 10 days after 25 December, and affected more than 15 villages. Notably, when Prime Minister Atal Bihari Vajpayee visited the Dangs, he did not reproach the government and the police for failing to protect religious minorities. Instead, he called for a national debate on inter-religious conversions.[58]

Ahmedabad was far from immune to the violence. Between November 1997 and August 1998, violence against Christians was reported from the industrial suburb of Naroda, where schools run by missionaries were vandalised.[59] There were similar attacks in western Ahmedabad on property owned by St Xavier's Social Service Society, a missionary body that provides health and education services in Ahmedabad's slums.[60]

From 1999, violence against Muslims in Ahmedabad increased rapidly, as did the government's unwillingness to respond.[61] In July 1999, the situation in the city became particularly tense in the wake of India's conflict with Pakistan over Kargil. One of the casualties of the Kargil War was Mukesh Rathod, a soldier who hailed from Meghaninagar in Ahmedabad.[62] Lal Krishna Advani, by then union home minister in the BJP-led National Democratic Alliance government at the centre, escorted the body of the slain soldier to the city.[63] Between 7 and 11 July, Advani, along with BJP MLA Harin Pathak, led mass rallies across the city and delivered provocative anti-Muslim speeches questioning the loyalty of Muslims to the country. The youth wing of the BJP, Bharatiya Yuva Morcha (Indian Youth Platform), painted provocative slogans, ostensibly targeted at Pakistan, on the walls of Muslim-dominated areas in the walled city, such as Vadigam. Meanwhile, the VHP and Bajrang Dal incited violence against Muslims. Several intelligence reports were submitted to Gujarat home minister Haren Pandya about the activities of these organisations. However, the government did not take any preventive steps.[64]

Anti-Muslim violence broke out on 20 July 1999. The immediate catalyst for the violence was a Muslim protest in the walled city, against the harassment of a mentally challenged Muslim boy by Hindu men. A clash ensued which soon developed into a 'free-for-all'.[65] Within hours, Dariapur, Kalupur, Saraspur, Gheekanta, Dabgarwad and Vadigam in the walled city were engulfed by violence. Armed mobs, reportedly led by leaders of the VHP, Bajrang Dal and BJP, attacked Muslims, burnt their homes and looted their property. A curfew was finally imposed and the violence brought to a halt.[66] On 21 July, however, violence erupted in Karanj, Gomtipur and Shah Alam in the industrial belt, Jamalpur in the walled city and in Paldi on the western side of the river. The curfew was extended to these areas to bring the violence under control.

The beginning of the twenty-first century was marked by more mobilisation and anti-Muslim violence in Ahmedabad. In the first week of January 2000, the RSS organised a massive *sankalp shibir* (resolution camp) in several parts of the city, including Naroda.[67] Over 30,000 people, including 5,000 government officials, participated in the camp, where

Hindu activists reaffirmed their commitment to the Hindutva cause. Here, the RSS pledged to open shakhas in every village in Gujarat by 2005, while the government provided transport, subsidised land and other municipal services such as electricity and water for the camp. Chief Minister Keshubhai Patel and Union Home Minister Lal Krishna Advani along with eight other ministers of Gujarat were among the participants.[68] In the same week, the Gujarat government lifted the 14-year-old ban on government officials joining the RSS, although it had to reinstate the ban a month later due to widespread condemnation of the decision. It cancelled most non-Hindu holidays and attempted to make subscription to the RSS mouthpiece, *Sadhana*, compulsory for schools.[69]

By 2000, violence over trivial issues such as cricket matches, parking spaces, rickshaw fares and the consumption of meat also rose, in line with the close alignment of large segments of the Gujarat government, police and society with the Hindu right's agenda. Ahmedabad's police commissioner P. C. Pandey likened the communal situation in Ahmedabad to 'sitting on a powder keg'.[70] The proverbial keg exploded in August 2000 after Lashkar-e-Taiba militants gunned down 33 Hindu pilgrims visiting the Amarnath shrine in northern India. As the news reached Gujarat, VHP general secretary Pravin Togadia declared on 1 August, 'we will avenge these attacks here' (i.e., in the state) (CCT 2002, 2:149). On 3 August, VHP and Bajrang Dal activists announced a Gujarat-wide strike to mourn the deaths of the 33 pilgrims and the 100 others who had died in the crossfire between the army and the militants.[71] According to a report by a citizens' tribunal:

> For the next ten days, the law and order machinery was held to ransom, as gangs of the RSS/VHP/BD [Bajrang Dal] led by elected representatives of the BJP destroyed Rs. 15 crore worth of Muslim property in Surat, Ahmedabad, Khhedbrahma, Lambadiya, Rajkot, Porbander and other Gujarat cities. Not a rupee in compensation was paid to any of the victims. Leaders and activists of RSS/VHP/BD figure in the FIRs of the police, yet no action has been initiated against them. (CCT 2002, 2:149)

Yet again, the violence started in Naroda, where the VHP, Bajrang Dal and the latest member of Gujarat's Hindu nationalist network, the Shiv Sena, had set up their main headquarters.

Meanwhile, Hindu activists led several campaigns to evict Muslims forcefully from mixed neighbourhoods in western Ahmedabad. In February 2000, the houses of two Muslim families, who had recently moved into Tulsi Apartments in the Paldi area, were vandalised (Engineer 2001). Allegedly led by BJP corporators, the attackers demanded that the families leave their homes or face dire consequences. Several other Muslim families of the area were told by VHP–BJP leaders to sell their houses and move out. Not only did the police not intervene, Deputy Commissioner of Police Bisht rationalised the violence by stating that 'this being a Hindu-dominated area, the locals got angry at the entry of two Muslim families. It's as simple as that'.[72] Similar evictions took place in the industrial suburb of Naroda, where 60 Muslim families (out of a total of 200) were forced to evacuate their property (Qaumi Ekta Trust et al. 2000: 9–14).

Attacks by al-Qaeda militants on the World Trade Center in New York on 11 September 2001, and the subsequent intensification of anti-Muslim sentiments across large parts of the world, afforded Hindu nationalists an opportunity to insert their agenda into a wider international narrative about terrorism. False statements such as, 'Every Muslim is not a terrorist, but every terrorist is a Muslim', became a part of the rhetorical repertoire of the Hindu right, especially the VHP.[73] This made curbing the 'Muslim threat' a pressing priority for two concurrent projects: establishing a glorious Hindu nation-state, and creating a safer global order.

Backlash and BJP response

By the end of 2000, the government had lost all control over the aggressive activities of Hindu cadres. Activists of the VHP and Bajrang Dal were extorting money from rich Hindu businessmen under the pretext of providing security from Muslims, and forcing the local government to protect temples.[74] They harassed Hindu families who wished to marry their children into Muslim families, and pressured them to retrieve their daughters 'trapped by Muslim men' (Engineer 2003: 16; see also Ghatwai 1998). Meanwhile, the ABVP repeatedly attacked middle-class girls wearing non-traditional clothes on university campuses in western Ahmedabad (International Initiative for Justice 2003: 182, Annexure V).[75] Violence against religious minorities had increased so markedly that Gujarat drew attention from civil rights groups both within India and abroad (such as the US-based Human Rights Watch).[76]

These aggressive actions, however, created a crisis of legitimacy for the incumbent Keshubhai Patel-led BJP government. It lost voters and elicited strong international and national rebuke. The party incurred major losses in the 2000 district panchayat elections. It won only 192 of 717 seats, and lost the 407 other seats it had won in 1998 to the Congress. The Congress registered a convincing victory, winning 513 seats (Yagnik and Sheth 2005: 270). However, the BJP managed to retain the AMC. In order to recover from these dismal results, the party replaced the so-called ideological moderates with hard-liners. In 2001, Chief Minister Keshubhai Patel was ousted and replaced by Narendra Modi, a former RSS pracharak. It was Modi's responsibility to defend 'the Hindu faith' and win the 2003 Gujarat elections (G. Patel 2002: 4833).

Following the arrival of Modi at the helm of Gujarat's government, the VHP restarted the Ramjanmabhoomi agitation in November 2001 with support from BJP leaders (International Initiative for Justice 2003: 155, Annexure I). The RSS, VHP and Bajrang Dal organised special ceremonies to arm their volunteers with swords, knives and tridents. The Bajrang Dal alone recruited over 300,000 people and distributed 400,000 tridents and knives among its activists.[77] Special camps to train people in the use of these weapons and other firearms were organised across the state (CCT 2002, 2:36–7). The groundwork for the 2002 massacre was being laid.

The massacre

The anti-Muslim massacre of 2002, an indelible scar on India's democratic history, followed a major tragedy that occurred on 27 February. On that day, the S6 compartment of the Sabarmati Express en route to Ahmedabad from Ayodhya was stoned and incinerated by a mob in Godhra, a small town some 100 miles east of Ahmedabad. At least 55 passengers – 16 men, 25 women and 14 children – were burnt to death; three more succumbed to their injuries a day later.[78] Most – though not all – of the dead were karsevaks returning after participating in the Ramjanmabhoomi movement in Ayodhya. Within hours, Chief Minister Narendra Modi, flanked by several cabinet ministers and BJP MLA Maya Kodnani, arrived in Godhra to inspect the site. Modi made a public broadcast describing the incident as a 'pre-planned, violent act of terrorism' (Bunsha 2002).[79] Union Home Minister Lal Krishna Advani went a step further, implicating Pakistan's Inter-Services Intelligence in the violence, even though there was no evidence to suggest the involvement of the agency or any other Pakistani state institution (CCT 2002, 2:17).

As the electronic media brought graphic and disturbing images of charred bodies and the incinerated train into people's homes in Ahmedabad and elsewhere in the country, public sentiment became increasingly sensitive. Modi, keen to generate political capital from these heightened sensitivities, insisted on bringing the charred remains to Ahmedabad for funeral rites, rejecting explicit warnings by Godhra's district collector not to do so (CCT 2002, 2:17).[80] The bodies of the 58 passengers were driven in a special cavalcade to Sola Hospital in the city, where a crowd of 500 VHP activists greeted them with slogans such as 'Long live the karsevaks' and 'Long live Hindu unity'. Thereafter, the Godhra victims were accorded a martyr's honour. The same evening, VHP general secretary Praveen Togadia, implying that the event was a calculated Muslim attack against Hindus, declared: 'Hindu society will avenge the Godhra killings. Muslims should accept the fact that Hindus are not wearing bangles. We will respond vigorously to all such incidents'.[81] Togadia's reference to bangles, a type of jewellery usually worn by women, suggests that for him the response to the violence in Godhra was to be a test of Hindu masculinity.

Most observers concur that the Godhra tragedy and its political manipulation sparked 'Gujarat 2002'. However, there is still considerable dispute over how the Godhra incident occurred in the first place, and why it should have sparked the massacre. Some observers argue that a mob of Muslim men torched the train compartment after karsevaks shouted provocative slogans and harassed Muslim women at the Godhra railway station (Jagori 2002: 4).[82] However, according to the official commission of inquiry led by Justice U. C. Banerjee, the fire on the train was an accident. Still others, especially senior leaders of Islamic organisations, suspect that the tragedy was a carefully executed conspiracy to stir anti-Muslim violence across the state with a view to winning the 2003 Gujarat elections (interview with S. Madani, state president of the Jamaat-e-Islami Hind, Ahmedabad, 20 November 2007). Historian Howard Spodek has advanced a similar explanation. According to him, 'the 2002 pogrom was not just a reaction to Godhra. It became part of the electoral campaign of the BJP and of its institutional allies, the RSS and the VHP' (2011: 261). In Spodek's view, the party had been factionalised between the so-called moderates and hard-liners, and was struggling to ensure good governance. It therefore 'accepted' pogroms as a way of securing victory in the imminent state assembly elections, due no later than March 2003 (ibid.).

Over a decade later, there is still no consensus on the causes of the Godhra incident, and the immediate motivations behind the 2002 massacre. Given the political significance of both these events (especially the latter), it is unlikely that such a consensus will ever emerge. Nonetheless, one fact is indisputable. Within 24 hours of the Godhra tragedy, Muslim men, women and children were made targets of horrific violence in large parts of Gujarat, especially its northern and central districts. According to Additional Director General of Police R. B. Sreekumar's deposition to India's Election Commission in August 2002, at least 151 towns and 993 villages were affected by the violence, covering 154 of Gujarat's 182 electoral constituencies.[83] The violence claimed the lives of up to 2,000 Muslims, and dozens of Muslim women suffered brutal sexual atrocities (Human Rights Watch 2002: 4). Gendered violence was so extreme, and its perpetration seemed so systematic, that a Citizens' Tribunal, formed in 2002 to conduct an independent inquiry into the violence, and led by former Supreme Court judge V. R. Krishna Iyer, spoke of a 'gory and military precision [...] evidence of some sick minds and a vicious ideology' (CCT 2002, 2:39).

Instigation: Familiar methods, new context

From the very first day of the 2002 massacre, as will be described in what follows, Hindu nationalist organisations and their allies incited Hindu men to inflict sexual violence against Muslim women. Their method for doing this was reminiscent of the 1969 riot. The propaganda began with the circulation, via the vernacular media, of imaginary stories of sexual attacks by Muslim men on Hindu women. Only this time the stories were published by *Sandesh*, one of the two most widely circulated Gujarati dailies, rather than its smaller afternoon edition. Moreover, these stories were markedly more inflammatory and crude than their 1969 equivalent.

On 28 February, *Sandesh* carried an article on its front page, alongside graphic images of the burnt S6 train compartment and charred bodies. The story read: 'Along with karsevaks of Sabarmati Express, children and ladies were massacred and fanatic miscreants dragged away some 10−15 ladies from the compartments, which has made the position of Godhra very tense'.[84] The same day, the police claimed that upon investigation, this account was found to be fictitious (Citizens' Initiative 2002: 80). Disregarding police findings and the press code of conduct, *Sandesh* carried a follow-up on 1 March. Entitled, 'From among those abducted from Sabarmati Express two dead bodies of Hindu girls found near Kalol in mutilated state', the article claimed: 'As part of a cruel inhuman act that would make even a devil weep, the breasts of both the dead bodies had been cut. Seeing the dead bodies one knows that the girls had been raped again and again, perhaps many times. There is speculation that during the act itself the girls might have died'.[85]

Sandesh retracted the story a couple of days later, but by then it was too late. From the morning of 28 February itself, photocopies of *Sandesh*'s front page were being circulated in Ahmedabad and the Panch Mahals,[86] and the story had acquired a life of its own. In some versions, Muslim men were alleged to have dragged women from the train into mosques and gang-raped them, while in others, the victimised Hindu women were identified as belonging to low-caste or tribal communities (Citizens' Initiative 2002: 80).

Once stories about Hindu women's sexual victimisation had been spread, Hindutva propaganda unhinged the Godhra events from their local and historical context and inserted them into a fabricated history of Muslim atrocities. It also invoked the dark history of Partition. For instance, in a pamphlet circulated by the VHP, the state leader of the organisation Chinubhai Patel exhorted:

At the time of the partition [. . .] [Muslims] went around shouting 'Allah-O-Akbar', 'Pakistan Zindabad!' and 'Kill the non-believers!' while carrying sticks, swords, knives and lighted torches, raped lakhs of Hindu mothers, sisters and daughters and killed them. To preserve their virginity many women jumped into wells or into fires [. . .]

In Pakistan the status of the Hindus is not just second class –
they are slaves there and that is going to happen to the Hindus in
India [. . .]

The Godhra incident is just one symptom of the cancer in this
country. This cancer is only the trailer – the entire film is still to
be seen.[87]

Yet, unlike in 1969, organisations such as the VHP called on
Hindutva's foot soldiers not only to defend their community and their
women, but apparently to annihilate Muslims altogether. These
changes reflected the increased assertiveness of Hindu activists in
Gujarat by 2002, and their confidence in the BJP government's ability
to provide their activities with a cover of impunity. One of the
pamphlets aimed at Scheduled Caste and backward communities
exclaimed:

We do not want to leave a single Muslim alive in Gujarat. The
people of villages as well as cities have now woken up and they are
ready to take an eye for an eye [to respond to stones with bricks].
To avenge murder [revenge for blood with blood] we will kill
Muslims wherever we see them [. . .]

Now the Hindus of the villages should join the Hindus of the
cities and complete the work of annihilation of Muslims. The
Muslims who consider the architect of Bharat, Baba Ambedkar, to
be an untouchable, do not know that they are not even fit to be his
footwear [. . .] All Hindu brethren are requested to destroy
Muslims without being afraid of any politician.[88]

Despite the wholly criminal content of such pamphlets and their
incendiary potential, the police did little to quell their circulation, or to
arrest their producers. Unlike in 1969, the commissioner of the
Information Department of the Gujarat government made no effort to
rebut the claims of sexual violence against Hindu women, or to establish
a special telephone line to disseminate correct information. Even though
the VHP often published the names of its leaders and the addresses of
their offices on these handouts, the government remained indifferent,
ordering neither the bureaucracy nor the police to take any preventive or
corrective measures.

However, the people who read such propaganda were anything but indifferent. Consider the testimony of Krishna Parmar, who identified himself as a Dalit member of the Bajrang Dal. He participated in the violence in rural Ahmedabad:

The RSS, VHP and Bajrang Dal have reached everywhere. They had told us so many stories that Muslims marry four wives, they rape and abduct Hindu women. In front of the youth, this issue is going to hurt the masculine pride very badly [...] this is not a small matter. If Muslims kidnap a Hindu girl, it is a big thing [...] On the 28th in areas where the RSS was not active, the newspapers took the information of what happened in Godhra. On reading this news, even people who were not ideologically with them, also joined them. They said, 'Gosh! Muslims have done this to our people [...] it is just like the Partition'. So the RSS people incited us saying that we have to take revenge on their women. They said that we must act otherwise India will become an Islamic Rashtra and the biggest weapon Hindus have to counter this threat is *rashtrabhakti* [devotion to the nation]. To prove this devotion, we must get rid of Muslims [...]

We had to prove our masculinity to them. If you break a man's arms and legs he will be temporarily weakened but that injury will heal over time. But if you rape his mother or sister then that injury will never ever heal. He will die bit-by-bit every day. (Interview, Ahmedabad, 20 October 2007)

Persecution with state complicity

Having provided the ideological motivation, leaders of Hindu nationalist organisations contributed to the perpetration of sexual violence by providing organisational leadership to the attackers. They mobilised foot soldiers, armed them and, as we will see in what follows, led them during attacks against Muslims.

In orchestrating sexual and other forms of violence against Muslims, the Hindu right received the support of a vast section of Ahmedabad's population. Many upper-caste, middle-class men and women, who had gradually gravitated towards Hindu nationalism since the 1960s, either condoned the violence or justified it as a necessary 'lesson' to the Muslim community. Some of them even participated in the violence by looting

Muslim shops situated in the affluent areas of the city (Bunsha 2003; CCT 2002, 2:31). The profile of the perpetrators of physical violence in 2002 was similar to that in 1969: Scheduled Castes, OBCs and some middle-class, upper-caste men. Yet there was a new entrant: Scheduled Tribe men (especially the denotified Chara tribe), who had been armed and mobilised by the VHP, the Bajrang Dal and their allies in the late 1990s and early 2000s. They killed and mutilated Muslim men, women and children, gang-raped Muslim girls and women, some as young as three, burnt them alive or dead to obliterate the evidence, and looted and destroyed Muslim homes and property. During the 1969 riot, sexual violence against Muslim women had constituted a symbolic subversion of the Congress's political and economic strategies, and an assertion of the sexual-religious power of various Hindu class and caste groups. By contrast, in 2002, attacks against Muslims and their property were conceived as symbolic affirmations of a political order characterised by an overt embrace of militant Hindu nationalism.

In order to understand how Hindutva foot soldiers were mobilised to inflict such violence, consider the case of the Gomtipur mill district. Home to daily-wage Scheduled Castes and Muslims, Gomtipur is located in the industrial region in eastern Ahmedabad. Several neighbourhoods in this region had witnessed brutal sexual violence against Muslim women during the 1969 riot. During the 1985 riot, however, Kshatriyas, Scheduled Castes and Muslims forged strategic alliances with one another in neighbourhoods where Muslims were a minority, in order to protect their own and each other's lives and property. The area had witnessed repeated bouts of communal violence throughout the 1990s, when Hindu nationalist leaders were aggressively mobilising unemployed Scheduled Caste youths from this region against Muslims. As a result, like most other neighbourhoods in the industrial region, Gomtipur was extensively segregated along community lines before the 2002 massacre began.

Violence started in Gomtipur on 1 March 2002. On that day, 260 Muslim homes were looted and burnt in Salatnagar and 200 each in Khokhara Housing Society, Soneni Chawl, Janata Nagar, Gafoor Basti and Ansar Nagar.[89] One of the men who participated in the attack on 1 March was Mohan Macwan who, as mentioned earlier, had joined the Bajrang Dal in the late 1980s. He explains how he was mobilised to participate in the violence:

On the 28th [of February] one of the members of the VHP came and collected all of us. He told us about what had happened in Godhra and said our people have been burnt [...] Muslims did this and that to our people. He asked, what do you think? Do you think what happened in Godhra was right? People collected on the roads and the atmosphere got very tense. No one went to work. He said that Muslims have been attacking us for hundreds of years, now we must teach them a lesson.

Later VHP leaders came to our *basti* [neighbourhood] and gave us weapons and told us that they will protect us in case police catches us or if there is any other problem [...] they said don't worry about anything. I also went to kill people [...] We thought that if we will kill Muslim men then their population will not reduce. But if we kill and rape women then it will. Even before the riot started, if a burqa-clad Muslim woman passed by, VHP men who socialise with us would challenge us and say 'if you are a man, then grab her [...] show us you have the guts to misbehave with her,' and we would. They told us that a Muslim woman is a thing to be enjoyed and gradually over time it got ingrained in our minds that this is a Muslim woman and such things should be done to her.

My grandfather used to say that during the reservation agitation [in 1985] Muslims had helped Dalits [...] they gave us food and protection. He said that the upper castes, together with the police attacked Dalits. Several others like my grandfather tried to reason with us and told us not to go out and do this. But we did not listen to him. No one listens to elders anyway. [Muslims] think we are eunuchs. We knew if we don't go out, Muslims would burn everything. They had done so much in Godhra we simply had to go out and do something. So we told our elders, you do what you have to do and sit at home. You don't even need to come out of the house. We will do whatever needs doing. We told them keep your mentality to yourself, we will go out. We are men, and we will ensure security. (Interview, Ahmedabad, 20 October 2007)

This testimony reveals how VHP leaders mobilised low castes by inserting the Godhra tragedy into an imaginary history of Muslim atrocities against the Hindu community, and by insisting on avenging those alleged crimes. Since distinctions between past and present atrocities allegedly committed by Muslims were blurred, any Muslim could be substituted for any other as a target of violence. Ostensibly on behalf of the entire Hindu community, Hindu men sought to prove that they were not 'eunuchs', and to 'teach a lesson' to their historical Muslim enemy. In order to prove their masculinity and avenge wrongs allegedly committed by Muslims for 'hundreds of years', men such as Mohan were also prepared to inflict sexual violence against Muslim women. Partly, they were prepared because they did not perceive sexual violence as a wholly criminal activity. After years of indoctrination, such violence had become for them a legitimate means of sexual gratification: 'a Muslim woman is a thing to be enjoyed'. Mohan's testimony also demonstrates the long-running Hindu anxiety about the 'burgeoning Muslim population'. Indeed, it appears that by 2002, the anxiety had deepened so considerably that Mohan did not see the killing of Muslim men as sufficient to solve the problem; only the rape and killing of Muslim women would do. To accomplish these aims, he was willing to disregard his own immediate family's experiences of the 1985 riot, when Muslim neighbours gave them food and protection. Mohan was now part of a much larger but ultimately imaginary Hindu family, whose members needed to prove that 'we are men'.

Once the foot soldiers had been mobilised and instigated to inflict sexual and other forms of violence against Muslims, Hindu nationalist organisations distributed more weapons among their activists. In a sting operation conducted by intrepid journalist Ashish Khetan in 2007, several VHP and Bajrang Dal leaders described how this was done. (The Central Bureau of Investigation in 2009 authenticated Ashish Khetan's audio-visual recordings, which were made secretly with a camera on his laptop.) Haresh Bhatt, vice president of the Bajrang Dal in 2002 and later BJP MLA from Godhra, described how the cadres were armed:

I have my own gun factory [...] I used to make firecrackers [...] We made all the bombs there [...] Diesel bombs, pipe bombs, we made them there [...] and we used to distribute them from there as well [...] We ordered two truckloads of swords from Punjab [...] right here, in a village called Dhariya, we readied everything there [...] and then we distributed the *samaan* [material] [...] At that time, the only thing was that the samaan was needed [...]

We distributed so many weapons that people were shocked to see how many there were [...] We would make them here and then test them.[90]

Many commentators have argued that these organisations received active support from sections of the government, bureaucracy and police in orchestrating the violence – not just in Ahmedabad but across Gujarat. After coming to power in 1998, the BJP seems to have placed special emphasis on installing compliant officers across the state apparatus. In Ahmedabad city itself, senior state BJP ministers – Minister of Urban Housing I. K. Jadeja and Minister of Health Ashok Bhatt – allegedly stayed in the police control room for several days, and interfered with police work (Khetan 2011). Although the army had arrived in Ahmedabad as early as 28 February, it was not provided the decisive instructions and support it needed to halt the violence in a timely fashion. The supply of voters' lists and tax lists to popular vernacular newspapers such as *Gujarat Samachar* and *Sandesh*, which published them in full, allowed Muslim homes and properties to be identified for attack.

The police were passive as Muslims were massacred; in some cases available data suggest that some police personnel may even have participated in the violence. Several VHP and Bajrang Dal leaders proudly narrated to Ashish Khetan stories about the assistance they received from the police. Anil Patel, VHP leader, for example, stated:

From time to time [...] there were some policemen we were in touch with [...] They would come and take the *samaan* and deliver it safely to the places it was supposed to go [...] The police here gave us so much support [...] Some even said, do something [...] loot them, break them, finish them.[91]

It is important to note that not all police officers were complicit in the violence. Several officers discharged their duties during the massacre by preventing violence within their jurisdiction, registering cases by Muslims and arresting culprits. However, many such officers seem to have been unceremoniously transferred to less consequential posts subsequently. Praveen Gondia, deputy commissioner of police, Zone IV, Ahmedabad city, was one such officer. During the massacre, he registered first information reports against prominent BJP and VHP leaders for their role in the violence. Apparently as a punishment for this, in April 2002 he was transferred to civil defence – the arm of the police department that ensures security in the event of a hostile attack against India by a foreign power. Similar transfer orders were given to police officials in several districts of Gujarat, including Banaskantha, Bharuch, Kachchh and Bhavnagar (Mazumdar and Menon 2003: 407–8). It is because of such acts of omission and, in some alleged instances, commission, on the part of certain members of the Gujarat government, the bureaucracy and the police, that 'Gujarat 2002' has been described by many observers as a 'state-sanctioned' massacre and not a 'communal riot'.[92]

Some trace the complicity of the state in the 2002 massacre all the way to the top leadership of the Gujarat government, including Modi himself. According to the report of the Citizen's Tribunal, established in 2002 for independently probing the massacre, Modi (together with at least three cabinet colleagues), 'instructed senior police personnel and civil administrators' that a 'Hindu reaction' to the burning of the Sabarmati Express in Godhra 'was to be expected and this must not be curtailed or controlled' (CCT 2002, 2:76). Zakia Jafri, who has been fighting a legal battle since 2006 seeking justice for the killing of her husband Ehsan Jafri during the 2002 massacre, has made similar allegations against Modi. Notably, in a special leave petition to the Supreme Court in 2008, Jafri claimed that, at a special meeting called by Modi at his residence on 27 February 2002, he gave orders to senior civil servants and government officials to go 'soft' on reprisal killings against Muslims.[93]

Jafri's claim was corroborated in 2010 by an Indian Police Services officer Sanjiv Bhatt, who was the deputy commissioner (intelligence) of the Gujarat Bureau of Investigation from December 1999 to September 2002. Bhatt was responsible for dispatching information to the various intelligence agencies and the army when the Godhra tragedy occurred. In his testimony to the Supreme Court-appointed Special Investigation Team (SIT), Sanjiv Bhatt explained that by virtue of the post occupied by him, late at night on 27 February he participated in the meeting where:

The Chief Minister Shri Narendra Modi said that the bandh call had already been given and that the party [the BJP] had decided to support the same, as incidents like the burnings of Kar-Sevaks at Godhra could not be tolerated. He further impressed upon the gathering that for too long the Gujarat Police had been following the principle of balancing the actions against Hindus and Muslims while dealing with the communal riots in Gujarat. This time the situation warranted that Muslims be taught a lesson to ensure that such incidents do not occur ever again. The Chief Minister Shri Narendra Modi expressed the view that emotions were running very high amongst Hindus and it was imperative that they be allowed to vent their anger.[94]

In 2012, the SIT, in its final report, confirmed that such a meeting had in fact taken place. However, on the grounds of insufficient corroborative evidence, it rejected Bhatt's allegation that Modi had ordered state officials to allow Hindus 'to vent their anger'.[95] In December 2013, a metropolitan court in Ahmedabad upheld the SIT's report, rejecting Jafri's protest petition against it.[96] Since Jafri intends to take her plea to higher courts,[97] questions regarding Modi's direct complicity in the 2002 massacre had not been conclusively answered when this book went to press. Regardless, one fact is indisputable: his government failed to prevent the massacre of Muslims, and some sections of his administration actively facilitated the violence through acts of commission and omission.

The Naroda tragedy

In Ahmedabad, sexual violence in the form of verbal abuse and intimidation was reported from Amraiwadi, Bapunagar, Danilimda, Behrampura and Vatva in the eastern industrial area. The geography of the violence replicated the pattern of the 1969 riot: Hindu activists did not attack Muslim-majority areas such as Juhapura in south-west Ahmedabad and Dariapur in the walled city. Instead, they targeted Muslims living on the fringes of mixed neighbourhoods. In the affluent Paldi area, in the western part of the city, the houses of the few Muslim residents, including the house of a retired Gujarat High Court judge, were attacked with the support of local VHP leaders and, allegedly, the police.[98] However, higher-class status appears to have had the affect of deterring Hindu activists from inflicting sexual violence upon Muslim women in Paldi. This claim cannot be made with certainty, since affluent

Muslim families did not seek refuge in relief camps in the aftermath of the 2002 massacre, as a result of which the experiences of wealthy Muslim women could not be recorded.

By far the worst forms of sexual violence against Muslim women in Ahmedabad were inflicted by Hindutva foot soldiers in the industrial areas of Naroda Patiya and Naroda Gaon. Therefore, the following discussion focuses on these areas to demonstrate how Muslim women were victimised during the carnage. Located along the eastern periphery of the city, these neighbourhoods are part of the Naroda constituency, which also includes Gulbarg Society and Gopinath Society. Home to migrant labourers from Maharashtra, Delhi and Karnataka, Naroda Patiya and Naroda Gaon had a substantial Scheduled Caste, Schedule Tribe and OBC population. Nearly 2,000 Muslim families earning daily wages also lived in the area, and depended on the nearby diamond cutting and polishing factories for their livelihood. Middle-class Patels, who lived in apartments in the Gulbarg and Gopinath Societies, dominated the constituency.

Like most parts of the eastern industrial region, Naroda Patiya and Naroda Gaon were extensively segregated along religious and caste lines before the carnage began. As discussed earlier, the VHP and the Bajrang Dal had actively mobilised Scheduled Castes, Scheduled Tribes and backward castes against their Muslim neighbours, and had orchestrated violence against religious minorities between 1998 and 2001. The constituency had become such a Hindutva stronghold that BJP leader Maya Kodnani won the AMC elections in 1995, and the Gujarat assembly elections in 2000, from Naroda with a convincing majority. The city's VHP and Bajrang Dal leadership resided in this area.

Around 9 a.m. on 28 February, a rumour spread in the Naroda area that Hindus were going to attack Muslims to avenge the Godhra tragedy. Most telephone lines had been snapped, and the supply of electricity and water to the area was temporarily suspended. By 10.00–10.30 a.m., a mob of 25,000 men, many of them wearing saffron headbands (frequently worn by Hindutva foot soldiers) and khaki shorts (the uniform of RSS volunteers) surrounded the neighbourhood. The people who constituted this mob were RSS, VHP and Bajrang Dal members from Naroda's slums and the neighbouring Gopinath and Gangotri Societies (Human Rights Watch 2002: 17–18; see also Citizens' Initiative 2002: 105). Armed with swords, tridents, spears, chemicals, petrol cans, kerosene bombs, gas cylinders, firearms and, in some instances, copies of *Sandesh*, the men arrived shouting slogans such as 'Burn the Muslims alive' and 'Victory to Lord Ram'. Bajrang Dal leader Babu Bajrangi (head of the Navchetan Group discussed earlier in this chapter), and BJP MLA from Naroda Maya Kodnani, were the leaders of the mob. According to Ashish Khetan's reports, 'Kodnani drove around Naroda all through the day, urging the mob to hunt Muslims down and kill them' (Khetan 2007b). Kodnani has since been convicted for her role in the violence, together with Babu Bajrangi.[99] Jaideep Patel, VHP general secretary, was also allegedly leading the Naroda rioters.

At first the mob threw stones, gas cylinders and crude bombs at Muslim houses and incinerated vehicles owned by Muslims. Then a massacre of Muslim men, women and children began. Petrol was poured into the mouths of children as young as six and matchsticks were lit, setting them on fire. Men and women were beaten and mutilated. Terrorised Muslim residents ran to the police station and pleaded with the police and the SRPF,[100] stationed less than 300 metres from the neighbourhood, for protection. Instead of ensuring their safety, Police Inspector K. K. Mysorewala fired tear-gas shells and told them, 'Go away, I have no orders to save you'.[101] Frantic calls made to the police headquarters and the office of the commissioner of police went unanswered. As Muslims, many of them women, tried to flee the area, some police constables redirected them towards Gopinath and Gangotri Societies, where a mob of several thousand was waiting for them. The Muslim residents were now caught between the high walls of the society buildings, the police and the mob.

Over the next 18 hours, the mob, composed mainly of Hindutva supporters, killed at least 100 Muslims, and subjected Muslim women to extreme sexual violence. One of the victims was Zarina, who was 25 years old in 2002. Her husband, Naimuddin Ibrahim Sheikh, whose family had migrated from Karnataka to Naroda in 1971, narrated his wife's harrowing experience:

It started at 9 am on February 28. That's when the mob arrived, shouting, 'Mian Bhai nikalo' ['Bring out the Muslims']. Many of them were wearing kesari chaddis [saffron shorts or underwear]. The mob included boys from the neighbouring buildings –

Gopinath Society and Gangotri Society. I ran out of my house with the entire family – mother, father, sister, sister's daughter, wife Zarina, my brother, my sister-in-law, and my niece [...] there were 11 of us. We all ran towards the police *chowki* [checkpost]. The police said, 'Go towards Gopinath and Gangotri'. In the melee, I was separated from my wife. What happened to her she told me later. She tried to escape the mobs by leaping over a wall. But found herself in a cul-de-sac. They [g]ang-raped her, and cut one arm. She was found naked. She was kept in the civil hospital for many days. (Citizens' Initiative 2002: 77)

Evidence of the active connivance of the police in the infliction of sexual violence emerges from numerous other survivors' testimonies as well. Witnesses reported that the police and the SRPF refused to defend and protect Muslims, instead facilitating the violence by directing them towards mobs of up to 5,000 heavily armed Hindu activists who massacred Muslim men, women and children over several hours with impunity. Consider the testimony of Jannat Sheikh, who lived in Kumbhaji Ni Chawli in Naroda Patiya. On 28 February she lost eight members of her family, of whom two were killed after being raped:

It was morning and I was cooking. My husband, my three children and I were in my house while my mother-in-law, brother-in-law and his wife with their three children were in the adjoining house. A mob of 5000 came and we started running. We were cornered from all the sides. SRP personnel were also chasing us. It was 6.30 in the evening by now. The mob caught hold of my husband and hit him on his head twice with the sword. They threw petrol in his eyes and then burned him. My sister-in-law was stripped and raped. She had [a] three-month baby in her lap. They threw petrol on her and the child from her lap was thrown in the fire. My brother-in-law was hit on the head with the sword and thrown in the fire. We were at that time hiding on the terrace of a building. My mother-in-law was not able to climb the steps so she was on the ground floor with her four-year-old grandson. She told them to take away whatever money she had but to spare the children. They took away all the money and jewellery and burnt the children with petrol. My mother-in-law was raped too. I witnessed all this. Unmarried girls from my street were stripped, raped and burnt. A 14 year old girl was killed by piercing an iron rod in her stomach. All this ended at 2.30 A.M. The ambulance came on the scene and I sat in it along with bodies of my husband and children. I have injury marks on my both my thighs and left hand that was caused by the police beating. My husband had 48 per cent burns, my daughter 95 per cent burns. Both my husband and daughter died in the hospital after three days. The police was on the spot but helping the mob. We fell at their feet but they said they were ordered from above not to help. Since the telephone wires were snapped we could not inform the fire brigade. (Citizens' Initiative 2002: 107)

Jannat Sheikh's chilling testimony sheds light on the organised and methodical nature of the violence in Naroda. The Hindu activists were well armed and inflicted brutal violence upon Muslim families, including aged women and young children. Muslims were looted, and then killed with arms such as swords and iron rods, and burnt with petrol. Sexual violence against women and girls appears to have been inflicted in a systematic manner, involving stripping, rape, mutilation and immolation to obliterate evidence.

The testimonies of other survivors also reveal that the perpetration of gory sexual violence against Muslim women, including girls between the ages of 12 and 16, was a widespread feature of the Naroda massacre. Kulsum Bibi, who lived in Jawan Nagar in Naroda Patiya before the massacre, told a women's group that:

The mob started chasing us with burning tyres after we were forced to leave Gangotri Society. It was then that they raped many girls. We saw about 8–10 rapes. We saw them strip 16-year-old Mehrunissa. They were stripping themselves and beckoning to the girls. They raped them right there on the road. We saw a girl's vagina being slit open. Then they were burnt. Now there is no evidence. (Citizens' Initiative 2002: 75–6)

Amina Appa, resident of Hussain Nagar in Naroda Patiya, similarly witnessed the rape and murder of several friends and neighbours:

Between Kalupur station and Naroda Patiya, I could see a crowd
stretching endlessly. All I could see were heads and more heads
everywhere. They seemed to be countless in number, maybe about
15,000. I could identify them as Bajrang Dalis, members of
Vishwa Hindu Parishad, because of their leaders who are known
members of these organisations and their saffron headbands. And
local people belonging to the Chara community [...]

That terrible day, I was hiding with some others on the roof of
my house. From there, I saw my dearest friend Kauser Bano
[resident of Pirojnagar, opposite Noorani Masjid, Kumbhajini
Chawl, Naroda Patiya] raped, her unborn baby slashed out from
her womb before being tossed into the fire to be roasted alive.
Thereafter, she too was brutally cut up and torched. She was 9
months pregnant. Kauser had a slight deformity on her upper lip,
which I had helped her rectify at the Civil Hospital. It was her
dream to get married and have a baby.

There is not a single woman resident of Hussain Nagar whose
dignity was left intact. They were all raped, cut to pieces and burnt
[...] Our women and children were denied even the possibility of a
decent burial.[102]

The men who perpetrated this violence against Muslims were
not faceless strangers in many cases, but the neighbours of their victims.
The testimony of Qudsiya, who lost her mother and sister in the carnage,
shows how 28 February marked the abrupt termination of all
neighbourhood ties. This is what she shared with me about that day:

That Bhavani [a neighbour] said come here, I am making rice and
kadhi [an Indian curry] for all of you. We cook rice and kadhi when
someone dies. Why was he cooking that while we were still alive?
My mother used to tie a *rakhi*[103] to that Bhavani [...] every year.
When on Id we would slaughter a goat and cook meat, she used
take some meat and feed him. When the riot started here, she
pleaded with him [...] she said that I am sure I will die, but keep
my young daughter. She is young and unmarried, save her. I am
sure I will die but at least protect my daughter. Don't protect me
but please give my young, unmarried daughter refuge in your
house. But he cut them with his sword there and then and burnt

them alive [. . .]

People who used to say that you are like my sister and you are like my mother, raped them that day. (Interview, Ahmedabad, 12 December 2007)

Unlike large parts of Ahmedabad, Naroda was a mixed colony: Muslims lived separately but in close proximity to Hindus. Qudsiya's testimony reveals how her family had established fictive kin ties with their Hindu neighbours over the years by participating in each other's festivals, such as Rakhi and Id. However, the day the mob attacked Naroda Patiya, these ties were abruptly terminated and replaced by hatred for Muslims.

Indeed, the perpetration of violence by neighbours, with whom the victims had had longstanding everyday ties, was an abiding feature of the 2002 massacre. Several other survivors knew the names of the Hindu activists who gang-raped Muslim girls. Azharuddin, who was 13 years old in 2002 and lived in Jawan Nagar in Naroda at the time, reported to a women's right group:

I saw Farzana being raped by Guddu Chara. Farzana was about 13 years old. She was a resident of Hussain Nagar. They a put a saria [rod] in Farzana's stomach. She was later burnt. 12 year old Noorjahan was also raped. The rapists were Guddu, Suresh and Naresh Chara and Haria. I also saw Bhawani Singh, who works in the State Transport Department kill 5 men and a boy. (Citizens' Initiative 2002: 76)

Outside Ahmedabad, where sexual violence took place, most of the victims recognised at least some of the perpetrators. A survey of Dahod and Panch Mahals districts found that in over half the incidents, Hindu neighbours of Muslim victims participated in the attacks (Raza and Hashmi 2002: 16). In a similar study of the violence in Sabarkantha district, a victim, on being asked whether she recognised the assailants, responded: 'Of course I can recognize them. I saw them everyday. I grew up with them' (Citizens' Initiative 2002: 89).

Suresh Chara, a Bajrang Dal member, was one of the men who engaged in sexual violence in Naroda. In his conversation with Ashish Khetan, he had this to say about his actions on 28 February:

When thousands of hungry men go in, they will eat some *fruit* or the other [...] in any case the fruit are going to be crushed and thrown away [...] Many Muslim girls were being killed and burnt to death anyway, some people must have helped themselves to the fruit. Might even have been more [...] then there were the rest of our brothers, our Hindu brothers, VHP people and RSS people. Anyone could have helped themselves, who wouldn't, when there's fruit? The more you harm them, the less it is. I really hate them [...] don't want to spare them. Look, my wife is sitting here but let me say [...] the fruit was there so it had to be eaten. I also ate [...] I ate once [...] Just once [...] then I had to go killing again [...] [About the girl he had raped] that scrap-dealer's girl [...] Naseemo [...] Naseemo that juicy plump one [...] I got on top [...] properly [...] then I pulped her [...] made her into a pickle.[104]

From this account, it is clear that the boundaries between sex and sexual violence, between human being and object, between a desirable sex object and the object of pathological hatred, were blurred in Chara's mind. For him, women's bodies were non-sentient pleasurable objects ('fruits'), which could be appropriated for sexual gratification. This understanding led him to perceive sexual violence against Muslim women as an erotic experience. He rationalised this sexual victimisation by insisting that the quest for 'sex', even when it requires brute force, is a natural male entitlement, and it is inevitable for men to act on these impulses: 'When thousands of hungry men go in, they *will* eat some fruit or the other [...] *who wouldn't, when there's fruit?*' The willingness to act on these 'impulses' was buttressed by Chara's deep hatred for Muslims and his desire to force himself on his victim; the violence enabled him simultaneously to humiliate the Muslim male 'enemy' and sexually gratify himself.

The confluence of these two ideas motivated several other men like Chara to perpetrate sexual violence. Some of the men who gang-raped Muslim women during the massacre were reported to have said, 'use her as much as you want now, we won't get her tomorrow'.[105] Others, including some policemen, referred to Muslim women as 'coloured TVs'[106] – an expensive but much-desired commodity in most households. Thus, Muslim women were viewed as expensive sexual commodities otherwise unavailable to Hindu men for the purposes of sexual gratification. This may have been related to the Hindu nationalist idea that Muslim women were hypersexual, or 'a thing to be enjoyed', as Mohan Macwan described them.

The alleged police connivance in the perpetration of sexual violence in Naroda was apparently not limited to facilitating rioters to inflict such violence. As in the case of the 1985 riot, testimonies from 2002 indicate that some police officers also seem to have themselves engaged in sexual violence against Muslim women, unzipping their trousers before them, hitting them with batons in their private parts and shouting sexual obscenities at them. Consider the testimony of Farida, a Muslim woman who lived in Behrampura before the massacre and was in her early 30s in 2007. She was one of the women who testified to having suffered sexual violence at the hands of police officials, and witnessed such actions being inflicted by rioters against others:

> During 2002 I saw [sexual violence] in front of my eyes. [Hindus] had captured me too. They hurled abuses at us, stripped in front of us, in front of me. The police also stripped in front of us [. . .] they hit us in such *kharab* [bad/wrong] places that I can't even tell you. And in Gomtipur in front of the fire brigade they cut a woman's breasts and removed all her clothes. But then some Muslim people came and saved her and took this woman away [. . .] In 2002, this has happened a lot [. . .] some 300 and 350 women were raped. Some women talk about this, some don't, so many died. (Interview, Ahmedabad, 8 December 2007)

Although Ahmedabad had witnessed extreme sexual violence against Muslim women during the 1969 riot as well, the events of 2002 were unprecedented, due perhaps to what many observers have alleged was the active complicity of large sections of the state apparatus, especially the police, in facilitating such violence. There is little evidence to suggest that police officials actively raped or mutilated Muslim women during the massacre; their criminal activities in this regard seem to have been restricted to verbal abuse, sexually intimidating behaviour and beating women in their private parts. However, this violence may have enhanced the impunity with which rioters raped, gang-raped, mutilated and killed Muslim women. Coupled with the ideological direction and organisational support provided by BJP politicians and state officials such as Maya Kodnani, such police connivance would have created a uniquely permissive environment for Hindu nationalists to pursue their belligerent anti-Muslim agenda.

Celebrating and Condoning Violence

In the aftermath of the massacre, the confidence of Hindu activists in 'their own government' manifested itself in public acceptance and an unprecedented celebration of the violence they had committed during the massacre. The most illustrative and disturbing example of this is a pamphlet called 'Jehad', which was circulated in Ahmedabad (cited previously in the Introduction to this volume):

> The people of Baroda and Ahmedabad have gone berserk
> Narendra Modi you have f****d the mother of miyas {Muslim men}
> The volcano which was inactive for years has erupted [...]
> We have widened the tight vaginas of the 'bibis' {Muslim women} [...]
> She was f****d standing while she kept shouting
> She enjoyed the uncircumcised penis.
> With a Hindu government the Hindus have the power to annihilate miyas.[107]

While anonymously published pamphlets such as 'Jehad' venerated extreme sexual violence – a glorification bordering on a dark, almost pathological obsession with Muslim female sexuality – Bajrang Dal and VHP leaders also glorified such actions in private discussions. These views were exposed in the sting operation conducted by Ashish Khetan in 2007. With a secret camera, Khetan made audio-visual recordings of VHP leader Suresh Chara (cited previously) openly rationalising the rape of a Muslim girl, and Bajrang Dal leader Babu Bajrangi proudly expounding on the horrific violence he had committed against Muslim women, men and children. Having boasted about the support he allegedly received from the police, from the Gujarat home minister Haren Pandya and from Modi in carrying out the violence, Babu Bajrangi said:

> It has been written in my FIR {First Information Report} [...] there was this pregnant woman, I slit her open, sisterf****r [...]

Showed them what's what [...] what kind of revenge we can take if
our people are killed [...] I am no feeble rice-eater] [...] didn't
spare anyone [...] they shouldn't even be allowed to breed [...]
I say that even today [...] Whoever they are, women, children,
whoever [...] Nothing to be done with them but cut them down.
Thrash them, slash them, burn the bastards [...] Hindus can be
bad [...] Hindus can be bad, and I'm saying that because, as I see
it, Hindus are as wicked as those people are [...] Many of them
wasted time looting [...] *Arrey*, [the idea is] don't keep them alive
at all, after that everything is ours.[108]

Other Hindu nationalist leaders in Gujarat have usually been more
cautious in their public discussions about sexual violence. While some
denied that such violence had occurred at all, others implicitly condoned
it. Rashtriya Sevika Samiti *pracharika* Sandhya Tipre, for example,
claimed that no Muslim woman had been raped during the 2002
massacre. Indeed, for her such violence could never occur in Ahmedabad,
because 'the good thing about Ahmedabad is that even during a riot, if
there is a single woman, even an auto rickshaw driver will drop you
home safely. They may overcharge you, but they will take you home
safely' (interview, Ahmedabad, 8 December 2007). Indumati Kaddare,
the joint general secretary of Vidya Bharati, a network of schools and
educational institutions run by the RSS, condoned sexual violence as an
almost necessary part of the Hindu struggle against Muslims: 'Even Lord
Ram had slashed out the nose and ears of [mythological female demons]
Tadka and Srupnakha' (interview, Ahmedabad, 12 October 2006).

The documented responses of various Hindu nationalist leaders reflect
their confidence in the ability of the Gujarat state apparatus to protect
the culprits. These responses also reflect their deep commitment to the
Hindutva project and, as in the case of Tipre and Kaddare, awareness of
the risk of legal reprisals associated with the violence committed during
the massacre. This was partly why the two female leaders sought to evade
direct questions during my interviews about how sexual violence had
occurred in Ahmedabad. Instead they offered vague answers that make it
impossible to apportion blame to any particular individual or
organisation. Despite this awareness, however, the 2002 responses
contrast with those advanced by Hindu nationalist organisations in the
aftermaths of the 1969 and 1985 riots, when they apportioned blame for

the violence to Muslims, strongly rejected claims about their own involvement, and were unable to take on the state.

Since 2002, testimonies and evidence regarding the culpability of particular individuals, organisations and institutions with regard to the violence have been bitterly contested in the public sphere and in courts, even as the Gujarat state government has condoned the violence, and in many cases allegedly obstructed formal investigations and perverted the course of justice. In such a context, the Muslims of Ahmedabad have found it increasingly difficult to rebuild their lives. The dark shadow of 2002 still looms large over them. The following chapter interrogates at length the trials and tribulations of the lives of the city's Muslims and the response of the state to 'Gujarat 2002'.

CHAPTER 4

AFTERMATH

'Gujarat 2002' is the most well-known episode of massive communal violence in India, after Partition. Images of large, armed mobs were shown 24 hours a day on national television channels and published by most newspapers, not just during the violence but for long afterwards. Countless media and civil society reports were published containing testimonies of men and women, adults and children who described the gory violence in mind-numbing detail. It was widely known that many Muslim women had been raped, gang-raped and genitally mutilated, and that some of them were as young as three. On the news, politicians and activists lamented how swords, sticks and tridents had been inserted into the vaginas of young girls, and how the heavily pregnant Kauser Bano's stomach had been ripped open with a sword, her foetus removed and thrown into the fire. Those who paid attention were aware that fathers, husbands, grandparents, brothers and uncles had been forced to watch the rapes of the women in their family, and mothers and daughters had witnessed each other being brutally gang-raped, beaten, stabbed and incinerated alive.

Fourteen years have passed since 2002, and during this period Muslims affected by the massacre have seen their lives irreversibly altered. They have suffered the losses of their loved ones and homes, the apathy of the Gujarat administration, and the denial of justice. In this chapter, I track the trials and tribulations of Muslims in Ahmedabad since 2002. The discussion proceeds along three broad lines. First, I examine the period between 2002 and 2003, during which some 100,000 Muslims were forced to live for months in poorly equipped, temporary relief camps across the state. Focusing on Ahmedabad, this section sheds light on a seldom-discussed aspect of life in the relief camps: the fact that some Muslim camp organisers coerced Muslim women into providing sexual services in exchange for basic aid. In discussing this aspect, the chapter examines the responses of civil society activists and Muslim leaders to such incidents.

Second, I delve into the period since 2003, when Islamic organisations took the lead in reconstructing the Muslim community. They established seven relief colonies to house 1,745 riot-affected Muslim refugees. They also pushed for the 'purification' of the Muslim community along more pious and socially traditional lines. While this process resulted in restrictions on women's mobility and life choices, it also created unexpected opportunities for them to flourish as agents of civil society beyond their previously subordinate roles in the family, neighbourhood and community.

Third, I analyse the response of the national government and the Gujarat administration to the infliction of sexual violence during the massacre. Authorities at both levels trivialised or condoned such violence through their rhetoric and practice. Moreover, many observers allege that the state government has obstructed official inquiries into the massacre, thus subverting the course of justice. This has resulted in the denial of justice to all but two victims of sexual violence in 2002.

In this chapter, I do not focus on how Muslim women who suffered sexual violence during the massacre have coped since 2002 at the personal level. I did not wish to undermine the coping mechanisms of such survivors by asking them to recount their experiences or reminding them of their suffering several years later (my field research was conducted between 2006 and 2008). I could not morally justify asking them to relive their violent experiences, or leaving such survivors in a worse emotional state than I had found them. Moreover, my engagement might have engendered expectations of justice and redress. As much as one would like one's contribution to have that impact, I cannot in good faith ignore the realities on the ground. Even though an estimated 150–200 women were raped or gang-raped in 2002, there had been not a single conviction for these offences when I was conducting my fieldwork. Since then the record has improved, but only marginally, with convictions emerging in two cases (more will be said about this in the last section of this chapter). With these factors in mind, I consciously avoided contacting survivors who had suffered aggravated sexual violence during 'Gujarat 2002'. Instead, my focus is on mapping the context within which such survivors are now living their lives.

Relief camps and sexual coercion

From 28 February 2002, Muslims themselves took the lead in organising relief for survivors in Ahmedabad and elsewhere in Gujarat. In the city, the initiative was taken by local strongmen who had the clout, network and financial resources to come forward as guardians of the community. Major shrines, mosques, community centres, school buildings, and even some Muslim cemeteries were temporarily converted into relief camps. In March 2002, there were at least 44 relief camps in the city, offering shelter to at least 66,292 survivors.[1] In the first week of March, NGOs and Jesuit groups formed a collective Citizens' Initiative to offer assistance in the camps. Ad-hoc arrangements were made, with the support of residents of localities close to the camps, to provide food, shelter, clothing, medical aid, psychological support, etc., to the survivors. The necessity of health-care support for survivors of sexual violence, in particular, can hardly be overstated, given that they suffered not only intense psychological trauma, but also major physical health problems, including genital injuries, reproductive tract infections, premature deliveries and miscarrriages (Khanna 2008: 147). Most relief camps lacked even basic facilities such as clean drinking water and sanitation. For example, at Shah-e-Alam, the largest camp in the city, there were only 22 toilets for 2,200 families or 8,000–10,000 Muslims (Citizens' Initiative 2002: 89). Yet such camps were the only refuge available to thousands of displaced Muslims in the scorching summer months of 2002.

The Gujarat government started offering some relief from 7 March in the form of monetary aid and food rations, but neither Chief Minister Narendra Modi nor any of his cabinet ministers visited any of the camps in Ahmedabad or elsewhere until the first week of April. In failing to visit the camps for nearly a month, the government neglected its obligations of governance and disregarded its constitutional duty to provide care to all citizens within its jurisdiction. The administration conveyed through this neglect that it was there primarily to cater to the Hindu majority, not to religious minorities. Modi and some ministers made a visit to the camps in April only to accompany Prime Minister Atal Bihari Vajpayee during his tour of the Shah-e-Alam camp.

By June, the government was keen to show that Gujarat had returned to normalcy and was ready for the assembly elections in December 2002. To that end, it began pressuring relief organisers to dismantle the camps. It discontinued food aid, rendering many camps unable to sustain themselves. It ordered organisers to shift inmates from smaller to larger camps, and pressed false charges against some camp managers under the 2002 Prevention of Terrorism Act (Jassani 2007: 90–9). It also ignored pleas for security, despite repeated attacks on some camps by Hindu nationalist goons. Under these multiple pressures, the number of camps in the city fell from 44 in March to 10 by early June, and that of inmates from over 66,000 to 13,685. Only four major camps remained in the city – Hajj House, Qureshi Hall Jamatkhana and Syedwadi camps in Khanpur (all located in the walled city), and the Jehangir relief camp in Vatva in the industrial area of Ahmedabad. However, these too were closed down in October 2003, leaving hundreds of survivors with nowhere to go (ibid.).

Victimisation in the relief camps: Jamila's story

In the immediate aftermath of the massacre, thousands of Muslims were utterly dependent on the relief camps for their continued survival. Those from poorer backgrounds, in particular, had no choice but to live in the camps for months, and some stayed until all the camps had been shut down in October 2003. As survivors attempted to cope with fear, trauma, and the intensely constrained realities of life in the camps, relief camps became sites for the sexual coercion of some Muslim women. Orphans, widows and those who had lost older male family members were especially vulnerable to repeated demands from camp organisers and other powerful men involved in relief work to give sexual services in exchange for basic aid.

Yet, at the same time, sexual favours became a means through which some Muslim women could negotiate better access to physical protection and material resources for themselves and their families. Consider the testimony of Jamila, who had lived in Ahmedabad's Jamalpur ward in the walled city before the 2002 massacre. Jamila was in her mid-20s in 2007. Immediately after violence broke out in her neighbourhood on 28 February, she and her family sought refuge in the Patrewali Masjid

relief camp in Saraspur (located in the industrial area), which housed 358
families and 1,728 people.[2] They were later transferred to one of the
three relief camps in the walled city that were open until October 2003,
since their home had not been rebuilt. (The name of the camp has been
withheld to protect Jamila's real identity.) Jamila had this to say about
her experience in the camp:

> When we lived in the camp, I restarted my education. I was small at
> the time [. . .] One day, the camp organiser called me, my sister and
> my mother to give us money for our education and books. My sister,
> who had already become an 'offering' in the riot [*dange ka bhog ban
> chuki thi*], was also there. So this *maulana* [Islamic priest] presented
> a proposal to my mother that you have so many daughters, you
> should take full advantage of everything. That maulana even called
> my elder sister for one night. I have such deep hatred for maulanas,
> that I feel angry whenever I see them. And I even know that person
> [the accused] because his father was such a big maulana, that he
> never came before women, he used to stay in *parda* [behind a veil].
> And his son called my mother and my elder sister to come to him
> for one night, in front of me! [. . .] I just knew that this person was
> wrong, so I just left the clothes and books there and returned [. . .]
> even though our house was completely burnt. We had saved
> ourselves from getting raped by Hindu mobs. The mobs had caught
> my sister to rape, but she was saved. We saved ourselves from there,
> but then our own people have left us worthless [*par hamare walon ne
> hi humein kahin ka nahi chhora*]. This has happened. (Interview,
> Ahmedabad, 17 October 2007)

This testimony exposes the acute constraints that some Muslim women
faced in aftermath of 'Gujarat 2002'. On the one hand, they had to cope
with the trauma of losing their homes and of living as refugees in their
own city, as well as the pain and shock of their family's experiences of
sexual and other forms of violence. On the other hand, they had to
navigate the predatory sexual behaviour of men who were tasked with
ensuring their security and well-being. Jamila's testimony sheds light on
both these constraints. In the relief camps, her family had to cope with
the bitter experience of the massacre as well as of being utterly
dependent on the camp and its leadership for sustenance. Although she

made conflicting statements about whether her sister had been raped during the massacre, Jamila's testimony at the very least points to the threat of gang-rape faced by her sister. Within this context of fear, pain and uncertainty, her mother and sister were pressured to exchange sexual favours for aid in the form of books, money for school fees and clothes.

For Jamila, the behaviour of the maulana in the relief camp differed from the acts of Hindu men during the massacre: the former was coercive but subtle, and the latter violent and overt. Instead of overtly making the aid contingent upon sexual favours, the maulana presented a 'proposal' to Jamila's mother and highlighted the 'full advantage' that acceptance would bring to herself and her daughters. As a result, despite the coercion and the abuse of power, his proposal created a minor scope for agency and choice for Jamila's mother. This predicament is reflected in the different words Jamila used to name what had occurred during the massacre and her experience in the relief camps, even though she appeared to be comparing the two. She described the sexual acts threatened or committed by Hindu men during the communal carnage as 'rape' at least once. However, her description of her own and her family's experience in the relief camps – 'our own people have left us worthless' – was more ambiguous, and reflected the constraints within which her mother and her sister had had to make sexual choices. However, the very marginal scope for choice was offset by a profound sense of betrayal, engendered both by the maulana's exploitation of the vulnerability of Jamila's family, and by the hypocrisy of his own religious piety. It is in this context that we must understand Jamila's reference to the asceticism of the maulana's father. The proposal presented by the camp organiser constituted for Jamila a symbolic 'unveiling' of his true nature, and his failure to follow in his own father's footsteps. At a time when Jamila's family needed support and compassion, the maulana became a source of anger and an object of hatred.

Jamila's family was one of many to experience such sexual coercion. Most of the activists I spoke with – ranging from local Muslim strongmen involved in relief to community activists and secular feminists – admitted that such incidents had occurred in several camps. Two activists, who wanted their identity withheld, actually went to the extent of stating that 'some [Muslim] women were raped once during the massacre, but if they stayed in the relief camps for 100 days, they were raped 100 times' (interviews, Ahmedabad, 10 December 2007). Another said, 'My name should not appear anywhere, but yes this has happened' (interview, Ahmedabad, 20 December 2007). However, there were notable exceptions: Alamdar Bukhari, joint editor of *Gujarat Today* and an active and prominent member of the Muslim community in Ahmedabad, denied that such events had occurred in the camps. So did two community workers who were active in the Jehangir relief camp in Vatva.[3] However, the latter did not deny that the potential for sexual coercion existed in their camp: 'We used to organise night vigils to ensure such incidents did not occur'.

These incidents have been absent from the public discourse on sexual violence during 'Gujarat 2002'. This is noteworthy because, even though activists such as those just cited labelled the incidents in the relief camps as 'rapes' (unlike Jamila), and claimed to be aware of their frequency, they failed to mention them in their reports on sexual violence committed during 'Gujarat 2002'.

Activists, community leaders and their politics

During my fieldwork I asked several activists about their reasons for not wanting to raise the issue of sexual coercion in the camps publicly. One of them, let us call her X, said the reason was that she and others like her thought that this was 'an internal matter of the community and they did not wish to politicise it' (interview, Ahmedabad, 20 January 2007).

X's response reflects the dilemma facing activists and Muslim relief organisers. Their concern that the issue of rape in relief camps could get 'politicised' must be understood in the context of the continuing communal climate of the city. As noted in previous chapters, Hindu nationalist propaganda had long demonised Muslims in their propaganda as rapists, and instigated sexual violence against Muslim women by circulating rumours that Muslim men had raped Hindu women. This propaganda reached its crescendo in 2002, paving the way for inhuman forms of sexual violence against Muslim women. Key parts of the state apparatus appear to have been complicit in this violence, or at least demonstrably apathetic towards it. Moreover, large sections of the Hindu community in the city condoned the massacre and were pleased that Muslims had been 'taught a lesson'.

Given this extent of anti-Muslim sentiment in the political, social and state realm, public discourse on sexual violence in the camps might have exposed the besieged Muslim community to more risks. First, it could have enabled Hindu nationalist organisations once again to blur the distinction between the criminal actions of some men in the camps and the characteristics of the entire community, and to validate their stereotypes about Muslim men. Second, disclosure might have distracted attention from the more severe sexual violence committed during the massacre. Worse still, any conflation of the violence committed in the camps with the sexual violence inflicted during the carnage might have blurred important distinctions between the context, nature and implications of the crimes, especially with regard to the role of the state, which turned a blind eye to the violence in 2002.[4] Third, such revelations could have given the Gujarat government another excuse to intensify pressure on the camp organisers to close down their facilities, removing the only source of sustenance available to thousands of Muslim refugees. Moreover, relief organisers and civil society groups pursuing documentation work and legal proceedings faced acute capacity constraints in the face of an apathetic and hostile Gujarat administration; understandably, they concentrated on issues they deemed most significant.

It must be stressed that in keeping silent about this aspect, feminist activists did not implicitly prioritise 'community interests' over 'women's rights'. Rehabilitation of Muslim women (including rape survivors) was a primary concern for many of them (see also Robinson 2005: 209–15). Rather, the difficult choice that several women's organisations had to make, it seems to me, was between addressing extreme and less extreme violations of (Muslim) women.

However, by not raising this issue, activists may have ignored some important considerations. A central aspect of Hindu nationalist propaganda has been to conflate the honour of the Hindu community with Hindu women's sexual chastity; this laid the basis for instigating 'retributive' and pre-emptive sexual violence against women from the 'enemy' community. The way to subvert this notion, and thus mitigate the risk of sexual violence in future conflicts, must surely then lie in dislodging discourses on women's rights from those on community. Treating sexual violence in camps as an 'internal community' matter could serve to reinforce the link, apart from doing little to curb the impunity with which women are often sexually exploited. Moreover, public silence on sexual coercion in camps could inadvertently discourage the state apparatus, especially law enforcement agencies, from taking responsibility for preventing sexual violence during such transitory phases of relief. The Gujarat administration ignored, and even condoned, the infliction of brutal sexual violence during the massacre, and remained oblivious to sexual coercion in the relief camps. Rights groups perhaps ought to have been more concerned about the implications of allowing the state to avoid its constitutional duty towards citizens, and about the denial of justice to those who suffered in the camps.

Furthermore, by not raising the issue of sexual coercion in the camps, activists may have unconsciously created for themselves a hierarchy of victimhood. Civil society and Muslim activists who were aware of the situation in the camps saw the sexual violence committed by Hindu men against Muslim women during the riots as more significant than the coercion in camps. This was partly because the former kind of violence, in many though not all cases, involved extreme physical brutality such as genital mutilation or worse. While such hierarchies do seem to have some merit, I am concerned about the implications they might have for combating less extreme forms of sexual assault and coercion, which not only damage the victim in profound ways but also act as pathways to such aggravated acts as rape and mutilation. For Jamila, the attack on her sister during the massacre was not necessarily worse than the proposition made to her family by the head of her relief camp. However, for those responding to the violence, pursuing redress for what occurred during the massacre was more important. This raises difficult questions about the ability of activists, writers and other interlocutors to evaluate women's subjective experiences of violence.

The responses of Muslim leaders of Islamic organisations to occurrences in the camps were somewhat different, but equally problematic. Referring to the cases of sexual violence and coercion in the camps, Fatima Tanveer, head of the women's wing of the Jamaat-e-Islami Hind, described violence against women as an unavoidable product of male desire: 'If you put so many women in front of a man, of course he will take advantage of it. That is his need. A man needs a woman's company [common euphemism for sex]. A single woman can spend her whole life by herself, but a man cannot' (interview, Ahmedabad, 21 November 2007). Such views, which are by no means unique to Tanveer, divest women of sexual agency, while ascribing uncontrollable sexual desire to men, thereby normalising the forceful expropriation of women's bodies for the sexual gratification of the heterosexual male.

Others such as Shafi Madani, Gujarat president of the Jamaat-e-Islami Hind, condemned the violence but also diffused responsibility. On being asked whether he had heard about such cases, he replied:

> We have not received anything on this [. . .] with evidence. Most of it is hearsay [. . .] But these stories have been fanned as well. It doesn't seem that something important/special [*khas*] like this has happened. Besides, something like this keeps happening [. . .] whether it be a neighbourhood, or a relief camp or a slum, because the environment is such. There are no methods to stop this[. . .]
>
> The other thing is that if something like this has happened in the camps or in the colonies, if women have been exploited, without their consent, then it is wrong. It is even more worrying [. . .]
>
> [. . .] a whole culture of nudity is developing [. . .] which is affecting our society. (Interview, Ahmedabad, 20 November 2007)

For Madani, the sexual 'exploitation' of women in relief camps and later in the relief colonies, was deeply worrying. Yet he appeared to have almost reconciled himself to accepting as inevitable the occurrence of such acts in the current 'environment'. He saw the issue as a wider cultural problem, where presumably traditional sexual restraint was being replaced by a 'whole culture of nudity'. Madani may be right in questioning the role of culture in promoting or undermining women's dignity, and in facilitating or deterring violence against women. However, this approach also obfuscated the responsibility of particular relief camp organisers in abusing their power by coercing Muslim women to exchange sexual services for aid. Displacing blame from individuals to sexual stereotypes about men (as in the case of Tanveer) or cultural norms (as in the case of Madani) thus serves to absolve the particular men of responsibility and to condone the sexual coercion of women in vulnerable situations.

Moreover, by normalising the prevalence of predatory male behaviour within a context of weakening cultural restraint, such leaders inadvertently make a case for tightening restrictions on women in order to 'protect' them from the sexual dangers ostensibly present beyond the confines of the regulated domestic sphere. As we will see in the following section, such views had a significant impact on the lives of Muslim women post-2002, in that they contributed to calls by Islamic organisations for a return to a more traditional social order and for greater regulation of women's mobility. The widespread incidence of brutal sexual violence during the carnage in 2002 intensified the sense of insecurity felt by Muslims, especially with regard to the safety of Muslim women (also see Robinson 2005: 209–18). This only reinforced the Muslim community's need to 'protect' *its* women (again identifying women with the community) and Muslim women's own attempts at self-regulation.

Yet attempts to turn the community onto a more traditional path also met with resistance. The 2002 massacre had an important role to play in this, for it created an enormous need to protect, rehabilitate and reconstruct affected families and the community as a whole. This formidable task engendered at first the desperate need, and later a genuine desire, among both women and men for the involvement of women as responsible agents of the community.

Rehabilitation, community purification and women's agency

Following the closure of the last four relief camps in Ahmedabad in October 2003, Muslims once again took the lead in organising the rehabilitation of the survivors. The initiative was taken primarily by Islamic religious organisations, in particular the Jamiat-Ulema-e-Hind, the Jamaat-e-Islami Hind and its relief wing, the Islamic Relief Committee, and the Tablighi Jamaat. These organisations had refrained from getting involved in the provision and running of relief camps immediately after the carnage, partly because they believed that local Muslim leaders and NGOs had paid sufficient attention to the immediate requirements (Jassani 2007: 99–100). Once the relief camps closed down, these organisations, specifically the Islamic Relief Committee, stepped in to establish rehabilitation colonies for survivors whose homes had been destroyed during the violence, or who were too scared to return to them.

The Islamic Relief Committee, with the support of NGOs and Muslim builders, established seven relief colonies – Arch Colony, Ekta Nagar I, Ekta Nagar II, Gupta Nagar, Javed Park, Siddikabad Colony and Yash Colony – which together housed 1,745 riot-affected Muslim refugees (Jaffrelot and Thomas 2012: 72). All these colonies were established in Juhapura, which in 2012 had an estimated 240,000 Muslim residents, or between 33 and 50 per cent of the city's Muslim population (ibid.: 68). Juhapura, located in the south-western part of the city, was established in 1973 to rehabilitate the 2,250 Hindu and Muslim slum dwellers affected by devastating floods the year before. Since the 1985 riot, the neighbourhood has become a refuge for Muslims fleeing communal violence and seeking safety in numbers. Juhapura has since the 1990s been referred to as 'mini-Pakistan' by locals, since it has the largest concentration of Muslims anywhere in India. Political scientists Christophe Jaffrelot and Charlotte Thomas (2012: 70) argue that Juhapura is a Muslim ghetto 'in the truest sense of the word':

> First, it gathers people who have mostly one thing in common, their religious identity, irrespectively of their socio-economic and socio-cultural status. Second, it is insulated from the rest of the city, not only because of one wall [that divides Hindu and Muslim colonies and is called the 'border'], but also because no bus connection had ever been established [to connect the area with the rest of the city]. Buses cross the area on the main road, but not a single one goes inside the locality. People are compelled to use private means of transportation like auto-rickshaws or scooters which are much more expensive. Third, the area had not benefitted from the same kind of attention from the state as other parts of the city. (Ibid.)

Although home mainly to lower-income and poor Muslims until the turn of the century, post-2002 Juhapura has also become home to middle-class Muslim professionals who no longer feel safe anywhere else in Ahmedabad. Unlike the poorer residents of the 'ghetto', who live in cramped, one- or two-room houses, middle-class Muslim families live in modern apartments with amenities such as proper roads, electricity and parking spaces.

The seven relief colonies are located along the outskirts of Juhapura, where the infrastructure deficit is even deeper than in the rest of the area. These colonies are enclaves of gated or ungated rows of small, single-room houses, most of whose residents lack access to basic amenities such as electricity and water. They house predominantly poor Muslims, since middle-class Muslims could utilise their family networks and draw on their personal savings to either rebuild their homes (as the Muslim residents of Gulbarg Society have done since 2002, for example), or relocate outside Ahmedabad.

Most of the residents of relief colonies struggle to find reliable employment. During my fieldwork between 2006 and 2008, respondents pointed to multiple reasons for this. The colonies are located far from the main business centres of Ahmedabad, and the survivors cannot afford to commute to areas where they could find employment. Or they are too scared to take routes that would cross Hindu neighbourhoods. They also frequently find that Hindu employers are unwilling to hire Muslims. The lack of skills, shortage of employment opportunities around the relief colonies, and intense competition over scarce jobs has put economic security beyond the reach of most residents. Restarting a previous occupation was difficult for those whose tools and equipment (bicycles, push-carts, sewing machines, etc.) had been destroyed during the violence. The economic boycott of Muslims, a central plank of Hindu nationalist organisations' agenda since the mid-1990s, shrank the market for survivors who had operated small service centres such as bakeries, repair shops and tailoring facilities prior to 2002. Low-income Muslim survivors who became community representatives and liaisons for NGOs active in medical or legal aid, resettlement, or education and documentation work post-2002, often work on a voluntary basis.

Due to these constraints, Muslims affected by the massacre have seen their income fall significantly over the last decade. Rachida, for instance, who lives in Ekta Nagar, confided to Jaffrelot and Thomas that her monthly household income had dropped from Rs 10,000 to Rs 3,000 rupees (2012: 72). Parveen and her two sons also live in Ekta Nagar. They were abandoned by Parveen's drug-addict husband after the carnage, because he was no longer able or willing to support the family. Although the Islamic Relief Committee gave Parveen a house, she has had to discontinue the education of her children and send them to work. Her 15-year-old elder son earns around Rs 50 per day doing odd jobs (interview, Ahmedabad, 16 January 2008).

Reviving piety and 'protecting' Muslim women

Although the active involvement of Islamic organisations such as the Jamaat-e-Islami Hind in establishing relief colonies helped alleviate some of the material difficulties of thousands of survivors of the 2002 massacre, it also resulted in renewed emphasis on 'community purification'. This emphasis arose out of a belief among Islamic organisations that the massacre had occurred partly because Muslims had strayed from their holy course, neglected their prayers and become ensnared in mundane desires. This discourse was particularly prominent between 2002 and 2006, and was extended to the inmates of the relief colonies as well as to Muslims in other parts of Ahmedabad (Jaffrelot and Thomas 2012: 73; Jassani 2007: 189). According to lawyer Sophia Khan, who heads an NGO called Social Action Forum Against Oppression in Ahmedabad, these organisations placed new emphasis on combining *dini taleem* (religious-spiritual education) with *dunyavi taleem* (worldly education) after 2002 (interview, Ahmedabad, 20 November 2007). They built mosques around relief colonies, downplayed Sufi and syncretic beliefs, and stressed the importance of regular prayer to their wards (Jaffrelot and Thomas 2012: 73).

These efforts were accompanied by moves to reinforce a more traditional and restrictive ethos with regard to women. Muslim women were encouraged or pressured to start wearing the full veil for the first time in their lives. Restrictions were placed on women's mobility outside the house. Some girls were married well before they had reached the age of 18, the legal age of consent in India. Jamila observed that 'girls aged 13, 14 and 15 were married off. Some girls who were already engaged, were married sooner than planned. Those that were not engaged, were also married off' (interview, Ahmedabad, 17 October 2007). Women who had been raped during the carnage were constrained not to disclose this information. Najma, who works as a community peace volunteer with an NGO called Aman Samudaya (Peace Community), added: 'Women who were raped in Faisal Park, Naroda were promptly married off. Those girls and widows were promptly married off [...] Now they live here in Vatva' (interview, Ahmedabad, 19 February 2008). Since Muslims from poorer backgrounds were dependent on Islamic organisations for security, survival and rehabilitation, their scope for resisting these restrictions was limited.

Restrictions on women's life choices and mobility were not entirely the result of the Islamic organisations' emphasis on religious piety and tradition. These restrictions also partly emerged out of fear for women's safety following the massacre, a fear that was intense and palpable among women themselves, even six years after the massacre. Consider the story and testimony of Farida, whose family had relocated from Gomtipur to Behrampura within the industrial area in the aftermath of the 1992–93 violence. She and her family relocated again to Muslim-dominated Jamalpur in the walled city after the 2002 massacre, in search of security. Farida is also associated with Aman Samudaya, and says she is fighting for 'justice for everyone affected by the 2002 genocide'. In 2008, she had this to say about the fear of rape that the conflict had instilled in her:

> Even today, Muslims are worried about this. I am also a Muslim woman. I am also worried that if I go to an area like Satellite [a Hindu-dominated area in western Ahmedabad], then on the way back I have to cross at least 10 Dalit neighbourhoods. If somewhere they catch me, then the first thing they will do to me is rape, then they will kill me or burn me. So rape is the foremost fear. (Interview, Ahmedabad, 8 December 2007)

Farida's family was directly affected by the repeated bouts of religion-based spatial segregation that Ahmedabad has witnessed after every major communal riot since the 1960s. The perpetration of horrific sexual violence against Muslim women during the 2002 massacre appears to have permanently sealed these spatial and psychological divides between Hindus and Muslims for Farida: she is now convinced that she could be attacked in any Dalit neighbourhood in Ahmedabad, and that, if she is attacked, she will be raped before being killed. Non-Muslim neighbourhoods have come to be associated with the fear of brutal sexual violence, humiliation and the killing of Muslim women.

Community agents: Naseem's experience

Despite the acute economic and spatial constraints faced by Muslim women in the aftermath of the massacre, and the external and self-imposed pressure to restrict their mobility, some female survivors challenged and sought to overcome these hurdles. Several of the Muslim women who survived the massacre – most of whom were poor and illiterate or semi-literate – became actively involved in organising relief for survivors soon after the massacre began on 28 February. One such woman is Naseem, a 29-year-old Muslim woman and mother of two from Vatva. On 28 February, when the violence began in her neighbourhood, Naseem first helped her husband, brothers-in-law and neighbours prevent the mob from entering their locality. Together with other women like her, she led children and the aged to safety, collected and pelted stones at the mobs, threw buckets of hot water with chilli powder at them, nursed the wounds of those who were injured, and called the police for help. Naseem recounted her experience to me in the following words:

> I had never stepped out of the main gate of my house ever before [she said pointing to the main door of her house]. But that day [28 February] we fought with all our might [...] we worked day and night to protect ourselves. Everyone was surprised with what we women were doing [...] they would say that men are doing what they have to do, but our women are proving as good as the men. (Interview, Ahmedabad, 20 October and 29 November 2007)

When the Jehangir camp was established in Vatva, Naseem and her sister-in-law joined their male relations in mobilising relief. They contributed to efforts to organise food for the thousands of people in the camps. They negotiated with the local bureaucracy for basic amenities such as water and electricity, and medical assistance for the survivors, and helped other survivors to register their cases with the police and human rights collectives. In organising relief for the victims, Muslim women such as Naseem were working as responsible agents of the community, rather than as subordinates. Simultaneously, by bringing the violence they had suffered into public view, they functioned not as the symbols of honour or as the sexual property of their religious community, but arguably as its guardians.

The ruptures created in the social order by 'Gujarat 2002' have survived. Naseem's activism continues to this day, even though she continues to shoulder most household responsibilities. By her own admission she is completely illiterate (*angutha chaap*), and cannot even write her own name. Yet she fulfils several functions that she was previously considered unfit for, and that were routinely assigned only to her husband or her male relations. The conflict has also significantly altered the hierarchy of power in the families of women such as Naseem, giving hitherto sheltered and marginalised women like her a say in family decisions, as well as access to the public sphere and the state. That the 2002 massacre precipitated some progressive changes in the gender-based allocation of responsibility within some affected families is not a unique occurrence: similar processes of social reordering have unfolded in the aftermath of several other major episodes of mass violence and displacement, including Partition and the 1992 riot in Bombay.[5]

Now Naseem goes to courts by herself, follows the legal proceedings of the cases her family has filed in relation to the massacre, and independently organises affidavits and ration cards. By engaging with the judicial apparatus, women such as Naseem are beginning to emerge as self-determining guardians of their family and the community. They are part of a wider collective of Muslim survivors who are pursuing legal redress for the violence committed against them in 2002. Since ration cards enable poorer families to access subsidised rations from the state distribution system, by obtaining and using these cards women are taking responsibility for supplying food to their families, a task usually entrusted to men. The continued activism of such Muslim women presages some internal shifts within the besieged Muslim community of Ahmedabad, especially with regard to women's life opportunities.

The involvement of dynamic, secular civil society organisations in community-level development in the city offers another source of hope for positive change. As mentioned earlier, in the immediate aftermath of the massacre, civil society organisations and NGOs across Ahmedabad had mobilised and distributed basic aid to survivors housed in the city's 44 relief camps, either independently or by joining the Citizens' Initiative. Since the closure of relief camps between March 2002 and October 2003, these organisations have shifted their focus to longer-term concerns, paying special attention to the constraints facing Muslim women.

Notably, AWAG, one of the most well-respected women's organisations in India since its establishment in 1981, has dedicated itself to instilling security among Muslim women affected directly or indirectly by the violence. For example, through interactive workshops, educational classes and counselling, Muslim women, especially fearful mothers, are encouraged to ease the restrictions on their daughters' mobility and to allow them to continue their education or maintain employment. The group also attempts to cultivate income-generating skills such as sewing and tailoring among women. Other organisations, such as the St Xavier Social Service Society (a Christian group working with social welfare) and Samerth (an NGO), concentrate on social reconciliation, seeing inter-religious engagement as key to the peaceful coexistence of different communities in the city. These organisations have a creative approach: they invite Muslims and Hindus to celebrate syncretic local festivals jointly, such as the kite festival of Uttarayan; they host inter-community feasts and organise friendly cricket matches (Oommen 2008). Art- and media-oriented NGOs such as Darshan and Drishti focus on educational theatre, film screenings and cultural events. Still others, such as Sanchetna, prioritise health, conducting extensive research in industrial neighbourhoods on women's health, domestic violence and alcohol abuse. They also offer some services such as counselling and medical assistance. Through such organisations, women such as Naseem will hopefully find support, recognition and new avenues for individual and collective growth.

State response to sexual violence

The state's handling of the brutal sexual violence against Muslim women during the 2002 massacre has, for the most part, been dismal. Senior public officials in the national government in Delhi and in the Gujarat government openly justified or condoned such occurrences, thus seeking to remove the issue altogether from the agenda of governance (this will be discussed further at a later stage in this chapter). Furthermore, the Gujarat administration has been widely criticised for actively obstructing official inquiries into the massacre, facilitated by the support of Hindu nationalist loyalists present at various levels within Gujarat's police and judicial apparatus (see the section 'Manipulating Official Inquiries' later in this chapter). At the time of publication (14 years after the massacre), one senior government official, Maya Kodnani, had been convicted for her complicity in orchestrating violence against Muslims.[6] Moreover, there are no official statistics on the number of women subjected to sexual violence in 2002; only two such cases have resulted in conviction as of March 2016.[7] This is particularly damning given the presence of extensive media documentation on the massacre, detailed national and international human rights reports, and numerous witnesses and survivors who have been able to recognise the perpetrators of the violence. Yet, the fact that for the first time in the history of communal conflict in India, a public official has been sentenced to 28 years in prison, and that for the first time two cases of sexual violence have resulted in convictions, offers hope for greater state accountability in the future. The following sections track some of the key prevailing and countervailing trends in the state's response to sexual violence in 2002.

Government, politicians and governance

At the time of the massacre, a BJP-led coalition led the national government in Delhi, and veteran RSS member and senior BJP leader Atal Bihari Vajpayee was Prime Minister. On 3 March, soon after the massacre had begun, the Prime Minister's Office issued the following statement: 'From Godhra to Ahmedabad, in so many places, there are so many incidents of people being burnt alive, including helpless women and children. This is a blot on the nation's forehead and has grievously harmed India's image in the eyes of the world' (quoted in CCT 2002, 1:299, Annexure 18). Having publicly accepted the gravity of the massacre, which elicited widespread international condemnation, Vajpayee on 4 April visited the Shah-e-Alam relief camp in Ahmedabad. There he bemoaned the violence, including the rapes of Muslim women. Yet he fell short of criticising the Gujarat government for failing in its constitutional duty to ensure the safety of religious minorities. Despite widespread calls for Modi's resignation from civil society activists, the political opposition and other prominent individuals, the Prime Minister's response was, at best, mild. He stated: 'My one message to the Chief Minister is that he should follow *raj dharma* [the duties and responsibilities of a ruler]. A ruler should not discriminate between his subjects on the basis of caste, creed and religion' (ibid.).

In less than three weeks, however, Vajpayee altered his discourse; he no longer chastised the government (howsoever mildly) or lamented the torture of hundreds of Muslims in Gujarat. Instead, he sought to appease hard-liners within the BJP by stressing that, without the attack in Godhra, the massacre would not have occurred. Speaking at the BJP's National Executive Meeting in Goa on 22 April, he said:

What happened in Gujarat? If a conspiracy had not been hatched to burn alive the innocent passengers of the Sabarmati Express, then the subsequent tragedy in Gujarat could have been averted. But this did not happen. People were torched alive. Who were those culprits? The Government is investigating into this. Intelligence agencies are collecting all the information. But we should not forget how the tragedy of Gujarat started. The subsequent developments were no doubt condemnable, but who lit the fire? How did the fire spread? (quoted in CCT 2002, 1:300, Annexure 18)

In pointing to the Godhra tragedy as the catalyst of the anti-Muslim massacre, Vajpayee was echoing Modi's infamous 'action–reaction theory'. This theory sought to portray the massacre as a mass, spontaneous, Hindu 'reaction' to the burning of some 58 passengers on board the Sabarmati Express in Godhra on 27 February. Modi expressed this view when asked about the violence in a television interview on 1 March 2002:

It is natural that what happened in Godhra the day before yesterday, where forty women and children were burnt alive, has shocked the country and the world. The people in that part of Godhra have had criminal tendencies. Earlier, these people had murdered women teachers. And now they have done this terrible crime for which a reaction is going on. (Quoted in Varadarajan 2002: 22)

Since the Godhra tragedy, as shown in the previous chapter, was accompanied by the circulation of rumours via newspapers and pamphlets about rapes of Hindu women by Muslim men, this 'action–reaction' discourse in effect also served to justify sexual brutalities against Muslim women in Ahmedabad and elsewhere in Gujarat. It deflected attention from the repeated failure of the Gujarat administration to ensure the safety of women in Godhra (if Modi's claim about past crimes in the region are correct), and its dismal failure to prevent violence against Muslims in the aftermath of the train tragedy. The discourse condoned lawlessness and large-scale violence as a 'natural' and thus acceptable state of affairs, disowning the state's duty to prevent and curb both.

Vajpayee and Modi were not alone in effectively condoning the violence against Muslims. Certain politicians from parties that were in coalition with the BJP in Parliament did the same, specifically with regard to the sexual victimisation of Muslim women. On 30 April 2002, a special parliamentary session was organised to debate the events in Gujarat. In his defence of the BJP-led national coalition government, George Fernandes, leader of the Samata Party and at the time union minister of defence, made a shocking statement on the floor of the lower house:

> All these sob stories being told to us, as if this is the first time the country has heard such stories – where a mother is killed and the foetus taken out of her stomach, where a daughter is raped in front of her mother, of someone being hurt. Is this the first time such things have happened? Didn't such things happen on the streets of Delhi in 1984? (Quoted in Dutt 2002: 214)

Fernandes's claims regarding the anti-Sikh riots in Delhi in 1984 are inaccurate in the light of evidence currently available in the public sphere.[8] Moreover, they demonstrate how, in the aftermath of the worst episode of communally motivated violence since Partition, sexual violence against Muslim women became, in Upendra Baxi's (2005: 340) words, merely a 'spectacular resource for doing competitive party politics'. Since the Congress Party was in power at the centre in 1984, and some senior government officials and allegedly even a few Congress leaders were complicit in the violence against Sikhs to which Fernandes referred, he was suggesting that the Congress had forfeited its right to criticise the BJP for failing to prevent sexual violence against Muslim women, since its own hands were not 'clean'. In so doing, Fernandes appeared to be demanding that 'each regime ought thus remain entitled to its own expanding quota of regime tolerated/sponsored collective political violence' (ibid.: 341). As a result, the issue of sexual violence in large-scale conflict has not been viewed as an unacceptable failure of governance. The repeated incidence of such violence is not seen as exposing the systematic failures of government, and the extremity of sexual violence is not understood as symptomatic of the extent of lawlessness. Instead, such violence is normalised as occurring beyond the remit of governance; the Congress's invocation of the moral and constitutional obligations of the BJP government was deemed inapposite.

The fact that sexual violence was indeed erased from the agenda of governance – and hence not seen as an issue that senior public officials should be held accountable for – is most palpably reflected in the response by the Gujarat government to Maya Kodnani between 2002 and her conviction in August 2012. A gynaecologist by training, Kodnani, as mentioned earlier, was the BJP MLA from Naroda, where some of the worst sexual atrocities were perpetrated against Muslim women on 28 February. In August 2012, a special fast-track sessions court established in Ahmedabad for 'Conducting Speedy Trial of Riot Cases' relating to the 2002 massacre found that Kodnani was the 'kingpin of the riot';[9] it sentenced her to 28 years' imprisonment for criminal conspiracy, murder and arson.

Well before her conviction, serious questions had been raised about Kodnani's complicity in the violence through acts of commission and omission. Several dozen Muslims survivors from Naroda had named her explicitly in their FIRs to the police, claiming that she had coordinated attacks against Muslims in the area. However, she dismissed the FIRs as being false, and the Gujarat government took no action against her. In her interviews with women's groups immediately after the massacre, and with me in 2007, she denied that any incidents of sexual violence had occurred in Naroda Patiya and Naroda Gaon on 28 February 2002 (Citizens' Initiative 2002: 82; author's interview, Ahmedabad, 10 November 2007).

In the immediate aftermath of the Godhra incident, Kodnani was one of the senior BJP leaders to visit the Sola hospital to receive the bodies of those killed on the Sabarmati Express. However, like Modi and all his cabinet ministers, she too decided not to visit any relief camps or to reassure members of her constituency, arguably disregarding her constitutional oath to serve Naroda's residents. In fact, when speaking to a fact-finding team in March 2002, she justified the massacre as a natural reflection of the 'essential nature of Gujarat' (Citizens' Initiative 2002: 109), and refused to accept her own failure and that of the government to govern Ahmedabad at the time. Referring to the marauding mobs on the streets of the city, she said: 'It was impossible to stop. There were between 50,000 and 1,00,000 people [out] on the streets. How could the police have stopped them? It was humanly impossible' (ibid.). Kodnani too echoed Modi's 'action–reaction theory', adding that 'there was nothing the State could do. There was natural *ghrina* [hatred] and *aakrosh* [anger] in the heart of every Hindu and we could not control it' (ibid.: 82).

Yet neither the BJP nor the Gujarat government was concerned by the fact that Kodnani had been implicated in, and was under investigation for, serious criminal activity, and did nothing to hold her accountable for the failures of government in Naroda. In 2007, she was once again allowed by the BJP to contest the Naroda constituency in the assembly elections. Following her victory, she was appointed state minister for women and child development – a post she held until 2009. However, by 2009, the pressure on the Gujarat government to take action against Kodnani had become irresistible. It filed an affidavit with the Gujarat High Court, accusing Kodnani of leading and instigating the mob to attack Muslims in Naroda, and of firing a pistol to incite the rioters.[10] In November 2012, the Gujarat High Court accepted Kodnani's appeal against her conviction in August of that year. Since then, the Court has granted her multiple bails, most recently in July 2015. Although the outcome of her appeal remains to be seen, the unwillingness of the Gujarat government, and of the BJP as a political party, to take any action against her for nearly seven years after the massacre constituted a violation of the norms of clean and non-partisan governance.

It is apposite and important to stress here that the BJP is not the only party to respond irresponsibly to the occurrence of sexual violence against women during communal conflicts. No major political party in India has prioritised the issue as part of its governance agenda. The Congress has led the central government in Delhi for two consecutive terms (2004–09 and 2009–14), and has criticised the BJP for its role in 'Gujarat 2002'. Yet its national government has repeatedly ignored calls for strong action from Indian and international civil society groups, and from the UN Committee on the Elimination of Discrimination Against Women (George and Kannabiran 2007). It has also prevaricated in Parliament on the anti-communal violence bill, which would, among other things, ensure greater government accountability for communal violence.

In addition, the record of left-wing parties with regard to sexual violence during political conflicts is hardly untarnished, although their past governments (in West Bengal and Kerala) have been credited with preventing communal riots. A Left Front coalition led by the CPI-M was in power in West Bengal, with the Congress-led United Progressive Alliance at Delhi, when the Nandigram massacre occurred in March 2007. The violence occurred on 14 March when the state government ordered a heavy-handed police crackdown on a peasant resistance movement in the rural area of Nandigram in West Bengal's East Midnapur district. The peasants of Nandigram had opposed the acquisition of their land for the creation of a Special Economic Zone, and had been involved in sporadic violent clashes with CPI-M activists and the police since 3 January 2007. Having repeatedly failed to capture the land, CPI-M activists and the police went on a rampage on 14 March to forcefully evict the peasants, leaving at least 14 people dead and hundreds injured. During the violence, police troops and CPI-M activists allegedly raped or gang-raped several women and mutilated their private parts (All India Citizens' Initiative 2012: 24, 31–2). However, these crimes have not led to any convictions or to the expulsion or resignation of any senior government or party official. Indeed, when some critics compared the Nandigram massacre to 'Gujarat 2002', then CPI-M general secretary Prakash Karat shunned responsibility, accusing the critics of being 'enemies of the people' (Krishnan 2008).

Regional parties have fared no better. In August 2013, at least five Muslim women were gang-raped during Hindu–Muslim riots in the Muzaffarnagar district of UP.[11] When the riot occurred, the Samajwadi Party (a caste-based regional party) led UP's state government, while the Congress-led United Progressive Alliance held the reins of power in Delhi. However, no concrete action had been taken by either government on this issue when this book went to press. Yet it is important to add that despite the dismal governance failures of the Congress, the CPI-M and the Samajwadi Party, none of them espouses a nationalist ideology that justifies sexual violence. By contrast, the BJP is the political front for the Hindu nationalist movement, whose ideological framework contains at its core an implicit, sometimes even overt incitement of sexual violence against 'enemy' women (see the discussion in the Introduction, this volume).

The level of irresponsibility among India's political class has outraged and dismayed civil society groups, feminists and academics. They warn of the emergence of a 'rape culture' in India, where sexual violence against disenfranchised (minority, poor or tribal) women is deployed as a 'central mode of stifling protests' (Chakravarti et al. 2007: 4), and where such gendered violence has become a means of political score-settling.

Manipulating official inquiries

Besides failing to hold the leadership accountable for gross violations against religious minorities, it has been alleged that, since 2002, the Gujarat administration has repeatedly attempted to obstruct the course of justice. The following paragraphs cite important developments in the period between March 2002 and March 2016 in this regard.

On 6 March 2002, within a week of the beginning of the carnage in Gujarat, Modi announced the establishment of a judicial commission of inquiry under retired Gujarat High Court judge K. G. Shah. The remit of this commission was restricted strictly to investigating the burning of the Sabarmati Express in Godhra on 27 February, and did not include the massacre that ensued. Moreover, the terms of reference excluded scrutiny of the role of the Chief Minister, his cabinet, top bureaucrats and police officials. After questions were raised about political interference, and about the neutrality of Justice K. G. Shah and his ability to examine such a deadly and protracted riot single-handedly, the Gujarat government on 21 May 2002 appointed retired Supreme Court judge G. T. Nanavati as the chair of the commission. However, the remit of the commission was left unaltered. Widespread protests against the exclusion of post-Godhra events from the purview of the inquiry forced the Gujarat government, on 3 June 2002, to take corrective steps. The commission would now also probe events that took place between 28 February and 30 March 2002. However, it would still not scrutinise the role of government officials, senior bureaucrats and top police officials.

The defeat of the BJP-led national coalition in the 2004 Lok Sabha elections by the Congress-led United Progressive Alliance constituted an important rejection of Hindu nationalism by the Indian electorate. Minister of Railways Laloo Prasad Yadav took advantage of his portfolio and appointed retired Supreme Court judge U. C. Banerjee to conduct a separate inquiry into the Godhra incident. Worried that the new central government might also appoint a committee to probe the anti-Muslim violence, the Gujarat government once again revised the terms of reference of the commission of inquiry. On 20 July 2004, it tasked the Nanavati Commission with also scrutinising the role of the Chief Minister, his cabinet, top bureaucrats and police officials. However, police officials and bureaucrats were allegedly pressured not to file their affidavits under these revised terms of reference; indeed, most of the affidavits continued to exclude information on the role of senior state officials.[12]

On 18 September 2008, the Nanavati Commission submitted the first part of its report, which aimed exclusively at probing the Godhra incident. Following Justice K. G. Shah's demise on 22 March 2008, the Gujarat government appointed retired Gujarat High Court judge Ashok Mehta as his replacement. The September report was submitted under the authority of Justices Nanavati and Mehta. This report concluded that the Godhra train burning incident was a 'pre-planned conspiracy' by Muslim terrorists, and that no senior Gujarat government official was involved (Government of Gujarat 2008). This conclusion was very different from the findings of the Justice U. C. Banerjee report, which in 2005 had concluded that the train fire was accidental (see Jaffrelot 2012). The Nanavati Commission requested more time to submit the second part of its report on the anti-Muslim violence between February and March 2002. On 10 May 2009, the Central Bureau of Investigation authenticated the tapes of a sting operation conducted in 2007 by journalist Ashish Khetan of *Tehelka* magazine, which indicate that neither Shah nor Nanavati were committed to conducting an impartial investigation. On the tapes (made with a hidden camera), the then advocate general of Gujarat Arvind Pandya (a Modi appointee) confided to the journalist that Shah was 'our man' and Nanavati was in the commission 'for the money'.[13]

On 31 March 2012, the Gujarat government granted the Nanavati Commission's request for an 18th extension, allowing it to delay the submission of Part II of its report until 31 December 2012. Meanwhile on 18 October 2012, the administration, via the additional director general (intelligence), admitted to the commission that some of the documents pertaining to the period February–March 2002 had been destroyed 'in routine course', and were thus no longer available for submission before the commission.[14] Following the BJP's re-election in the Gujarat state assembly elections in 2012, the government on

31 December 2012 granted the Nanavati Commission its 19th extension. The publication of the report on the massacre was then scheduled for 30 June 2013. A day before this deadline, on 29 June 2013, the commission was granted its 20th six-month extension. On 31 December 2013, the Gujarat government granted the commission its 21st extension, until 30 June 2014, thereby preventing the finalisation of the report before the 2014 parliamentary elections. The elections saw the BJP win a clear majority in the lower house of parliament, delivering Modi to the Prime Minister's office. On 18 November 2014, about six months after Modi was sworn in, the Nanavati Commission submitted Part II of its report to the Gujarat government. The latter had not made the report public as of March 2016. This delay may be an attempt to prevent 'Gujarat 2002' from casting a shadow over Modi's national image and agenda.

These developments are disturbing because official commissions of inquiry embody the state's commitment, at least in principle, to truth and justice. As Rowena Robinson (2005: 45) has noted, they also allow survivors to articulate their suffering publicly and legitimately. By restricting the remit of the commission until June 2002 to the Godhra tragedy, whose victims were Hindus, the Gujarat administration demonstrated the extent to which its priorities and agenda were fashioned by Hindu right ideology. The violation suffered by Muslim men and women during the massacre was not deemed worthy of investigation. This was in sharp contrast to the investigations conducted in the wake of the 1969 and 1985 riots in Gujarat, where the commissions were tasked with undertaking a comprehensive review of the violence. In 1969, the Reddy Commission examined events that occurred during the entire course of the violence (18–30 September), and in 1985 the Dave Commission devoted equal attention to the anti-reservation agitation and the communal riot.

In preventing inquiries into the role of senior state officials, the Modi administration unabashedly violated two of the most fundamental norms of a democracy: equality before the law, and government accountability. Again, this marks a sharp departure from precedent. In both 1969 and 1985, the primary brief of the Reddy and Dave Commissions was to scrutinise the role of the state in preventing and quelling the violence. Both reports harshly criticised the incumbent administrations for their failures. The unwillingness of the Gujarat administration to submit itself to independent, rigorous scrutiny with regard to its role in communal riots had become apparent as early as 1992, following violence in Surat and Ahmedabad. The BJP–Janata Dal coalition government in Gujarat disbanded the Chauhan Commission in 1996 before its report into the violence could be finalised and released. In the wake of the 2002 massacre, its appetite for impartial judicial inquiries appears to have shrunk even further. Since the government could not resist political pressure to establish a commission of inquiry, it seems to have appointed an extremely weak one (Jaffrelot 2012: 79–80). Serious concerns have been expressed about the commitment and ability of the Nanavati Commission to conduct a thorough and impartial investigation.

Furthermore, in willingly granting multiple extensions to the Nanavati Commission, the Gujarat government has allowed investigations to be compromised (since some documents have already been destroyed), and the process of justice to be delayed. It is noteworthy that the Reddy Commission submitted its report to the Gujarat government within a year of the riot (in October 1970), and the Dave Commission did so by May 1990, within five years of the 1985 riot. Despite the political significance and brutality of the 2002 massacre, the Nanavati Commission took nearly 13 years to submit its report on events that occurred between February and March of that year. It showed greater haste with regard to the Godhra tragedy, submitting Part I of its report in 2008. The Gujarat government released the Reddy Commission's report to the public on 9 March 1971, within two years of the riot, while the Dave Commission's report was released on 4 September 1991, within six years of the riot. Although Part II of the Nanavati Commission's report was submitted in mid-November 2014, there are no signs that the current Gujarat government, led by Chief Minister Anandiben Patel, intends to release it any time soon. This, and the fact that the Gujarat government disregarded the findings of the U. C. Banerjee report, would suggest that neither the national nor the Gujarat government have the motivation to pursue justice with regard to the 2002 massacre.

Quest for justice

When the investigating agency helps the accused, the witnesses are threatened to depose falsely and the prosecutor acts in a manner as if he was defending the accused, and the court was acting merely as an onlooker and there is no fair trial at all, justice becomes the victim.

> – Supreme Court to Gujarat's judiciary on its handling
> of the high-profile Best Bakery case
> (Quoted in Robinson 2005: 26)

Besides manipulating the Nanavati Commission, as Christophe Jaffrelot (2012) argues, Hindu nationalist loyalists and supporters within Gujarat's bureaucratic, police and judicial apparatus seem to have obstructed the course of justice at every stage of police and judicial inquiries.[15] Previous chapters have tracked the growing communalisation of Gujarat's state apparatus. The Indian legal system has four constituents: investigation, prosecution, adjudication and appeal, the police being the administrative authority in charge of investigations. In several cases pertaining to 2002, the Gujarat police has allegedly destroyed key evidence (such as radio communications), or allowed such evidence to be destroyed.[16] In other cases, it has failed to preserve evidence that could be presented to the Nanavati Commission or to the courts at a later date. The aforementioned admission of the additional director general (intelligence) in October 2012 that vital evidence had been destroyed 'in routine course' is a case in point.

The police also allegedly prevailed on victims not to lodge complaints, and when the complainants persevered, key details such as the name of the accused or other details about the crime seem to have been excluded from their FIRs. In numerous cases, the police may have specifically omitted complaints about sexual violence and the names of those who committed it. For example, Medina Shaikh witnessed the brutal gang-rape, mutilation and murder of three girls, one of them her daughter Shabana, by a mob of men on 3 March 2002 in Eral village of Kalol taluka, Panch Mahals district. When a group of civil society activists and journalists recorded Medina's testimony on 30 March at Kalol camp, they noted that the police had excluded information about sexual violence from Medina's testimony, obfuscating vital details in her FIR:

> We saw a copy of Medina's FIR, where the police has charged 5 persons with murder under section 302. Charges of rape have not

been included. The FIR uses the colloquial phrase 'bura kaam' [bad/wrong acts] rather than the specific term 'rape'. We were also given the case report prepared by the camp leaders. The names of some of the accused are mentioned in the FIR. (Citizens' Initiative 2002: 77)[17]

The government also arguably leveraged its administrative control on another important component of the judicial process: prosecution. Since 2002, it has appointed Hindu nationalist sympathisers, BJP supporters, RSS members and VHP leaders as public prosecutors in districts badly affected by the 2002 violence, including Ahmedabad, Sabarkantha, Anand, Vadodara, Panch Mahals and Mehsana (Jaffrelot 2012). These prosecutors obtained acquittals and bail for members of Hindu nationalist cadres indicted for crimes including rape and murder. Muslim complainants have been prevailed upon to withdraw their cases, apparently through intimidation or offers of money. Cases filed by Muslims were often dismissed at the lower levels of the judiciary (e.g., in sessions courts). Many of the accused would thus seem to have received strong support from sympathetic judges in the sessions courts and the Gujarat High Court. These judges have allegedly even advised prosecutors on the manner in which they should present their cases, on what date, etc. (ibid.: 81).

The alleged collusion between such prosecutors and judges, coupled with faulty and incomplete police records, has not only deprived victims of sexual violence of justice, but has also had the effect of deterring some from pursuing it. This became most apparent in the aftermath of the 'Best Bakery case'.[18] The Best Bakery case centred on the testimonies of 73 eyewitnesses, including a Muslim woman, Zahira Shaikh, who witnessed 14 Muslims being burnt alive on 1 March in a bakery (whose name gave the case its title) in Vadodara. Initially, Zahira pursued her case in court. The trial began in February 2003, with a VHP sympathiser Raghuvir Pandya as the public prosecutor. However, in June 2003, Zahira as well as her mother and brothers retracted their testimonies after they received death threats.

Following this, the legal rights group Citizens for Justice and Peace (CJP) helped Zahira record her testimony before the National Human Rights Commission. Jointly with Zahira, CJP petitioned the Supreme Court for reopening the case and conducting a retrial outside Gujarat.

The Supreme Court persuaded the Gujarat government to request a retrial before the Gujarat High Court. However, the latter rejected the appeal in December 2003. In January 2004, Zahira appealed directly to the Supreme Court, which granted her request, thereby annulling the ruling of the Gujarat High Court, and ordered a retrial in Maharashtra. The Gujarat judiciary's mishandling of the Best Bakery case is what led the Supreme Court to issue the damning statement quoted in the beginning of this section.

However, in November 2004, a month after the retrial began in Mumbai, Zahira and her family once again retracted their statements, allegedly after being bribed by a BJP MLA from Vadodara. This time the trial continued nonetheless, and culminated in the conviction in February 2006 of nine of the 17 accused, who were sentenced to life imprisonment. The Supreme Court also sentenced Zahira to one year's imprisonment for lying under oath. The pronouncement of a one-year sentence for Zahira outraged various women's groups and concerned citizens, who stressed that even though she had repeatedly changed her statements to the courts, she was an 'injured witness' rather than a 'routine hostile witness' (Saheli et al. 2006). They insisted, rightly in my view, that we must remember that 'she is a survivor first and foremost and her "hostility" to the prosecution is a product of surviving in a highly hostile and insecure environment' (ibid.: 934).

Conviction in the Best Bakery case constituted an important landmark in judicial accountability for the 2002 massacre. This is because, for the first time in the history of independent India, involvement in communal rioting had resulted in a life sentence. Since then there have been four more landmark verdicts. A total of 79 accused were given life sentences for crimes committed against Muslims during the massacre in Sardarpura (Mehsana district), Odh (Anand district) and Deepda Darwaza (Mehsana district). These verdicts were delivered between November 2011 and July 2012. In August 2012, a total of 32 accused in the Naroda massacre were given life imprisonment.[19]

However, these victories have been bittersweet. Zahira's predicament, and her subsequent imprisonment, had a chilling effect in Ahmedabad on some victims of sexual violence and activists engaged in rehabilitation work. Zahira's case highlighted the pressures faced by victims post-2002. They bore the trauma of surviving gruesome violence against themselves and their families, and many lived in poverty after losing everything in the violence. They were torn between fighting a tough and protracted legal battle with no assurance of justice at the end, and risking widespread public condemnation by acquiescing to pressure to withdraw their cases and trading their silence for financial resources. Legal justice would heal some wounds, but surrender would ease the fear they lived with after the violence. It would also possibly generate material resources with which to rebuild their lives.

The difficulty of choosing between the two, and the media attention that Zahira's case received, deterred some survivors of sexual violence and activists engaged in rehabilitation work from seeking judicial redress. Consider the testimony of an activist involved in reconciliation work among Dalit and Muslim women in Ahmedabad. Some of these Muslim women were raped during the massacre. When asked why her organisation had decided not to pursue legal justice for rapes and other forms of sexual violence committed during the riots, the activist said:

> You have seen that a woman's stomach was ripped open and a baby was taken out with a sword. We used to keep banging on about this story saying that this has happened and there is such a woman, this has happened. Now the *Tehelka* people have shown it [in the sting operation by Ashish Khetan] so it has become true. So we have to find proof like this, but we don't have money for it. Today, I am ready to throw a challenge that if the 32 women I work with are assured justice, then they will speak. But we need that justice. These women cannot become like Zahira. Zahira, poor thing, was pulled in different directions, got so much publicity. [She was under pressure] sometimes to say yes, sometimes to say no. They said she took a lot of money and bribes. What money, what bribe has she taken? She has suffered. Look what has become of that delicate girl? Why would we want our girls to suffer like that? (Interview, Ahmedabad, 10 December 2007)

The activist's words speak volumes about the compulsions faced by survivors of sexual violence after the conflict, as well as the constraints confronting those helping them to rebuild their lives. On the one hand, both had to grapple with securing reliable evidence and pursuing the protracted and expensive legal battle, while being aware that the prospect of justice was remote. On the other hand, Zahira's experience suggested that, should they decide to pursue a case, they too might suffer like her, first in the massacre and then under the unforgiving, incessant public gaze. By shunning the judicial course, these women were seeking self-preservation from what might have been tantamount to a second violation; it was an attempt to preserve what still remained 'delicate'. This is a damning verdict on the ability of the judicial apparatus to deliver justice to victims of sexual violence.

The decision by some women not to seek judicial redress (willingly or under family and community pressure), together with the administration's efforts to subvert legal proceedings, has meant that all but two cases of sexual violence committed during the massacre have gone unpunished. The first ever conviction in India for sexual violence during communal violence was achieved by Bilkees Yakoob Rasool in 2008.[20] The difficulties she faced in her legal battle for justice would have caused most people to surrender, making her triumph all the more astounding.

Bilkees was five months pregnant when she was gang-raped on 1 March 2002, during the peak of the violence, by neighbours who were familiar to her. On that day she also witnessed the rape of three of her family members and the murder of 14 relatives, including her three-year-old daughter. She survived because she was left for dead. When the police found her on 2 March and took her to the hospital, the medical examination confirmed rape. She attempted to lodge an FIR on 4 March, but the police recorded only seven of the 14 killings. They also refused to lodge her complaint regarding rape, even though her medical examination had confirmed it and she knew the names of the three men who had raped her (AIDWA 2002: 63–4; Jaffrelot 2012: 82).[21] The case was closed in January 2003 for lack of evidence.

However, with the support of NGOs including Jan Vikas and the National Human Rights Commission, Bilkees petitioned the Supreme Court, which in turn ordered the Gujarat government to conduct fresh investigations and reopen the case. Following this, the Gujarat police allegedly sought to harass her so that she would withdraw her case. One of the tactics included 'waking her in the middle of the night to return to the location of the rape and murders to re-enact the events' (Jaffrelot 2012: 82). In 2003, the Supreme Court ordered the Central Bureau of Investigation to reinvestigate the case. This led to the arrest of 12 men for rape and murder, and of two police officers for the obstruction of justice. Bilkees then successfully fought for the transfer of her case to Mumbai, and the central government appointed a public prosecutor for her in August 2004. In 2008, six long years after the massacre, 13 of the 20 accused were convicted, and 11 were condemned to life imprisonment.

With regard to the cases of sexual violence in Ahmedabad, there is a ray of hope, its rarity making it all the more precious. In August 2012, the special fast-track sessions court established in Ahmedabad for cases relating to the 2002 massacre delivered a remarkable judgement on the violence committed in Naroda Patiya, the worst-affected area in Gujarat. Here, at least 95 Muslims, including 30 men, 32 women and 33 children, were killed and burnt, and many Muslim girls and women were mutilated, raped, gang-raped and murdered on 28 February 2002. The presiding judge Jyotsna Yagnik ruled that it had been proven beyond reasonable doubt that in Naroda Patiya, 'offences of rape, gang-rape and even outraging the modesty of women did take place on that day'.[22]

The court found Bajrang Dal leader Suresh Chara, who was arrested in May 2002 but released on bail in October 2002, guilty of the rape of a Muslim girl, Naseemo, who was around 16 years old in 2002. Chara is the same individual who had boasted to *Tehelka* journalist Ashish Khetan about how he had raped Naseemo: 'Naseemo that juicy plump one [...] I got on top [...] properly [...] then I pulped her [...] made her into a pickle'.[23] Chara was sentenced to rigorous punishment for 12 years for offences related to sexual violence: a two-year jail sentence for the use of criminal force with the intent to 'outrage the modesty of a woman' (under section 354 of the Indian Penal Code), and 10 years for rape (under section 376). Since he was also convicted for murder, his total prison sentence was 31 years. Tough sentences were given to 31 accused besides Chara for committing non-sexual offences, notably Bajrang Dal leader Babu Bajrangi (life imprisonment till death) and BJP leader and former Gujarat cabinet minister Maya Kodnani (28 years' imprisonment). Both Bajrangi and Kodnani have been granted multiple bails by the Gujarat High Court.

The conviction of Chara is the first – and, as of March 2016, the only – conviction for sexual violence committed in Ahmedabad during the 2002 massacre. His conviction builds on the Bilkees judgement. It constitutes a major triumph for the survivors of Naroda Patiya, who persevered with their cases for more than ten years even though they had to cope with fear and intimidation, resist monetary allurements, and repeat harrowing accounts of their families' suffering in courts. It is also a salutary accomplishment of civil society groups such as CJP (the group that pursued the Naroda Patiya cases), who persevered in the face of a hostile Gujarat administration, strong anti-Muslim sentiment within Gujarat, the decline in national and international public attention with regard to 2002, and, perhaps most importantly, limited hope.

However, the prospects of further convictions for sexual violence are remote. The quality of evidence, especially the reliability of witness accounts, is likely to deteriorate further, both for natural reasons and because of the inability and/or unwillingness of the Gujarat police to prevent evidence from being destroyed or contaminated. The impact of the deteriorating evidence has already been felt in the case of the Naroda Patiya judgement. Due to the lack of sufficient reliable evidence, the court gave Chara the benefit of the doubt for the offence of gang-rape against Naseemo, even though it found him individually guilty of rape. Eight others accused of rape and gang-rape were acquitted on a similar basis, since 'in none of the other cases of rape or outraging the modesty of a Muslim women has it been proved beyond reasonable doubt as to who the tormentor was'.[24] While individual convictions for rape are important in themselves, convictions for gang-rapes are crucial for establishing in courts the severity of violence committed against Muslim women in 2002. The deterioration in the quality of the evidence makes this increasingly difficult.

Moreover, the culpability of organisations such as the Bajrang Dal in orchestrating violence against Muslims during February–March 2002 has yet to be established by the judiciary, even though individual members of the outfit, such as Suresh Chara and Babu Bajrangi, have been given tough sentences for crimes they committed. Holding organisations accountable is particularly important for bringing within the judicial purview the political networks through which sexual and other forms of violence were orchestrated and inflicted. Two precedents offer some hope in this regard. First, the Congress-led national government imposed a nationwide ban on organisations such as the RSS in 1993, after the demolition of the Babri Mosque sparked communal riots in large parts of India. Establishment of the culpability of Hindu right organisations in the 2002 massacre may pave the way for a similar ban. Second, in the Naroda verdict in August 2012, the presiding judge held Maya Kodnani guilty of 'criminal conspiracy' as well as murder and arson, thereby establishing that violence committed during the massacre was carefully orchestrated, rather than a product of individual actions by Hindu nationalist foot soldiers. The admission of this notion in the criminal jurisprudence around communal violence may well have implications for on-going cases, such the one being pursued by Ehsan Jafri's widow Zakia Jafri, in which complainants have accused Modi, Kodnani and other senior government and police officials of 'criminal conspiracy to commit mass murders'.[25] Ehsan Jafri, former Congress MP from Gujarat, was killed on 28 February by Hindu activists in Gulberg Society, Chamanpura. His widow is pursuing a legal battle on his behalf (see the discussion in Chapter 3).

A verdict that establishes the culpability of particular Hindu nationalist organisations or sections of the Gujarat state apparatus would act as a strong deterrent to the production of such violence in the future, and create an important legal precedent. It may also enhance the confidence of religious minorities in the resilience of the Indian state's commitment to the rule of law and secularism in the face of a powerful and strident Hindu right. It might also go some way towards healing the scars of the thousands of victims who have been denied justice for crimes committed by Hindu nationalist activists in previous episodes of large-scale conflict in India.

Concluding remarks

Sexual violence against women and girls, and in some cases against men and boys,[26] has become an all but ubiquitous feature of armed conflict across the world. According to a comprehensive recent study, sexual violence during armed conflict was reported from no less than 51 countries across the world between 1987 and 2007, including 20 countries in Africa, six in Latin America, eight in Asia (including India), six in Europe and five in the Middle East (Bastick et al. 2007). Ethnic polarisation (for example, between Hutus and Tutsis during the 1994 Rwandan genocide), mobilisation of large, armed paramilitary forces (such as during the civil war in Sierra Leone between 1991 and 2002), and a partisan state apparatus (for example, the Pakistani military during Bangladesh's independence war in 1971) have been identified as recurring aspects of the context in which such violence occurs. The experience of Gujarat, even in 2002, was not as extreme as that of regions such as Rwanda, where within 100 days of the genocide in 1994, up to one million people were killed and between 100,000 and 250,000 women were raped. However, 'Gujarat 2002' illuminates the role of communalism, of Hindu nationalist activists and the state apparatus in the incidence of sexual violence during communal conflict. Consequently, I hope that the findings reported in this book will facilitate comparative work on different jurisdictions within India, as well as on variations in the incidence of such violence within the same territory.

The production of sexual violence during communal conflict in Ahmedabad, as I have argued, must be understood with reference to the interplay between Hindu nationalist ideology and the local dynamics in operation in particular neighbourhoods or localities. This enables us to understand how the work of specific outfits such as the RSS, VHP and the Bajrang Dal can inspire rioters and give their collective and individual sexual-political agendas focus and direction. The interplay varies from conflict to conflict, causing the presence or absence of more or less extreme forms of sexual violence in each instance of strife. In 1969, and particularly in 2002, the conflict was communally motivated from the very outset, and Hindu nationalist propaganda and activities encountered few challenges. The ideological instigation of sexual violence against Muslim women was not subverted by an alternative rhetoric; efforts to mobilise Hindus against Muslims were not impeded by the mobilisation of people under different identity rubrics; and violence at the neighbourhood level was inflicted almost exclusively along gendered communal lines.

However, in 1985, caste- and religion-based violence occurred simultaneously, diluting the potency of Hindu nationalist propaganda to mobilise people exclusively along communal lines. The impact of inflammatory propaganda material inciting violence against Muslims was diminished by campaigns mounted by upper-caste Hindus, who called for violence against low castes as well as Muslims, but did not encourage sexual violence. Due to the eruption of tensions along multiple axes, a 'Hindu collective' could not be forged: upper castes attacked backward castes, low castes and Muslims, and the police targeted upper-caste women. Consequently, backward castes, low castes and Muslims, who at the time lived in close proximity to one another, forged mutual alliances, protecting each other's lives and property and avoiding extreme sexual violence. To conclude, understanding sexual violence against minority women entails that, beyond an exclusive focus on majoritarian rhetoric, we grasp the way nationalist ideology becomes imbricated in the lives of individual people – as victims, rioters and leaders, and as neighbours, workers and family members – at the local level.

APPENDIX

HINDU NATIONALIST
PROPAGANDA MATERIALS

કર્યા પછી એક જ મહિનામાં તે જ મુસ્લિમે બીજા લગ્ન કરતાં હિન્દુ યુવતીએ ઝેર ગટગટાવ્યું.

★ કર્ણાવતીના એક કરોડપતિ હિન્દુ પરિવારની શિક્ષીત યુવતીને કાર ડ્રાઈવીંગ શીખવતા મુસ્લિમે ફસાવી તેનું અપહરણ કર્યું.

★ સુરત જીલ્લામાં બસમાં અપડાઉન કરતી સગીરવયની અનેક હિન્દુ યુવતીઓને-વિદ્યાર્થીનીઓને મુસ્લિમ ડ્રાયવરો ફસાવી રહ્યા છે.

★ કર્ણાવતીમાં કોલેજના દરવાજેથી ગ્રેજ્યુએટ યુવતીને 'રાજુ' નામધારી મુસ્લિમે ફસાવી લગ્ન કર્યા પછી હિન્દુ યુવતીને જાણ થઈ કે તે મુસ્લિમના હાથમાં ફસાઈ છે.

★ કર્ણાવતીમાં સૌંદર્ય પ્રસાધનોની દુકાન ચલાવનાર મુસ્લિમે તેની ગ્રાહક એવી હિન્દુ યુવતીઓને ફસાવી.

★ રાજકોટની બ્યુટી પાર્લર ચલાવતી હિન્દુ યુવતી પાસે સામાન વેચવા આવનાર મુસ્લિમ ફેરિયાએ તેને ફસાવી

★ ભરૂચમાં મુસ્લિમ સિનીયર વકીલે તેની જુનિયર તરીકે કામ કરતી હિન્દુ યુવતીને ફસાવીને તેની બીજી પત્ની બનાવી.

★ કર્ણાવતીમાં શિક્ષિત હિન્દુ યુવતી સોનલને મુસ્લિમે બીજાનો બંગલો પોતાનો છે એમ કહીને, પોતે સારી નોકરી કરે છે, તેવી ખોટી વાતોમાં ભરમાવીને લગ્ન કરી લીધા પરંતુ લગ્ન પછી તેને ગોમતીપુરની ઝુપ્પડપટ્ટીમાં રાખી. ત્યાંથી સોનલ ઘરે પરત ભાગી આવી.

★ નવસારીમાં મુસ્લિમ ડોક્ટરે તેની સાથે કામ કરનાર હિન્દુ ડોક્ટર બહેનને ફસાવ્યાં.

★ બારડોલીનાં હિન્દુ વહેપારીનાં મુસ્લિમ પાર્ટનરે હિન્દુ વેપારીની બહેન વર્ષાને ફસાવી, અપહરણ કરી લગ્ન કરી લીધા.

હિન્દુ માતા-પિતાને આહ્વાન

● જો તમે આવી દુર્ઘટનાનો ભોગ બન્યા હોવ તો લોકલાજની ચિંતા વગર તરત જ પોલીસ કેસ કરો.

● આપણી દીકરીને સન્માન સહિત ઘેર પાછી લાવો.

● સંકટ સમયે વિશ્વ હિન્દુ પરિષદ, બજરંગદળ, દુર્ગાવાહિનીનો સંપર્ક કરો.

● આપની જાણમાં આવેલ જુના અથવા નવા આવા કિસ્સા વિગતવાર લખીને નીચે જણાવેલ સરનામે મોકલીને કાર્યમાં સહયોગ આપો.

> હિન્દુ સમાજમાંથી એક વ્યક્તિ મુસલમાન કે ખ્રિસ્તી બને એટલે એક હિન્દુ ઘટ્યો એમ નહી પણ હિન્દુ સમાજનો એક દુશ્મન વધ્યો.
> —સ્વામી વિવેકાનંદ

વિશ્વ હિન્દુ પરિષદ

ડૉ. વણીકર સ્મારક ભાવન, ૧૧, મહાલક્ષ્મી સોસાયટી,
મહાલક્ષ્મી ચાર રસ્તા, પાલડી, કર્ણાવતી.

પ્રકાશક : વિશ્વ હિન્દુ પરિષદ ડૉ. વણીકર સ્મારક ભાવન, ૧૧, મહાલક્ષ્મી સોસાયટી, પ્લાલડી, કર્ણાવતી. ફોન - ૬૬૦૪૦૧૫
મુદ્રક : એલાઈડ ઓફસેટ પ્રિન્ટર્સ (ગુ.) પ્રા. લિ. ૧૪/૨, કાબીદાસ મીલ કમ્પાઉન્ડ, ગોમતીપુર, અમદાવાદ-૨૧ ● ફોન : ૨૧૪૧૨૩૮, ૨૧૬૫૦૫૦, ૨૧૬૬૧૪

Figure A.1   Reverse Of Pamphlet in Fig. 3.1 (*Source*: Vishwa Hindu Parishad. 'Savadhan Campaign' (Ahmedabad: VHP, 1998))

भारतके इसाईकरणका षडयंत्र

भारतके निम्म प्रदेशोंमें इसाईकरणकी वृध्धि हिन्दुओकी तुलनामें बहुत ज्यादा है ।

१९८१- १९९१ की वृध्धि

प्रदेश	हिन्दु वृध्धि %	इसाई वृध्धि %
अरुणाचल प्रदेश	७३.३४ %	२२५.९८ %
गुजरात	२९.१२ %	३६.९६ %
मणीपुर	२४.१८ %	४८.६ %
मेघालय	४८.३४ %	६३.६ %
उडिसा	३६.८३ %	३८.६७ %
पंजाब	१२.७३ %	२९.७५ %
सिक्किम	३०.६ %	९९.२ %
त्रिपुरा	३०.२ %	८६.८४ %
लक्षदिप	२९.९९ %	१२४.८ %

अत्तर पूर्वांचलमें इसाई वृध्धिका दर गत ९० सालमें

साल	इसाई
१९०१	१.२३%
१९०५	७.८%
१९७१	१२.५%
१९९१	३१.८%

रिजर्व बेंक के अनुसार इसाईको मिल रहे विदेशी धन

- १९५०-५४ - २९.२७ करोड रूपिया
- १९८०-८६ - २००० करोड रूपिया
- अत्तु - नवे, डिसें १९९८ - १४ करोड रूपिया

वर्ल्ड क्रिश्चियन एनसाइक्लोपिडीया के अनुसार

- विश्वमें इसाईयतका वार्षिक बजट ६५,००० करोड रूपिया
- पूर्णकालिन इसाई प्रचारक ४१,००,००० (इकतालीस लाख)
- चर्च के द्वारा चलाई जा रही लायब्रेरी - १३०००
- चर्च के द्वारा चलाई जा रही युनिवसीर्टी - १५००
- चर्च के प्राइवेट टीव्ही रेडियो - १८००
- विविध भाषा के मेगेजीन - २२,०००
- बडी मीशन संस्थाए - ४,०००
- विदेशमें जाकर काम कर रहे पादरी - २,६२,३००

७८८ मतांतरकी बडी योजनामें

- १ करोड कार्यकर्ता वर्षमें काम करते है ।
- १८,००० करोड रूपियाका बजट - वार्षिक

१५५ मतांतरके वैश्विक योजनाए

- १५,५०,०० कार्यकर्ता
- ६२०० करोड रूपियाका वार्षिक बजट

Figure A.2 Bharat ke Isaikaranka Shadyantra (*Source*: Vishwa Hindu Parishad (Ahmedabad: VHP, 1998))

३३ मतांतरके राक्षसी वैश्विक योजनाएं

- ३३,००,००० (तैंतीत लाख) कार्यकर्ता
- ११,५०० करोड़ रुपियकत वार्षिक   बजट

चर्चकी भारतमें भावि योजनाएं

इसाईकी मीशन मेन्डेट पुस्तकके अनुसार

- भारतमें १,००,००० नये चर्च बनना
- हर गांवमें एक चर्च
- हर हाथमें एक बाइबल

हिन्दुओंकी बनबासी एवं दलित जातिओंको मतांतर करके हिन्दुओं प्रति घिक्कारकी व्यापक योजना बनी है ।

इसाईयोंकी Why North India - documents में से

- / उत्तर भारतमें नये - ७५००० चर्च
- नये १,००,००० मिशनरीज तैयार करनेकी योजना बनी है ।
- भारत के ५९२ जिल्लोमें चर्च बनानेकी योजना 'क्रिस्मेटीक न्यु लाईफ' चर्चने बनाई है ।

OM India (Operation Mobilisation)

- भारत के १० करोड लोगों तक इसा मसीह के संदेश पहुंचाने की योजना
- मध्यप्रदेशमें ३०,००० नये चर्चकी योजना
- राजस्थान : प्रत्येक ब्लोकमें एक चर्च
- हरियाणा : प्रत्येक ब्लोकमें एक चर्च
- भारतमें इसाईओंकी मतातंरकी ताकत

  १,९९,२५० इसाई पादरी

  ९०,००० इसाई नन्स

  १०,०० विविध शिक्षाकी संस्थाए   { २२, नवेम्बर १९९५ -

  २४०, कोलेज   Indian Express }

  ७०४ अस्पाल

  १७९२ मेडीकल डिस्पेनारी

- भारत के २.२५ करोड इसाईमें २-लाख (एक प्रतिशत) मतातंर के कार्यमें लगें है ।

हिन्दुओं के देवताओं का अपमान

- राम कृष्ण..... मुक्तिदाता नही हो सकते, क्योंकी सबके सब.... बुराइओंमें लिप्त थे ।

  - वह (कृष्ण) चोर... था

  - राम.. पापी था ।

नियोगी कमिशनने पान नं. ११९-१२० पर इसाईयोंकी पत्रिकामें से उपरोक्त लिया है

Why North India के इसाईओंके डोक्युमेन्टमें हमारी तिर्थ नगरी बनारस के शेतानकी नगरी कहा है ।

इसाई मेगेजीन के Operation Agape अक्तुबर १९९८ के अंकमें

- भारत देशको - शत्रु भुमि कहा है ।
- भारत देशको जितना है - एसा कहा है

एसी युध्धकी भाषाका प्रयोग भारत ओर हिन्दुओं के विरोधमें कीया गया है ।

प्रकाशक :

विश्व हिन्दु परिषद, गुजराज. ११ महालक्ष्मी सोसायटी, पालडी, कर्णावती - ३८० ००७.

Figure A.3   Reverse of Pamphlet in Figure A.2 (*Source*: Vishwa Hindu Parishad (Ahmedabad: VHP, 1998))

જય શ્રી રામ

વંદે માતરમ્   "ધર્મ: રક્ષિતમ્ રક્ષિતઃ"   ભારત માતા કી જય

બજરંગ દળ - વિશ્વ હિન્દુ પરિષદ

મણીનગર સ્ટેશન, પ્રખંડ દક્ષિણ કર્ણાવતી.

પ્રિય ધર્મબંધુઓ,

પ્રિય ધર્મપ્રેમી માતાઓ, બંધુઓ, બહેનો આપ સૌ વિશ્વ હિન્દુ પરિષદ અંતર્ગત સંસ્થા "બજરંગ દળ" વિશે આપ કશું પણ જાણતા જ હશો. છતાં, વિશેષ જાણકારી આપવા માંગીએ છીએ.

"બજરંગ દળ" યુવકોનું વિશાળ સંગઠન છે.

"બજરંગ દળ" નું ધ્યેય

- o દેશની રક્ષા એટલે ભારત માતાની રક્ષા કરવી.
- o હિન્દુ સમાજની ઉપેક્ષા કરનાર સામે બુલંદ અવાજ ઉભો કરવો.
- o ધર્મ, સંસ્કૃતિની રક્ષા કરવી.
- o હિન્દુ બેન-બેટીની રક્ષાર્થે કામ કરવું.
- o રાષ્ટ્ર વિરોધી તત્વો સામે ઝઝુમવું.
- o ગૌહત્યા સામે જેહાદ જગાવવી
- o હિન્દુ કન્યાની મુસ્લીમો દ્વારા ફસામણી તેમજ ખ્રિસ્તી મીશીનરીની રાષ્ટ્ર વિરોધી કામગીરી સામે જન જાગૃતિ અભિયાન.
- o બજરંગ દળ એટલે રાષ્ટ્ર શક્તિ - હિન્દુ શક્તિ.
- o જગત જનની માં જગદંબા, એ જ દુર્ગા માતા એ જ માં ભારત માતા તો તેમના રક્ષણ માટે

ચાલો રાષ્ટ્ર હિત માટે જોડાવ "બજરંગ દળ" માં

"દેશનું અસ્તિત્વ તો, આપણું અસ્તિત્વ"

તો દેશ માટે ચાલો યુવાનો ઉમટી પડો.

"બજરંગ દળ" માં જોડાઈ ભારત માતાનું ઋણ અદા કરીએ.

❀ ત્રિશૂલ દિક્ષાન્ત વિધિ કાર્યક્રમ ❀

મહોદ્ય શ્રી

મુખ્ય મહેમાન : શ્રી હસમુખભાઈ પટેલ (મુખ્ય વક્તા - કર્ણાવતી-બજરંગદળ સંયોજક)

અતિથિ વિશેષ : શ્રી દિલીપભાઈ પટેલ (કર્ણાવતી દક્ષિણ જીલ્લો બજરંગદળ સંયોજક)

શ્રી બચુભાઈ લાડવા (વિશ્વ હિન્દુ પરિષદ દક્ષિણ જીલ્લો - મંત્રી)

દિનાંક : ૧૫-૯-૯૮   વાર : મંગળવાર

સ્થળ : સ્વામિનારાયણ મંદિર,   સમય : સાંજે ૭:૦૦ કલાકે

રામબાગ, મણીનગર કર્ણાવતી.

● નિમંત્રક ●

શંકરરાવ મોરે (કાર્યકારી અધ્યક્ષ વિ.હી.પ)   સુધીર સૈની (બજરંગ દળ સંયોજક)

ભીખાભાઈ પ્રજાપતિ (મંત્રી)   અમૃત દેસાઈ (બજરંગ દળ સહ સંયોજક)

ડૉ. દેવેન્દ્ર શર્મા (સંયોજક, વિ.હિ પ પ્રમુખ)

નોંધ : વરસાદ હશે તો પણ કાર્યક્રમ ચાલુ રહેશે.

પ્રાંતીય કાર્યાલય : વિશ્વ હિન્દુ પરિષદ ડૉ. વझીકર ભવન, ૧૧, મહાલક્ષ્મી સોસાયટી, પાલડી, કર્ણાવતી. દૂરભાષ : ૪૧૪૦૧૫

મુદ્રકઃ શ્રી સાંઈનાથ પ્રિન્ટર્સ અમીનભુવન મણીનગર, અમદાવાદ-૮.

Figure A.4 Bajrang Dal-Vishwa Hindu Parishad (*Source*: Vishwa Hindu Parishad (Ahmedabad: VHP, 1998))

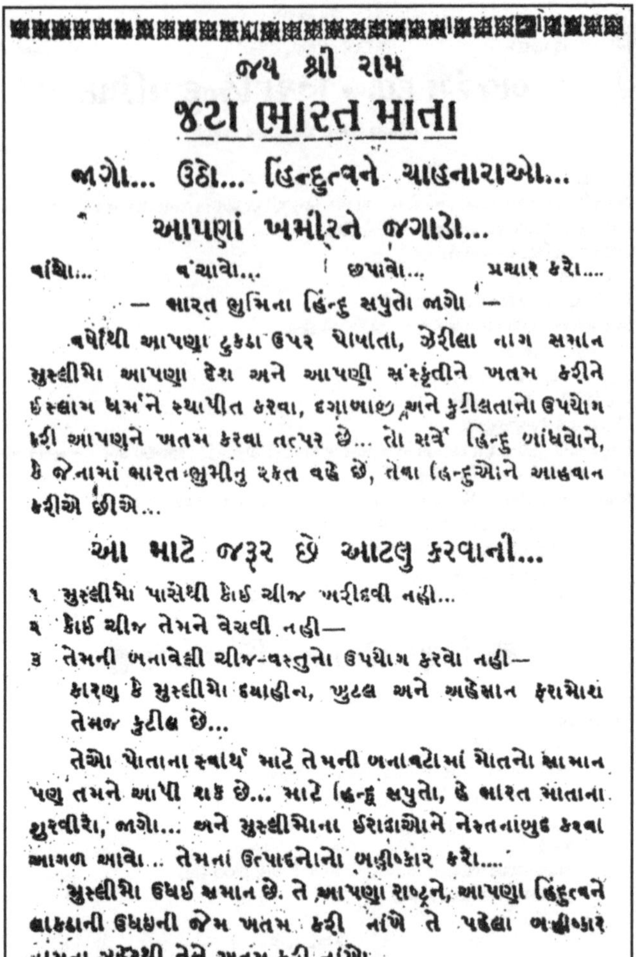

જય શ્રી રામ

જય ભારત માતા

જાગો... ઉઠો... હિન્દુત્વને ચાહનારાઓ...

આપણાં ખમીરને જગાડો...

વાંચો... વંચાવો... છપાવો... પ્રચાર કરો....

— ભારત ભુમિના હિંન્દુ સપુતો જાગો —

વર્ષોથી આપણા ટુકડા ઉપર પોષાતા, ઝેરીલા નાગ સમાન મુસ્લીમો આપણા દેશ અને આપણી સંસ્કૃતીને ખતમ કરીને ઈસ્લામ ધર્મને સ્થાપીત કરવા, દગાબાજી અને કુટીલતાનો ઉપયોગ કરી આપણને ખતમ કરવા તત્પર છે... તો સર્વે હિન્દુ બાંધવોને, કે જેનામાં ભારત ભુમીનુ રક્ત વહે છે, તેવા હિન્દુઓને આહવાન કરીએ છીએ...

આ માટે જરૂર છે આટલુ કરવાની...

૧ મુસ્લીમો પાસેથી કોઈ ચીજ ખરીદવી નહી...
૨ કોઈ ચીજ તેમને વેચવી નહી—
૩ તેમની બનાવેલી ચીજ-વસ્તુનો ઉપયોગ કરવો નહી—
કારણ કે મુસ્લીમો દયાહીન, જુટલ અને અહેસાન ફરામોશ તેમજ કુટીલ છે...

તેઓ પોતાના સ્વાર્થ માટે તેમની બનાવટોમાં મોતનો સામાન પણ તમને આપી શકે છે... માટે હિન્દુ સપુતો, હે ભારત માતાના શુરવીરો, જાગો... અને મુસ્લીમોના ઈરાદાઓને નેસ્તનાબુદ કરવા આગળ આવો... તેમનાં ઉત્પાદનોનો બહીષ્કાર કરો....

મુસ્લીમો ઉધઈ સમાન છે. તે આપણા રાષ્ટ્રને, આપણા હિંદુત્વને લાકડાની ઉધઈની જેમ ખતમ કરી નાંખે તે પહેલા બહીષ્કાર નામના ઝહેરથી તેને ખતમ કરી નાંખો...

જય શ્રી રામ

Figure A.5 Jai Bharat Mata (*Source*: Anonymous (Ahmedabad, n.d.))

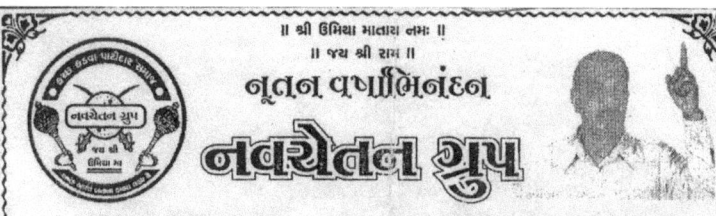

॥ શ્રી ઉમિયા માતાય નમઃ ॥
॥ જય શ્રી રામ ॥
નૂતન વર્ષાભિનંદન
નવચેતન ગ્રુપ

હર ઘરમાં એક જીવતો બૉમ્બ છે. ગમે ત્યારે ફાટી શરૂ છે. જીવતો બૉમ્બ કોણ છે ? આપણી દીકરી.

ઈતિહાસ સાક્ષી છે કે આપણા પૂર્વજો જે જમીન અને જોરૂ માટે લડતા રહ્યા છે. પણ આજનો જમાનો અલગ અને વિચિત્ર બની ગયો છે. હર વ્યક્તિને એવો આરામની જરૂરિયાત કરતાં પણ અતિ સંપત્તિ પાછળ દોડી રહ્યો છે. ક્યારે નથી વિચાર્યું કે પૈસા પાછળ પાગલ છું પણ મારા પૂર્વજોના સંસ્કારો ભારતીય સંસ્કૃતિના સંસ્કાર, હિન્દુ સંસ્કૃતિના સંસ્કારો અને ઋષિમુનિઓના સંસ્કારોની તરફ ક્યારે વિચાર કરીને નથી જોયું તેથી આજના યુગનું પરિણામ છે કે આપણી દીકરી ક્યાં ભટકતી હોય છે. તમારી દીકરી સવારથી નીકળે છે. કૉલેજ જવા માટે કાં તો જૉબ કરવા માટે નીકળે છે. મિત્રને મળવા માટે જાય છે. આપણું ધ્યાન ના હોવાથી આપણી દીકરીને બદમાશો આજના લફંગાઓ ફોસલાવી પટાવી ઊંધે રસ્તે લઈ જાય છે. દીકરીને એવી રીતે ખોટી લાગણીઓથી ફસાવે છે કે દીકરી એમની બની જાય છે. અને માબાપને ઓળખવા તૈયાર નથી હોતી.

આ નાદાન દીકરી સમાજ..... કાર્ય કરતી હોય છે. આપણા ઘરની દીકરીને સંસ્કારોથી વંચિત રાખીએ છીએ. કાલે એ દિકરાને જન્મ આપે છે. ત્યારે.... નિર્મલ કરવાનું કામ કરત હોય છે. પણ જ્યારે આજના યુગના દિકરા દિકરીઓને વડીલોના સંસ્કારો આપવાનું કામ.... ..કર્યું હોય તો આવતી પેઢીને સંસ્કાર શિખવવાનું કામ નહીં કરીએ તો હિન્દુ સમાજનું પતન ચોક્કસ છે.

ભાઈઓ-બહેનો આજ અ...... જોઈ રહ્યા છો ટીવી ચેનલો અમેરિકન પશ્ચિમી વિસ્તારનું આક્રમણ આપણા ઉપર થઈ રહ્યું છે. એના કારણે આપણી દીકરી અ.... હિન્દુ સમાજની દીકરીઓ હુંકા કપડાં પહેરી નીકળતી હોય છે. ત્યારે એમને સમજાવવાનું કામ કોણ છે ? ભારતમાં રહેતા હર ....જવાબદારી બને છે. આપણે જોઈ રહ્યા છીએ. આ યુગનું પતન થઈ રહ્યું છે. પણ આપણે બધા ચુપ છીએ.

દીકરીને શિક્ષણ આપવા જોઈએ એક તરાજુમાં શિક્ષણ અને વ... તરાજુમાં ભારતીય સંસ્કૃતિ અને સંસ્કારો આપવા જોઈએ. જો માતા પિતાને પોતાની દીકરીને કૉલેજમાં મોકલવાની હોય અથવા તો આપણા દિકરા કૉલેજમાં ભણતી હોય ત્યારે કેવી રીતે આપણે પંપાળમાં સવારથી સાંજ સુધી એ લાલચી બની એના પાછળ દોડતા હોઈએ એ આતો આપણું અમૂલ્ય ધન છે. તો એના પાછળ આપણે ધ્યાન આપવું જોઈએ.

એક બાપની દીકરી જ્યારે પરણે છે. ત્યારે વિદાય આપવાના સાંકે દિકરીનો બાપ ગમે તેટલો મર્દ હોય પણ વિદાય વખતે બાપના આંખમાંથી અને હૃદયમાંથી આંસુઓનો વરસાદ વરસે છે. એ ઘડી કંઈ અનોખી હોય છે. પણ એજ બાપની બીજી દીકરી કોઈ લફંગાના ષડયંત્ર (પ્રેમ)માં આવી ગઈ હોય અને એ એના સાથે ભાગી જાય ત્યારે એ દીકરી વિદાય થઈ કહેવાય પણ ત્યારે એના બાપના આંખમાં આંસુ તો આવે પણ કેવા આવે એમની સમાજમાં ઈજ્જતદાર લોકો આંગલી ચીંધે કે જોવા પેલાની દીકરી એક લફંગા સાથે ભાગી ગઈ છે. તેનો બાપ જાય છે. સમાજના લોકો અને પરિવારના લોકો રોજ સંભળાવે છે કે તમે દીકરીને સંસ્કારો નથી આપ્યા તેનું આ પરિણામ છે. હવે તમે ભોગવો.

જો કોઈ દીકરી પોતાનું ઘર કે સમાજ ભૂલી ગઈ હોય તો તેને સમજાવવાનું કામ વિનામૂલ્ય કરે છે નવચેતન ગ્રુપ. જો કોઈ આપના એરિયામાં કોઈપણ દીકરી ઘર ભૂલી ગઈ હોય તો દીકરીને પુછો કે બેટા તું કોણ છે. તારા મા બાપ કોણ છે અને એને સમજાવો જો ના સમજે તો આપશ્રી અમારો સીધ.. સંપર્ક કરો. જો આપ એક દિકરી બચાવો છો તો સમજો કે આપ સો ગામમાતા બચાવતા છો. એક દિકરી બરાબર સો ગાય માન.. છે. દિકરીને આપણા ઘર અને સમાજની ઈજ્જત છે. એને બચાવી આપણે હિન્દુ ધર્મ છે. અને હિન્દુ સંસ્કૃતિ છે.

દિકરી ભાગવાની ભુલ કરે છે એ આપણાને ડંખે છે સમાજ વિના પુરી જિંદગી દુ:ખી થાય છે એ ક્યારે ચલાવી લેવાય નહીં.

તો આવો આપણે ભેગા થઈને બૉમ્બ બચાવવાનું કામ કરીએ બૉમ્બ કોણ છે. આપણી દીકરીઓ.

સર્વ ભાઈબહેનો દિવાળીના શુભકામનાઓ સાથે બૉમ્બ બચાવવાનું કામ કરીએ.

બાબુભાઈ બજરંગી
રાષ્ટ્રીય અધ્યક્ષ
નવચેતન ગ્રુપ

॥ જય શ્રી રામ ॥
તથા નવચેતન ગ્રુપ સમગ્ર ભારતના કાર્યકર્તાઓ

રજનીભાઈ એમ. ચટેલ
કેન્દ્રીય મહામંત્રી,
નવચેતન ગ્રુપ

સૌજન્ય : ઘનશ્યામભાઈ પટેલ તથા ભુપેન્દ્રભાઈ એડવોકેટ (કિરણ પટેલ)

કેન્દ્રિય કાર્યાલય : શ્રીજી માળ, અનંટા ઈલોરા શોપીંગ સેન્ટર, ગેવડ઼ી સિનેમા પાસે, નરોડા, અમદાવાદ. મો. ૯૮૯૧૯૮૨૫૦૧

Figure A.6 Navchetan Group (*Source*: Babu Bajrangi, 'Navchetan Group' (Ahmedabad: Navchetan Group, n.d.))

GLOSSARY

aakrosh	anger
Adivasi	indigenous people; used to describe the Scheduled Tribes
ahimsa	non-violence
akhada	gymnasium, wrestling den, centre of physical culture, the organisation or the site of activities and training of any specialised group
angutha chaap	literally, thumb-print; someone who is illiterate
badli	a temporary worker, casual worker, a substitute
Bajrang Dal	Army of the monkey deity Hanuman
bandh	strike, shutting down of businesses, shops and offices
basti	slum
beizzati	literally 'insult'; the term is often used as a euphemism for rape
bhai	brother
bhaiya	elder brother
bhakti	Hindu devotionalism
bhavna	feeling, sentiment
bibi	a Muslim woman
budha; *budhe*	a derogatory term for an old man
burqa	veil worn by Muslim women
chacha	a term of respect and endearment; literally refers to father's younger brother

chawl; chawli	a form of neighbourhood: a row of rooms with either no sanitary conveniences, or with community facilities built for labourers around the textile mills; tenement
chowki	checkpost
Corporation	commonly used short form for the Ahmedabad Municipal Corporation
crore	10,000,000
Dalit	literally, oppressed; former untouchables; in legal parlance called Scheduled Castes
danga	local term for riot
dharma	religion or religious duty
dini taleem	Islamic religious-spiritual education
dunyavi taleem	worldly education
ghar ke log	members of the family
ghrina	hatred
Gita; Bhagavad Gita	Hindu mythological text that recounts the conversation between warrior-prince Arjuna and Lord Krishna on idealism and practical wisdom
gumraha karna	lead astray
gunda; goonda	thug, local muscleman, tough
Harijan	literally, children of God; term coined by Gandhi for the former untouchables
Hindutva	term coined by Savarkar in 1923 that roughly translates as 'Hindu-ness'; the essence of being a Hindu
jamaat	religious and occupation-based associations
janmabhoomi	birthplace
kaam ki cheez	useful object
kadhi	Indian yoghurt-based curry
karsevak	Hindu religious volunteers
kharab	bad, wrong
khas	special, significant
laj	sexual purity, modesty, chastity
lakh	100,000
lathi	cane, wooden staff, pole, truncheon
maha arti	grand Hindu ceremony of worship
mandir	temple

mangal sutra	sacred thread worn by married Hindu women
masjid	mosque
matrubhumi	motherland
mazdoor	labourer, worker
miya	Muslim man
mrityughant	death knell, symbolised by the banging of kitchen utensils
parda	veil
patrika	booklet; pamphlet
pitribhumi	fatherland
pol	traditional neighbourhood in the walled city of Ahmedabad, consisting of narrow streets lined with buildings
pracharak/pracharika	preacher, propagandist (male/female)
punyabhumi	holy land
purush nirman	creation of an ideal man
Qur'an	Islamic scripture
Rabari	a lower-caste community who traditionally work as milk producers and distributors
raj dharma	the duties or responsibilities of a ruler
Rakhi	a Hindu festival that is marked by the tying of a rakhi, or holy thread, by the sister on the wrist of her brother. The brother in return vows to protect her.
Ramayana	ancient Hindu mythological epic
Ramlila	a dramatic folk re-enactment of the life of the mythological god Rama as described in Hindu epic *Ramayana*. In most parts of northern and western India, local troupes perform the *Ramayana* over 10–15 days.
rashtra	nation-state
rath yatra	Hindu religious procession
roti	Indian flat bread
sabha	association
sadhu	Hindu ascetic or mendicant
safa	turban
samaan	weapons, arms
samskara	good virtues, cultivation

sari	a female garment worn in the Indian subcontinent. It is a strip of unstitched cloth, ranging from 4 to 9 metres in length, that is draped over the body
sarkar	government
sarsanghchalak	supreme philosopher-guide of the RSS
sati	self-immolation by a woman on the pyre of her deceased husband
savadhan	warning/caution
shakha	branch
swayamsevak	(RSS) volunteer
UP *ka bhaiya*	labour immigrants from the north Indian state of Uttar Pradesh
Urs	Sufi religious ceremony

NOTES

Introduction

1. *Communalism Combat*, vol. 8, no. 76, March–April 2002, p. 17. Available online at: http://www.sabrang.com/cc/archive/2002/marapril/ (last accessed on 19 February 2014).
2. Megha Kumar, field notes from the Gujarat relief camps, 2002.
3. Ibid. Also cited in Citizens' Initiative (2002: 106–7).
4. For a critique of previous sexual violence laws, see N. Menon (2004).
5. Females under the age of 18, the legal age of consent in India, will be referred to as 'girls' throughout this study.
6. The draft of the 'communal violence' bill has been amended multiple times since it was first introduced in Parliament in 2005. Its latest version has been awaiting parliamentary approval since 2011.
7. This account is based on numerous print and electronic media reports, of which I cite here some of the most representative: 'Delhi rape protests continue unabated, barricades breached at Manmohan's residence', *India Today*, 21 April 2013. Available online at: http://indiatoday.intoday.in/story/delhi-child-rape-case-protests-outside-sonia-gandhis-house/1/266933.html (last accessed on 17 February 2014). 'Second arrest made after Delhi child rape but anger at police rises', Reuters, 22 April 2013. Available online at: http://in.reuters.com/article/2013/04/22/india-delhi-child-rape-arrest-protest-idINDEE93L05T20130422 (last accessed on 17 February 2014). 'Probe confirms SHO tried to bribe five-year-old Gudiya's kin', *India Today*, 28 April 2013. Available online at: http://indiatoday.intoday.in/story/delhi-child-rape-case-sho-tried-to-bribe-victims-kin/1/268184.html (last accessed on 17 February 2014). 'Five months on, gang-rape survivor Gudiya's trauma forgotten?' NDTV, 5 September 2013. Available online at: http://www.ndtv.com/video/player/news/five-months-on-gang-rape-survivor-gudiya-s-trauma-forgotten/289485 (last accessed on 17 February 2014).

8. 'Delhi gangrape prime accused remorseless during interrogation, says police', *India Today*, 21 December 2012. Available online at: http://indiatoday.intoday.i n/story/delhi-gangrape-prime-accused-remorseless/1/238740.html (last accessed on 17 February 2014).

9. Interview with S. Chara, in 'The RSS will tell you how Chharas killed Muslims', *Tehelka*, 3 November 2007. Available online at: http://www.tehelka.com/s tory_main35.asp?filename=Ne031107The_RSS_will.asp (last accessed on 17 February 2014). The detailed judgement may be found in Sessions Case Nos 235/09, 236/09, 241/09, 242/09, 243/09, 245/09, 246/09 & 270/09, COMMON JUDGMENT, pp. 1707–8. Available online at: http://www.cjponline.org/gujaratTrials/narodapatiya/NP%20Full%20Judgmnt/Naroda%20Patiya%20-%20Common%20Judgment.pdf (last accessed on 17 February 2014).

10. See the various reports included in Indian Social Institute (2002). Notably, two members of the Hindu nationalist outfit Bajrang Dal, namely, Babu Bajrangi and Suresh Chara, have been convicted for their direct participation in the 2002 massacre. Babu Bajrangi was sentenced to life imprisonment until death for non-sexual offences, whereas Chara has been imprisoned for 12 years for raping the 16-year-old Muslim girl Naseemo. See Sessions Case Nos 235/09, 236/09, 241/09, 242/09, 243/09, 245/09, 246/09 & 270/09, COMMON JUDGMENT, p. 1699.

11. For the complete legal definition of genocide, see Office of the UN Special Adviser on the Prevention of Genocide, 'Analysis Framework'. Available online at: http://www.un.org/en/preventgenocide/adviser/pdf/osapg_analysis_framework.pdf (last accessed on 14 January 2013).

12. See 'Ahmedabad: Carnage capital', *Tehelka*, 3 November 2007. Available online at: http://www.tehelka.com/story_main35.asp?filename=Ne031107Ahm edabad.asp (last accessed on 17 February 2014). See also: Forum against Oppression of Women and Awaaz-e-Niswaan (2002); Hashmi and Kumar (2002); Jaffrelot (2012); Jagori (2002); T. Sarkar (2002); Spodek (2011); and *Communalism Combat*, vol. 8, no. 76, March–April 2002. Culpability at the highest levels has not been established by the judiciary, except for former Gujarat state minister and senior BJP politician Maya Kodnani. Kodnani was sentenced to 28 years' imprisonment for her direct involvement in the violence in Ahmedabad's Naroda Patiya area in 2002 by a special fast-track sessions court established in Ahmedabad for 'Conducting Speedy Trial of Riot Cases' relating to the 2002 massacre. See Sessions Case Nos 235/09, 236/09, 241/09, 242/09, 243/09, 245/09, 246/09 & 270/09, COMMON JUDGMENT, p. 602. Kodnani had been granted bail by the Gujarat High Court when this book went to press.

Convictions of police officials for their involvement in violence against Muslims in 2002 have been few and far between. Notably, in 2008, head constable of the Limkheda police station, Somabhai Gori, was sentenced to three years' imprisonment for falsifying records and refusing to lodge the first complaint of Bilkees Yakoob Rasool, who was gang-raped on 1 March 2002 in

Randhikpur village of Gujarat's Dahod district. In 2012, Ahmedabad's police was strongly criticised for 'indirectly facilitating' violence against Muslims. The criticism came from the special fast-track sessions court established in Ahmedabad for 'Conducting Speedy Trial of Riot Cases'. See Sessions Case Nos 235/09, 236/09, 241/09, 242/09, 243/09, 245/09, 246/09 & 270/09, COMMON JUDGMENT, pp. 485 and 489–90. Several human rights organisations have also alleged police complicity in the violence, particularly the People's Union for Civil Liberties, Gujarat. See PUCL, Gujarat, 'An Interim Report to the National Human Rights Commission', in Indian Social Institute (2002: 160–1). Several of my interviewees also mentioned that some police constables unzipped their trousers and used sexually abusive language when Muslim women pleaded for protection during the 2002 massacre.

13. A citizens' tribunal set up in the aftermath of the 2002 violence concluded that the Gujarat police failed to 'fulfill their constitutional duty and prevent mass massacre, rape and arson – in short, to maintain law and order. Worse still is the evidence of their active connivance and brutality, their indulgence in vulgar and obscene conduct against women and children in full public view. It is as if, instead of being impartial keepers of the rule of law, they were a part of the Hindutva brigade targeting helpless Muslims' (CCT 2002, 2:81). See also 'They'd deliver our arms safely for us', *Tehelka*, 13 June 2007. Available online at: http://www.tehelka.com/story_main35.asp?filename=Ne031107TheyDeli ver.asp (last accessed on 14 January 2013). See also the discussion in Chapter 3, this volume.

14. 'Rapes occur in India, not Bharat', *Times of India*, 4 January 2013. Available online at: http://articles.timesofindia.indiatimes.com/2013-01-04/india/ 36147879_1_mohanrao-bhagwat-rss-supremo-rss-leader (last accessed on 14 January 2013).

15. For details regarding these incidents, see Citizens' Initiative (2002); Forum against Oppression of Women and Awaaz-e-Niswaan (2002); Hashmi and Kumar (2002); Jagori (2002); and *Communalism Combat*, March–April 2002.

16. On 27 December 2013, Modi wrote on his blog that he had been 'shaken to the core' by the 2002 massacre, while welcoming the Ahmedabad Metropolitan Court's rejection of the petition of Zakia Jafri, whose husband Ehsan Jafri was killed during the 2002 massacre. He called the judgement a 'victory for peace, unity & brotherhood'. See 'Narendra Modi says he was shaken to the core by 2002 Gujarat riots but does not offer apology', *India Today*, 27 December 2013. Available online at: http://indiatoday.intoday.in/story/narendra-modi-says-sorry-without-saying-sorry-blog-2002-gujarat-riots/1/333239.html (last accessed on 17 February 2014).

17. 'Delhi gang-rape: Women's safety a matter of concern, says Narendra Modi', Zee News, 27 December 2012. Available online at: http://zeenews.india.com/news/ delhi/delhi-gang-rape-womens-security-issue-should-be-above-politics-says-narendra-modi_819151.html (last accessed on 14 January 2013).

18. 'Sushma Swaraj seeks death penalty in child rape cases', *DNA*, 20 April 2013. Available online at: http://www.dnaindia.com/india/report-sushma-swaraj-s eeks-tougher-law-death-sentence-in-rape-of-children-1824847 (last accessed on 14 January 2013).

19. In 2008, 13 men were convicted (of whom 11 were sentenced to life imprisonment) for the rape of Bilkees Yakoob Rasool on 1 March 2002 in Randhikpur village of Dahod district (see Jaffrelot 2012: 82), and for murder (ibid.). In 2012, as mentioned earlier, Suresh Chara was sentenced to rigorous punishment for 12 years for the rape of Naseemo on 28 February 2002 in Ahmedabad's Naroda area. See note 10 above.

20. The Citizens' Initiative report was released on 16 April 2002.

21. 'Gujarat Muslim women "rape victims"', BBC News, 16 April 2002. Available online at: http://news.bbc.co.uk/1/hi/world/south_asia/1933521.stm (last accessed on 17 February 2014).

22. '5-year-old Delhi rape victim's condition gradually improving: Doctor', *Hindustan Times*, 21 April, 2013. Available online at: http://www.hindustantim es.com/india-news/newdelhi/delhi-minor-rape-victim-s-condition-improving-doctor/article1-1048048.aspx (last accessed on 14 January 2013).

23. Based on G. Shah (1970: 195), and my own interviews with survivors, particularly with 'Jamila', resident of Jamalpur (Ahmedabad, 16 November 2007); 'Amina Sheikh', resident of Gomtipur and daughter of a former mill worker (Ahmedabad, 16 November 2007); and Rashida Bano and 'Khurshida Bano', residents of Gomtipur (Ahmedabad, 29 November 2007 and 30 January 2007). The term 'communal riot' is frequently used in the extant historiography to refer to large-scale, religiously motivated violence in India, especially between Hindus and Muslims. The term does not imply that both communities participated equally or suffered proportionately in the violence.

24. Spellings of the names of major cities throughout this book reflect earlier or current usages depending on the historical contexts under discussion.

25. 'Kandhamal rape case: Nun identifies the third accused', *Indian Express*, 23 June 2009. Available online at: http://www.indianexpress.com/news/kandhamal-rape-case-nun-identifies-the-third-accused/480360/ (last accessed on 15 January 2013).

26. The most notable studies are: Turshen (2005) on the conflict in Mozambique and Rwanda; Brownmiller (1975) and Grech (1993) on the 1971 Bangladesh war.

27. That such opportunistic violence has occurred during large-scale conflict beyond Ahmedabad is suggested by Jan Breman's study on the 1992 riot in Surat; this idea has featured more explicitly in studies on conflict elsewhere in the world. See Breman (1993). For studies of conflicts outside India, see, for instance, Brownmiller (1975) and Seifert (1994). However, Brownmiller's conceptions of masculinity have been largely rejected. For a critique of her position, see Skjelsbæk (2001) and Gerecke (2009).

28. Paul Brass, on the basis of extensive work on Uttar Pradesh, has long argued that communal violence in India is actively produced by a wide variety of non-state and state agents (see Brass 2003). Brass's work focuses largely on UP. More recently, Ward Berenschot has done work on the role of political networks in fomenting communal violence in his *Riot Politics* (2011). None of these studies, however, examines the production of sexual violence.

29. Scheduled Castes are the former 'untouchables'. In Gujarat, they are hierarchically organised into the communities of Garodas (Scheduled Caste Brahmins), Vankars (hand weavers), Chamars (a leather tanning caste) and Bhangis (scavengers).

30. Scheduled Tribes is the legal term for 'indigenous people' or Adivasis.

31. On 20 September 1969, *Sevak*, the afternoon edition of *Sandesh*, one of the two most widely circulated vernacular dailies in Gujarat, carried a false report about sexual violence against Hindu women. The newspaper subsequently retracted the report (see Reddy Commission 1971: 106). On 28 February and 1 March 2002, *Sandesh* similarly carried false reports about brutal sexual violence against Hindu women by Muslim men in Godhra; both reports were retracted a couple of days later (see *Sandesh*, Ahmedabad edition, 28 February 2002, p. 1, and 1 March 2002, p. 16).

32. In 1969, Hindu nationalist propaganda materials were published and circulated primarily by the Hindu Sangram Samiti, and by the Hindu Dharma Raksha Samiti, which, according to the Reddy Commission, was formed by the RSS, Jana Sangh, Hindu Mahasabha and some religious priests (see Reddy Commission 1971: 107–9). In 2002, the VHP, Bajrang Dal and Hindu Jagran Morcha took the lead in circulating inflammatory pamphlets (see 'Pamphlet poison', *Communalism Combat*, March–April 2002, p. 133).

33. In its inquiry into the 1969 riot, the Reddy Commission recorded that several witnesses saw Jana Sangh and RSS members leading the crowds, pointing out Muslim properties to the attackers with the help of voters' lists, and otherwise instigating violence (see Reddy Commission 1971: 162, 216, 218). The commission also took note of police reports that several Jana Sangh leaders and workers, and Hindu Mahasabha members, had actively participated in the riot in Ahmedabad and in other parts of Gujarat (ibid.).

In 2002, Haresh Bhatt, vice-president of the Bajrang Dal in 2002 and later BJP MLA from Godhra, reportedly took an active part in arming Hindu men. See 'We made a complete rocket launcher here', *Tehelka*, 1 June 2007. Available online at: http://www.tehelka.com/story_main35.asp?filename=Ne031107WeMade.asp (last accessed on 17 February 2014). Senior BJP ministers in the Gujarat administration–Minister of Urban Housing I. K. Jadeja and Minister of Health Ashok Bhatt–allegedly stayed in the police control room for several days after the 2002 massacre began on 28 February

2002, and interfered with police work (Khetan 2011). Some VHP leaders such as Anil Patel were also reported to have coordinated attacks against Muslims with support from the police. See 'They'd deliver our arms safely for us', *Tehelka*, 13 June 2007.

Several eyewitnesses and survivors also identified members of various Hindu nationalist organisations among the rioters. Their testimonies have been recorded in reports published by human rights groups. See the reports included in *The Gujarat Pogrom: Compilations of Various Reports* (Indian Social Institute 2002). Of these, Bajrang Dal leaders Babu Bajrangi and Suresh Chara have been convicted for their direct participation in the 2002 massacre (see note 10 in this Introduction).

34. See 'Dateline Gujarat', *Communalism Combat*, March–April 2002.

35. In August 2012, as cited previously, former Gujarat minister of state and senior BJP politician Maya Kodnani was sentenced to 28 years' imprisonment for her direct involvement in the violence in Ahmedabad's Naroda Patiya region in 2002. For the judgement, see note 12 in this Introduction.

36. Sessions Case Nos 235/09, 236/09, 241/09, 242/09, 243/09, 245/09, 246/09 & 270/09, COMMON JUDGMENT, pp. 489–90.

37. Ibid., p. 485.

38. In some cases, the police deliberately omitted complaints of sexual violence in the first information reports filed by victims (see the discussion on the police handling of Medina Shaikh's complaint in Citizens' Initiative (2002: 77)). In one instance, police officials harassed a rape victim to pressure her into withdrawing her complaint (see the discussion on Bilkees Yakoob Rasool's case in Jaffrelot (2012: 82)). In the high-profile Best Bakery case, the main complainant was allegedly bribed by a BJP MLA from Vadodara to withdraw her case (see the discussion on this case in ibid.). The Gujarat government has repeatedly been found unwilling to subject its handling of the 2002 violence to independent, rigorous inquiry. Notably, between February and June 2002, the government refused to task the Nanavati Commission with investigating the anti-Muslim violence committed in the aftermath of the Godhra tragedy on 27 February 2002; the commission's remit was confined to the events in Godhra. The government finally relented in June 2002, following strong public pressure, but barred the commission from scrutinising the role of government officials, senior bureaucrats and top police officials in relation to the massacre. Meanwhile, the administration displayed remarkable leniency towards the Nanavati Commission's delay in completing its probe into the anti-Muslim carnage. It had granted 24 extensions before the commission finally submitted its report to the Gujarat government for consideration in mid-November 2014. The Gujarat government has yet to make this report public. These issues have been discussed extensively in Chapter 4.

39. Part II of the Nanavati Commission report has yet to be made public.

40. The first successful conviction took place in 2008 for the rape of Muslim woman Bilkees Yakoob Rasool, and the second in 2012 for the rape of a Muslim girl, Naseemo. Both convictions relate to violence inflicted during the 2002 anti-Muslim carnage. For a discussion of the first case, see Jaffrelot (2012: 82). The judgement on the second case is cited in note 10 in this Introduction.

41. Pamphlet entitled 'Awake, Oh Hindus: Awake, Oh Youths', published by the Hindu Sangram Samiti, reproduced and translated in Reddy Commission (1971: 108–9).

42. Reproduced and translated in 'Pamphlet poison', *Communalism Combat*, vol. 8, no. 76, March–April 2002, p. 137.

43. Ibid., p. 135.

44. In an article published in 2004, political scientist Ashutosh Varshney argues that in order to better understand communal violence in India, academics and the media need to 'compare systematically the episodes of mass violence with episodes of peace' (see Varshney 2004). His appeal resonates in some senses with my own attention to the absence of extreme sexual violence in certain riot contexts.

45. In October 2002, the UN released a special bulletin on this issue (see Bastick et al. 2007: 171).

46. A notable exception is Purushottam Agarwal's (1996) study, 'Surat, Savarkar and Draupadi'. However, Agarwal's article focuses only on Savarkar's *Six Glorious Epochs of Indian History.*

47. See note 12 in this Introduction.

48. An earlier version of this discussion of Hindu nationalist ideology was published as 'History and Gender in Savarkar's Nationalist Writings', *Social Scientist*, vol. 34, nos 402–3 (2006), pp. 33–50.

49. Here, 'humiliation' refers to sexual violation, because in the original text Hedgewar uses the term *laj*, which in India usually refers to sexual purity.

50. Like much of gendered national/colonial politics, 'Mother India' belonged within a long tradition of imperialist propaganda that cynically exploited the condition of women against the political demands of nationalists in India. See Sinha (2000: 627).

51. In some Indian accounts of the colonial era, the nation was imagined as Goddess Durga, the invincible protector of righteousness and the moral order (see Ramaswamy 2010: 106–7). However, in the writings of Hindu nationalist ideologues such as Savarkar, the motherland was identified primarily with stereotypical feminine virtues of beauty, sensitivity and fragility.

52. Nothing substantial is said in any of these texts about the children born of such a union.

Chapter 1   1969

1. There is a major lacuna in the existing archives on the incidence of sexual violence during the 1969 riot, which makes it impossible to determine its scale. This issue is discussed in detail later in the present section.

2. For a discussion of Gujarat's experience of Partition, see Yagnik and Sheth (2005: 224–5).

3. *Communalism Combat*, vol. 8, no. 76, March–April 2002, p. 17.

4. Due to the sub-division of districts, the total number of districts in Gujarat had risen to 25 by the time of the 1985 riots, and to 26 in 2002. No further increase had occurred in the number of districts when this book went to press.

5. The rise in communal polarisation in Ahmedabad between the late 1960s and the early 2000s is examined in detail in the next two chapters.

6. For reports and judgements pertaining to state and police complicity in the 2002 carnage, see Introduction, note 12.

7. Due to the lack of alternative sources, this chapter relies heavily on the testimonies, affidavits, speeches, newspaper reports and propaganda materials reproduced by the Reddy Commission. *Gujarat Samachar*, one of the two most widely circulated vernacular dailies in the state, is among the few contemporary Gujarati newspaper sources available to researchers, and its reports have been referenced where appropriate. The newspaper did not carry any mention of sexual violence against women in its coverage of the riot.

8. Shani (2007), Spodek (2011) and Sud (2012) discuss the 1969 riot in their respective works, drawing on the report of the Reddy Commission and Ghanshyam Shah's (1970) article, but these studies do not examine the incidents of sexual violence.

9. These statistics have been collated from the *Annual Records of Jyoti Sangh* (various years).

10. For a more detailed analysis of different jamaats in Ahmedabad, see Jassani (2007: 61).

11. Between 1968 and 1969, 62.7 per cent of all girls were enrolled in primary schools and 24.7 per cent in middle schools in Gujarat. However, women constituted only 0.21 per cent of university students and 0.04 per cent of those attending professional and special colleges. Computed from Table XXI: Enrolment (Percentage of Girls in Relevant Age Groups) by Stage of Education for Girls: Comparison between 1956–57 and 1968–69; and Table XXII: Enrolment Ratios (Percentages) by Stage of Education for Girls: Comparison between 1956–57 and 1968–69, Government of India (1974: 267–8).

12. *Gujarat Samachar*, 26 June 1967, p. 3.

13. See National Crime Bureau, 'Snapshot 1953–2006'. Available online at: http://ncrb.nic.in/ciiprevious/Data/CD-CII2006/cii-2006/Snapshots%201953-2006.pdf (last accessed on 28 January 2014).

14. For an excellent discussion on Gandhi's views on ideal masculinity and femininity, see Kishwar (1985).

15. Interview with lawyer and eminent political commentator Girish Patel, Ahmedabad, 27 November 2006.

16. *Gujarat Samachar*, 4 September 1969, p. 9.

17. *Sadhana*, 28 January 1968, p. 10.

18. *Organiser*, 26 July 1969, p. 3.

19. *Sadhana*, 4 January 1959, p. 2.
20. *Organiser*, 6 December 1969, p. 15.
21. *Sadhana*, 14 January 1968, p. 7.
22. Instances of such narratives are discussed later in this chapter.
23. *Gujarat Samachar*, 12 March 1969, p. 10.
24. *Gujarat Samachar*, 10 September 1969; reproduced and translated in Reddy Commission (1971: 56).
25. The *Gujarat Samachar* sold 63,688 copies daily in 1968. See Government of India (1969, 1:109).
26. The Ramlila is a dramatic folk re-enactment of the life of the mythological warrior-prince Rama as described in the Hindu epic *Ramayana*. In most parts of northern and western India, local troupes perform the *Ramayana* over 10 to 15 days.
27. Ghanshyam Shah (1970) makes a similar argument about the causes of the riot.
28. Except for parts of Chapter 2, this book focuses on violence committed against Muslims during communal riots in Ahmedabad since the 1960s. In doing so, I am not seeking to minimise the significance of violence committed against Hindus in any way. On the contrary, a study examining the incidence of sexual and other forms of violence against Hindus during communal riots would constitute a valuable addition to the literature on communalism in India.
29. In 1968, *Sevak* had a daily circulation of 6,367 copies, while the main newspaper *Sandesh* claimed a circulation of 70,988 copies. Government of India (1969, 1:83, 107).
30. In fact, the vernacular media played a similar role during the anti-Muslim massacre in 2002. *Sandesh* published a similar story about the sexual victimisation of Hindu women by Muslim men in February 2002 (see the discussion in Chapter 3).
31. *Gujarat Samachar*, 20 September 1969, p. 1; emphasis added.
32. Affidavit of C.P. Deboo (Reddy Commission 1971: 106).
33. In Ahmedabad's neighbourhoods, especially the pols, blackboards are installed in the most public part of the locality for publicising special government notices, daily news, etc. During the riot, these boards were used for anti-Muslim propaganda.
34. The nature of propaganda during the 1985 riot, which we shall examine in the following chapter, differed from that in 1969 in crucial respects. This in turn altered the nature of the violence.
35. These statistics are not disaggregated on the basis of the community of the victims.
36. Collated from data published in Reddy Commission (1971: 151–66).
37. Interviews with 'Jamila', resident of Jamalpur, on 16 November 2007; 'Amina Sheikh', resident of Gomtipur and daughter of a former mill worker, on 16 November 2007; Rashida Bano and 'Khurshida Bano', residents of Gomtipur, on 29 November 2007 and 30 January 2007.

38. 'Jamila', a resident of Jamalpur, is currently the president of the Adarsh Mahila Mandal. Interview, Ahmedabad, 16 November 2007.

39. The strength of the crowd fluctuated throughout the day, the number of men in the mob usually declining in the early hours of the day or late at night.

40. *Hindustan Times*, 22 September 1969.

41. Rabaris are a low-caste community who traditionally work as milk producers and distributors.

42. The term *bhaiya* literally means elder brother, and usually refers to labour immigrants from the northern Indian state of UP, but Rashida used the term in a derogatory way.

43. *Organiser*, 3 January 1970, pp. 8–9.

44. Affidavit of P. M. Raval on behalf of the HPSS, Reddy Commission (1971: Appendix III, p. 29).

45. Om Prakash Tyagi (Jana Sangh MP) in an interview to *Hindustan Times*, 28 September 1969, p. 4.

46. Affidavit of S. K. Acharya, for the Hindu Dharma Raksha Samiti, Reddy Commission (1971: Appendix III, p. 32).

47. The Reddy Commission dedicated an entire chapter to the examination of propaganda materials circulated during the riot. See especially Reddy Commission (1971), Chapter X, 'Part Played by Newspapers, Pamphlets and Rumours in Fanning the Riots', pp. 102–13.

Chapter 2   1985

1. For details about police culpability with respect to the incidence of sexual crimes in 2002, see PUCL Gujarat, 'An Interim Report to the National Human Rights Commission', in Indian Social Institute (2002: 160–1). Several of my interviewees also mentioned that some police constables had unzipped their trousers and used sexually abusive language when Muslim women pleaded with them for protection during the 2002 massacre. In 2008, head constable of the Limkheda police station Somabhai Gori was sentenced to three years' imprisonment for falsifying records and refusing to lodge the first complaint of Bilkees Yakoob Rasool, who was gang-raped on 1 March 2002 in Randhikpur village of Gujarat's Dahod district. With regard to the 2002 cases from Ahmedabad, no police officer has been convicted for complicity in the violence or for dereliction of duty. However, Ahmedabad's police has been strongly criticised for 'indirectly facilitating' violence against Muslims by a special fast-track sessions court established in Ahmedabad for 'Conducting Speedy Trial of Riot Cases'. See Sessions Case Nos 235/09, 236/09, 241/09, 242/09, 243/09, 245/09, 246/09 & 270/09, COMMON JUDGMENT, pp. 485 and 48–90.

2. The Jyoti Sangh recorded two incidents of rape in 1981; one in 1982; two in 1983; one in 1984 and one in 1985. *Annual Records of Jyoti Sangh* (various years).

3. The religious background of the remaining 120 killed out of 220 total casualties is unavailable.

4. For a more exhaustive list of factors that contributed to the decline of the composite textile mill industry, see Breman (2004: 144).

5. For example, in Gujarat the wholesale price of coarse rice, a staple, rose 294 per cent from Rs 56.77 per quintal in 1962 to Rs 223.40 in 1981. The price of groundnut oil per quintal increased 649 per cent from Rs 190.95 to Rs 1,431.18, and that of sugar increased 493 per cent from Rs 114.95 per quintal to Rs 682.68. During the same period, the average daily wage of cobblers in Gujarat increased 250 per cent from Rs 4 to Rs 14, and that of skilled carpenters by 255 per cent from under Rs 5 to Rs 17.77 (Government of Gujarat 1985a: 97).

6. The Calico Mill was owned by one of Ahmedabad's most prominent families, the Sarabhais. This mill was one of the last to be closed, in 1998.

7. Other respondents made similar claims. See Dave Commission (1990, 1:209).

8. The death knell was sounded by the banging of kitchen utensils from rooftops.

9. Also see Dave Commission (1990, 3: 200–61, Annexure 35).

10. *Times of India*, Ahmedabad, 30 July 1985, cited in Spodek (2011: 214).

11. The other three provinces that have a prohibition policy are Mizoram, Nagaland and Manipur. Lakshadweep, a union territory, also prohibits alcohol sale, purchase and consumption. In Gujarat, a prohibition policy has been in place since the creation of the state on 1 May 1960 out of deference to Gandhi, who held alcohol consumption responsible for many social ills, such as domestic violence.

12. Reproduced in Gujarati in Dave Commission (1990, 3:24, Annexure 7), and translated in Shani (2007: 111–12).

13. The *Bhagavad Gita* (*c.* 500 B.C.) is an Indian scripture that is part of the mythological epic *Mahabharata*. Crafted as a poem, the *Gita* recounts the conversation between the warrior-prince Arjuna and Lord Krishna on idealism and practical wisdom.

14. Reproduced in Gujarati in Dave Commission (1991, 3:23, Annexure 7); translated in S. Patel (1986: 146).

15. Ibid.

16. This understanding of the 'Hindu brotherhood' draws on Gupta and Ferguson (2001: 13), who argue that a sense of community is often forged through a process of exclusion and othering.

17. Reproduced in Gujarati in Dave Commission (1990, 3:22, Annexure 7); translated in Shani (2007: 130–1).

18. *Gujarat Samachar*, 10 April 1985, p. 1.

19. Affidavit of B. K. Jha, Police Commissioner of Ahmedabad, reproduced in Dave Commission (1990, 1:264–7).

20. Hindu women of the neighbourhood gave similar statements, but added that even the police and SRPF personnel were guilty of such behaviour. See Women's Research Group (1985: 1727).

21. AWAG report, cited in S. Patel (1985: 66–8). In its testimony to the Dave Commission (1990, 1:62), the Lok Swaraj Manch representative also stated that

policemen had misbehaved and removed their clothing, although he did not mention the specific case.

22. The word *dalit* literally means oppressed in Sanskrit. 'Dalit' is a political identity adopted by many Scheduled Castes across India.

23. Interview with an anonymous Muslim man, Aman Chowk Relief Camp, 1 June 1985, recorded in a documentary film by Yagnik and Jani (1985).

Chapter 3   2002

1. 'Relief and rehabilitation of victims of communal riots in Gujarat of 2002', Press Information Bureau, Government of India, 22 March 2007. Available online at: http://pib.nic.in/newsite/erelease.aspx?relid=26352 (last accessed on 3 February 2014).

2. *Times of India*, 11 May 2005.

3. *Communalism Combat*, March–April 2002, p. 17.

4. *Times of India*, 11 May 2005. According to some press reports and media commentators, there were also some attacks by Muslims mobs against Hindus after 2 March 2002. However, these reports note that the majority of Hindu fatalities were a result of police firing, or of attacks by Hindu nationalist mobs who punished Hindus for working with or being friends of Muslims. See Varadarajan (2002: 83) and Swami (2002).

5. *Communalism Combat*, March–April 2002, pp. 45–53.

6. Teesta Setalvad, Expert Witness to the Concerned Citizens' Tribunal (CCT 2002, 1:226).

7. Hashmi and Kumar (2002); Megha Kumar, field notes from the Gujarat relief camps, 2002.

8. Data for 2009–13 are unavailable.

9. For literature on attacks against Christians, see Forum against Oppression of Women and Awaaz-e-Niswaan (2002); Human Rights Watch (1999); 'Dateline Gujarat', *Communalism Combat*, March–April 2002, p. 103. See also 'Welcome to Hindu Rashtra', *Communalism Combat*, October 1998. Available online at: http://www.sabrang.com/cc/comold/octob98/story.htm (last accessed on 25 February 2014).

10. 'Dateline Gujarat', *Communalism Combat*, March–April 2002, p. 104.

11. See, for example, pamphlets such as Vishwa Hindu Parishad's 'Savadhan Abhiyaan' (Ahmedabad: VHP, 1998) (see Figure 3.1 in this chapter and Figure A1, Appendix); 'Jai Bharat Mata' (anonymous pamphlet, Ahmedabad, n.d.); Hindu Jagruti Morcha, 'Hindu Jagriti Se Sanskriti Rakhsha' (Ahmedabad: HJM, n.d.), Part 2, p. 15.

12. Interviews with Mohan Macwan and Krishna Parmar, members of the Bajrang Dal, Ahmedabad, 20 October 2007; see also Banerjee (2005).

13. Interview with Mohan Macwan, a member of the Bajrang Dal, Ahmedabad, 20 October 2007; see also Quami Ekta Trust (2000: 9–10).

14. In 2007, Babu Bajrangi claimed that he had 'rescued' 957 such Hindu women on behalf of their families. Interview with Babu Bajrangi, quoted in Ashish Khetan (2007a).

15. This issue will be discussed in greater detail shortly, particularly with reference to the Ramjanmabhoomi movement.

16. Based on my interviews with survivors, especially S. Pathan, Ahmedabad, 15 January 2007; I. Yaqub, Ahmedabad, 29 January 2007; and A. Rafiq, Ahmedabad, 18 January 2007. None of the human rights activists I spoke with during my fieldwork mentioned any case of extreme sexual violence in the 1992–93 riot in Ahmedabad (interviews with G. Shah (5 January 2007), C. Prakash (11 December 2006), I. Pathak (26 December 2006), M. Mansuri (4 November 2007), S. Khan (20 November 2007), S. George (4 November 2007), P. Ginwala (1 November 2007) and S. Dhruv (21 October 2007)). However, this claim cannot be made with absolute certainty, not least due to the absence of official records. The official commission of inquiry established to probe the violence in Ahmedabad and Surat in 1992–93 was disbanded in 1996 before its report could be finalised and made public.

17. The census defines 'main workers' as people who were employed for at least six months during the year that preceded the census year.

18. During my field trip in 2006–08, I spotted several such billboards in Ahmedabad, Surat and Vadodara.

19. Shahabuddin, interviewed at the Aman Chowk Relief Camp, 1 June 1985, by Yagnik and Jani (1985).

20. Interviews with local community leaders S. Khan (Juhapura, Ahmedabad, 21 December 2007) and J. Ahir (Gupta Nagar, Ahmedabad, 23 December 2007).

21. 'Face to face with fascism', *Communalism Combat*, April 2000. Available online at: www.sabrang.com/cc/comold/april00/co-story.htm (last accessed on 3 February 2014).

22. For an excellent discussion of the Shah Bano case, see Pathak and Sunder Rajan (1989).

23. Vishwa Hindu Parishad, 'Shri Ramjanmabhoomi ni vyatha katha' (unpublished pamphlet, Ahmedabad, 1987), reproduced and translated in Sud (2007: 233–4).

24. On a related theme, also see Davis (1996).

25. Sadhavi Rithambara's speech recorded in Anand Patwardhan's (1994) documentary film, *Father, Son and the Holy War*.

26. Vishwa Hindu Parishad, 'Antankvadnu Bharat par akraman' (Ahmedabad: VHP, 1990).

27. Ruqayya is a common name among Muslim women.

28. Lal Krishna Advani, quoted in *Times of India*, 1 December 1992.

29. Based on reports published in *Times of India* between 6 December 1992 and 1 February 1993.

30. These estimates are based on reports published in the Ahmedabad editions of the *Times of India* and *Indian Express* during 6–12 December 1992, 24–5 December 1992, 6–30 January 1993, and data provided by A. Bhatt (1992).

31. Ibid.

32. 'Flag marches' are orderly marches of army columns or convoys. They are organised to instil a sense of security among people, usually during war or civil unrest.

33. Interviews with S. Pathan, Ahmedabad, 15 January 2007; I. Yaqub, Ahmedabad, 29 January 2007; and A. Rafiq, Ahmedabad, 18 January 2007.

34. The edited volume by Gayer and Jaffrelot (2012) contains articles on 11 Indian cities where a similar process of communalisation has occurred. In particular, see the articles on Jaipur, Bhopal, Delhi and Hyderabad.

35. For example, the Ministry of Home Affairs (Government of India) Notification No. II/14034/2 (iii) 92-IS (DV) placed a ban on the VHP; No. II/14034/2 (iv) 92-IS (DV) on the RSS; and No. II/14034/2 (v) 92-IS (DV) on the Bajrang Dal on 11 December 1992. Quoted in *Times of India*, 17 December 1992, p. 5.

36. Jeemol Unni, 'Urban Informal Sector: Size and Income Generation Processes in Gujarat (Report on the First Stage)', SEWA-GIDR-ISST-NCAER, Report No. 2 (National Council of Applied Economic Research, New Delhi, April 2000), quoted in Mahadevia (2002: 4853).

37. The AMC's *Revised Development Plan 1975–1985* (1985) provides details on only those areas that fall under the jurisdiction of the AMC. Had the slums located outside this area been surveyed, the figures for the late 1990s would be higher still.

38. Interviews with two Dalit members of the Bajrang Dal in Gomtipur, Ahmedabad, 20 October 2007.

39. Interviews with RSS members in Ahwa town, the Dangs district, quoted in Human Rights Watch (1999: 20).

40. Quoted in *Outlook*, 18 March 2002, p. 28.

41. Sacred marital thread worn primarily by upper-caste Hindu women.

42. From the BJP's 1996 election manifesto, 'For a Strong and Prosperous India: Election Manifesto 1996', quoted in Indian Social Institute (2002: 1).

43. *Sadhana*, 8 June 1996, p. 8.

44. Vishwa Hindu Parishad, 'Savadhan Campaign' (Ahmedabad: VHP, 1998).

45. Babu Bajrangi, 'Navchetan Group' (Ahmedabad: Navchetan Group, n.d.).

46. Vishwa Hindu Parishad, 'Savadhan Campaign' (Ahmedabad: VHP, 1998).

47. Between 1998 and 2002, the organisation received at least 17 such complaints. These statistics have been collated from the *Annual Records of Jyoti Sangh* (various years).

48. Interview with Babu Bajrangi, quoted in Khetan (2007a).

49. 'Welcome to Hindu Rashtra', *Communalism Combat*, October 1998.

50. Ibid.

51. See also Vishwa Hindu Parishad, *Isaiyan par tathakathit atyachar keval dushprachar hi dushprachar. Satye ye hai* (Ahmedabad: VHP, 1999), p. 11.

52. Ibid.; Vishwa Hindu Parishad, *Bharatke Isaikaranka shadyantra* (Ahmedabad: VHP, 1998).

53. Hindu Jagruti Morcha, *Hindu jagriti se sanskriti rakhsha*, Part I and II (Ahmedabad: HJM, n.d.).

54. Vishwa Hindu Parishad, 'Bajrang Dal–Vishwa Hindu Parishad' (Ahmedabad: VHP, 1998b).

55. 'Dateline Gujarat', *Communalism Combat*, March–April 2002, p. 104.

56. Ibid.

57. Violence against Christians was recorded from some other parts of the country as well. Notably, in the Jhabua district of Madhya Pradesh, four nuns were raped, allegedly by Hindu nationalist foot soldiers in 1998.

58. *The Hindu*, 26 January 1999, p. 1.

59. 'Dateline Gujarat', *Communalism Combat*, March–April 2002, p. 104.

60. 'Welcome to Hindu Rashtra', *Communalism Combat*, October 1998.

61. The following account is based on 'Dateline Gujarat', *Communalism Combat*, March–April 2002, pp. 104–6, and media reports that comment on the period.

62. 'State loses three more sons in Kargil', *Indian Express*, 8 July 1999. Available online at: http://expressindia.indianexpress.com/ie/daily/19990708/i ge08085.html (last accessed on 25 February 2014).

63. 'Advani returns with a hero's ashes', Rediff News, 3 July 1999. Available online at: http://in.rediff.com/news/1999/jul/03rath.htm (last accessed on 26 February 2014).

64. 'Dateline Gujarat', *Communalism Combat*, March–April 2002.

65. 'Riots in city areas', *Indian Express*, Ahmedabad, 21 July 1999, p. 1.

66. Committee for Protection of Democratic Rights (CPDR) report, quoted in 'CPDR report sees saffron hand in Ahmedabad riots', *Indian Express*, 22 August 1999. Available online at: http://expressindia.indianexpress.com/ie/ daily/19990822/ige22015.html (last accessed on 25 February 2014). See also 'A fragile peace rules in Ahmedabad', Rediff News, 31 July 1999. Available online at: http://m.rediff.com/news/1999/jul/31ganga.htm (last accessed on 25 February 2014). 'Gujarat: A communal cauldron', *Outlook*, 27 February 2002. Available online at: http://www.outlookindia.com/printarticle.aspx? 214727 (last accessed on 25 February 2014).

67. 'Dateline Gujarat', *Communalism Combat*, March–April 2002, p. 105; International Initiative for Justice (2003: 228); and 'Saffron promises and performance', *Communalism Combat*, September 2000. Available online at: http://www.sabrang.com/cc/comold/sep00/cover1.htm (last accessed on 4 February 2014).

68. Ibid.

69. Ibid.

70. Quoted in 'Riots in city areas', *Indian Express*, Ahmedabad, 21 July 1999, p. 1.

71. 'Kashmir killings impact rest of the country: Report', *Pioneer*, 9 November 2000. Available online at: http://www.jammu-kashmir.com/archives/archives 2000/kashmir20001109c.html (last accessed on 26 February 2014).

72. 'Face to face with fascism', *Communalism Combat*, April 2000.

73. Speeches of VHP leaders recorded in the film by Rakesh Sharma (2003).

74. 'Dateline Gujarat', *Communalism Combat*, March–April 2002.

75. The ABVP, together with the BJP, carried out similar assaults on girls wearing western outfits in other Indian cities, such as Kanpur (see K. Sharma 2000).

76. Human Rights Watch reported on violence in the Dangs in its 1999 report, *Politics by Other Means*.

77. 'People who wanted revenge and got it', *Outlook*, 18 March 2002, p. 28.

78. 'Death toll in Indian train inferno rises to 58', Reuters, 28 February 2002.

79. Also quoted in 'Godhra', *Communalism Combat*, March–April 2002, p. 12.

80. See also: 'Modi said, bring Godhra bodies to Ahmedabad', *Times of India*, 22 August 2004. Available online at: http://timesofindia.indiatimes.com/india/Modi-said-bring-Godhra-bodies-to-Ahmedabad/articleshow/823413.cms?referral=PM (last accessed on 25 February 2014). 'Godhra', *Communalism Combat*, March–April 2002, p. 12.

81. Togadia made this statement in an interview to Hotline, in Ayodhya. Quoted in 'Call to arms', *Communalism Combat*, March–April 2002, p. 16.

82. See also 'Godhra', *Communalism Combat*, March–April 2002, p. 14; *Times of India*, Ahmedabad and Delhi, 28 February 2002, p. 1.

83. Election Commission of India, 'General Elections to the Gujarat Legislative Assembly', Press Note No. ECI/PN/35/2002/MCPS, 16 August 2002, p. 15. Available online at: http://eci.nic.in/eci_main1/current/PN_16082002.pdf (last accessed on 25 February 2014).

84. *Sandesh*, 28 February 2002, p. 1.

85. *Sandesh*, 1 March 2002, p. 16.

86. *Communalism Combat*, March–April 2002, p. 49.

87. VHP pamphlet reproduced and translated in 'Pamphlet poison', *Communalism Combat*, March–April 2002, p. 133.

88. Reproduced and translated in 'Pamphlet poison', *Communalism Combat*, March–April 2002, p. 135.

89. *Communalism Combat*, March–April 2002, p. 39.

90. 'We made a complete rocket launcher here', *Tehelka*, 1 June 2007.

91. 'They'd deliver our arms safely for us', *Tehelka*, 13 June 2007.

92. Interviews with: T. Setalvad, Mumbai, 24 December 2007; Dr A. A. Engineer, Mumbai, 28 December 2007; P. Ginwala, Ahmedabad, 1 November 2007; S. George, Ahmedabad, 4 November 2007; and C. Prakash, Ahmedabad, 11 October 2006. Also see *Communalism Combat*, March–April 2002, pp. 108–14; and International Initiative for Justice (2003).

93. Zakia Jafri's special leave petition against the judgement and order dated 2 November 2007 in Special Criminal Application No. 421 of 2007 passed by

the High Court of Gujarat at Ahmedabad, pp. 66–7. Available online at: http://www.cjponline.org/zakia/Zakia%20CJP%20SLP%201088%20of% 202008%20final.pdf (last accessed on 25 February 2014).

94. Sanjiv Bhatt's affidavit submitted to the Supreme Court of India, Special Leave Petition no. 1088 of 2008. *Zakia Jafri and ANR – Petitioners vs. State of Gujarat & ORS – Respondents*, 14 April 2011, p. 12.

95. Comments of the Chairman, SIT, Gujarat, on the Enquiry Report in the SPL (Crl.) 1088/2088 filed by Smt. Jakia Nassim, pp. 3–5. Available online at: http://www.cjponline.org/zakia/Chairman%20Raghavans%20Comments% 2014.5.2010.pdf (last accessed on 25 February 2014).

96. 'Gulbarg massacre: Narendra Modi gets a clean chit', *Economic Times*, 26 December 2013. Available online at: http://articles.economictimes.indiatim es.com/2013-12-26/news/45592887_1_zakia-jafri-protest-petition-sit-report (last accessed on 25 February 2014).

97. '2002 riots: BJP euphoric over clean chit to Modi, Zakia vows to fight on', IBN-Live, 6 January 2014. Available online at: http://ibnlive.in.com/news/ 2002-riots-bjp-euphoric-over-clean-chit-to-modi-zakia-vows-to-fight-on/ 441765-3-238.html (last accessed on 25 February 2014).

98. *Communalism Combat*, March–April 2002, pp. 36–8.

99. These events are discussed in greater detail in the following chapter. See also the Introduction to this volume.

100. The SRPF is a special armed police force that reinforces the general police's ability to ensure the internal security of each state.

101. For the court ruling on Mysorewala's actions, see Sessions Case Nos 235/09, 236/09, 241/09, 242/09, 243/09, 245/09, 246/09 & 270/09, COMMON JUDGMENT, pp. 489–90.

102. *Communalism Combat*, March–April 2002, p. 21.

103. Rakhi is a Hindu festival that is celebrated by the tying of a *rakhi*, or holy thread, by the sister on the wrist of her brother. The brother in return vows to protect her.

104. Charas are an OBC group. Interview with S. Chara, quoted in 'The RSS will tell you how Chharas killed Muslims', *Tehelka*, 12 August 2007.

105. Interviews by the author with survivors of sexual violence in relief camps, Ahmedabad, May 2002.

106. Interviews with survivors of the 2002 massacre in Ahmedabad: one survivor from Behrampura on 5 December 2007; four survivors from Vatva during 29 October–3 November 2007; and one survivor from Jamalpur on 20 October 2007.

107. Reproduced and translated in *Communalism Combat*, March–April 2002, p. 137.

108. 'After killing them, I felt like Maharana Pratap', *Tehelka*, 1 November 2007. Available online at: http://archive.tehelka.com/story_main35.asp? filename=Ne031107After_killing.asp (last accessed on 10 February 2014).

Chapter 4 Aftermath

1. *Communalism Combat*, March–April 2002, p. 17.
2. 'Nothing "voluntary" about it', *Communalism Combat*, July 2002. Available online at: http://www.sabrang.com/cc/archive/2002/july02/cover3.htm (last accessed on 23 December 2012).
3. Alamdar Bukhari, interview, Ahmedabad, 18 October 2007. Interviews with A. Jahan and A. Bhai, Ahmedabad, 15 December 2007.
4. The direct involvement of some members of the state apparatus in the violence has been documented in the Introduction, and will be taken up for discussion again later in this chapter.
5. On Partition, see R. Menon and Bhasin (1998) and Das (1995). On the 1992 riots in Bombay, see Robinson (2005), especially Chapter 6.
6. See Sessions Case Nos 235/09, 236/09, 241/09, 242/09, 243/09, 245/09, 246/09 & 270/09, COMMON JUDGMENT, p. 602. Kodnani had been released on bail when this book went to press.
7. See Jaffrelot (2012: 82) for a discussion of the Bilkees Yakoob Rasool case. For the judgement relating to Suresh Chara, see Sessions Case Nos 235/09, 236/09, 241/09, 242/09, 243/09, 245/09, 246/09 & 270/09, COMMON JUDGMENT, p. 1707–8.
8. Studies published thus far suggest that sexual violence was not an integral feature of the 1984 riots, even though some isolated incidents of rape may have occurred. For a more detailed account of the events in 1984, see Chakravarti and Haksar (1987). Also see Das (2006).
9. Sessions Case Nos 235/09, 236/09, 241/09, 242/09, 243/09, 245/09, 246/09 and 270/09, COMMON JUDGMENT, p. 602.
10. 'Maya Kodnani led mob to carry out Naroda riot: Gujarat govt to HC', *Economic Times*, 21 February 2009. Available online at: http://articles.economic times.indiatimes.com/2009-02-21/news/28413366_1_kodnani-affidavit-mla-and-allegations (last accessed on 25 February 2012).
11. 'Muzaffarnagar riots show a dangerous trend', *Times of India*, 9 October 2013. Available online at: http://articles.timesofindia.indiatimes.com/2013-10-09/india/42861638_1_aidwa-riot-victims-muzaffarnagar (last accessed on 11 February 2014).
12. 'Truth and the Nanavati-Shah Commission', *Communalism Combat*, vol. 13, no. 124, July 2007. Available online at: http://www.sabrang.com/cc/archive/2007/july07/statecomp4.html (last accessed on 11 February 2014).
13. 'KG Shah is our man. Nanavati is only after money. Gujarat Advocate General Arvind Pandya claims the accused have nothing to fear from the Nanavati-Shah Commission', *Tehelka*, 8 June 2007. Available online at: http://archive.tehelka.com/story_main35.asp?filename=Ne031107KG.asp (last accessed on 11 February 2014).
14. 'Some '02 riots documents were destroyed: Gujarat govt', *Outlook*, 2 November 2012. Available online at: http://news.outlookindia.com/items.aspx?artid=779819 (last accessed on 11 February 2014).

15. This discussion on the role of the police and the Gujarat judiciary draws on Jaffrelot (2012).

16. 'Legal experts question destruction of papers relating to 2002 communal riots', *Hindu*, 1 July 2011. Available online at: http://www.thehindu.com/news/nati onal/legal-experts-question-destruction-of-papers-relating-to-2002-comm unal-riots/article2147413.ece (last accessed on 25 February 2014). 'Gujarat riots: NGO plans to move court for the "destruction of evidence"', *India Today*, 2 July 2011. Available online at: http://indiatoday.intoday.in/story/gujarat-riots-ngo-plans-to-move-court-for-the-destruction-of-evidence/1/143404.html (last accessed on 25 February 2014).

17. Several other survivors also reported to human rights organisations that the police was unwilling to lodge FIRs, or that key details from their complaints were omitted. See, for example, Citizens' Initiative (2002: 83), and PUCL Gujarat, 'An Interim Report to the National Human Rights Commission', in Indian Social Institute (2002: 161).

18. The facts of the Best Bakery case have been drawn from Jaffrelot (2012: 82).

19. 'Editors' Note', *Communalism Combat*, vol. 19, no. 168, November 2012, p. 3. Available online at: http://www.sabrang.com/cc/archive/2012/nov2012/Com Nov2012.pdf (last accessed on 11 February 2014).

20. In 2008, 13 men were convicted (of whom 11 were sentenced to life imprisonment) for the rape of Bilkees Yakoob Rasool on 1 March 2002 in Randhikpur village of Dahod district (see Jaffrelot 2012: 82), and for murder (ibid.)

21. See also 'Bilkis Bano's brave fight', *Tehelka*, 2 February 2008. Available online at: http://archive.tehelka.com/story_main37.asp?filename=Ne020208bilkis.asp (last accessed on 11 February 2014).

22. Sessions Case Nos 235/09, 236/09, 241/09, 242/09, 243/09, 245/09, 246/09 & 270/09, COMMON JUDGMENT, p. 1699.

23. 'The RSS will tell you how Chharas killed Muslims', *Tehelka*, 12 August 2007.

24. Sessions Case Nos 235/09, 236/09, 241/09, 242/09, 243/09, 245/09, 246/09 & 270/09, COMMON JUDGMENT, p. 1708.

25. 'Editors' Note', *Communalism Combat*, November 2012, p. 3.

26. Literature on sexual violence against men and boys is scarce. Nonetheless, an article by Dubravka Zarkov (2005) constitutes an important intervention.

BIBLIOGRAPHY

Agarwal, Purushottam. 1996. 'Surat, Savarkar and Draupadi: Legitimising Rape as a Political Weapon', in Tanika Sarkar and Urvashi Butalia (eds), *Women and the Hindu Right* (New Delhi: Kali for Women).

Agnes, Flavia. 1992. 'Protecting Women against Violence? Review of a Decade of Legislation 1980–90', *Economic and Political Weekly*, vol. 27, no. 17 (April), pp. 19–33.

AIDWA (All India Democratic Women's Association). 2002. 'Gujarat Carnage Report', in *The Gujarat Pogrom: Compilations of Various Reports* (New Delhi: Indian Social Institute).

AIDWA (All India Democratic Women's Association), Centre for Women's Development Studies, Mahila Dakshata Samiti and National Federation of Indian Women. 1996. 'Report of Women's Delegation', in Tanika Sarkar and Urvashi Butalia (eds), *Women and the Hindu Right* (New Delhi: Kali for Women).

All India Citizens' Initiative. 2012. *Nandigram: What Really Happened? Based on the Report of the People's Tribunal on Nandigram, 26–28 May 2007* (New Delhi: Daanish Books).

AMC (Ahmedabad Municipal Corporation). 1976. *Report of the Census of Slums Ahmedabad City, 1976* (Ahmedabad: AMC).

—— 1985. *Revised Development Plan 1975–1985* (Ahmedabad: AMC).

Anand, Javed. 2001. 'Publishers Note: Who's Afraid of the Commission's Report?' Available online at: http://www.sabrang.com/srikrish/pubnote.htm (last accessed on 11 February 2014).

Anderson, Benedict. 1983. *Imagined Communities: Reflections on the Origin and Spread of Nationalism* (London: Verso).

Andersen, Walter K., and Shridhar D. Damle. 1987. *A Brotherhood in Saffron: The Rashtriya Swayamsevak Sangh and Hindu Revivalism* (Boulder: Westview Press).

Annual Records of Jyoti Sangh. 1937–2005. Jyoti Sangh Archives, Ahmedabad.

Atkins, Stephen. 2004. *Encyclopaedia of Modern Worldwide Extremists and Extremist Groups* (Westport: Greenwood Press).

Bacchetta, Paola. 1994. 'Communal Property/Sexual Property: On Representations of Muslim Women in a Hindu Nationalist Discourse', in Zoya Hasan (ed.), *Forging Identities* (New Delhi: Kali for Women).

—— 2005. 'Hindu Nationalist Women as Ideologues: The "Sangh" and the "Samiti" and Their Differential Concepts of the Hindu Nation', in Christophe Jaffrelot (ed.), *The Sangh Parivar: A Reader* (New Delhi: Oxford University Press).

Bagchi, Jasodhara, and Subodhoranjan Dasgupta (eds). 2006 [2003]. *The Trauma and the Triumph: Gender and Partition in Eastern India* (New Delhi: Stree).

Balakrishnan, Pulapre. 2010. *Economic Growth in India: History and Prospect* (New Delhi: Oxford University Press).

Banerjee, Sikata. 1996. 'The Feminization of Violence in Bombay: Women in the Politics of the Shiv Sena', *Asian Survey*, vol. 36, no. 12 (December), pp. 1213–25.

—— 2005. *Make Me a Man! Masculinity, Hinduism, and Nationalism in India* (Albany: SUNY Press).

Bastick, Megan, Karin Grimm and Rahel Kunz. 2007. *Sexual Violence in Armed Conflict: Global Overview and Implications for the Security Sector* (Geneva: Geneva Centre for the Democratic Control of Armed Forces).

Basu, Amrita. 1996. 'Mass Movement or Elite Conspiracy? The Puzzle of Hindu Nationalism', in David Ludden (ed.), *Contesting the Nation: Religion, Community and the Politics of Democracy in India* (Philadelphia: University of Pennsylvania Press).

—— 1998. 'Hindu Women's Activism in India and the Questions It Raises', in Patricia Jeffery and Amrita Basu (eds), *Appropriating Gender: Women's Activism and Politicized Religion in South Asia* (New York: Routledge).

Basu, Tapan, Pradip Datta, Sumit Sarkar, Tanika Sarkar and Sambuddha Sen. 1993. *Khaki Shorts and Saffron Flags: A Critique of the Hindu Right*, Tracts for the Times, vol. 1 (New Delhi: Orient BlackSwan).

Baxi, Pratiksha. 2004. 'The Social and Juridical Framework of Rape in India: Case Studies in Gujarat'. Unpublished PhD thesis, University of Delhi.

—— 2009. 'Violence of Political Rhetoric on Rape', *Economic and Political Weekly*, vol. 44, no. 32 (August), pp. 15–16.

Baxi, Upendra. 2005. 'The Gujarat Catastrophe: Notes on Reading Politics as Democidal Rape Culture', in Kalpana Kannabiran (ed.), *The Violence of Normal Times: Essays on Women's Lived Realities* (New Delhi: Women Unlimited).

Berenschot, Ward. 2011. *Riot Politics: India's Hindu–Muslim Violence and the Everyday Mediation of the State* (London: Hurst, and New York: Columbia University Press).

Bhatt, Arunkumar. 1991. 'Polishing the claws: What is the VHP up to?' *Frontline*, vol. 8, no. 21 (12–25 October).

—— 1992. 'Ahmedabad carnage: Rioters rip Gujarat's premier city apart', *Frontline*, vol. 10, no. 3 (30 January), pp. 18–20.

Bhatt, Chetan. 2001. *Hindu Nationalism: Origins, Ideologies and Modern Myths* (Oxford: Berg, and New York: New York University Press).

Bhatt, Mahesh, and V. K. Chawda. 1976. 'Housing the Poor in Ahmedabad', *Economic and Political Weekly*, vol. 11, no. 19 (May), pp. 706–11.

BJP (Bharatiya Janata Party). 1995. *Sankalp Patra: Vidhansabha Chutni* (Ahmedabad: BJP, Gujarat Pradesh).

Brass, Paul. 2003. *The Production of Hindu–Muslim Violence in Contemporary India* (New Delhi: Oxford University Press).

—— 2004. *The Politics of India since Independence* (Cambridge: Cambridge University Press), 2nd edn.

Breman, Jan. 1993. 'Anti-Muslim Pogrom in Surat', *Economic and Political Weekly*, vol. 28, no. 16 (April), pp. 737–41.

—— 2004. *The Making and Unmaking of an Industrial Working Class: Sliding Down the Labour Hierarchy in Ahmedabad, India* (New Delhi: Oxford University Press).

Brown, Judith. 1989. *Gandhi: Prisoner of Hope* (New Haven: Yale University Press).

Brownmiller, Susan. 1975. *Against Our Will: Men, Women and Rape* (London: Secker and Warburg).

Bunsha, Dione. 2002. 'The Modi road show', *Frontline*, vol. 19, no. 21 (12–25 October). Available online at: http://www.frontline.in/static/html/fl1921/stories/20021025006900900.htm (last accessed on 25 February 2014).

—— 2003. 'Riding the hate wave', *Frontline*, vol. 19, no. 26 (21 December). Available online at: http://www.frontline.in/static/html/fl1926/stories/200301030078 12600.htm (last accessed on 26 December 2011).

—— 2007. '"I don't believe in love marriages": An Indian serial kidnapper interviewed', *New Internationalist*, no. 400. Available online at: http://newint.org/columns/currents/2007/05/01/fundamentalism/ (last accessed on 11 February 2014).

Burton, Antoinette. 1994. *Burdens of History: British Feminists, Indian Women and Imperial Culture* (Chapel Hill: University of North Carolina Press).

Butalia, Urvashi. 1996. 'Muslim and Hindu Men and Women: Communal Stereotypes and Partition of India', in Tanika Sarkar and Urvashi Butalia (eds), *Women and the Hindu Right* (New Delhi: Kali for Women).

—— 1998. *The Other Side of Silence: Voices from the Partition of India* (New Delhi: Penguin).

Butler, Judith. 1990. *Gender Trouble* (New York: Routledge).

—— 2004. *Undoing Gender* (New York: Routledge).

Cahill, Ann. 2000. 'Foucault, Rape, and the Construction of the Feminine Body', *Hypatia*, vol. 15, no. 1 (Winter), pp. 43–63.

Carroll, Lucy. 1989. 'Law, Custom and Statutory Social Reform: The Hindu Widows' Remarriage Act of 1856', in Jayasankar Krishnamurthy (ed.), *Women in Colonial India: Essays on Survival, Work and the State* (New Delhi: Oxford University Press).

Carvalho, Nirmala. 2006. 'Hindu Fanatics Abduct and Rape Christian Women', National Confederation of Human Rights Organizations, 1 June 2006. Available online at: http://www.nchro.org/index.php?option=com_content&view=article&id=3528:hindu-fanatics-abduct-and-rape-christian-women&catid=7:fascism&Itemid=16 (last accessed on 15 January 2013).

Casolari, Marzia. 2000. 'Hindutva's Foreign Tie-Up in the 1930s: Archival Evidence', *Economic and Political Weekly*, vol. 35, no. 4 (January), pp. 218–28.

CCT (Concerned Citizens' Tribunal) (Justice V. R. Krishna Iyer, Justice P. B. Sawant, Justice Hosbet Suresh, K. G. Kannabiran, Aruna Roy, K. S. Subramanian, Ghanshyam Shah and Tanika Sarkar). 2002. *Crime against Humanity: An Inquiry into the Carnage in Gujarat*, vol. 1: *List of Incidents and Evidence*; vol. 2: *Findings and Recommendations*; vol. 3: *List of Annexures* (Mumbai: CCT).

Chakravarti, Uma, and Nandita Haksar. 1987. *The Delhi Riots: Three Days in the Life of a Nation* (New Delhi: Lancer International).

Chakravarti, Uma, Urvashi Butalia, Pratiksha Baxi, Xonzoi Barbora, Ashley Tellis, Anand Chakravarti, Mohinder Singh, N. R. Levin and Sarovar Zaidi. 2007. 'Rape Culture', *Economic and Political Weekly*, vol. 42, no. 50 (December), p. 4.

Chandra, Sudhir. 1993. 'Communal Consciousness and Communal Violence: Impressions from Post-Riot Surat', *Economic and Political Weekly*, vol. 28, no. 36 (September), pp. 1883–7.

Chartier, Roger. 1982. 'Intellectual History or Sociocultural History?' in Dominick LaCapra and Steven L. Kaplan (eds), *Modern European Intellectual History: Reappraisals and New Perspectives* (Ithaca: Cornell University Press).

Chaudhary, N. K. 1995. *Assembly Elections 1994–1995: An Analysis and Results* (New Delhi: Shipra Publications).

Choudhari, K. K. 1985. *Maharashtra and Indian Freedom Struggle* (Mumbai: Director General of Information and Public Relations, Government of Maharashtra).

Citizens' Initiative (Syeda Hameed, Ruth Manorama, Malini Ghose, Sheba George, Farah Naqvi and Mari Thekaekara). 2002. 'How Has the Gujarat Massacre Affected Minority Women? The Survivors Speak. Fact-Finding by a Women's Panel', in *The Gujarat Pogrom: Compilations of Various Reports* (New Delhi: Indian Social Institute).

Citizens' Tribunal (Justice S. M. Daud and Justice Hosbet Suresh). 2002. *People's Verdict* (Mumbai: Sabrang).

Cockburn, Cynthia. 2004. 'The Continuum of Violence', in Wenona Giles and Jennifer Hyndman (eds), *States of Conflict: Gender, Violence and Resistance* (Berkeley: University of California Press).

Croizier, Ralph. 1970. 'Medicine, Modernization, and Cultural Crisis in China and India', *Comparative Studies in Society and History*, vol. 12, no. 3 (July), pp. 275–91.

Daiya, Kavita. 2008. *Violent Belongings: Partition, Gender and National Culture in Postcolonial India* (Philadelphia: Temple University Press).

Das, Veena. 1995. *Critical Events: An Anthropological Perspective on Contemporary India* (Oxford: Oxford University Press).

—— 1996. 'Sexual Violence, Discursive Formations and the State', *Economic and Political Weekly*, vol. 31, nos 35–7 (September), pp. 2411–13, 2415–18, 2420–3.

—— 2006. *Life and Words: Violence and the Descent into the Ordinary* (Oxford: Oxford University Press).

Datta, Pradip K. 2003. '*Hindutva* and the New Indian Middle Class', in Indira Chandrasekhar and Peter Seel (eds), *Body.City: Siting Contemporary Culture in India* (New Delhi: Tulika).

Dave Commission. 1990. *Report of the Commission of Inquiry into the Incidents of Violence and Disturbances which Took Place at Various Places in the State of Gujarat since February, 1985 to 18th July, 1985*, 3 vols (Ahmedabad: Government of Gujarat).

Davis, Richard. 1996. 'The Iconography of Rama's Chariot', in David Ludden (ed.), *Contesting the Nation: Religion, Community, and the Politics of Democracy in India*, South Asian Seminar Series (Philadelphia: University of Philadelphia Press).

Dayal, John (ed.). 2002. *Gujarat 2002: Untold and Re-told Stories of the Hindutva Lab* (New Delhi: Media House).

Desai, Ishwarlal P. 1981. 'Anti-reservation Agitation and Structure of Gujarat Society', *Economic and Political Weekly*, vol. 16, no. 18 (May), pp. 819–23.

Deshpande, B. V., and S. R. Ramaswamy. 1981. *Dr Hedgewar, the Epoch-Maker: A Biography* (Bangalore: Sahitya Sindhu).

Devji, Faisal F. 1991. 'Gender and the Politics of Space: The Movement for Women's Reform in Muslim India, 1857–1900', *South Asia: Journal of South Asian Studies*, vol. 14, no. 1, pp. 141–53.

Dutt, Barkha. 2002. 'Nothing New? Women as Victims', in Siddharth Varadarajan (ed.), *Gujarat: The Making of a Tragedy* (New Delhi: Penguin).

Engineer, Asghar Ali, 1985a. 'From Caste to Communal Violence', *Economic and Political Weekly*, vol. 20, no. 15 (April), pp. 628–30.

—— 1985b. 'Communal Fire Engulfs Ahmedabad Once Again', *Economic and Political Weekly*, vol. 20, no. 27 (July), pp. 1116–20.

—— 1989. *Communalism and Communal Violence in India: An Analytical Approach to Hindu–Muslim Conflict* (New Delhi: Ajanta).

—— 1990. 'Communal Riots in Recent Months', *Economic and Political Weekly*, vol. 25, no. 40 (October), pp. 2234–6.

—— 1992. 'Communal Riots in Ahmedabad', *Economic and Political Weekly*, vol. 27, nos 31–2 (August), pp. 1641–3.

—— 2001. 'Communal Riots—2000', Centre for Study of Society and Secularism, 1–15 January. Available online at: http://www.csss-isla.com/arch%20211.htm (last accessed on 26 February 2014).

—— (ed.). 2003. *The Gujarat Carnage* (New Delhi: Orient Longman).

Fisher, Siobhan. 1996. 'Occupation of the Womb: Forced Impregnation as Genocide', *Duke Law Journal*, vol. 46, no. 1 (October), pp. 91–133.

Forum against Oppression of Women and Awaaz-e-Niswaan. 2002. *Genocide in Rural Gujarat: The Experience of Dahod District* (Mumbai: Forum against Oppression of Women and Awaaz-e-Niswaan). Available online at: http://www.onlinevolunteers.org/gujarat/reports/rural/rural-gujarat-12.htm (last accessed on 11 February 2014).

Fox, Adam. 2000. *Oral and Literate Culture in England, 1500–1700* (Oxford: Clarendon Press).

Ganguli, Amulya. 2007. 'Mumbai Riots of 1992–93: Letting Sleeping Dogs Lie', 11 August. Available online at: http://www.boloji.com/index.cfm?md=Content&sd=Articles&ArticleID=6665 (last accessed on 11 February 2014).

Gayer, Laurent, and Christophe Jaffrelot (eds). 2012. *Muslims in Indian Cities: Trajectories of Marginalisation* (London: C. Hurst & Co.).

George, Sheba, and Kalpana Kannabiran. 2007. 'What Is Justice for Survivors of Gujarat 2002?' *Economic and Political Weekly*, vol. 42, no. 11 (March), pp. 923–5.

Gerecke, Megan. 2009. 'Explaining Sexual Violence in Conflict Situations: Preliminary Findings from Bosnia and Herzegovina, Rwanda and Sierra Leone'. Paper presented at the annual meeting of ISA's 50th Annual Convention, 'Exploring the Past, Anticipating the Future', New York Marriott Marquis, New York, 15 February 2009, pp. 1–62. Available online at: http://citation.allacademic.com/meta/p313164_index.html (last accessed on 11 February 2014).

Ghatwai, Milind. 1998. 'VHP matrimonials fix up "misguided" Hindu girls'. *Indian Express* (6 August). Available online at: http://expressindia.indianexpress.com/ie/daily/19980806/21850124.html (last accessed on 26 February 2014).

Ghosh, Papiya. 1994. 'The Virile and the Chaste in Community and Nation Making: Bihar 1920's to 1940's', *Social Scientist*, vol. 22, nos 1–2 (January–February), pp. 80–94.

Gillion, Kenneth. 1968. *Ahmedabad: A Study in Urban History* (Berkeley: University of California Press).

Gilmartin, David. 1998. 'A Magnificent Gift: Muslim Nationalism and the Election Process in Colonial Punjab', *Comparative Studies in Society and History*, vol. 40, no. 3 (July), pp. 415–36.

Golwalkar, Madhav S. 1947 [1939]. *We or Our Nationhood Defined* (Nagpur: Bharat Prakashan), 4th edn.

—— 1996 [1966]. *Bunch of Thoughts* (New Delhi: Sahitya Sindhu Prakashan), 3rd edn.

Gooptu, Nandini. 2001. *The Politics of the Urban Poor in Early Twentieth-Century India* (Cambridge: Cambridge University Press).

Government of Gujarat. 1978. *Handbook of Basic Statistics, Gujarat State 1969 to 1976* (Gandhinagar: Bureau of Economics and Statistics, Government of Gujarat).

—— 1982. *General Elections: Gujarat Legislative Assembly 1962–1980* (Gandhinagar: Chief Electoral Officer, Government of Gujarat).

—— 1985a. *Ahmedabad District Gazette* (Gandhinagar: Government of Gujarat).

—— 1985b. *Report on the General Elections to the Gujarat Legislative Assembly, March 1985 (Statistical Review)* (Gandhinagar: Chief Electoral Officer, Government of Gujarat).

—— 1995. *Location of Industries in Gujarat State 1975, 1980 and 1985*, 3 vols (Gandhinagar: Directorate of Economics and Statistics, Government of Gujarat).

—— 2008. *Inquiry into the facts, circumstances and all the course of events of the incidents that led to setting on fire some coaches of the Sabarmati Express Train on 27.2.2002 near Godhra Railway Station and the subsequent incidents of violence in the State in the aftermath of the Godhra incident. Report by the Commission of Inquiry consisting of Mr Justice G. T. Nanavati and Mr Justice Akshay H. Mehta*, Part I (Sabarmati Express Train Incident at Godhra), Ahmedabad, 18 September. Government of Gujarat, Home Department. Available online at: home.gujarat.gov.in/home department/downloads/godharaincident.pdf (last accessed on 11 February 2014).

—— n.d. 'Ahmedabad' (Gandhinagar: Industries Commissionerate, Government of Gujarat). Available online at: http://www.vibrantgujarat.com/images/pdf/ahmedabad-district-profile.pdf (last accessed on 23 November 2012).

Government of India. 1961. *Census of India 1961: Gujarat District Census Handbook, Ahmedabad District* (New Delhi: Office of the Registrar General, Government of India).

—— 1969. *Press in India 1968: Annual Report on the Press Compiled by the Registrar of Newspapers for India under the PRB Act for the Year*, 2 vols (New Delhi: Ministry of Information and Broadcasting, Government of India).

—— 1971. *Census of India 1971: Gujarat District Census Handbook, Ahmedabad District* (New Delhi: Office of the Registrar General, Government of India).

—— 1974. *Towards Equality: Report of the Committee on the Status of Women in India* (New Delhi: Ministry of Education and Social Welfare, Government of India).

—— 1981. *Census of India 1981: Gujarat District Census Handbook, Village and Townwise Primary Census Abstract (Ahmedabad)* (New Delhi: Office of the Registrar General, Government of India).

—— 1991. *Census of India 1991: Gujarat District Census Handbook, Village and Townwise Primary Census Abstract (Ahmedabad)* (New Delhi: Office of the Registrar General, Government of India).

—— 1997. *Estimates of Poverty in India* (New Delhi: Planning Commission, Government of India).

—— 2001. *Census of India 2001: Gujarat District Census Handbook, Ahmedabad District* (New Delhi: Office of the Registrar General, Government of India).

—— 2013. 'The Criminal Law (Amendment) Act 2013', *Gazette of India* (New Delhi: Ministry of Home Affairs, Legislative Department, Government of India), pp. 2–6. Available online at: http://egazette.nic.in/WriteReadData/2013/E_ 17_2013_212.pdf (last accessed on 11 February 2014).

Graham, Bruce. 2005. 'The Leadership and Organisation of the Jana Sangh, 1951– 1967', in Christophe Jaffrelot (ed.), *The Sangh Parivar: A Reader* (New Delhi: Oxford University Press).

Grech, Joyoti. 1993. 'Resisting War Rape in Bangladesh', *Trouble and Strife*, no. 26 (Summer), pp. 17–21.

Gupta, Akhil, and James Ferguson (eds). 2001. *Culture, Power, Place: Explorations in Critical Anthropology* (Durham: Duke University Press).

Gupta, Charu. 2001. *Sexuality, Obscenity, Community: Women, Muslims and the Hindu Public in Colonial India* (New Delhi: Permanent Black).

—— 2004. 'Censuses, Communalism, Gender and Identity: A Historical Perspective', *Economic and Political Weekly*, vol. 39, no. 39 (September), pp. 4302–4.

Hansen, Thomas B., and Christophe Jaffrelot (eds). 1998. *The BJP and the Compulsion of Politics in India* (New Delhi: Oxford University Press).

Harding, Sandra. 1997. 'Is There a Feminist Method?' in Sandra Kemp and Judith Squires (eds), *Feminisms* (Oxford: Oxford University Press).

Harris, Ruth. 1993. 'The "Child of the Barbarian": Rape, Race and Nationalism in France during the First World War', *Past and Present*, no. 141 (November), pp. 170–206.

Hasan, Mushirul. 1996. 'The Myth of Unity: Colonial and National Narratives', in David Ludden (ed.), *Making India Hindu: Religion, Community and the Politics of Democracy in India* (New Delhi: Oxford University Press).

Hashmi, Shabnam, and Megha Kumar. 2002. *Break the Silence: Stories and Testimonies from Gujarat* (New Delhi: SAHMAT).

Hawkins, Mike. 2000. 'Social Darwinism and European Thought 1860–1945', *Journal of the History of Ideas*, vol. 61, no. 2 (April), pp. 223–40.

Hedgewar, Keshav B. 1972. *Rashtriya Swayamsevak Sangh: Tatva aur vyavhar* (Lucknow: Lokhit Prakashan).

Heitzman, James. 2008. *The City in South Asia* (London: Routledge).

Hirway, Indira, and Piet Terhal. 2002. 'The Contradictions of Growth', in Ghanshyam Shah, Mario Rutten and Hein Streefkerk (eds), *Development and Deprivation in Gujarat: In Honour of Jan Breman* (New Delhi: Sage).

Human Rights Watch. 1999. *Politics by Other Means: Attacks against Christians in India* (New York: Human Rights Watch).

—— 2002. *"We Have No Orders to Save You": State Participation and Complicity in Communal Violence in Gujarat* (New York: Human Rights Watch).

Indian Social Institute. 2002. *The Gujarat Pogrom: Compilations of Various Reports* (New Delhi: Indian Social Institute).

International Initiative for Justice (Anissa Helie, Gabriele Mischkowski, Nira Yuval-Davis, Sunila Abeysekara, Vahida Nainar, Farah Naqvi, Meera Vellayudan, Rhonda Copelan and Uma Chakravarti). 2003. *Threatened Existence: A Feminist Analysis of the Genocide in Gujarat* (Mumbai: International Initiative for Justice).

Islam, Shamsul. 2000. *The Freedom Struggle and the RSS: A Story of Betrayal* (New Delhi: Joshi-Adhikari Institute of Social Studies).

Jaffrelot, Christophe (ed.). 2005. *The Sangh Parivar: A Reader* (New Delhi: Oxford University Press).

—— 2012. 'Gujarat 2002: What Justice for the Victims? The Supreme Court, the SIT, the Police and the State Judiciary', *Economic and Political Weekly*, vol. 40, no. 8 (February), pp. 77–89.

Jaffrelot, Christophe, and Charlotte Thomas. 2012. 'Facing Ghettoisation in "Riot-City": Old Ahmedabad and Juhapura between Victimisation and Self-Help', in Laurent Gayer and Christophe Jaffrelot (eds), *Muslims in Indian Cities: Trajectories of Marginalisation* (London: C. Hurst & Co.).

Jagori. 2002. *What Happened in Gujarat? The Facts* (New Delhi: Jagori).

Jani, Manishi. 1984. 'Textile Workers: Jobless and Miserable'. SETU, Ahmedabad.

Jassani, Rubina. 2007. 'Communal Violence, Displacement and Muslim Identities: Negotiating Survival and Reconstruction in Ahmedabad, Western India'. Unpublished thesis, University of Warwick.

Jones, Dawn E., and Rodney W. Jones. 1976. 'Urban Upheaval in India: The 1974 Nav Nirman Riots in Gujarat', *Asian Survey*, vol. 16, no. 11 (November), pp. 1012–33.

Joshi, Chitra. 2003. *Lost Worlds: Indian Labour and Its Forgotten Histories* (New Delhi: Permanent Black).

Kakar, Sudhir. 1995. *The Colours of Violence* (New Delhi: Penguin).

Kannabiran, Kalpana, and Vasanth Kannabiran. 1996. 'The Frying Pan or the Fire? Endangered Identities, Gendered Institutions and Women's Survival', in Tanika Sarkar and Urvashi Butalia (eds), *Women and the Hindu Right* (New Delhi: Kali for Women).

—— 2002. *De-eroticizing Assault: Essays on Modesty, Honour and Power* (Kolkata: STREE).

Kapur, Anuradha. 1993. 'Deity to Crusader: The Changing Iconography of Ram', in Gyanendra Pandey (ed.), *Hindus and Others: The Question of Identity in India Today* (New Delhi: Viking).

Keer, Dhananjay. 1950. *Savarkar and His Times* (Mumbai: A. V. Keer).

—— 1966. *Veer Savarkar* (Mumbai: Popular Prakashan).

Kelly, Liz. 1988. *Surviving Sexual Violence* (Cambridge: Polity Press).

—— 2000. 'Wars against Women: Sexual Violence, Sexual Politics and the Militarized State', in Susie Jacobs, Ruth Jacobson and Jennifer Marchbank (eds), *States of Conflict: Gender, Violence and Resistance* (London: Zed Books).

Khan, Yasmin. 2007. *The Great Partition: The Making of India and Pakistan* (New Haven: Yale University Press).

Khanna, Renu. 2008. 'Communal Violence in Gujarat, India: Impact of Sexual Violence and Responsibilities of the Health Care System', Conflict and Crisis Settings: Promoting Sexual and Reproductive Rights, *Reproductive Health Matters*, vol. 16, no. 31 (May), pp. 142–52.

Khetan, Ashish. 2007a. 'Muslims, they don't deserve to live', *Tehelka* (3 November). Available online at: http://tehelka.com/muslims-they-dont-deserve-to-live/ (last accessed on 26 February 2014).

—— 2007b. 'Conspirators and rioters. Ahmedabad: Carnage capital', *Tehelka* (3 November). Available online at: http://www.tehelka.com/story_main35.asp?filename=Ne031107Ahmedabad.asp (last accessed on 10 February 2014).

—— 2011. 'The truth about the Godhra SIT report', *Tehelka* (12 February). Available online at: http://tehelka.com/story_main48.asp?filename=Ne120211coverstory.asp (last accessed on 26 February 2014).

Kishwar, Madhu. 1985. 'Women and Gandhi', *Economic and Political Weekly*, vol. 20, no. 40 (October), pp. 1691–702 and vol. 20, no. 41 (October), pp. 1753–8.
—— 1993. 'Safety Is Indivisible: The Warning from Bombay Riots', *Manushi*, nos 74–5, pp. 1–3.
Klein, Dorie. 1981. 'Violence against Women: Some Considerations regarding Its Causes and Its Elimination', *Crime and Delinquency*, vol. 27, no. 1, pp. 64–80.
Kleinman, Arthur. 2001. 'The Violences of Everyday Life: The Multiple Forms and Dynamics of Social Violence', in Veena Das, Arthur Kleinman, Mamphela Ramphele and Pamela Reynolds (eds), *Violence and Subjectivity* (Berkeley: University of California Press).
Krishnan, Kavita. 2008. 'Nandigram and CPI(M)'s Response to Its Left Critics', *Liberation* (January). Available online at: http://www.cpiml.org/liberation/year_2008/january/nandigram_and_cpim.html (last accessed on 11 February 2014).
Lahkar, Abhinash, and Uma Dhanushkodi. 2002. *Troubled Times: Communal Fascism Arrives* (Bengaluru: Bhumika).
Lobo, Lancy, and Paul D'Souza. 1993. 'Surat Riots II — Images of Violence', *Economic and Political Weekly*, vol. 28, no. 5 (January), pp. 152–4.
Mahadevia, Darshini. 2002. 'Communal Space over Life Space: Saga of Increasing Vulnerability in Ahmedabad', *Economic and Political Weekly*, vol. 37, no. 48 (November), pp. 4850–8.
Mahadevia, Darshini, and Wilfred D'Costa. 1997. 'Poverty and Vulnerability in Ahmedabad'. Unpublished report, Oxford Urban Poverty Research Programme (Ahmedabad: Oxfam India Trust).
Mani, Lata. 1989. 'Contentious Traditions: The Debate on *Sati* in Colonial India', in Kumkum Sangari and Sudesh Vaid (eds), *Recasting Women: Essays in Colonial History* (New Delhi: Kali for Women).
Marcus, Sharon. 1992. 'Fighting Bodies, Fighting Words: A Theory and Politics of Rape Prevention', in Judith Butler and Joan Scott (eds), *Feminists Theorize the Political* (New York: Routledge).
Mazumdar, Monojit, and Vinay Menon. 2003. 'This Man Is the Real Culprit. He Got Our People Killed', in Asghar Ali Engineer (ed.), *The Gujarat Carnage* (Hyderabad: Orient Longman).
Mehta, Bhavana, and Trupti Shah. 1992. 'Gender and Communal Riots', *Economic and Political Weekly*, vol. 27, no. 47 (November), pp. 2252–4.
Mehta, Deepak, and Roma Chatterji. 2001. 'Boundaries, Names, Alterities: A Case Study of a "Communal Riot" in Dharavi, Bombay', in Veena Das, Arthur Kleinman, Margaret Lock, Mamphela Ramphele and Pamela Reynolds (eds), *Remaking a World: Violence, Social Suffering and Recovery* (Berkeley: University of California Press).
Menon, Nivedita. 2004. *Recovering Subversion: Feminist Politics beyond Law* (Ranikhet: Permanent Black).
Menon, Ritu, and Kamla Bhasin. 1998. *Borders and Boundaries: Women in India's Partition* (New Delhi: Kali for Women).
Moser, Caroline, and Fiona Clark (eds). 2005. *Victims, Perpetrators or Actors? Gender, Armed Conflict and Political Violence* (New Delhi: Zubaan).
Mosse, George L. 1982. 'Nationalism and Respectability: Normal and Abnormal Sexuality in the Nineteenth Century', Sexuality in History, *Journal of Contemporary History*, vol. 17, no. 2 (April), pp. 221–46.

Nandy, Ashis, Shikha Trivedi, Shail Mayaram and Achyut Yagnik (eds). 1995. *Creating a Nationality: The Ramjanmabhumi Movement and Fear of the Self* (New Delhi: Oxford University Press).

Noorani, Abdul G. 2002. *Savarkar and Hindutva: The Godse Connection* (New Delhi: Leftword Books).

O'Hanlon, Rosalind. 1991. 'Issues of Widowhood: Gender and Resistance in Colonial Western India', in Douglas Haynes and Gyan Prakash (eds), *Contesting Power: Resistance and Everyday Social Relations in South Asia* (New Delhi: Oxford University Press).

—— 1994. *A Comparison between Women and Men: Tarabai Shinde and the Critique of Gender Relations in Colonial India* (Oxford: Oxford University Press).

Omvedt, Gail. 1975. 'Rural Origins of Women's Liberation in India', Special Number on Women, *Social Scientist*, vol. 4, nos 4–5 (November–December), pp. 40–54.

Oommen, T. K. 2008. *Reconciliation in Post-Godhra Gujarat: The Role of Civil Society* (New Delhi: Pearson Longman).

Pandey, Gyanendra. 1991. 'Hindus and Others: The Militant Hindu Construction', *Economic and Political Weekly*, vol. 26, no. 52 (December), pp. 2997–3009.

—— 2001. *Remembering Partition: Violence, Nationalism and History in India* (Cambridge: Cambridge University Press).

Parekh, Bhikhu. 1989. *Colonialism, Tradition and Reform: An Analysis of Gandhi's Political Discourse* (New Delhi: Sage).

Patel, B. B. 1988. *Workers of Closed Textile Mills* (New Delhi: Oxford and IBH).

Patel, Girish. 2002. 'Narendra Modi's One-Day Cricket: What and Why?' *Economic and Political Weekly*, vol. 37, no. 48 (November), pp. 4826–37.

Patel, Sujata. 1985. 'The Ahmedabad Riots, 1985: An Analysis'. Unpublished monograph, Centre of Social Studies, Surat.

—— 2002. 'Urbanization, Development and Communalisation of Society in Gujarat', in Takashi Shinoda (ed.), *The Other Gujarat: Social Transformations among Weaker Sections* (Mumbai: Popular Prakashan).

Pathak, Ila. 2006. 'History of Jyoti Sangh', *Guidelines for Counsellors of Family Counselling Centres* (Ahmedabad: Ahmedabad Women's Action Group).

Pathak, Zakia, and Rajeswari Sunder Rajan. 1989. 'Shahbano', *Signs*, vol. 14, no. 3 (Spring), pp. 558–82.

Patwardhan, Anand. 1994. *Father, Son and the Holy War*, documentary film.

Qaumi Ekta Trust, *Communalism Combat*, Dakshin Gujarat Adivasi Sangh, Vikas Adhyayan Kendra, Samvad, Insaf, Institute for Initiative in Education, Sahrwaru, Vote and People's Union for Human Rights. 2000. *Saffron on the Rampage: Gujarat's Muslims Pay for Lakshar's Deeds* (Mumbai: Sabrang).

Rajagopal, Arvind. 2001. *Politics after Television: Hindu Nationalism and the Reshaping of the Public in India* (Cambridge: Cambridge University Press).

Ramaswamy, Sumathi. 2010. *The Goddess and the Nation: Mapping Mother India* (Durham, NC: Duke University Press).

Ray, Raka. 2007. 'A Slap from the Hindu Nation', in Amrita Basu and Srirupa Roy (eds), *Violence and Democracy in India* (Oxford: Seagull Books).

Raza, Gauhar, and Shabnam Hashmi. 2002. *State of Ruins: The Dispossessed at the Vortex of Communal Whirlpool in Gujarat. A Report* (Ahmedabad: Prashant, and Delhi: SAHMAT).

Reddy Commission (Commission of Inquiry headed by Justice P. Jaganmohan Reddy). 1971. *Inquiry into the Communal Disturbances at Ahmedabad and Other*

Places in Gujarat on and after 18th September 1969, Report and Appendices (Ahmedabad: Government of Gujarat).

Robinson, Rowena. 2005. *Tremors of Violence: Muslim Survivors of Ethnic Strife in Western India* (New Delhi: Sage).

Roy, Tirthankar. 2005. *Rethinking Economic Change in India: Labour and Livelihood* (Oxford: Routledge).

Rudolph, Lloyd I. 1992. 'The Media and Culture Politics', in S. K. Mitra and J. Chiririyankandath (eds), *Electoral Politics in India: A Changing Landscape* (New Delhi: Segment Books).

Rudolph, Lloyd I., and Susanne Hoeber Rudolph. 1987. *In Pursuit of Lakshmi: The Political Economy of the Indian State* (Chicago: University of Chicago Press).

Saheli, Sama, Nirantar, Uma Chakravarti, Farah Naqvi and Pratiksha Baxi. 2006. 'Zahira Shaikh: "Victim" of Justice', *Economic and Political Weekly*, vol. 41, no. 11 (March), p. 934.

Sangari, Kumkum. 2002. 'Violent Routes: The Traffic between Patriarchies and Communalism', in K. N. Panikkar and Sukumar Murlidharan (eds), *Communalism, Civil Society and the State: Reflections on a Decade of Turbulence* (Delhi: SAHMAT).

Sarkar, Sumit. 1996. 'Indian Nationalism and Politics of Hindutva', in David Ludden (ed.), *Making India Hindu: Religion, Community, and the Politics of Democracy in India* (Oxford: Oxford University Press).

Sarkar, Tanika. 1991. 'The Woman as Communal Subject: Rashtrasevika Samiti and Ran Janmabhoomi Movement', *Economic and Political Weekly*, vol. 26, no. 35 (August), pp. 2057–62.

—— 1992. 'The Hindu Wife and the Hindu Nation: Domesticity and Nationalism in 19th century Bengal', *Studies in History*, vol. 8, no. 2, pp. 213–35.

—— 2001. *Hindu Wife, Hindu Nation: Community, Religion and Cultural Nationalism* (New Delhi: Permanent Black).

—— 2002. 'Semiotics of Terror: Muslim Children and Women in Hindu Rashtra', *Economic and Political Weekly*, vol. 37, no. 28 (July), pp. 2872–6.

—— 2005. 'The Gender Predicament of the Hindu Right', in Christophe Jaffrelot (ed.), *The Sangh Parivar: A Reader* (New Delhi: Oxford University Press).

Savarkar, Vinayak D. 1940. *Hindu Sangathan: Its Ideology and Immediate Programme – A Collection of His Three Presidential Speeches at Karnavati, Nagpur and Calcutta* (Bombay: N. V. Damle).

—— 1949 [1923]. *Hindutva: Who Is a Hindu?* (New Delhi: Hindi Sahitya Sadan), 4th edn.

—— 1970. *Six Glorious Epochs of Indian History* (New Delhi: Rajdhani Granthagar).

—— 1983 [1905]. *Vande Mataram* (Chennai: Spectra).

Seifert, Ruth. 1994. 'War and Rape: A Preliminary Analysis', in Alexandra Stiglmayer (ed.), *Mass Rape: The War against Women in Bosnia-Herzegovina* (Lincoln: University of Nebraska Press).

Seshadri, Hongasadra V. (ed.). 1981. *Dr. Hedgewar the Epoch Maker: A Biography* (compiled by B. V. Deshpande and S. R. Ramaswamy) (Bengaluru: Sahitya Sindhu Prakashana).

Sethi, Manisha. 2002. 'Avenging Angels and Nurturing Mothers', *Economic and Political Weekly*, vol. 37, no. 16 (April), pp. 1545–52.

Shah, A. M. 2002. 'For a More Humane Society', Society under Siege: A Symposium on the Breakdown of Civil Society in Ahmedabad, *Seminar*, no. 513, pp. 58–60.

Shah, Ghanshyam. 1970. 'Communal Riots in Gujarat: Report of a Preliminary Investigation', *Economic and Political Weekly*, vol. 5, nos 3–5 (January), pp. 187–200.

—— 1974a. 'Anatomy of Urban Riots: Ahmedabad 1973', *Economic and Political Weekly*, vol. 9, nos 6–8 (February), pp. 233, 235, 237, 239–40.

—— 1974b. 'The Upsurge in Gujarat', *Economic and Political Weekly*, Special Number, vol. 9, nos 32–4 (August), pp. 1429–54.

—— 1991 [1984]. 'The 1969 Communal Riots in Ahmedabad: A Case Study', in Asghar Ali Engineer (ed.), *Communal Riots in Post-Independence India* (Hyderabad: Sangam Books).

Shani, Ornit. 2007. *Communalism, Caste and Hindu Nationalism: The Violence in Gujarat* (Cambridge: Cambridge University Press).

Sharma, Kalpana. 2000. 'Good girls do not wear jeans', *Hindu* (12 March). Available online at: http://www.hindu.com/2000/03/12/stories/13120615.htm (last accessed on 26 February 2014).

Sharma, Rakesh. 2003. *Final Solution*, documentary film.

Shaw, Graham, and Mary Lloyd (eds). 1985. *Publications proscribed by the Government of India: A catalogue of the collections in the India Office Library and Records and the Department of Oriental Manuscripts and Printed Books*, British Library Reference Division (London: British Library).

Sheth, Pravin. 1998. *Political Development in Gujarat* (Ahmedabad: Karnavati Publications).

Shukla, Gajendraprasad. 1991. 'Rajkiya Pakshni Vicharsarani Ane Tena Aadhar: Gujarat Bharatiya Janta Pakshno Ekam Abhyas'. Unpublished thesis, University of South Gujarat.

Sinha, Mrinalini. 1995. *Colonial Masculinity: The 'Manly Englishman' and the 'Effeminate Bengali' in the Late Nineteenth Century* (Manchester: Manchester University Press).

—— 2000. 'Refashioning Mother India: Feminism and Nationalism in Late-Colonial India', Points of Departure: India and the South Asian Diaspora, *Feminist Studies*, vol. 26, no. 3 (Autumn), pp. 623–44.

Skinner, Quentin. 1988. 'Meaning and Understanding in the History of Ideas', in James Tully (ed.), *Meaning and Context: Quentin Skinner and His Critics* (Cambridge: Polity Press).

Skjelsbæk, Inger. 2001. 'Sexual Violence and War: Mapping Out a Complex Relationship', *European Journal of International Relations*, vol. 7, no. 2, pp. 211–37.

Spodek, Howard. 1989. 'From Gandhi to Violence: Ahmedabad's 1985 Riots in Historical Perspective', *Modern Asian Studies*, vol. 23, no. 4, pp. 765–95.

—— 2010. 'In the Hindutva Laboratory: Pogrom and Politics in Gujarat, 2002', *Modern Asian Studies*, vol. 44, no. 2, pp. 349–99.

—— 2011. *Ahmedabad: Shock City of Twentieth-Century India* (Bloomington, Indianapolis: Indiana University Press).

Srikrishna, Justice B. N. 1998. *Damning Verdict: B. N. Srikrishna Commission Appointed for Inquiry into the Riots at Mumbai during December 1992–January 1993 and the March 12, 1993 Bomb Blasts* (Mumbai: Sabrang).

Sud, Nikita. 2007. 'Gujarat: From Developmental State to Hindu Rashtra?' Unpublished thesis, University of Oxford.

—— 2012. *Liberalization, Hindu Nationalism and the State: A Biography of Gujarat* (Oxford: Oxford University Press).

Sunder Rajan, Rajeswari. 2000. 'Women between Community and State: Some Implications of the Uniform Civil Code Debates in India', *Social Text*, vol. 18, no. 4 (Winter), pp. 55–82.

Swami, Pravin. 2002. 'Saffron Terror', *Frontline*, vol. 19, no. 6 (16–29 March). Available online at: http://www.frontline.in/static/html/fl1906/19060080.htm (last accessed on 26 February 2014).

Trivedi, Lisa. 2003. 'Visually Mapping the "Nation": Swadeshi Politics in Nationalist India, 1920–1930', *Journal of Asian Studies*, vol. 26, no. 1 (February), pp. 11–41.

Turshen, Meredith. 2005. 'The Political Economy of Rape: An Analysis of Systematic Rape and Sexual Abuse of Women during Armed Conflict in Africa', in Caroline O. N. Moser and Fiona Clark (eds), *Victims, Perpetrators or Actors? Gender, Armed Conflict and Political Violence* (New Delhi: Zubaan).

Udaykumar, S. P. 2005. *Presenting the Past: Anxious History and Ancient Future in Hindutva India* (Westport: Praeger Publishers).

Varadarajan, Siddharth. 2002. 'Chronicle of a Tragedy Foretold', in Siddharth Varadarajan (ed.), *Gujarat: The Making of a Tragedy* (New Delhi: Penguin).

Varshney, Ashutosh. 2002. *Ethnic Conflict and Civic Life* (New Haven: Yale University Press).

—— 2004. 'Understanding Gujarat Violence' (26 March). Available online at: http://conconflicts.ssrc.org/archives/gujarat/varshney/index.html#e5 (last accessed on 12 February 2014).

Venkatesan, V. 1998. 'Communal outrages in M.P.'., *Frontline*, vol. 15, no. 21 (10–23 October). Available online at: http://www.frontline.in/static/html/fl1521/15210300.htm (last accessed on 15 January 2013).

Watt, Carey A. 1997. 'Education for National Efficiency: Constructive Nationalism in North India, 1909–1916', *Modern Asian Studies*, vol. 31, no. 2 (May), pp. 339–74.

Women's Research Group. 1985. 'Impact of Ahmedabad Disturbances on Women: A Report', *Economic and Political Weekly*, vol. 20, no. 41 (October), pp. 1726–31.

Women's Studies Research Centre. 2003. 'Profile of Women in Gujarat' (Vadodara: M.S. University of Baroda).

Wood, John R. 1984. 'Congress Restored? The "KHAM" Strategy and Gujarat', in John R. Wood (ed.), *State Politics in Contemporary India: Crisis or Continuity?* (Boulder: Westview Press).

Yagnik, Achyut, and Manishi Jani. 1985. *The 1985 Riot in Ahmedabad*, documentary film, SETU: Centre for Social Knowledge and Action, Ahmedabad.

Yagnik, Achyut, and Nikita Sud. 2004. 'Hindutva and Beyond: The Political Topography of Gujarat'. Paper presented at the conference on State Politics in India in the 1990s: Political Mobilisation and Political Competition, Developing Countries Research Centre, University of Delhi and London School of Economics, 13–17 December. Available online at: www.crisisstates.com/download/india/yagnik&sud (last accessed on 20 June 2009).

Yagnik, Achyut, and Suchitra Sheth. 2005. *Shaping of Modern Gujarat: Plurality, Hindutva and Beyond* (New Delhi: Penguin).

—— 2011. *Ahmedabad: From Royal City to Megacity* (New Delhi: Penguin).

Yanagizawa-Drott, David. 2012. 'Propaganda and Conflict: Theory and Evidence from the Rwandan Genocide'. Unpublished paper, Harvard University.

Yechuri, Sitaram. 1993. 'What is this Hindu Rashtra: On Golwalkar's fascistic ideology and the saffron brigade's practice', *Frontline* (12 March).

Yuval-Davis, Nira. 1997. *Gender and Nation* (London: Sage).

Zarkov, Dubravka. 2005. 'The Body of the Other Man: Sexual Violence and the Construction of Masculinity, Sexuality and Ethnicity in Croatian Media', in Caroline O. N. Moser and Fiona Clark (eds), *Victims, Perpetrators or Actors? Gender, Armed Conflict and Political Violence* (New Delhi: Zubaan).

Periodicals

Communalism Combat, Mumbai

Gujarat Samachar, Ahmedabad edition

Hindu, Chennai edition

Hindustan Times, Delhi edition

Indian Express, Delhi edition

Jansatta, Delhi edition

Outlook, Delhi edition

Pioneer, Delhi edition

Sadhana, Ahmedabad

Sandesh, Ahmedabad edition

Tehelka Magazine

Times of India, Delhi and Ahmedabad editions

INDEX

'abolition of untouchability', *see* untouchability, abolition of
Acharya Mandal (Teachers' Group), 124
Adultery, 63
Advani, Lal Krishna, 168, 172, 191–2, 195
Agarwal, Purushottam, 11, 272n46
ahimsa (non-violence), 48
Ahmedabad
    civic amenities, 60–2, 182
    communal polarisation, 26, 273n5
    Congress Party, disintegration of, 65–9
    'correct' sexual order in society, 190
    economic conditions in, 62
    education for women, 62
    emergence as a riot city, 14–17
    foundation of, 15, 60
    Hindu nationalism in, 71–6
    industrial belt, walled city and western enclave, 60–5
    industrial workers in, 57–60
    Islamic legacy of, 15
    living conditions, deterioration of, 180
    political and social life of, 180
    population, 14–16, 111–13
    sessions court, fast-track, 21, 238, 246, 250
    sexual violence in, 14–17
    Shah, Ahmad, 15, 60
    slum housing, 180
    social insecurity, 181
    socio-cultural stratification, 15
    socio-economic insecurity, 119, 121, 182
    spatial segregation, 58, 181, 231
    textile mills in, *see* textile mills, in Ahmedabad
Ahmedabad Municipal Corporation (AMC), 65, 69, 97, 113, 167, 178, 180, 183, 194, 206
Ahmedabad Relief Committee, 101
Ahmedabad Women's Action Group (AWAG), 140
Akhil Bharatiya Vidyarthi Parishad (ABVP), 118, 121, 122, 123, 126, 131, 156, 163, 166, 189, 193
    anti-reservation policy, 126
    attack on 'Western dress', 152, 189
    support for upper-caste, 133
Akhil Gujarat Navrachna Samiti (AGRS), 124, 133, 135, 134
Akhil Gujarat Vaali Maha Mandal, 133
All Gujarat Committee for Reconstruction, *see* Akhil Gujarat Navrachna Samiti (AGRS)

All India Muslim Majlis-e-Musawarat, 146
Al-Qaeda, 193
Aman Samudaya, 230–1
Ambedkar, B. R., 157–8, 198
anti-caste movements, 37, 157
anti-communal violence bill, 239
'anti-rape law', 3, 8
anti-reservation riots (1981), 125, 127, 133
  'darkest period' of, 141
  see also Mandal Commission

Babri Mosque, demolition of
  (6 December 1992), 10, 19, 146, 149, 154, 167–8, 181, 251
  and its aftermath, 172–6
  see also Ramjanmabhoomi movement
Bacchetta, Paola, 160
Bajrang Dal, 20, 31, 152–3, 156–8, 167, 173–4, 177, 181, 189–94, 199–200, 202, 206–7, 211, 214, 250–1, 253
  national membership of, 182
  offences against minorities, 183–7
  rise in social support for, 163
Bajrangi, Babu, 152, 186, 187, 207, 214, 250–1, 267n10
Balance of payments crisis, 154
Banerjee, U.C., 195, 241, 242, 244
Baxi, Upendra, 149, 237
Best Bakery case (2003), 246, 247, 271n38, 284n18
Bhagavad Gita, 129
Bhagwat, Mohan, 8
Bharatiya Jana Sangh, see Jana Sangh
Bharatiya Janata Party (BJP), 8–9, 19, 31, 34–5, 55, 67, 71, 116–21, 126, 133, 138, 141, 147, 150, 177, 192, 235, 243
  anti-reservation policy, 126
  BJP–Janata Dal coalition government, 167, 244
  election manifesto, 182

election victory, 167
inter-party defections, 178
Mahila Morcha (Women's Forum), 9, 160
National Democratic Alliance, 191
political rise of, 165–7
Ramjanmabhoomi campaign, see Ramjanmabhoomi movement
rise to power in Gujarat, 153
Bharatiya Mazdoor Sangh, 126
Bharatiya Yuva Morcha, 191
Bhatt, Haresh, 182, 202, 270n33
Bhatt, Sanjiv, 204
Bhilwada neighbourhood, experience of, 96–100
Bombay Presidency, 15, 37, 70
  territorial reorganisation of, 68
Breman, Jan, 59
Brownmiller, Susan, 12

caste-based discrimination, 58, 72, 121, 157
caste-based hostilities, 23
caste hierarchy, 15, 38, 116, 162, 183
Central Bureau of Investigation, 202, 242, 249
Central Relief Committee, 101, 146
Chara, Suresh, 6–7, 211, 214, 250, 251, 267n10
Chara tribe, 200, 210, 212
Chauhan Commission, 244
child marriage, 63
Chinoy, M. J., 76–7
Chirandas, Dattatreya Narain, 147
Citizens for Justice and Peace (CJP), 246
Citizens' Initiative, 219, 233, 271n38
civil society organisations, 3, 36, 233
Citizens' Council, 88
Code of Ethics for Press in Reporting and Commenting on Communal Incidents, 84
Committee for Hindu Struggle, see Hindu Sangram Samiti

Committee for the Protection of the
  Hindu Religion, *see* Hindu
  Dharma Raksha Samiti (HDRS)
communalisation, of trivial events,
  78–80, 116, 245
communalism
  and advent of economic liberalism,
    154–63
  spread of, 116
Communist Party of India (CPI), 88
community purification, 227–9
Concerned Citizens' Tribunal (CCT),
  5–6
Congress Party
  anti-corruption protests, 119
  anti-reservation quotas and
    anti-Muslim riots, 122–8
  disintegration of, 65–9
  factionalism within, 66, 69
  hold over electoral politics, 68
  under Indira Gandhi, 66–7
  inter-party defections, 178
  KHAM strategy, 116–22, 124,
    130–1, 141, 143, 158, 166
  'minority appeasement' efforts, 166
  political decline of, 165
  reservation policies, 109, 120–1,
    124
  social transformation for the
    marginalised, 120
  support among Ahmedabad's middle
    class, 69
  United Progressive Alliance, 240–1
  upper-caste anger against, 120
consumer price index, 61
conviction, for sexual violence, 249–51
cow slaughtering, 128
Criminal Law (Amendment) Act
  (2013), 3

Dalit Panthers, 121
Darshan (non-governmental
  organisation), 234
Das, Veena, 18

Dave Commission, 106, 108, 123, 128,
  134, 136, 140, 146, 243–4
  report on 1985 riot, 116
Dave, Vinod Shanker, 106
'democidal rape culture', emergence of,
  149
Desai, Morarji, 66
dini taleem (religious-spiritual
  education), 230
'distress sales', of houses, 164
domestic violence, 36–8, 65–6, 126,
  231
dowry deaths, 64
Drishti (non-governmental
  organisation), 234
dunyavi taleem (worldly education), 230
Durga Vahini, 74, 153, 156, 158–9,
  163, 167, 181, 186
  rise in social support for, 163

economic boycott, against Muslim
  community, 130, 184, 229
economic insecurity, 65, 70, 104, 115,
  180, 182
economic liberalism, advent of, 154–63
education for women, 62
Emergency (1975), 117–19, 121, 126
employment
  female work participation rate, 156
  job security, 58, 156
  labour market, 156
  survivors struggle for, 229
Ethnic Conflict and Civic Life (2002), 26
ethnic identity, 4, 7
  role in motivating sexual violence, 6

fanaticism, religious, 40
fatherland, notion of, 39, 45, 132
female bodies and male weakness,
  characterisations of, 43–4
female sexuality
  characterisation of, 43
  definition of, 39
  desirable and repulsive, 169

forceful appropriation of, 11
Muslim, 214
notion of, 41, 170
Fernandes, George, 118, 237
    claims regarding the anti-Sikh
        riots, 237
Fisher, Siobhan, 12
forced marriages, 184, 190

Gandhi, Indira
    administration of, 66
    assassination of, 110, 123, 166
    Congress Party under, 66
    election victory, 166
    'Garibi Hatao' slogan, 67
    imposition of Emergency, 118
    KHAM strategy, 119
    loyality to, 117
Gandhi, Mahatma, 14, 102
    assassination of, 70
    views on ideal feminine and
        masculine behaviour, 64
Gandhi, Rajiv, 110, 119, 166
gender-specific crimes, incidents of,
    63–4
genital mutilation, 17, 20, 27, 91,
    106–8, 148, 173, 225
genocide
    definition of, 7
    gendered violence, analysis of,
        12–13
    of Muslims, 94
    in Rwanda, 12, 88, 107, 252, 253
    in Yugoslavia, 12, 88
'ghetto', characteristics of, 32, 164,
    228–9
Godhra incident (27 February 2002),
    53, 123, 152, 194–206, 235, 236,
    241–4
Godse, Nathuram, 70
Golwalkar, Madhav Sadashiv, 29,
    37–9, 44, 46–51, 66, 70, 71,
    73, 76
Gondia, Praveen, 203

Grand Gujarat People's Council, see
    Maha Gujarat Janata Parishad
    (MGJP)
Gudiya, story of, 4–9
'Gujarat 2002', see Hindu–Muslim
    conflict (2002)
Gujarat Bureau of Investigation, 204
Gujarati Congress, 66
Gujarat Samachar, 62, 63, 78–9, 83–4,
    135, 136, 203

Harijans, 15, 95, 117, 119, 123,
    130–1, 133–4, 136, 144–5
Hedgewar, Keshav Baliram, 29, 37–8,
    44, 49–51, 74
Hindu brotherhood, 130–2, 134
Hindu communalism, 39
Hindu Dharma Raksha Samiti (HDRS),
    80–1, 87, 101–3
    'Ramayana incident', 80
Hindu identity, 95, 169
    definition of, 39
Hindu Jagran Morcha, 183, 187, 190,
    270n32
Hindu Mahasabha, 80, 87, 90, 270n32
Hindu–Muslim conflict (1947), 52–4
    'Recovery Operation', 54
Hindu–Muslim conflict (1969),
    16–18, 20, 22, 24, 26, 79–81,
    162, 171, 213
    anti-Muslim propaganda, 86
    Bhilwada neighbourhood, experience
        of, 96–100
    communalisation, of trivial events,
        78–80
    communal propaganda and sexual
        violence, 82–9
    difference with 2002 riots, 52
    diffusing responsibility and denying
        culpability during, 101–3
    fatalities during, 53
    Gandhi Park incident, 83–4, 89
    inflammatory propaganda material,
        circulation of, 103

Jagannath Temple incident, 81, 91, 94, 102–3, 123, 137
  Khurshida Bano's account, 96, 98–9, 269n23
  organisation of, 89–95
  police inaction against, 94
  Rashida Bano's account, 96–7
  rebuilding life after, 103–4
  relief camps, 103–4
  sexual violence, infliction of, 96–100
Hindu–Muslim conflict (1985), 25, 27, 173
  anti-Muslim mobilisation, impact of, 132
  anti-reservation agitation and, 122–8, 134
  compulsions of survival and ideological alliances, 141–6
  Congress and the KHAM alliance, 116–21
  'darkest period' of, 141
  defensive Hindu nationalism and, 146–7
  events triggering, 122–8
  and Indian citizenship of Muslims, 134
  instigation and infliction of sexual violence, 137
  militant rhetoric and plural focus, 128–37
  'Patels of Gujarat Awake' pamphlet, 133–4
  police criminality and, 139–41
  rath yatra, 106, 137–8
  sexual violence against Muslim women, 105–6
  textile mills and predicament of mill workers, 110–16
Hindu–Muslim conflict (1993), 150, 154, 173–4
  see also Babri Mosque, demolition of (6 December 1992)
Hindu–Muslim conflict (1999), 191

Hindu–Muslim conflict (2002), 18, 24, 52–3, 71, 118
  anti-Muslim massacre, 194–6
  celebrating and condoning violence, 214–16
  connivance of the police, 208, 214
  conviction for sexual violence, 250
  culpability of Hindu right organisations in, 251
  'democidal rape culture', 149
  distribution of weapons, 199, 201–3
  failure of the state in preventing, 20
  Godhra incident (27 February 2002), 195–6, 198, 238, 241–2
  government, politicians and governance in aftermath of, 235–41
  instigation, familiar methods for, 196–9
  Naroda tragedy, 205–14
  and national ascent of the Hindu right, 153–4
  official inquiries, manipulation of, 241–2
  origins of, 149
  persecution with state complicity, 199–205
  political significance and brutality of, 244
  quest for justice, 244–6
  relief and rehabilitation of victims, 28
  relief camps, see relief camps
  relief for survivors, 219, 232
  sessions court, fast-track, 21, 238, 246, 250
  sexual violence against Muslim women, 177
  Special Investigation Team (SIT), 204
  state response to sexual violence, 234–5
  'state-sanctioned' massacre, 204

Hindu nationalism, 27, 29, 38, 39,
    66, 110, 132, 146–7, 169, 172,
    178, 241
  anti-minority ideology, 176
  anti-Muslim rhetoric, 171
  assertiveness of, in Gujarat, 163–5
  defensive aspects of, 146–7
  development of, 176–8
  Hindu nationalist 'laboratory',
    making of, 19, 176–7
  image of the ideal Hindu woman,
    170
  militancy in, 171
  Ramjanmabhoomi movement, see
    Ramjanmabhoomi movement
  and removal of secular impediments,
    177–9
Hindu nationalist, ideologues of,
    17–23, 29, 30, 36, 44, 81, 93,
    103, 109–10, 115, 126, 128
  and instigation of sexual violence,
    37–9
  sexual violence against Muslim
    women, 87, 96
  tenets of, 87
Hindu nationalist mobilisation, 73,
    121, 147
Hindu nationalist movement, 7, 8,
    19, 29, 37–9, 149, 150–3, 160,
    176, 240
  development of, 176–7
Hindu nationalist organisations, 36, 81,
    89, 101, 126, 133, 145, 147, 153,
    156, 158, 165, 181, 199, 202,
    224, 252
  backlash and BJP response, 193–4
  communal mobilisation, 100, 156,
    164, 178, 181
  infiltration of the state machinery,
    182–3
  instigation of riots, familiar methods
    for, 196–9
  mill workers, support of, 114
  network of, 153, 167

offences against minorities, 183–7
organisation of riots of 1969, 89–95
partitioning of space and segregation
    of lives by, 163–5
popularity of, 116
preparation of Hindu foot soldiers,
    187–9
propaganda material circulated by,
    103
religious minorities, violence against,
    153
rise in membership of, 165
state indifference and complicity
    against, 189–93
street activities organised by, 154
Hindu nation-state, see Hindu rashtra
Hindu rashtra, 37, 46, 163–5
  restoration of, 50
Hindu right, 158, 169, 184, 188
  ABVP, 189
  combating of Muslim threat, 187
  culpability of, 251
  efforts to co-opt Ambedkar's legacy,
    158
  goals and ideology of, 176
  ideological agenda of, 190
  mobilisation strategy, 110, 153, 154
  national ascent of, 153–4
  outfits affiliated to, 182
  political, social and cultural goals, 177
Hindu Sangram Samiti, 22, 85, 87–8,
    102, 270n32
Hindu sexuality, concept of, 13, 40
Hindutva, 45
Hindutva foot soldiers, 109, 157,
    184–7, 196, 198, 200, 204–5,
    248
Hindutva network, 177, 178, 182
Hindutva project, 215
Hindu women
  degeneration and violation of, 43
  forced abductions of, 43–4
  Muslim atrocities committed
    against, 70, 79–80

sexual chastity and virtues of, 42, 100, 140, 190, 224
Hindu Yuvak Mandal, 128, 133
holy war of religion, 131
honour, notions of, 11, 18, 34, 42
Hullad Pidit Sahayta Samiti (HPSS), 101–2, 104

impregnation, policy of, 13, 50
Indian feminist movement, 108
Indian People's Theatre Association, 96
India–Pakistan war (1965), 67, 71, 75
Indo–China war (1962), 67
inter-caste marriages, 186
inter-community interactions, 26, 72
International Monetary Fund (IMF), 154
inter-religious marriages, 186, 190
Inter-Services Intelligence, Pakistan, 195
Islamic Relief Committee, 227, 229
Islamic religious organisations, 227
 community agents, 231–2
 involvement in establishing relief colonies, 230
 reviving piety and 'protecting' Muslim women, 230
Islamic Sevak Sangh, 177

Jaffrelot, Christophe, 228, 229, 245
Jafri, Zakia, 204–5, 252, 268n16
Jamaat-e-Islami Hind, 177, 196, 225, 226, 230
Jamaats, 60–1, 273n10
Jamiat-Ulema-e-Hind, 76, 88, 104, 227
Jana Sangh, 66, 68, 70–1, 74–6, 79–81, 85, 87–90, 101, 104, 116–19, 124
 electoral performance, 124
 electoral support for, 68
 Hindu Sangram Samiti, 22, 85, 87, 88, 102, 270n32

Janata Dal, 150, 166–7, 178, 244
Jan Vikas (non-governmental organisation), 249
'Jehad', 23, 214
job security, 58, 156
Jyoti Sangh, 35, 59, 63–4, 77, 108, 186

Kakar, Sudhir, 25–6
Karat, Prakash, 240
Kargil war (1999), 191
Karseva (religious service), 172, 173, 194–7
Khan, Sophia, 230
Khetan, Ashish, 202–3, 207, 211, 214, 242, 248, 250
Khosla, G. D., 9
kidnapping and abduction, 35, 64
 cases of rape under, 78
Kodnani, Maya, 9, 182, 195, 206–7, 214, 234, 238–9, 250, 252
Kshatriya Sabha, 117

Lashkar-e-Taiba, 192
Liberation Tigers of Tamil Eelam, 166
'love marriages', 186

Macwan, Mohan, 156, 188, 200, 213
Madani, Shafi, 195, 226
Madhok, Balraj, 71, 75
Maha Gujarat Janata Parishad (MGJP), 68–9
Mahila Morcha (Women's Forum), 9, 160
male sexuality, notion of, 51
Mandal Commission, 160
marital rape, 3
masculinity, notions of, 18, 41, 44, 50, 70, 100, 152, 170, 195
mass propaganda campaigns, 20, 81, 183
Mehta, Harubhai, 88
migration, intra-city, 165
'Mini-Pakistan', 164, 181, 228

minority women, victimisation of, 14, 16, 18, 19, 147, 154, 254
Modi, Narendra, 8, 23, 38, 194–5, 204–5, 214, 219, 235–9, 241, 243, 252
molestation, 49, 64, 87
motherland, notion of, 45–7, 72–3
Muslim communalism, 39
Muslim identity, definition of, 40
'Muslim threat', perception of, 38–9, 44–6, 51, 95, 130, 133, 187, 193
Muslim Women (Protection of Rights on Divorce) Act (1986), 166
Muzaffarnagar Hindu–Muslim riots, 240
Mysorewala, K. K., 22, 207

Nagrik Sangathan (Citizens' Association), 133
Nanavati Commission, 242–5, 271n38
Nanavati, G. T., 241, 242
Nandigram violence (2007), West Bengal, 28, 240
Naranpura Patel Youth Committee (NPYC), 133
Narasimha Rao, P. V., 154, 177
Narayan, Jayaprakash, 117–18
National Crime Records Bureau, India, 64
National Democratic Alliance, 191
National Human Rights Commission, 246, 249
National Women's Commission, 148
Navchetan Group, 152, 186, 187, 207, 261
Nav Nirman (social reconstruction) movement, 117, 126, 166
Navrachna Nirman Samiti, 128
Nehru, Jawaharlal, 54, 65–6
Nirbhaya, story of, 2–3, 5–6, 8
non-governmental organisations (NGOs), 31–3, 35, 219, 227, 229, 233, 249
Nutan MGJP (New MGJP), 69

official inquiries, manipulation of, 218, 234, 241–2
Organiser (news magazine), 71–3, 101–2
Other Backward Class (OBC), 111
as Hindutva foot soldiers, 187–9
reservation policies favouring, 124

Pakistan
Bangladesh independence from, 12
creation of, 44, 47, 67
demand for, 67
India's war with, 67, 71, 75, 191
Inter-Services Intelligence, 195
'Mini-Pakistan', 164, 181, 228
Palanpuri, A. R., 76–7
Pandya, Haren, 190, 191, 214
Parmar, Satish, 114
Parmar, Vinod, 72
partition of India (1947), 5, 9–10, 52–4, 71, 86, 233
Patel, Chimanbhai, 117–18, 166–7, 178
Patel, Keshubhai, 178–9, 183, 192, 194
pogrom, 7, 196
police sensitivity, in handling sexual crimes, 3
Prevention of Communal and Targeted Violence (Access to Justice and Reparations) Bill, 4
Prevention of Terrorism Act (2002), 220
Protection of Women from Domestic Violence Act (2005), 33–4

Radcliffe Line, 54
Ramayana, 48–9, 80, 87, 159, 169–70
Ramjanmabhoomi movement, 149, 153, 177–8, 194–5
in Gujarat, 167–8
and normalisation of sexual violence, 167–72

rath yatra, 168
see also Babri Mosque, demolition of
  (6 December 1992)
Ramjanmabhoomi Trust, 168
rape, 19, 65
  'anti-rape law', 3, 8
  definition of, 4
  'democidal rape culture', 149
  gang rape, 1–2, 4, 9–10, 16, 20, 23,
    96, 106–8, 137, 148–50, 154,
    171, 173, 188, 200, 212, 245,
    249–51
  Gudiya, story of, 5–9
  marital rape, 3
  Nirbhaya, story of, 2–9
  punishment for offence of, 4, 250
  'rape culture' in India, 241
  in relief camps, 220–3
Rashtriya Janata Party, 179
Rashtriya Sevika Samiti, 31, 74, 152,
  160–1, 182, 215
  rise in social support for, 163
  women's participation in, 161–2
Rashtriya Swayamsevak Sangh (RSS), 8,
  20, 31, 66, 70, 76, 90, 97,
  113–14, 118, 121, 153, 167,
  177, 183
  and anti-Congress sentiment, 118
  anti-reservation policy, 126
  cultivation of an aggressive
    masculinity, 70
  as fascist organisation, 38
  founding ideologues of, 41, 51, 87
  Hindutva, ideologues of, 46
  mobilisation of low castes, 156
  and 'Muslim threat' of further
    violation, 44–7
  pracharika (female propagandist),
    161
  Rashtriya Sevika Samiti, 31, 74, 152,
    160–1, 182, 215
  revival of Hindu militancy, 38
  sankalp shibir, 191
  self-defence training, 74–5, 128

sexual violence, instigation of,
  49–52
shakha model, 38, 153
  women's wing, establishment of, 74
Rasool, Bilkees Yakoob, 249, 271n38,
  272n40, 275n1
rath yatra, 106, 115, 136–7, 168
'Recovery Operation', 54
Reddy Commission (1969), 55, 76, 78,
  80, 83–5, 87, 88, 90, 94, 101,
  103–4, 106, 244
Reddy, P. Jaganmohan, 55
Relief and rehabilitation of victims, 28
  Naseem's experience, 231–4
relief camps, 31, 103, 215
  activists, community leaders and
    their politics at, 223–7
  basic facilities, lack of, 219
  denial of justice, 217–8, 225
  dismantaling of, 220, 227
  issue of rape in, 223
  Jamila, story of, 220–3
  rehabilitation, community purifi-
    cation and women's agency, 227–9
  and rehabilitation of Muslim women,
    224
  for reviving piety and 'protecting'
    Muslim women, 230–1
  sexual 'exploitation' of women in, 29,
    226
  sexual services in exchange for basic
    aid, 218, 220
  Shah-e-Alam camp, 219, 220, 235
  victimisation in, 220–3
Relief Committee for Riot Victims,
  see Hullad Pidit Sahayta Samiti
  (HPSS)
religion-based discrimination, 67, 72
religion-based spatial segregation, 60
religious conversion, 86, 189, 190
religious identity, 42, 83, 84, 115, 121,
  122, 228
  politicisation of, 69–78
  preservation of, 42

religious minorities, 120, 122, 241,
        252
    in Gujarat, 16
    Hindutva and, 183
    method of destroying, 149
    one-sided offences against, 176
    political-social order, 183
    rights of, 37
    safety of, 235
    and strategic replacement of
        'Hindus', 188
    violence against, 153, 178, 190,
        193, 206
religious polarisation, in Ahmedabad,
        26
religious reform movements, 37
reservation policies, of Congress party,
        120
    anti-reservation forums, 135
    anti-reservation riots (1981), 121
    implementation of, 125
    reservation quota, increase in, 122–8
riot-time alliances, 26
Rithambara, Sadhvi, 170, 182
Robinson, Rowena, 14, 243

Sabarmati Express tragedy, see Godhra
        incident (27 February 2002)
Sadhana (news magazine), 71–2, 75,
        101, 183, 192
St Xavier Social Service Society, 234
Samajwadi Party, 240
Samerth (non-governmental organis-
        ation), 234
samskaras (good virtues), 160
Sangh Parivar, 19
sankalp shibir, 191
Sarela, Akbar S., 55
Sarkar, Tanika, 13, 18, 160
Savarkar, Vinayak Damodar, 39–43, 49
    female sexuality, definition of, 42
    Hindu, definition of, 40
    Hindu men, characterisation of, 41
    Hindutva, 45

Muslim men, characterisation of, 41
    nation, concept of, 45
    Six Glorious Epochs of Indian History
        (1970), 40
Scheduled Castes (SCs), 15, 19, 24, 36,
        57–62, 66–7, 72–4, 91, 95, 97,
        105–6, 110–11, 113–22, 127,
        132, 138, 141, 146, 157, 162,
        166, 180–1, 187–8, 198, 200,
        206
    as Hindutva foot soldiers, 187–9
    reservation quota for, 122
    social respectability for, 158
Schedule Tribes (STs), 206
    as Hindutva foot soldiers, 187–9
    reservation quota for, 122
self and the other, creation of, 39–43
sessions court, fast-track, 21, 238,
        246, 250
sexual atrocities, motivations for,
        10–11, 17, 27, 85, 86, 171,
        196, 238
sexual chastity, 42, 100, 140,
        190, 224
sexual gratification, 18, 95, 100,
        202, 212–13, 226
sexual harassment, 3, 24, 64
'sexual immorality' of Muslims, 40
sexual purity of women, 11
sexual-religious segregation, 188
sexual violence, against men, 3
sexual violence, against women
    during armed conflict, 252
    Bhilwada neighbourhood, experience
        of, 96–100
    categories of, 3
    celebrating and condoning, 214–16
    during communal riots, 10, 14, 16,
        26–7, 154
    conviction for, 249
    cruelty by husbands and relatives, 64
    ethnic identity in motivating, role
        of, 6
    'everyday crimes', 2–9

forced abductions of Hindu women, 45–6
Gudiya, story of, 4–9
ideological instigation of, 253
instigation of, 48–51
Jamila, story of, 93, 220–3
as method of destroying religious minorities, 149
minority women, victimisation of, 14, 16, 18, 19, 147, 154, 254
motivations for, during conflict, 14
Naroda tragedy (2002), 205–14
Nirbhaya, story of, 2–9
'peace-time' and 'conflict-time', 6
production of extreme forms of, 17–29
Ramjanmabhoomi movement and normalisation of, 167–72
relief and justice for the victims of, 28
in relief camps, 28, 30
state response to, 7, 234–5
stigma and shame associated with, 64
as 'weapon of war', 12
sexual violence laws
'anti-rape law', 3, 8
Criminal Law (Amendment) Act (2013), 3
Muslim Women (Protection of Rights on Divorce) Act (1986), 166
Prevention of Communal and Targeted Violence (Access to Justice and Reparations) Bill, 4
Protection of Women from Domestic Violence Act (2005), 33–4
structural and legal reforms in, 4–5
Shah Bano case (1978), 166
Shah, Ghanshyam, 56, 61, 87, 91, 96, 107
Shah, K. G., 241–2
Shaikh, Zahira, 246–9
Shani, Ornit, 107, 113
Shekavat, Bhairon Singh, 178

Shishu Mandir (Children's Temple), 181
Shiv Sena, 192
Six Glorious Epochs of Indian History (1970), 40
Social Action Forum Against Oppression in Ahmedabad, 230
social brotherhood, 145
social marginalisation, 70, 76
social reconciliation, 234
socio-economic inequality, 69
Solanki, Madhavsinh, 119, 126, 138, 147
Special Economic Zone, 240
Special Investigation Team (SIT), 204
Spodek, Howard, 107, 196
Sreekumar, R. B., 196
State Reserve Police Force (SRPF), 138–9
Sturmabteilung (Nazi paramilitary wing), 38
Swaraj, Sushma, 8, 269n18
Swatantra Party, 66–8

Tablighi Jamaat, 227
Tanveer, Fatima, 225–6
'Terrorism Attacks India', 171–2
Textile Labour Association (TLA), 58, 72, 111–14, 121
Textile mills, in Ahmedabad, 15, 104
closure of and predicament of mill workers, 104, 110–16, 158
cultural homogeneity in, 58
decline of, 19, 57–60
economic and housing strife, 112
economic stagnation, impact of, 57
employment opportunities, 58
female work participation rate, 156
Hindu mobilisation, scope for, 114
and Hindu nationalist organisations, 114–15
industrial relations, structure and mechanisms of, 115
labour insecurity, 111

laid-off mill workers, economic
    difficulties of, 112
wages of workers, 156
Thakkar, Bacchubhai, 70
Thomas, Charlotte, 228
Togadia, Pravin, 192, 195
Turshen, Meredith, 12

United Nations
    Committee on the Elimination of
        Discrimination Against Women,
        239
    International Criminal Tribunal, 107
    Office of Internal Oversight Services,
        28
United Progressive Alliance, 240–1
untouchability, abolition of, 156–8
upper-caste Hindus, 25, 49, 61–2, 110,
    116–17, 141–2, 161, 165, 253
    in Congress leadership, 66
    hegemony of, 37
    Hindu religious festivals, 138
    jobs and social respectability,
        59–60
    sexual violence against, 17, 137, 139
    supremacy of, 37
    victimisation of minorities, 19
    violence against backward castes, 24

Vaghela, Shankersinh, 175, 179
Vajpayee, Atal Bihari, 71, 102, 183,
    190, 220, 235–7
Vakil, Nusservanji K., 55
Vanikar, Vishwa Nath Ananth, 146

Vanvasi Kalyan Ashram, 181
Varshney, Ashutosh, 26, 73, 272n44
Verma, J. S., 3
Vidya Bharati (India's Knowledge),
    181, 215
Violence against women
    domestic violence, 32–4, 63, 234
    dowry deaths, 64
    lack of police sensitivity in
        handling, 3
    sexual violence, see sexual violence,
        against women
    state responsiveness to, 3, 234–5
Vishwa Hindu Parishad (VHP), 20, 31,
    73, 76, 102, 113–15, 126, 128,
    134, 138, 146, 152, 156–8, 165,
    168, 171, 177, 210
    Jagannath yatra, 171
    mobilisation of low castes against
        Muslims, 201–2
    offences against minorities, 183–7
    Ramjanmabhoomi agitation, 194
    rise in social support for, 163
    'Savadhan Campaign', 185, 256
Voluntary Militia for National Security,
    Italy, 38

women's life choices, restrictions on,
    231
Women's Research Group, 107

Yadav, Laloo Prasad, 241
Yagnik, Indulal, 69
Yagnik, Jyotsna, 21, 250